THE NATIONAL UNIVERSITY OF IRELAND

ROLL *of* HONOUR

A doctor dresses the wounds of Lieutenant Guy Vaughan Morgan of the 2nd Battalion, Irish Guards at an RAMC aid post during the Battle of Pilckem Ridge, 31 July 1917.

(Courtesy of Imperial War Musuem)

FIRST WORLD WAR CENTENARY

ROLL *of* HONOUR

AND ESSAYS

Published in 2024 by
The National University of Ireland
49 Merrion Square, Dublin 2, Ireland

www.nui.ie

Hardback ISBN 978-0-901510-983
Paperback ISBN 978-0-901510-990

Cover design, text design, typesetting and layout by Lyn Davies Design
lyndaviesdesignfolio.com
Printed by CRM Design + Print Ltd

NUI CENTENARY PUBLICATION

Contents

Foreword

In 1919, the National University of Ireland compiled a war list of all students, graduates, and staff of University College Cork, University College Dublin, and University College Galway, who had died or served in the Great War. At the beginning of the First World War, many Irish men were persuaded to enlist with the promise of Home Rule, while others may have joined to secure a decent living; however, by 1918 and the end of the war, the political landscape in Ireland had changed radically and those who had served in the war found themselves relegated to the shadows of a war that was rarely, if ever, discussed.

The republication of the National University of Ireland's Roll of Honour forms a central part of NUI's ambitious and broad-based commemorative programme for the Decade of Centenaries. From the outset it was decided that, as part of the programme, the university would honour figures associated with NUI who had made significant contributions to the building of the new Irish state such as Douglas Hyde, Eoin MacNeill, Éamon de Valera and Patrick McGilligan. NUI's commemoration programme began in 2013 with a seminar 'Douglas Hyde: The professor who became president of Ireland', and the proceedings were published in 2016. In 2013, NUI published a facsimile reproduction of Lia Fáil: Irisleabhar Gaeilge Ollscoil na hÉireann launched by President Michael D. Higgins. In 2018, the inaugural Hyde lecture/Léacht de hÍde (in partnership with the School of Irish, Celtic Studies and Folklore, UCD) took place when a paper 'The Legacy of Douglas Hyde' was delivered by President Higgins in UCD. The second Hyde lecture, 'Douglas Hyde's American Tour 1905–6', was delivered by Professor Liam Mac Mathúna in UCD in 2019 and in 2024 after a COVID pandemic hiatus, Professor Mary Harris delivered the third lecture, 'Douglas Hyde and Eoin MacNeill: Visions and realities'.

Éamon de Valera, the second chancellor of the university, who presided over its affairs from his election in 1921 until his death in 1975, was remembered in 2016, when two additional scholarships were offered in his name. In that year, a specially commissioned Éamon de Valera medal was presented to each of the 2016 NUI award winners. As 2021 marked the centenary of de Valera's election as chancellor, a lecture series, 'DevTalks: Towards an assessment of his legacy,' was jointly hosted by NUI and Dublin Institute of Advanced Studies. Given his strong personal, and continuing family, connections with NUI, the university felt it particularly appropriate to honour Eoin MacNeill. To mark the centenary of the publication of MacNeill's article, 'The North Began,' HistoryHub.ie, UCD's public history website, produced an eight-part online series, 'Eoin MacNeill: Revolutionary and scholar' in November 2013. In 2016, NUI held a seminar 'Eoin MacNeill: A reassessment of the scholar revolutionary'. The two programmes combined provided a ready-made framework for a publication that, with the addition of invited contributions, formed a fresh re-evaluation of MacNeill's contribution to the shaping of modern Ireland and Irish academia: Eoin MacNeill: The Pen and the Sword edited by Conor Mulvagh and Emer Purcell was published in 2022.

'John Redmond and the Irish Parliamentary Party: A Centenary Symposium' was held in the National Gallery of Ireland on 6 March 2018. The symposium was organised by the Department of Tourism, Culture, Arts, the Gaeltacht, Sport and Media and the National University of Ireland, in collaboration with the Royal Irish Academy and the School of History, University College Dublin, as part of the John Redmond State commemorative programme. The symposium set out to reassess John Redmond and the achievements of the Irish Parliamentary Party under his leadership. The Decade of Centenaries provided the opportunity to consider issues and events relevant to the Irish Parliamentary Party (IPP) such as Home Rule, the First World War, women's suffrage, and parliamentary democracy. John Redmond and Irish Parliamentary Traditions edited by Martin O'Donoghue and Emer Purcell will be published by UCD Press in 2024. In July 2022, NUI held a seminar that examined the contribution of Patrick McGilligan, who succeeded MacNeill as TD for NUI in 1923. He also served on the NUI Senate. McGilligan was a key player in two of the major developments of the 1920s: the establishment of the ESB and the constitutional developments in the British Commonwealth that led to the Statute of Westminster in 1931. NUI's Decade of Centenary programme was determined to acknowledge and foreground the contribution of Irish women and NUI graduates to the formation of the state. In December

2018, in collaboration with Maynooth University, NUI marked the centenary of women's suffrage with a symposium, 'Political Voices: The participation of women in Irish public life, 1918–2018', the proceedings of which will be published in due course.

In this volume, reproduction of the NUI Roll of Honour is accompanied by five essays. Two essays are by Ronan McGreevy; the first is a substantial introduction to the roll itself and the second provides individual profiles of NUI men who died in the war and a selection of men who served. Drawing upon the work of Tom Burnell and the database of Irish in the Great War Archive, and following threads in publications and online sources, Ronan brings these men, their service, and their lives after the war to life. Fionnuala Walsh writes a chapter on NUI women, including those who graduated from the Royal University of Ireland. For the first time, she brings together details of the lives of women students, graduates, and staff, and discusses the many ways in which they contributed to the war effort. Patrick Casey, Kevin Cullen, and Joe Duignan present here a summary of their book, Irish Doctors in the First World War, focusing on NUI doctors who served in the war and discussing advances in medical practice and the realities of practicing medicine in a war zone. In addition to NUI's list, the Royal College of Surgeon in Ireland's Roll of Honour is also reproduced here. RCSI is a recognised college of NUI, and this book presented the ideal opportunity to publish the names of their students, graduates, and staff who served in the war. For the first time, a list of the chaplains, who ministered to the men in the war, from St Patrick's College Maynooth is presented. The list, compiled by Barbara McCormack, is accompanied by an introduction and a selection of chaplain profiles.

Until recent decades, the history of the Irish men and women who served in the First World War was often neglected, especially in the first years of the fledgling Irish state. In 1919, NUI's Roll of Honour preserved the names of these men; over one hundred years later, this book shines a bright light on the people who gave their lives and made huge personal sacrifices during the First World War.

The Decade of Centenaries will be seen as a golden age in the study of Irish history. Never before has our history been subject to such study and analysis, never before has the range of study been so wide and so comprehensive, never before have so-called 'no go' areas and taboo topics been opened up to the most intense scrutiny. And never before has a people embraced the revelations and reflections of often difficult and painful memories and differences with such openness and maturity. Of all the legacies of the Decade of Centenaries, that may well be the greatest. And it is interesting now to note how many there were a decade ago who said this could never happen.

As previous volumes in the NUI centenary series have shown, NUI and its graduates played a significant role in the events leading up to the foundation of and the shaping of the new State. But NUI was also of its time. It did not speak with one voice. Its Senate was a Home Rule Senate and some of its staff – most notably Tom Kettle – and many of its graduates volunteered to serve in the Great War. Many died and some who returned did not find the new Ireland a congenial place. But they are no less a part of the story of those years as their classmates and colleagues who chose differently.

This is an important and timely book which fits into the comprehensive and inclusive reach of the Decade of Centenaries.

The editor of the series Dr Emer Purcell has given us a handsome volume edited to the highest standards.

MAURICE MANNING
Chancellor NUI, 2009–2024

Contributors

TOM BURNELL is an army veteran, a military historian, and a lexicographer. He has published widely on Irish history and the First World War. His publications include: *The Anglicised Words of Irish Placenames: Gaillimh to Galway* (2023), *Irishmen in the Great War: Reports from the Front 1914 and 1915* (2020), as well as *26 Counties Casualties of the Great War* (2008-2017). He has compiled an extensive database of all Irish men who died serving, or as a result of service, in the Great War *https://irelandsgreatwardead.ie/*.

PATRICK CASEY is a founding member of the Medal Society of Ireland. He is a life-long military medal collector with a keen interest in the profiles of those awarded military honours. Co-author with Kevin Cullen and Joe Duignan of *Irish Doctors in the First World War* (2015).

KEVIN CULLEN is a retired geologist and past President of the Institute of Geologists of Ireland. Co-author with Patrick Casey and Joe Duignan of *Irish Doctors in the First World War* (2015).

JOE DUIGNAN is a retired surgeon and former Council Member of the Royal College of Surgeons in Ireland. He has lectured on the nature and treatment of wounds and diseases of past military campaigns from the Crimean War to World War Two. Co-author with Patrick Casey and Kevin Cullen of *Irish Doctors in the First World War* (2015).

BARBARA MCCORMACK is the Librarian of the Royal Irish Academy. She is responsible for the strategic direction of the Library and Archive, the information services provided by the Library, and the curation of the world's largest collection of manuscripts in the Irish language, as well as numerous other manuscript and archival collections, and books. She previously worked as Special Collections Librarian at Maynooth University

Library, where she had responsibility for the early printed books, manuscripts, and archives of St Patrick's College Maynooth and Maynooth University. She has also worked at the British Library and Trinity College Library, Dublin, and has published on book collecting in Ireland and Britain and Irish religious history.

RONAN MCGREEVY is a senior journalist with the *Irish Times*. He is the author of *Wherever the Firing Line Extends: Ireland and the Western Front* (2016), *Great Hatred: The Assassination of Field Marshall Sir Henry Wilson MP* (2022), and the co-author of *The Kidnapping: A hostage, a desperate manhunt and a bloody rescue that shocked Ireland* (2023) with Tommy Conlon. He was made a Chevalier des Arts et des Lettres by the French government in 2018 for his work on remembrance of the First World War.

EMER PURCELL is Publications Manager at the National University of Ireland. She is responsible for NUI's Decade of Centenaries programme of events and publications. She was previously a part-time lecturer in the School of History, University College Cork. She is the general editor of *Clerics, Kings, and Vikings* (2015) and co-editor with Carrie Griffin of *Text, Transmission, and Transformation in the European Middle Ages, c.1000–1500* (2018). She is co-editor of two other books in NUI's Decade of Centenary publication series: with Conor Mulvagh, *Eoin MacNeill: The Pen and the Sword* (2022), and with Martin O'Donoghue, *John Redmond and Irish Parliamentary Traditions* (2024).

FIONNUALA WALSH is Associate Professor of Modern Irish History at University College Dublin. She completed her PhD and Irish Research Council Postdoctoral Fellowship at Trinity College Dublin. Her first book, *Irish Women and the Great War* (2020), was joint winner of the National University of Ireland Publication Prize for Irish History in 2021. She has published extensively in the fields of Irish First World War studies and late nineteenth and early twentieth century women's history. She is also the editor of *America in Ireland: Culture and Society 1841–1925* (2024).

Acknowledgements

IN 2018, the National University of Ireland decided to republish its 1919 Roll of Honour, with an introduction, in time for the centenary of the original publication in 2019. Ronan McGreevy agreed to write the introduction, and he suggested the inclusion of a chapter with detailed profiles of the men who died and served in the First World War. Keen to acknowledge the role of women, NUI invited Fionnuala Walsh to write a chapter on NUI women and their contribution to the war effort. Patrick Casey, Kevin Cullen, and Joe Duignan had already published a book on Irish doctors in the First World War, so it seemed appropriate to ask them to write a chapter on NUI doctors. The final part of the puzzle was complete when we learned of Barbara McCormack's research on Maynooth chaplains. Six years and a pandemic later, the book is finally going to print. Not quite hitting the centenary year of 2019, but landing in time, almost to the day, for the 106th anniversary of the end of the war on 11 November 2024.

Over the course of the six years and the evolution of this book, one very positive development is the publication of a number of books on women graduates, and staff of the Royal University of Ireland and the National University of Ireland: Joyce Padbury's book on Mary Hayden, Mary McAuliffe and Harriet Wheelock's edition of the diaries of Kathleen Lynn, Margaret Ward's book on Hanna Sheehy-Skeffington, and Jackie Uí Chionna's book on the lesser known, but fascinating, Emily Anderson. All of these women feature in this book in their own right.

Emily Anderson serves as an interesting case of how multiple members of the same family often served in the war. The daughter of University College Galway President, Alex Anderson, she joined the Foreign Office and worked as a codebreaker in the Middle East. Her brother, Alex Jr, was reported missing in November 1916, and remained a prisoner until the end of the war. Other families suffered multiple fatalities, like the Flanigan family. Three brothers lost their lives in the war: Gerald in April

1916, Edmund in June 1916, and Dominic in November 1917. They had already lost a brother to natural causes before the war.

The effect on families must have been enormous, and herein lies the breadth and appeal of this book, from the personal and familial impact of the war, to the wider bearing on early twentieth-century Ireland: from Home Rule and the Easter Rising, through to the subsequent War of Independence and the Civil War, and to the wider context of the devastating impact of the war on Europe. Many veterans took part in all three wars; World, Independence, and Civil.

In 2018, NUI did not possess a printed copy of the Roll of Honour, and so Special Collections, University College Cork, not only supplied a copy, but very kindly digitised the entire book for republication here. Many thanks to the staff of UCC library, particularly, Elaine Harrington and Catherine McKenna. We would also like to thank the staff of the libraries and repositories that facilitated research for this book: our constituent university libraries and archives (UCC, University College Dublin, University of Galway, and Maynooth University); the Military Archives, Ireland; the National Archives of Ireland; the National Library of Ireland; the National Archives, UK; and the British Red Cross Archives.

We are very grateful to the Imperial War Museum, the Library of Congress, Washington, the National Library of Ireland, and the Wellcome Library for permission to reproduce the images used to illustrate this book, and to Ronan McGreevy and Cora Lenihan for allowing the use of their photographs. Thank you to the NUI IT and Records Office: John Foley (retired), Eric Lambe (retired), Myles Kehoe, Gerry Penston, and Edward Smyth for their assistance with records and the digitisation of material from the NUI archives. As part of a UCD Internship programme, five students have worked in NUI and have helped with researching images and proofing the text at various stages: Sarah Droney, Eileen Hogan, Kendra Onuorah, Amber Sullivan, and Djamel White. To my colleagues in NUI, especially Cora Lenihan and Helen Scanlon who proofread this book and supported the project through drafting, editing and, finally, publication. Many thanks to Attracta Halpin (former Registrar of NUI), Patrick O'Leary (Registrar of NUI), and Maurice Manning (former Chancellor of NUI), for their support of this project.

A special word of thanks to Dr John Borgonovo, School of History, UCC, who reviewed the text as part of the peer review process. He made invaluable suggestions that greatly enhanced each chapter of the book and resulted in a stronger publication. I will be forever grateful to Lyn Davies, designer and typesetter, who shared his advice and experience in the making of this book, and for his patience in the long gestation of the final publication. To Eileen O'Neill for producing a detailed and complex index. To Richard Kelly, of CRM Print + Design for sharing the benefit of his experience in the print trade, and for production and printing. And, to Anthony Tierney and the team at Four Courts Press who manage our sales and distribution.

It remains to record our gratitude to my fellow editors and the contributors to this volume, who have brought the men and women of NUI who served in the war, and supported the war effort, to life.

EMER PURCELL
Publications Office, NUI

Illustrations

Abbreviations

AMS	Army Medical Service
ANZAC	Australia and New Zealand Army Corps
BEF	British Expeditionary Force
BMH	Bureau of Military History
CCS	Casualty Clearing Station
CO	Commanding Officer
MC	Military Cross
CEF	Canadian Expeditionary Force
CSO	Chief Secretary's Office (Ireland)
CWGC	Commonwealth War Graves Commission
DFA	Department of Foreign Affairs (Ireland)
DIAS	Dublin Institute for Advanced Studies
DIB	*Dictionary of Irish Biography*
DSM	Distinguished Service Medal
DSO	Distinguished Service Order
DIFP	*Documents on Irish Foreign Policy*
DMP	Dublin Metropolitan Police
EEF	Egyptian Expeditionary Forces
IHS	*Irish Historical Studies*
IMS	Indian Medical Service
INWMR	Irish National War Memorial Record
IPP	Irish Parliamentary Party
IRA	Irish Republican Army
IRB	Irish Republican Brotherhood
IWFL	Irishwomen's Franchise League
MAI	Military Archives, Ireland
MC	Military Cross
MDS	Main Dressing Station
MEF	Mediterranean/Marine Expeditionary Force
MSPC	Military Service Pensions Collection
NAI	National Archives, Ireland
NCO	Non-commissioned Officer
NLI	National Library of Ireland
NUI	National University of Ireland
POW	Prisoner of war
OBE	Order of the British Empire
ODNB	*Oxford Dictionary of National Biography*
OTC	Officers' Training Corps
QUB	Queen's University Belfast
PRIA	*Proceedings of the Royal Irish Academy*
PRONI	Public Record Office of Northern Ireland
RAP	Regimental Aid Posts
RAChD	Royal Army Chaplains' Department
RAMC	Royal Army Medical Corps
RAVC	Royal Army Veterinary Corps
RDF	Royal Dublin Fusiliers
RFC	Royal Flying Corps
RIA	Royal Irish Academy
RIC	Royal Irish Constabulary
RCPI	Royal College of Physicians in Ireland
RCSI	Royal College of Surgeons in Ireland
RUI	Royal University of Ireland
RN	Royal Navy
RNVR	Royal Navy Volunteer Reserve
TCD	Trinity College Dublin
TCDA	Trinity College Dublin Archives
UCC	University College Cork
UCD	University College Dublin
UCDA	University College Dublin Archives
UCG	University College Galway
UVF	Ulster Volunteer Force
WHO	World Health Organisation
WS	Witness Statement

Arthur J. Beveridge

Maurice.R.J. Hayes

Desmond T. McWeeney

William Lombard Murphy

William.A. Redmond

FIGURE 1.1 *Portraits of five NUI men.*

1. *Introduction*

The National University of Ireland Roll of Honour

RONAN MCGREEVY

IN 1919, the National University of Ireland published a Roll of Honour of its students, staff, and alumni who served in the First World War, eighty of whom lost their lives in service. Remembrance of the conflict began as soon as it ended, a conflict so vast in its scale and suffering that it became known as 'The Great War'.

The Great War coincided with the most significant decade in modern Irish political history between 1912 and 1922, with constitutional changes that endure to this day. The limited form of autonomy granted under the Home Rule settlement was due to come into force in 1914, but its implementation was thwarted, fatally, as it turns out, first by resistance from Ulster Unionists and then by the outbreak of war in August 1914. Irish Parliamentary Party leader John Redmond's call for Irishmen to go and join the British Army, unprecedented for a nationalist leader, led to an irrevocable split in the Irish Volunteers. This was an armed militia set up in 1913 to defend Home Rule and to act as a counterpart to the loyalist Ulster Volunteers founded in 1912.

The establishment of NUI in 1908 marked a new departure for education in Ireland. As John Coolahan points out: 'the Irish university question was one of the three great issues in Anglo-Irish relations, the others being the land question and Home Rule, in the late-nineteenth and early-twentieth century'.[1] The foundation of NUI marked the end of a century-long struggle to find a university education system acceptable to Catholics in Ireland and to the Catholic Church. Rising expectations made the issue of third-level education a critical one in the nineteenth and early-twentieth century, though the numbers involved represented a tiny elite in Irish society. Just 7.5% of children between the ages of twelve and fourteen went to secondary school, according to the 1911 UK census that included Ireland.[2] The numbers going on to university at the turn of the century in Ireland, 3,2% according to the 1901 census, represented an even smaller segment of Irish society.[3]

Nevertheless, the creation of an educated Catholic middle-class was a key goal for nationalists who wanted parity with what they believed were the historic unfair advantages enjoyed by the Protestant minority in Ireland. It was also a priority for the British Government. It believed solving the university problem would help reconcile Ireland to the union, by providing a British-educated Irish elite capable of self-government, albeit the limited form of it as envisaged by Home Rule. Successive British governments had grappled with the problem. The Queen's University Colleges of Cork, Galway, and Belfast were created in 1845 'to afford a university education of members of all religious denominations' in Ireland and as an alternative to the Church of Ireland administered Trinity College Dublin.[4]

The Queen's Colleges incurred the wrath of the Catholic Church who regarded them as 'godless institutions', though it did not deter Catholics from sending their children there. The Catholic University of Ireland in Dublin (now University College Dublin) was created in 1851 to offer an explicitly Catholic third-level education to students in Ireland, but its degrees were not initially recognised by the British state. It was a relatively minor issue on a UK basis and yet the Irish universities saga was one of the factors that brought down the Liberal government of William Gladstone in 1873. The Irish Universities Bill, which would have created one university for the whole island including TCD, was defeated by three votes. Gladstone resigned and subsequently lost the 1874 British general election.

The Royal University of Ireland (RUI) was a first attempt to accommodate the concerns of Catholics. It was created in 1879 as an examination and degree conferring body. The Catholic University became UCD as a consequence.[5] A multiplicity of educational institutions, both second and third level, sent their students for examination to RUI. It was the first university in Ireland to confer degrees on women.[6] As Senia Pašeta points out, the Royal University was not set up with women in mind, but skilful lobbying by female educationalists meant it was 'something of a blessing for women who were as yet barred from attending the other Irish universities and the Royal was their only Irish option'.[7]

Yet, the Royal's arrangements were not optimal. Nationalist Ireland wanted more than just an examinations body. It wanted a university to rival Trinity. The National University of Ireland, as originally constituted in 1908, consisted of UCD, University College Cork (UCC) and University College Galway (UCG). Both UCD and UCC had designs on being independent universities, but it did not happen, and the federalised university system has remained to this day.

Of the three universities, UCD was the most Catholic in ethos, founded as it was by the Catholic convert and now saint, John Henry Newman. It struggled until its degrees were recognised by the Royal University of Ireland. However, its medical school founded in 1855 and based in Cecilia Street, was the 'Catholic university's great success. By the end of the century, it had become the largest medical school in the country'.[8] Many of the older graduates who feature in the Roll of Honour studied there.

Maynooth College, then the national seminary for the Catholic Church, became an affiliated college of NUI in 1910. Maynooth is the oldest institution within NUI. It was founded in 1795 and endowed by the British Government who feared that Irish priests educated on the continent would spread sedition at home. More than fifty Maynooth graduates served as army chaplains in the war, though they do not appear in the Roll of Honour unless they have a connection with UCD, UCC, or UCG.[9] Maynooth-educated priests included the remarkable Fr Tom Duggan, who served as a British Army chaplain in both world wars and allied himself with the republican movement in the Irish War of Independence.[10]

Another was Fr Francis Gleeson who inspired the most famous Irish painting of the First World War. Gleeson was a priest in the Dublin diocese when he volunteered to serve in the British Army in 1914. He was commissioned into the 2nd battalion of the Royal Munster Fusiliers. On 8 May 1915, Fr Gleeson accompanied his battalion on the way to the frontline before the start of what became known as the Battle of Aubers Ridge in northern France. They stopped at a wayside chapel where Fr Gleeson gave general absolution to the 800 men in the battalion, the vast majority of whom were Catholic. The result, by the Italian artist Fortunino Matania, was the *Last General Absolution of the Munsters at Rue du Bois* with its menacing foreboding of an impending battle; the painting is used to illustrate the cover of this book.

Throughout the nineteenth- and early twentieth-century Irish participation in the British Armed Forces never fell below the Irish percentage of the UK population at the time and usually exceeded it. The British Army had eight regiments from Ireland covering every county: the Royal Irish Fusiliers, the Royal Irish Rifles, the Royal Inniskilling Fusiliers, the Royal

Dublin Fusiliers, the Royal Munster Fusiliers, the Royal Irish Regiment, the Leinster Regiment, and the Connaught Rangers. Many Irish towns such as Tralee, Clonmel, and Birr were known as garrison towns. In 1900, Queen Victoria sanctioned the establishment of the Irish Guards, an elite regiment in the British Army, in recognition of Irish service in the Anglo-Boer War. The Royal Navy too had a substantial presence in coastal Irish towns.

The Roll of Honour reflects the commitment of middle-class Irish Catholics to the British war effort, as evidenced by the contribution of many of the elite Catholic secondary schools at the time: some 604 ex-pupils of Clongowes Wood College served in the war and ninety-five died;[11] from Belvedere College 300 served and forty-nine were killed;[12] at Castleknock College 356 served and fifty-one were killed.[13] These schools were not unique in their commitment to the British war effort.

In his autobiography, *India as I Knew It,* the Jesuit-educated Sir Michael O'Dwyer, lieutenant-governor of the Punjab, held responsible for the 1919 Amritsar massacre, stated that prior to the Easter Rising, Clongowes had been renowned for producing men who worked in the service of the British Empire:

> Till the unfortunate revulsion of feeling that followed the Easter rebellion of 1916, the Jesuit schools prided themselves on the numbers that passed into the service of the Crown, in the army and civil service. This was, of course, good business, but it was also based on a spirit of loyal support of constituted authority. The Roll of Honour of Clongowes College in the Great War perhaps surpassed that of any Irish school, Catholic or Protestant, and for the first two years of the war, the spirit was admirable.[14]

In 1940, O'Dwyer was assassinated in London by a Sikh nationalist, Udham Singh, for his role twenty-one years earlier in the Amritsar massacre.

Catholic secondary schools were part of a revolution in learning which occurred in the nineteenth century and continued into the twentieth century in Ireland.[15] The burgeoning Catholic middle-classes saw the number of secondary schools double from twenty-four to forty-eight between 1850 and 1870. Many of those represented here in the NUI Roll of Honour saw the British Empire as a professional opportunity. Some also saw it, in the context of the time, as a civilising force. Their world view was best expressed by Dr Patrick Heffernan, a former student of Blackrock College, who spent his war years in the Indian Medical Service, British India's military medical service. His book *An Irish Doctor's Memories* was published in 1947:[16]

> The narrow, atavistic and reactionary section of the Irish of today will, doubtless, sneer as us as 'Shawneens'[17] and West-Britons but at the time we regarded ourselves as Irish Europeans, cosmopolitan and citizens of the world, who hoped to find in a liberalised and democratised British Empire in which Ireland occupied her worthy place, a métier in which we could live satisfying lives, and perhaps contribute a share, great or small, to human progress and human civilisation.[18]

The connection with Empire was prized by the universities too. In *From Queen's College to National University*, James P. Murray notes the placing of UCG graduates in the entrance examinations to the British Armed Forces medical services was important in establishing the reputation of the university's medical faculty: 'At that time, the sons of many middle-class families in Ireland aspired to careers in the public service at home and abroad. There was a special social cachet attached to a career in the Indian medical and civil services'.[19]

The Black Lives Matter movement, which began globally following the murder of George Floyd in 2020, brought a renewed focus worldwide on the legacy of colonialism. Ireland was not an independent nation during the heyday of European colonialisation in the eighteenth and nineteenth centuries, but as this book and others attest, the Irish participated in colonial enterprises. Jane Ohlmeyer, in *Making Empire. Ireland, Imperialism and the Early Modern World*, examines how Ireland was colonised by the English, but through the Easter Rising and the War of Independence provided a template for other British colonies to become independent nations.

> In this – and in so many other ways – Ireland served as a laboratory for the British Empire. It was in Ireland that imperial and anglicising policies were formulated. Race-based ideologies were developed and 'tools of empire', such as mapping, were tested. Just as the Irish were victims of English imperialism, some – Catholics as well as Protestants – actively engaged in the business of empire or served in imperial armies and administrations. As well as making empires, Ireland served as an exemplar for resistance to imperial rule and inspired freedom fighters across the British and other European empires.[20]

Those who appear in this Roll of Honour grew up in a country that was barely recognisable from the one that followed the tumult of the Irish Revolution. Those pre-war years were chronicled from a Republican perspective by Christopher 'Todd' Andrews, who went on to play a significant role in the new State. Born in 1901, he recalled that the Ireland he grew up in had lost its 'consciousness as a separate identity'. His native Dublin was a 'British city and accepted itself as one' and it was a society divided on distinctly British class lines.[21]

Catholics with means, mostly from the landed Catholic gentry, sent their boys to Clongowes Wood College or to Catholic boarding schools in England. The next group, Andrews recounted, was the 'middle middle-classes' who sent their boys to schools like Belvedere College, Blackrock College, or St Mary's College. A rung further down the social scale were the boys who were sent to Christian Brothers' schools. These schools were much more nationalistic in outlook, sceptical of the British Empire, and produced a disproportionate number of those who involved themselves in the Irish Revolution. They also produced many of the leaders of the new Irish State.

The men (they were all men) listed in the Roll of Honour were the sons and grandsons of prosperous Irish businessmen, doctors, and solicitors. They were from the class that Andrews described as 'the top of the heap'. He listed them as 'the medical specialists, fashionable dentists, barristers, solicitors, wholesale tea and wine merchants, owners of large drapery stores and a very few owners or directors of large business firms'. Those from the lower strata of Irish society, Andrews recalled, 'sent their children to the national school for as short a time as possible and a great many emerged from these schools illiterate and remained so'. They also, he observed, filled the ranks of the Royal Dublin Fusiliers. In the First World War these under-educated men were mostly private soldiers and Non-Commissioned Officers (NCOs) at best.[22]

Many of those who feature here were the vanished tribe of Catholic loyalists who saw no contradiction between their faith, their desire for Home Rule for Ireland, and their loyalty both to the United Kingdom in time of war and the British Empire. Many of them were 'imperialist nationalists', as Major Willie Redmond, who died in the war, described himself.

Yet, neither could they be immune to the changes that occurred afterwards. The decision by Dr Joseph O'Carroll, a member of the NUI Senate, to hand back his OBE in 1920 in protest at the behaviour of the Black and

Tans in Ireland demonstrated a sense of betrayal that was keenly felt among many who served in British uniforms in the war. Writing nearly forty years after the war ended, Eugene Sheehy, who also features in this Roll of Honour, recalled the profound impact of the Easter Rising on the Irish serving at the front:

> The Rising in Easter Week was a source of heartbreak for me and to the many tens of thousands of Irish nationalists who had joined the British Army. We had done so at the request of our leaders who were the elected representatives of the people and the vast majority of the people had applauded our actions. As the tide of Irish public opinion gradually changed and hostility to England grew, we did not quite know where we stood, where our duty lay.[23]

The motivations of the Irish who served in the First World War are complicated, but those in this Roll of Honour were not compelled by 'economic conscription', to use James Connolly's famous phrase, to go and fight. They left promising studies, doctors' practices, careers at the bar and engineering jobs. They had everything to lose from participation in their war and eighty of them lost their lives. These men were invariably the sons of small-town prosperous merchants, large farmers, and the professional classes. These also included Dr William Lombard Murphy*, the son of one of Ireland's most successful businessmen, William Martin Murphy, and Dr John Donal (J.D.) Carroll from the famous cigarette dynasty. They were not motivated by boredom or limited opportunities at home.

Irish middle-class support for the war, most notably D Company of the 7th Royal Dublin Fusiliers, the so-called 'Posh pals' drawn from the city's more privileged denizen, was noted by Charles Casey who later became Attorney-General and a judge of the High Court. Castleknock College educated, he served in the 7th Leinsters during the war before going on to have a successful career at the Bar. There were many like him, he said to 'dispel the myth that all who fought and died in the Great War came from the ranks of the unemployed, uneducated and deprived'.[24]

The events of the summer of 1914, which began with the shooting of Archduke Franz Ferdinand on 28 June plunged the continent into war within thirty-seven days. Yet in Ireland, the coming catastrophe was barely noticed as nationalist and unionist politicians debated how the Home Rule Act, due presently to come into force, could be implemented. A conference at Buckingham Place in July 1914 between the leaders of nationalist and unionist Ireland ended without agreement. Six days later the United Kingdom, which then included Ireland, was at war.

The declaration of war on 4 August 1914 came as a profound shock to the university community in Ireland as it did to wider European society.[25] The minutes of NUI's governing body, the Senate, in July 1914, before the great cataclysm, were preoccupied with such matters as the drains in NUI headquarters in Merrion Square and a payment of £4 to the designer of the degree parchments. The extraordinary Senate meeting on Wednesday, 19 August, two weeks after the war broke out, was preoccupied with the war. Everything had changed. The Senate cleared the way for students to participate in Crown forces by agreeing that the 'studentship shall be kept open without prejudice during such service so that the student may resume his tenure on the termination of his (war) service'.[26] This was confirmed at another extraordinary meeting of the Senate on 1 September when it adopted a resolution 'that any student of the university who may be employed in the service of the Crown during the war shall not be prejudiced in any way in his university course on account of such service'.[27] Additionally, it passed a motion allowing members of staff of the university to serve during the war and to keep open their posts.

The relatively neutral language used in these pronouncements was dispensed with when Senate member, Dr George Sigerson, who gives his name to the Sigerson Cup, the Irish universities' premier Gaelic football competition, proposed a motion which was unanimously adopted condemning the burning of the library at Louvain by German forces in the early weeks of the war. It was, he stated, 'a calamity without parallel in history since the destruction of the library of Alexandria'.[28] The burning of Louvain, with its close academic and ecclesiastical ties to Ireland, was keenly felt especially in academic circles. The fate of Belgium, a small Catholic country, also exercised the conscience of many in Ireland in the initial stages of the war. As Tom Kettle put it: 'It is impossible not to be with Belgium in this struggle'.[29]

The British war effort won the immediate backing of the presidents of the respective colleges.[30] UCD's first President Professor Denis Coffey encouraged students to join up, though the university had prominent separatists in its ranks. These included Eoin MacNeill, the founder of the Irish Volunteers and Professor of Early (including Medieval) Irish History, and Thomas MacDonagh, a lecturer in English in UCD, and one of the signatories of the Proclamation, but they were in the minority.

George O'Brien in his *History of the Literary and Historical Society* wrote that those involved in the UCD society were content with the Home Rule settlement as proposed and expected to prosper from it:

> Our professors, without knowing it, were forming the minds of a new governing class ... We all took it for granted that, if Home Rule was achieved, we should be among the politicians of the New Ireland. So certain were we of the approach of Home Rule that some of the students neglected to prepare for a profession, believing that they would get a good job when self-government came.[31]

As Donal McCartney notes too: 'The college authorities and almost all the senior staff were Home Rulers who were grateful to Redmond, Dillon, and the Irish Party for the Irish Universities Act. It was not surprising, therefore, that the college generally was prepared to assist in the war effort'.[32] In 1914, UCD, the largest of the NUI colleges, had 946 students; 722 men and 224 women.[33]

When war broke out, the university's academic council recommended the setting up of an Officers' Training Corps (OTC) to aid the British war effort.[34] Most UK universities and the best private schools had an OTC to give basic military training to men who could reasonably expect a commission in the event of a major war.[35] In April 1915, Coffey asked the British Army's Irish Command to sanction an OTC for the college. He estimated that 500 students, excluding women and ecclesiastical students, were available for war service. Of the 500, he suggested 120 would join an OTC straight away and 'I'm certain that this number would quickly grow to be twice as great'. Significantly though, Coffey was realistic enough to know that a majority of eligible students would not join up in what was predominantly a nationalist-dominated institution.

The War Office turned down the UCD request on the basis that a review of all OTCs had been due to take place before war broke out and that was now postponed indefinitely. 'It not anticipated that such an opportunity will occur before cessation of hostilities,' Brigadier General Richard Greenfield wrote to Coffey later that month.[36] This was not the end of the matter as UCD wrote again to the War Office in October, but the same response came back. The matter was subsequently dropped, but there remained a lingering suspicion that the real reason was a reluctance on the part of the War Office to give military training to nationalists who might use it one day against the Crown.

In Todd Andrews' memoir, Coffey is described as someone who held his position 'by grace of the Irish Party and the Catholic Church'. He was a 'lowsized, extremely dapper, white-haired man' who knew the name of every student. Andrews, who enrolled in UCD shortly after the end of the war, did not hold Coffey's support for the British war effort against him as other advanced nationalists had done. 'The criticism was unjustified. His primary obligation was to keep the college open and in this he had a difficult job considering the state of the country'.[37]

UCC's President Sir Bertram Windle was an English-born Professor of Medicine, but a committed Home Rule nationalist and supporter of both the Irish Party and the Gaelic League. An enthusiastic supporter of the war effort, he detested the Easter Rising and the separatist turn nationalist Ireland took after it.[38] He discerned strong support in UCC initially for the British war effort writing in his diary on 10 August 1914:

> Redmond's speech (in the House of Commons on 3 August) was magnificent and except for a few sore-headed dissentients, Ireland is a united country and what a Godsend that is! And it is boiling with patriotic fervour and a desire to fight for the Empire! Deputation from students wanting to form a Volunteer Corps. Highly approved. I felt it my duty to place the college at the disposal of the military and naval authorities as a base hospital with myself as its administrator and my medical professors as its surgeons. [39]

His disillusionment with the war set in early. He was shocked by the casualties, the chaos it created in his own university and the restlessness that followed the Easter Rising. He was a member of the Irish Convention that failed in 1917 to reconcile nationalist and unionist positions over the Home Rule impasse. Windle sought from the foundation of NUI to have UCC as an independent, self-governing university, but this effort was ultimately unsuccessful.[40] John A. Murphy suggests that there was a suspicion in Sinn Féin that 'Windle was trying to consolidate pro-British, pro-unionist control of UCC', but Windle, who was a father-in-law of Cork Irish Party leader J.J. Horgan, had a more nuanced view of the university's role than that. Deeply disillusioned, Windle eventually left Ireland in 1919.[41]

UCG's President Alexander Anderson was personally invested in the war as his son Alex Jr served in the British Army and was taken prisoner. The college's academic council minutes from May 1915 demonstrated the lengths to which NUI colleges went to in order to facilitate students who participated in the war:

> Students who join the Army are to be allowed, when they return, to take up the same academic position they had at time of leaving as regards college standing and fees: unpaid instalments of scholarships to be retained for them and special consideration to be given them as regards the period of college session at which they come back.[42]

In December 1914, twenty-seven students from UCD asked that their final medical exam be brought forward to the end of June 1915 to enable them to offer their services to the Royal Army Medical Corps (RAMC) at the earliest possible date. The request was granted.[43] The Senate decided that a special examination be held for medical students from the three colleges to enable them to join the RAMC or its Royal Navy equivalent.

In February 1915, the Senate agreed to defer the grant of £6,000 for building works because of the war. The universities were bluntly told by the British administration in Dublin Castle that embarking upon building works is 'undesirable during the continuance of the war … both because of the necessity of postponing all non-urgent expenditure and by reason of the difficulty of securing reasonable tenders for the execution of the work'.[44] Though deprived of funding for much-needed building works, the Senate penned a particularly obsequious letter to the newly-installed Lord Lieutenant Viscount Wimbourne reminding him that 'many of our graduates and undergraduates are on active service in the momentous struggle in which the Empire is at present engaged'.[45] In response, Wimbourne said it was a 'source of satisfaction to the university authorities that many of your graduates and undergraduates have already gone to the front, where they are doing great service to their country and giving good example to their fellows'.[46]

The students who signed up to fight encountered obstacles that other university students in the UK did not face. A completed secondary school education was usually enough to obtain a commission in the British Armed Forces in the First World War and a third-level education was a virtual guarantee. However, this was not the case for all the students and graduates of NUI. The difficulty for many was the absence of prior military training. As has already been noted for UCD, none of the constituent colleges of NUI had an OTC, though the Royal College of Surgeons in Ireland (RCSI) did.

The absence of OTCs in NUI colleges proved to be a source of political embarrassment to John Redmond. The 16th (Irish) Division was formed in the autumn of 1914 as a political imperative and a Catholic, nationalist counterpoint to the unionist and Protestant-dominated 36th (Ulster) Division.[47] The officer commanding the 16th, Lieutenant General Laurence Parsons, showed a tin ear to Irish nationalist sensibilities to the extent that Redmond's deputy John Dillon called him an 'Orange ass'. Parsons refused to offer commissions to candidates who did not have prior military experience.[48] No such qualification was demanded to those given commissions in the 36th (Ulster) Division. Not for the first time, nationalists suspected that one set of rules applied to them and another to unionists. Consequentially, William Archer Redmond, John Redmond's son, signed up as a private in the ranks before obtaining a commission in the Royal Dublin Fusiliers. Eugene Sheehy also recalled how difficult it was for him to get a commission:

> I, as the son of an Irish nationalist member of Parliament (David Sheehy), felt that it was incumbent on me to answer the call, and I applied for a commission in an Irish regiment. The War Office evidently did not approve of Irish nationalists as officers and I discovered that so long as my application was sponsored by Mr (Joe) Devlin MP or Mr T.P. O'Connor MP it achieved no success other than a futile journey to Reigate in Surrey to interview with a major of the London Irish Rifles. It was not until I met Mr Maurice Healy (barrister and solicitor) in Dublin in March 1915 that I received the hint that sponsorship was a hindrance rather than a help.[49]

Eventually Sheehy secured a commission in the 4th Royal Dublin Fusiliers. The British relented partially out of political expediency and partially out of necessity given the high rate of attrition among officers in the initial stages of the war. Almost every man listed in this Roll of Honour was either a commissioned or non-commissioned officer.

The most striking feature of the Roll of Honour is the number of medics who appear on it.[50] This reflected the large number of Irish doctors and medical students who served in the war: 3,336 in total, of whom 261 died, according to *Irish Doctors in the First World War*.[51] Some 808 Irish-born doctors already had commissions in the Royal Army Medical Corps prior to the war. They represented 20% of serving officers in the RAMC, though Ireland was just 10% of the population of the United Kingdom at the time.

Many in Britain grumbled at the relatively low level of recruitment from Ireland in the early stages of the war, but the response from doctors was more enthusiastic.[52] Within two days of the outbreak of the war, sixty Irish doctors had applied for commission in the British Army, according to an article in the *British Medical Journal* published in November 1914.[53] In *The Irish Medical Profession and the First World War*, David Durnin estimates that 20% of all Irish doctors who participated in the war had signed up by December 1914.

In 1915, the Irish Medical War Committee was set up to maximise recruitment among medical personnel. Those targeted included workhouse and dispensary medical officers followed by doctors who worked for the Local Government Board for Ireland (LGBI). The committee issued regular appeals to doctors, and a letter was sent to every serving doctor in November 1915 asking them to join up. The committee also offered doctors protection for the posts they were in, and they were allowed to nominate their own locums.[54] According to Durnin, approximately half of all Ireland's doctors had enlisted in the armed services, in line with England, Scotland and Wales. The absence of doctors was keenly felt in rural parts of Ireland during the war. He concluded: 'An important element of self-mobilisation among the professions was the consistent peer pressure, stemming primarily from senior figures, which sustained enlistment rates. Friends and educational mentors successfully encouraged Ireland's medical men to join'.[55]

Remarkably, Irish doctors remained disproportionately represented in the British Armed Forces long after independence.[56] Between 1922 and 1945, 16.4% of the doctors in the RAMC were from the Irish Free State with an additional 7.2% of the total from Northern Ireland, triple the equivalent number for the size of population. Steven O'Connor points out that the pattern was established long before the First World War with one study suggesting that just a third of Irish doctors who graduated between 1860 and 1905 stayed in Ireland.[57]

> The origins of this recruitment to the British Army lay in a wider medical emigration out of Ireland due to the inability of the predominantly rural and shrinking population to absorb the large number of Irish medical graduates. From the nineteenth century onwards, the sons of upwardly mobile families were increasingly attracted to the income prospects and social status of the medical profession which meant that Irish universities expanded unevenly

and became dependent on the medical school for much of their revenue. Hence, they routinely produced many more medical graduates than could be employed in Ireland and the majority settled in Britain or in Empire.[58]

The men listed in this Roll of Honour were pitched into a conflict that had no parallels before in scale or suffering.[59] The British Empire sustained almost 1.15 million dead in the war, of whom 885,135 were from Great Britain and Ireland. The First World War was also one of the largest conflicts in modern Irish history. More Irish men served (approximately 270,000 between the British Armed Forces and the armed services of Canada, the United States, Australia, New Zealand, and South Africa)[60] than in any war before or since representing, according to Keith Jeffery, between a quarter and a third of the male population of military age (16–35) in Ireland.[61] The exact number of Irish dead remains contested.[62] The Irish National War Memorial Records compiled in 1922 acknowledges 49,647 who were killed, but that figure includes non-Irish personnel who served in Irish regiments.[63]

Tom Burnell's 15 volume series, *26 County Casualties of the Great War*, lists 29,450 people from what is now the Republic of Ireland who died in the war. The criteria for inclusion is born in, died in, address in or next of kin in, what is now the Republic of Ireland.[64] This would indicate a total figure of 49,000 fatalities for the whole of Ireland on a pro-rata (60:40) basis between what is now the Republic of Ireland and Northern Ireland, very close to the original figure in the memorial records, but with substantially different personnel.

The First World War was also a catalyst for many changes that have had a lasting impact. As Jeffery has pointed out, the Easter Rising was an event which occurred during, and as a result of, the First World War and not part of some separate narrative.[65] Therefore, he concluded, the war was the 'single most central experience of twentieth-century Ireland'. It was already contested memory in Ireland by the time it ended in November 1918. There were clashes between republicans and loyalists on the streets of Dublin on Armistice Day.[66] Republicans decided to stage a counterdemonstration in the middle of the reverie and fights broke out with ex-soldiers. For years afterwards the day was a source of rancour in Irish society.

A month after Armistice Day, nationalist Ireland voted overwhelmingly for Sinn Féin in the December 1918 British general election. The party won seventy-three of the 105 seats and outpolled the Irish Parliamentary Party (IPP), which had dominated Irish politics from the 1870s, by more than two to one. Sinn Féin's success was in large part due to the party's opposition to Irish participation in the war especially after the conscription crisis of the spring of 1918. Significantly, the only Irish Parliamentary Party MP returned in the south of Ireland in the 1918 general election was Captain William Archer Redmond, who features in the Roll of Honour. He was returned in the Waterford constituency, which he had won in a by-election to replace his late father John earlier that year.

The students of the National University of Ireland reflected the decisive separatist turn Ireland took in the 1918 election.[67] Professor Eoin MacNeill, standing for Sinn Féin, polled twice as many votes (1,644) as his challenger Professor Arthur Conway (813) who stood for the Irish Parliamentary Party in the NUI constituency.[68] MacNeill had explicitly repudiated Redmond's call in September 1914 for Irishmen to join the British Army and the Irish Volunteers split over the issue.

In his celebrated memoir *On Another Man's Wound*, Ernie O'Malley, a medical student in UCD during the war, recounted how he had gone to the university in 1915 with his classmates: 'There one heard little of the Volunteers or the various other movements'.[69] He had considered joining the British Army as his brother had done, but the Easter Rising made that impossible for him as it did for most nationalist-minded students:

> The university was changed now for me – new associations, new affiliations. Some of the boys had been out and escaped arrest; others who had been in the country had not received orders. I reconstructed my world slowly. We were being hammered red-hot in the furnace of the spirit and a spark was bound to fly and disclose us to each other, with a word, a look, a chance remark.[70]

During the War of Independence, two UCD students were executed by the British. Kevin Barry entered the university in 1919 as a first-year medical student and was hanged a year later as 'just a lad of 18 summers' for his role in an ambush in which three British soldiers were killed. Less well known is Frank Flood, an honours engineering student, who was hanged in March 1921 for his part in an ambush of the Dublin Metropolitan Police in January of that year.

The NUI Roll of Honour was both an act of remembrance and a political act in the context of post-war Ireland. Some members of the NUI Senate were unionists, most were Home Rule nationalists, and there were a few who had separatist sympathies, most notably, the Archbishop of Dublin,

Dr Willie Walsh, the first NUI Chancellor. However, the governing body remained supportive of the students and staff who fought in the war. In 1917, a resolution was passed by the NUI Senate recognising course work or examinations completed by students who were prisoners of war (POWs) and allowed the rest to sit examinations they had missed.[71] This was to be done 'in a manner suited to their circumstances' and in a 'liberal spirit'. The Senate concluded that prisoners of war 'have made great efforts to pursue systematic courses of study and that arrangements are in existence for the work done by them and in most cases for examining them'.[72]

At the end of hostilities, NUI, like all universities in the UK at the time, was anxious to accommodate students who had their studies disrupted because of the war. In December 1918, the NUI Senate agreed that medical students who had served in the armed forces should be allowed to obtain their qualifications 'without undue prolongation'. Students were also given exemptions to sit their first medical examination if they spent one term in practical laboratory instruction.

The deans of the medical faculties were given discretion to allow exemptions from study or examinations to certain students. Exemptions too were made for first, second-, and third-year medical students who had their studies interrupted by the war. Students who had passed their third-year medical examination but had missed lectures in fourth year because of war service were also exempted from the six-months hospital placement. Similarly, students who had attended certain courses while in the pay of the armed forces were accepted into NUI colleges though they had not matriculated in the usual way, as were students sent to the university by the Ministry of Munitions.[73]

In December 1917, a sub-committee of the Senate was set up to examine how best to acknowledge those who had distinguished themselves in the war with the intention of giving some of them an honorary degree. UCD, UCC, and UCG all contributed long lists of names. In February 1918, UCC delivered a list of names of those who had won various distinctions for bravery in the war or were mentioned in dispatches. According to supporting documentation for the Senate minutes, UCG provided a list of students who fought in the war without mentioning any distinctions. UCD published its list of alumni and students who fought in the war in its 1918/1919 calendar. The list is published verbatim in the NUI Roll of Honour. UCC also produced a list of its graduates who fought in the war separately in its official gazette published in July 1919.

It would appear that these publications were the origins of the war list that was published later in 1919 by NUI and is reproduced here. It was a considerable logistical feat given the administrative chaos that followed the war's end. The Roll of Honour remains a valuable reference point to this day. It remembers 914 students, graduates, and staff who fought in the war. Of those, 443 were from UCD (48%), 335 (37%) from UCC and the rest 136 (15%) from UCG. Some eighty are listed here as having died, forty-three from UCD (54%), twenty-six from UCC (32%) and eleven (14%) from UCG.[75] In the First World War an average of one in eight British servicemen (12.3%) were killed. The death rate of those from NUI who participated in the war was 8.75%. This reflects the preponderance of doctors and engineers on the list who by definition were not in the front line though the risk of death or injury were far from trivial.

Those who returned from the war did so with some trepidation. In his 1964 tribute to the economist and First World War veteran, John Busteed, Denis Gwynn remarked that 'military service in the British Army during those years usually became a handicap for future careers in Ireland'.[76] Busteed, he stated, was an exception in that regard. Gwynn took a keen interest in the fate of those from the professional classes who served in the war and was always on hand to pay tributes in his popular *Cork Examiner* column *Now and Then*. Many of his observations appear here. And yet the experience of Busteed and that of himself would appear to contradict his claim that military service in the First World War was a barrier to employment in the Irish Free State.[77] Busteed became one of the country's best-known economists and was appointed Professor of Economics in UCC just six years after the war ended. Gwynn's war service and his staunch defence of John Redmond was no barrier to him becoming Professor of Modern Irish History at UCC in 1946, a position he held for seventeen years.[78]

The biographical profiles of a selection of NUI students and graduates who survived the war would also suggest that there was no discernible penalty in the Irish Free State for those who served in the war. The new state was not so endowed with professional talent that it could turn its back on those who had served in British Armed Services. Neither did it. Many of those who appear in the Roll of Honour achieved high office after independence. The case of Dr Maurice Hayes is instructive.[79] When he died in 1930, many members of the cabinet, including the President of the Executive Council, William T. Cosgrave, and the former chief-of-staff of the IRA, Richard Mulcahy, attended his funeral. During the Civil War,

Hayes was appointed by Michael Collins as the Director-General of the Irish Free State Army Medical Corps and set about recruiting many of his fellow British veterans.

Similarly, Lieutenant Francis Joseph Morrin became the first Director of medical services in the National Army. His war service in a British uniform was no bar to his appointment as surgeon and officer in charge at the Curragh Hospital during the Civil War. When he retired as Director of medical services in 1924, an official dinner was held in his honour in which he was praised for his 'true and loyal service to the State, the Army and the Corps'.[80] This was in keeping with the willingness of the nascent Irish state to use the services of British Army veterans to fight against anti-Treaty forces in the Civil War.[81] According to Liam Tobin, one of the leading figures in the National Army, half of those who served in it were ex-British servicemen.

Other doctors on the Roll of Honour secured important public positions in the new State.[82] Dr Edmond McWeeney became the first Irish civil servant to work for the United Nations when he moved to the World Health Organization (WHO) to work in tuberculosis research. Casey et al., in *Irish Doctors in the First World War,* concluded those who served were not:

> ... in any way disadvantaged in civilian life on account of their military service. On the contrary, it is obvious from the lists of the presidents of both the RCSI (Royal College of Surgeons in Ireland) and the RCPI (Royal College of Physicians in Ireland) in the years following the war that military service was no hindrance to advancement in their chosen career.[83]

Durnin states that there was an oversupply of doctors in Ireland after the war. Those who had posts before the war were able to return to them, but those who had gone straight from medical school to the Royal Army Medical Corps (RAMC) found that it 'was an impediment to career development for many Irish doctors ... it has been posited here that returning doctors sometimes experienced difficulty in securing positions as a consequence of their ties to the British Army'. He adds: 'However, in other cases, the IRA ultimately coveted army doctors for their professional skill and wartime experience'.

If anything, the status of army chaplains in the new State was enhanced by their wartime service. Fr Joseph Scannell went from the Irish Guards to become the first chaplain of the National Army in Cork. When Michael Collins died during the Civil War in August 1922, Scannell recited the funeral prayers over his body. His fellow Cork prelate Fr Duggan recalled the ambiguities and competing loyalties of the time:

> My generation in Maynooth embraced the ideals of Easter Week 1916 with a hundred per cent fervour. That did not prevent us from become chaplains in the British Army. In the First World War there were well over 100,000 Irish Catholics in the fighting ranks. Everyone admitted that these boys were spiritually intractable to anyone save to an Irish priest. Hence, when in 1917, Cardinal Logue issued a special appeal for Irish chaplains, I volunteered. And I went off to France with the blessing and the encouragement of every friend I had in advanced Sinn Féin circles in Dublin.[84]

Duggan later enlisted as a chaplain in the British forces in the Second World War though he was overage.

Eugene Sheehy was active in post-war veterans' politics, and then became legal officer to the Free State army after the Civil War and later a judge.[85] He was even appointed as a military referee in adjudicating on the pension claims of veterans of the War of Independence and Civil War. The hardships suffered by veterans were considerable, but nobody had it easy in the impoverished state that followed independence. British Armed Forces' veterans had pensions and access in some cases to housing through the Soldiers and Sailors Trust. There were also considerably more of them than there were those who served in the IRA during the war.

Many of these men were able to pick up their lives from where they left off, but none could have been immune to the horrors that they witnessed. Alex Anderson Jr, the son of Alexander Anderson who was University College Galway (UCG) President for thirty-five years (1899–1934) set up a car dealership in London after the war. The business went bankrupt after two years. Anderson walked all the way from London to Liverpool, changed his name to Arthur Andrews and cut all ties with his family. His sister Emily's biographer, Jackie Uí Chionna, suggested Anderson's decision to change his name was motivated by the trauma of his wartime experience, the shooting down of his plane, the death of his pilot and his subsequent incarceration in a German prisoner-of-war camp: 'Having tried and failed in his initial attempt to overcome his wartime experience, he sought another way to deal with the trauma and reinvent himself'.[86]

In a debate in the Dáil in 1927, William Archer Redmond moved a private motion calling for a commission to be set up to examine the circumstances of British ex-servicemen in the Irish Free State:

> When it is remembered that there are, as has been stated many times, from 150,000 to 200,000 British ex-servicemen in Ireland, and when one realises that their dependents, taking the dependents on a very low plane as three, would make the total sum of citizens of this country involved in this motion in or about half a million, I think that the House will recognise its gravity.[87]

There was safety in numbers. The men listed in this Roll of Honour who survived and who are profiled here resumed their careers afterwards. Even Dr Charles Nyhan, who was targeted during the War of Independence by the IRA for being the doctor available to Crown forces in Clonakilty, Co Cork, remained as the dispensary doctor in the town. It is also undeniable, though, that official commemorations of the Irish who fought in the war became more difficult as the years went on. The fate of the memory of Tom Kettle came to encapsulate the ambivalence among the public in general and official hostility to those Irishmen who served in British uniforms in the First World War.

The Easter Rising had a profound effect on the Irish psyche and on the remembrance of those Irishmen who fought in the First World War. Before he died, Kettle famously prophesised that those who fought against the British 'will go down to history as heroes and martyrs and I will go down – if I go down at all – as a bloody British soldier'.[88]

Shortly after his death, a T.M. Kettle Memorial Committee was set up by his friends. It commissioned a sculptor, Albert Power, to create a bust of Kettle with a view to putting it in a public place. A public fund for the memorial was oversubscribed. The bust was not ready until March 1921, by which time the War of Independence made it politically impossible to erect any memorial to a former British Army soldier and especially to someone who was among the most prominent Irish recruiters during the First World War.[89] In 1927, the ceremony was fixed for 25 March of that year, but difficulties arose with the Commissioner of the Board of Works as to the inscription. The commissioner objected to the final words of Kettle's poem *To My Daughter Betty, the Gift of God*: 'Died not for flag nor king nor emperor/But for a dream born in a herdsman's shed and for the secret scripture of the poor'. It was further stipulated that there be no public announcement of the unveiling ceremony and that the former Irish Parliamentary Party MP Joe Devlin, who had been a supporter of the British war effort, was not to make any comments of a political nature.[90] These strictures proved to be unacceptable to Kettle's widow Mary. The plinth on which the bust was supposed to stand remained unoccupied until the memorial was eventually unveiled without any public ceremony in 1937 in St Stephen's Green. The inscription on it satisfied nobody. It reads:

THOMAS M. KETTLE
1880–1916
Born in County Dublin
3rd February 1880.
Killed At Guinchy
9th September 1916.
Poet. Essayist. Patriot.

The centenary of Kettle's death in 2016, coinciding with the centenary of the Easter Rising, was a demonstration of how much attitudes had changed in Ireland in recent decades towards those Irishmen who died in the First World War.[91] A memorial service was held in Kettle's honour in St Stephen's Green; a commemoration event was also held in the Palace of Westminster. UCD unveiled a bronze plaque on the centenary of his death and hosted a conference dedicated to his life and writings. At the plaque unveiling, UCD President Professor Andrew Deeks, acknowledged that the university had links to the Easter Rising, but also noted:

> The experience of service in the First World War was in many ways the more typical experience for UCD students of this era. Today, in this place of quiet contemplation, we remember not merely the stellar figure of Tom Kettle but also those from UCD who fought and fell in the terrible European conflagration which engulfed the continent for more than four years a century ago. We remember those who went to tend to the wounded as well as those who went to fight. One of my predecessors, the University's first president, Dr Denis Coffey, was, like Tom Kettle, a committed Irish nationalist who saw his duty to support the war effort. UCD made a significant contribution to the list of Irishmen who served in the First World War.[92]

In 2016, UCD digitised its Roll of Honour, made it publicly available online, and set up a Twitter account that tweeted the names of its students killed in the war.[93] At the same time, UCD acknowledged its not inconsiderable contribution to the Easter Rising by hosting a public exhibition about its former student and lecturer, Thomas MacDonagh, who was executed as one of the signatories of the Proclamation.[94]

In 2014, UCC hosted a conference on the origins of the war that included Dr Andrew Murrison, the special representative on commemorations for the then British Prime Minister David Cameron. Since 2011, the university has staged an annual concert in honour of the twenty-six students and staff from UCC who died in the war.[95] University of Galway produced both a physical and online exhibition about the college's role during the Irish Revolution, which included a section on its students and staff in the war, and also an online biography of the eleven students from UCG who were killed.[96] Maynooth University held an exhibition in 2015 to remember the chaplains from the college who served in the war, at least one of whom was killed.[97]

NUI's decision to republish this Roll of Honour is an act of remembrance extended to those Irishmen who served in the First World War in British uniforms. It is a timely reminder that all Irishmen who fought in the war were volunteers. They joined for varied reasons. They had agency and they exercised it in the belief that they were doing the right thing, even if it may be hard for us, at one hundred years' remove, to understand their motivations. As the Irish Party MP and volunteer Stephen Gwynn, the father of Denis, wrote: 'It is very difficult now, after all that has crowded in upon us, to reconstitute the frame of mind in which we passed those days'.[98]

In 1966, when nationalist Ireland was gripped by the fervour surrounding the commemorations to mark the 50th anniversary of the Easter Rising, the then Taoiseach Seán Lemass remarked, 'In later years it was common – and I also was guilty in this respect – to question the motives of those men who joined the new British armies formed at the outbreak of war, but it must, in their honour and in fairness to their memory, be said that they were motivated by the highest purpose.'[99] The Lemass family exemplified the differing allegiances of Irish families at that time. While he and his brother Noel were both involved in the Easter Rising and War of Independence, their cousin Herbert Lemass was killed during the Battle of the Somme.

All eighty men who are listed as having died in the Roll of Honour are profiled in Chapter 2, along with forty-two who survived. Of the eighty who died, there are no listings for Donal Barry, Wilfred Dixon, or George Naylor, all UCC students who served with the RAMC, in either the Irish National War Memorial Records or the Commonwealth War Graves Commission website. They are listed, though, in *Irish Doctors in the First World War*.[100] It may be the case that these men died of natural causes and are therefore not regarded as having died on active service or as a consequence of active service.

Men from the officer classes who died were usually well memorialised particularly in the newspaper *Irish Life*. Similarly, De Ruvigny's Roll of Honour chronicled more than 25,000 commissioned and non-commissioned officers who died in the war. This was in contrast to many of those who enlisted as privates from the lower ranks in Irish society at the time and whose deaths never merited anything more than a footnote or a death notice in the newspapers of the time. In *The University at War*, Tomás Irish concludes that 'few institutions were as profoundly impacted by the First World War as universities. The mass mobilization of student populations into belligerent armies from 1914 transformed the university campus and the scholarly community, causing a rupture from which it would take almost a decade to recover'. [101]

They were at the vanguard of a total industrial war where all the resources of modern European states were marshalled to the collective war effort. Tens of thousands of young men in universities in the combatant nations joined up to fight. Students from German universities were slaughtered at the first Battle of Ypres in the autumn of 1914. The long, melancholy list of names is carved into the walls of the entrance to the Langemarck German Military Cemetery. It became known as the *kindermord* (the massacre of the innocents).

The war claimed the children of the elite as much as it did the ruled. Among those killed in the war was Raymond Asquith, the son of the British Prime Minister Herbert Asquith and an alumnus of Oxford. [102] The university lost a staggering 2,716 men during the war, 19.2% of those who served. Andrew Bonar Law, the Conservative leader during the war and afterwards prime minister, two sons were killed. Two of the stepsons of German's principal military strategist Erich Ludendorff were killed, as was the son of the Allied supreme commander Ferdinand Foch.

The First World War was a war in which the commissioned British officer was more likely to be killed than the private soldier. [103] An average of one in six died in the war compared to one in eight privates. [104] The war had a devastating impact on Britain's public schools and universities. As John Lewis-Stempel observed in 2014: 'The more exclusive your education, the more likely you were to die'. [105] Of the students who served in the war, 18% from Oxford, 16.6% from Cambridge, 15% from Edinburgh and 12.8% from St Andrew's University in Scotland were killed. War memorials were built in these universities after the war.

Trinity College Dublin also suffered devastating losses in the war. [106] Of the 3,000 who enlisted, 471 (15%) were killed. TCD's commitment to the British war effort reflected its status as a bastion of unionism in the nationalist South. [107] The dead are remembered by name in the Hall of Honour, now a vestibule to the Reading Room, which was closed off to the public for many years.

There is no such memorial for NUI graduates who died in the war. Their numbers were more modest, but they faced unique circumstances coming from a more ambivalent place than university students and graduates in the rest of the UK as it was then. The survivors listed here are a sample of those who distinguished themselves either in Irish society or in Britain after the war. Despite the horrors they witnessed, many fulfilled their potential and went on to live long productive lives. The men in this Roll of Honour were no less patriotic for their war service and many of them made a significant contribution to their professions and their country. It is right that they are remembered.

The National University of Ireland

1919 ROLL OF HONOUR

REPRODUCTION

THE NATIONAL UNIVERSITY OF IRELAND.

WAR LIST.

ROLL OF HONOUR.

DUBLIN:
PRINTED FOR THE NATIONAL UNIVERSITY
BY ALEX. THOM & CO. (LIMITED), CROW STREET.
1919.

THE NATIONAL UNIVERSITY OF IRELAND

WAR LIST

ROLL OF HONOUR

The National University of Ireland.

WAR LIST.

ROLL OF HONOUR.

UNIVERSITY COLLEGE, DUBLIN.

KILLED IN ACTION, OR DIED ON ACTIVE SERVICE.

James Barrett, M.B., B.Ch. (1907), Staff Surgeon, R.N.

James O'S. Beveridge, M.B., B.Ch. (1915), Captain, R.A.M.C.

Jeremiah Brennan, B.A., LL.B. (1914), Second Lieutenant, Lancashire Hussars.

Patrick Anthony L. Byrne (1912-14), D.S.O., Captain, R.F.C.

Joseph P. Coghlan, M.Sc. (1914), Military Cross, Lieut., Royal Engineers.

Ambrose J. S. Davoren, B.A., LL.B (1914), Lieut., Royal Artillery.

John J. Doyle (1911-14), Lieut., 6th Batt. Royal Dublin Fusiliers.

Thomas A. Duggan (1912-14), Second-Lieut., 10th Batt. Lancashire Fusiliers.

James St. J. Dundon, M.B., B.Ch. (1915), Lieut., R.A.M.C.

James Jameson Dwyer, L.R.C.P.S.I. (1909), D.S.O., Captain, R.A.M.C.

Thomas L. Enright, L.R.C.P.S.I. (1914), Captain, R.A.M.C.

Godwin Swifte O'Flahertie (1913-14), Sec.-Lieut., Shropshire Light Infantry.

Edmund H. Flanigan, M.B., B.Ch. (1908), Lieut., R.A.M.C.

Arthur H. Flannery, M.B., B.Ch. (1915), Surgeon, R.N.

Gerald J. Fogarty (1912-1915), Second-Lieut., 3rd Batt. R.I.R Observer, R.F.C.

Joseph Garry, M.B., B.Ch. (1914), Surgeon, *Lusitania.*

John Joseph Gilligan (1913-14), Second-Lieut., R.F.A.

Captain The Rev. John Gwynn, S.J., Army Chaplain.

Timothy J. Hartigan, M.B., B.Ch. (1901), Surgeon, Royal Navy.

Dermot Healy (1912), Second-Lieut., Royal Dublin Fusiliers.

Thomas O. Kavanagh (1913), 3rd Batt. Royal Irish Fusiliers.
Thomas J. Keating (1912-14), Captain, R.F.A.
Joseph F. Kelly, M.B., B.Ch. (1891), Lieut.-Colonel, R.A.M.C.
Professor Thomas M. Kettle, Lieut., 9th Dublin Fusiliers.
Thomas J. Lacy (1912-15), Second-Lieut., R.F.A.
Patrick S. Lynch (1910-1913), Military Cross with Bar, Lieut., 7th Batt. Leinster Regiment.
Hugh O'N. Maguire (1912-14), Second-Lieut., 3rd Batt. Connaught Rangers.
Edmund J. Mahony (1908), Lieut., 9th Batt. Munster Fusiliers.
William Mallen (1915), Lieut., Royal Dublin Fusiliers.
Michael J. Moynihan (1909-10), London Rifles.
Roger M'Grath, M.B., B.Ch. (1914), Captain, R.A.M.C.
Louis L. M'Keever, L.R.C.P.S.I. (1914), Captain, R.A.M.C.
James P. M'Loughlin (1910-1913), Lieut., 4th Batt. Royal Dublin Fusiliers.
William J. M'Veigh (1910-11), Lieut., Royal Munster Fusiliers.
John Neligan, M.B., B.Ch. (1915), Lieut., R.A.M.C.
James J. Nolan (1913-15), Surgical Probationer, Royal Navy.
Francis B. E. O'Carroll (1913-14), Second-Lieut., 6th Batt. Royal Dublin Fusiliers.
Patrick J. O'Reilly, L.R.C.P.S.I. (1914), M.C., Captain, R.A.M.C.
Bernard Reid, B.A. (1911), Second-Lieut., 9th Batt. Royal Dublin Fusiliers.
Gerald C. Rooney (1893), Major, Royal Marine Light Infantry.
Herbert Tierney, B.A. (1908), Lieut., Cheshire Regiment—Missing, believed killed.
Joseph G. Walsh (1911-14), Gunner, Royal Field Artillery.
Stephen B. Walsh, B.A., M.D. (1905), Lieut., R.A.M.C.

MILITARY DISTINCTIONS.

Award of C.M.G.

Bernard Forde, M.B., B.Ch. (1886), Lieut.-Colonel, R.A.M.C.

Award of D.S.O.

Patrick A. L. Byrne (1912), Captain, R.F.C.—Missing.
Robert Cahill, M.B., B.Ch. (1903), Major, R.A.M.C.
Walter Coppinger, B.A., M.B., B.Ch. (1897), Major, Royal Army Medical Corps (Indian Med. Service).

James Jameson Dwyer, L.R.C.P.S.I. (1909), Captain, R.A.M.C.
William Egan, M.B., B.Ch. (1904), Major, R.A.M.C.
Frederick Garland, M.B., B.Ch. (1901), Major, R.A.M.C.
James Geoffrey Gill, L.R.C.P.S.I. (1896), Lieut.-Colonel, R.A.M.C.
Rev. Henry Gill, S.J., Chaplain
Patrick J. Hanafin (With Bar), L.R.C.P.S.I. (1901), Lieut.-Colonel, R.A.M.C.
Edward Kavanagh, M.B., B.Ch. (1906), Major, R.A.M.C.
Peter Burrowes Kelly, L.R.C.P.S.I., Surgeon, R.N.
Edmund M'Allister (1895), Major, Army Service Corps.
Sir Christopher W. Nixon, Bart. (1896), Major, R.F.A.
Arthur D. O'Carroll, M.B., B.Ch. (1904), Lieut.-Colonel, R.A.M.C.
Charles O'Gorman, L.R.C.P.S.I. (1894), Lieut.-Colonel, R.A.M.C.
Edward M. O'Neill, M.B., B.Ch. (1905), Major, R.A.M.C.
Michael Power, L.R.C.P.S.I. (1902-6), Major, South African Army Medical Corps.
Francis C. Sampson, M.B., B.Ch. (1903), R.A.M.C. With Bar.
William A. Redmond, B.A. (1907), Captain, Inniskilling Fusiliers.
Joseph F. Whelan, M.B., B.Ch. (1896), Major, R.A.M.C.

Award of D.F.C.

Oscar A. Heron (1916), Captain, R.A.F.

Award of Military Cross.

Charles Bannigan, M.B., B.Ch. (1913), Captain, R.A.M.C.
Arthur J. Beveridge, M.B., B.Ch. (1915), Captain, R.A.M.C.
Arthur M. J. Blake L.R.C.P.S.I. (1910) Captain R.A.M.C. (With B r).
John Burke, L.R.C.P.S.I. (1908), Captain, R.A.M.C.
Leo Blake, M.B., B.Ch. (1916), Captain, R.A.M.C.
John Donal Carroll, B.Sc., M.B., B.Ch. (1913), Captain, R.A.M.C.
Philip Carney, M.B., B.Ch. (1914), Captain, R.A.M.C.
John A. Coghlan (1913), Lieut., Tank Corps.
Joseph P. Coghlan, M.Sc. (1914), Lieut., Royal Engineers—Killed in action.
Joseph M. A. Costello, M.B., B.Ch. (1907), M.D. (1917), Major, R.A.M.C.
Thomas J. Costello, B.Sc., M.B., B.Ch. (1913), Captain, R.A.M.C.
Eugene H. Coyne, M.B., B.Ch. (1915), Captain, R.A.M.C.
Cecil Dillon-Kelly, L.R.C.P.S.I., Captain, R.A.M.C.
Lomond Dillon-Kelly, L.R.C.P.S.I., Captain, R.A.M.C.
Patrick Dwyer, M.B., B.Ch. (1903), Captain, R.A.M.C.

A 1

George C. Gaynor, M.B., B.Ch. (1915), Captain, R.A.M.C.
Rev. Henry J. Gill, M.A., Army Chaplain.
William E. Graham, M.B., B.Ch. (1911), Captain, R.A.M.C.
Bartholomew Hackett, M.B., B.Ch. (1899),Captain, R.A.M.C.
Charles J. Hannigan, B.A., M.B., B.Ch. (1914), Captain, R.A.M.C
Henry A. Harbinson, M.B., B.Ch. (1913) (With Bar), Captain, R.A.M.C.
William Hickey, M.B., B.Ch. (1917), Lieut., R.A.M.C.
Edward Kavanagh, M.B., B.Ch. (1916), Major, R.A.M.C.
Richard Kenefick, M.B., B.Ch. (1912), Captain, R.A.M.C.
Alphonsus P. M. Kennedy (1914), Second-Lieut.
Ernest W. O'G. Kirwan, M.B., B.Ch. (1909), Major, I.M.S.
Patrick J. Lane, M.B., B.Ch. (1915), Captain, R.A.M.C.
Patrick S. Lynch (1910-13) (With Bar), Lieut., 7th Leinsters—Killed in action.
John P. Marren (1915), 2nd Lieut.
Timothy Meagher, M.B., B.Ch. (1906), Captain, R.A.M.C.
Joseph B. M'Arevey (1913-15), Captain, Royal Irish Rifles.
Louis L. M'Keever, L.R.C.P.S.I. (1914), Captain, R.A.M.C.
John D. McCormack, L.R.C.P.S.I. (1914), Captain, R.A.M.C.
Desmond M'Weeney (1915-16), Second-Lieut., Connaught Rangers.
Arthur P. O'Connor, B.A., M.B., B.Ch. (1908), Captain R.A.M.C.
Joseph P. O'Reilly (1914), Sec.-Lieut., Royal Munster Fusiliers.
Patrick J. O'Reilly, L.R.C.P.S.I. (1914), Captain, R.A.M.C. With Bar.
Gerard Petit, L.R.C.P.S.I. (1906), Captain, R.A.M.C.
James Power, B.Sc., B.E. (1914), Lieutenant, R.E.
Maurice A. Power, M.B., B.Ch. (1906), with 2nd Bar, Captain, R.A.M.C.
John J. Reynolds, M.B., B.Ch. (1914), Captain, R.A.M.C.
Walter N. Rishworth, M.B., B.Ch. (1911), Captain, R.A.M.C.
John M. Rowe, M.B., B.Ch., Captain, R.A.M.C.
Charles Roche, L.R.C.P.S.I. (1914) (With Bar), Captain, R.A.M.C.
Peter J. Ryan, B.A., M.B., B.Ch., Captain, R.A.M.C.
James Shelly, B.E. (1914), Second-Lieut., Royal Engineers.
Christopher T. Sullivan, F.R.C.S.I. (L. 1900), Captain, R.A.M.C.

Award of Croix de Guerre.

Timothy Meagher, M.B., B.Ch. (1906), Captain, R.A.M.C.
William L. Murphy, B.A., M.B. (Cantab.) (1907), Captain, R.A.M.C.
Joseph M. A. Costello, M.D., M.C.

Arthur M. J. Blake, L.R.C.P.S.I., M.C.
John M. Rowe, M.B., B.Ch., M.C.
Peter John Ryan, B.A., M.B., B.Ch., M.C.
Oscar A. Heron, D.F.C.

Award of Medaille des Epidémies (en Vermeil).

Edward M. O'Neill, M.B., B.Ch., D.S.O.

Award of O.B.E.

Col. Joseph F. O'Carroll, M.B., F.R.C.P.I. (Professor).
Lieut.-Col. Thomas Potter, L.R.C.P.S.I.
Major Charles F. White, M.B., B.Ch.
Capt. Richard F. O'T. Dickinson, L.R.C.P.&S.I.
Lieut.-Col. Thomas McDermott, M.B., B.Ch.
Major Bertram J. Collingwood (Professor).
Capt. William A. Frost, M.B., B.Ch.

Award of M.B.E.

Major J. Bayley Butler, M.A., M.B., B.Ch. (Professor).
Lieut. Vincent A. Cox, B.A.

Egyptian Order.

Capt. Percy M. Brett, M.B., B.Ch.

Award of C.I.E.

Major John B. Hanafin, F.R.C.P.S.I., I.M.S.

Award of Serbian Order of St. Sava.

Lieut.-Col. Bernard Forde, M.B., B.Ch., R.A.M.C. 3rd Order.
Capt. Richard V. Slattery, M.B., B.Ch., R.A.M.C. 4th Order.

PAST AND PRESENT STUDENTS OF THE COLLEGE AND OF THE MEDICAL SCHOOL, CECILIA STREET, SERVING 1914-1918.

(Owing to the difficulty in obtaining the names of Past Students, this list is incomplete.)

The Titles of Rank and Unit are given provisionally, as it has not been possible to refer fully to Official Publications.

Those who were members of the Army or Navy previous to the War are marked †

The dates indicate the year of taking Degree or qualification, or of entering College.

Members of the College Staff.

Blaney, Alexander J. M'A., M.A., M.B., B.Ch., F.R.C.S.I., Assistant in Surgery, Major, Royal Army Medical Corps.

Butler, J. Bayley, M.A., M.B., B.Ch., Professor of Botany, Lieut., Royal Army Medical Corps, Promoted Captain.

Collingwood, Bertram J., B.A., M.D., Professor of Physiology, Major, Royal Army Medical Corps. With special appointment in Gas Instruction.

Crofton, William M., B.A., M.D., Lecturer on Special Pathology, Capt., Royal Army Medical Corps.

Gwynn, Rev. John, B.A., Member of the Governing Body, Chaplain. *Killed.*

Hayes, Maurice, F.R.C.S.I., Assistant in Pharmacy, Capt., Royal Army Medical Corps.

Kettle, Thomas M., B.A., Professor of National Economics, Lieut , 9th Batt. R. Dublin Fusiliers. *Killed.*

Meade, Henry S., F.R.C.S.I., Demonstrator of Anatomy, Capt., Royal Army Medical Corps, 1915. In 1914 with French Red Cross and French Army.

O'Hanlon, Oriel J., M.B., B.Ch., Demonstrator of Anatomy. *Mentioned in Despatches.* Lieut., Royal Army Medical Corps. Promoted Captain.

Slattery, Richard V., B.A., M.B., B.Ch., Hon. Demonstrator of Anatomy. *Mentioned in Despatches. Serbian Award, 4th Class, Order of St. Sava.* Capt., Royal Army Medical Corps (T.F.).

PAST AND PRESENT STUDENTS.

Adye-Curran, John. (Entered 1913). Motor Service.

†Adye-Curran, Stafford, L.R.C.P&S.I., 1900, Major, Royal Army Medical Corps.

†Adye-Curran, William, J.P., L.R.C.P.&S.I., 1898. *Mentioned in Despatches.* Major, Royal Army Medical Corps. Promoted Lieut.-Col.

Ahern, John M., M.B., B.Ch., 1902, Lieut., Royal Army Medical Corps.

†Ahern, Michael D., L.R.C.P.&S.E. (Entered 1901). Capt., Royal Army Medical Corps.

Bannigan, Charles, M.B., B.Ch., 1913. *Awarded Military Cross. Mentioned in Despatches.* Lieut., Royal Army Medical Corps. Promoted Captain.

†Barrett, James, M.B., B.Ch., 1907, Staff Surgeon, Royal Navy. *Died on Active Service.*

Barrett, Jeremiah, L.R.C.P.&S.I., 1913, Lieut., Royal Army Medical Corps.

Barrett, Joseph H. P. B., M.D., 1912, Lieut., Royal Army Medical Corps.

Beveridge, Arthur J., M.B., B.Ch., 1915. *Awarded Military Cross. Mentioned in Despatches.* Lieut., Royal Army Medical Corps. Promoted Captain and Acting Major. *Wounded.*

Beveridge, Gerald O. (Entered 1902). *Mentioned in Despatches. Meritorious Service Medal Special Reserve Service Medal (Large).* Sergt.-Major, M.M.P.

Beveridge, James O'S., M.B., B.Ch., 1915, Lieut., Royal Army Medical Corps. Promoted Captain. *Killed.*

Beveridge, William John, L.R.C.P.&S.I., 1896, M.D. (Brux), Major, Australian Army Medical Corps.

Blake, Arthur M. J., L.R.C.P.&S.I., 1910. *Awarded Military Cross. with Bar. Mentioned in Despatches.* Lieut., Royal Army Medical Corps. Promoted Captain.

Blake, Leo, M.B., B.Ch., 1916, Lieut., Royal Army Medical Corps. Promoted Captain.

Bobbett, James C. (Entered 1901), Artists' Training Corps.

†Bourke, John J., M.A., M.B., 1891, Lt.-Col., Indian Med. Service.

Boylan, Daniel, M.B., B.Ch., 1907, Lieut., Royal Army Medical Corps.

Boyle, Cornelius C., M.B., B.Ch., 1913, Lieut., Royal Army Medical Corps.

Brennan, Garrett. (Entered 1912), in the Ranks.

Brennan, Jeremiah, B.A., LL.B., 1914, Sec.-Lieut., Lancashire Hussars. *Killed.*

Brennan, Richard D., M.B., B.Ch., 1915, Lieut., Royal Army Medical Corps.

Brereton-Barry, James, L. A. H., 1915, Lieut., Royal Army Medical Corps. Promoted Captain. *Wounded.*

†Brett, Percy Morgan J., M.B., B.Ch., 1909, Capt., Royal Army Medical Corps.

Broderick, Simon L. N., Lieut., Army Medical Corps.

Browne, James M., M.B., B.Ch., 1894, Lieut., Royal Army Medical Corps. Promoted Captain.

†Burke, Francis, M.B., B.Ch., 1910, Lieut., Royal Army Medical Corps.

Burke, John William. (Entered 1911). Royal Army Medical Corps. Promoted 2nd-Lieut., Royal Irish Rifles. *Wounded.*

Burke, John, L.R.C.P&S.I., 1908, Lieut., Royal Army Medical Corps. Promoted Captain and Acting Major.

Burke, Michael J., L.R.C.P.&S.I., 1915, Lieut., Royal Army Medical Corps.

Byrne, Francis M. J., L.R.C.P.&S.I., 1914, Lieut., Royal Army Medical Corps. Promoted Captain.

Byrne, Patrick Anthony L. (Entered 1912). *Awarded D.S.O. Mentioned in Despatches.* Sec.-Lieut., Royal Field Artillery. *Wounded.* Royal Flying Corps. *Missing, believed killed.*

Byrne, Patrick J., 1912-16, Surgical Probationer, Royal Navy.

Burns, Michael, M.B., B.Ch., Lieut., Royal Army Medical Corps.

Burke-Gaffney, Edward, B.E., 1911, Sec.-Lieut., Royal Engineers

Burke-Gaffney, P. O'D., B.E., B.Sc., 1912, Trooper, Canadian Fort Garry Horse.

†Cahill, Robert, M.B., B.Ch., 1903. *Mentioned in Despatches Awarded D.S.O.* Capt., Royal Army Medical Corps *Prisoner of War—repatriated.* Promoted Major and Lieut.-Col.

Cahir, John P., M.B., B.Ch., 1908. *Mentioned in Despatches.* Lieut., Royal Army Medical Corps. Promoted Captain and Acting Major.

Camac, Rev. Joseph P., B.A., 1911, Chaplain.

Campbell, Charles M. G., L.R.C.P.&S.I., 1914, Lieut., Royal Army Medical Corps. Promoted Captain.

Cane, Richard J., L.R.C.P.&S.I., 1900, Lieut., Royal Army Medical Corps. Promoted Captain.

Cannon, Dominick J., B.A., M.B., B.Ch., 1913, Lieut., Royal Army Medical Corps.

Carey, Edward P., B.A., B.Sc., M.B., B.Ch., 1914, Lieut., Royal Army Medical Corps. Promoted Captain.

Carey, Thomas V., Surgical Probationer, Royal Navy.

Carney, Philip, M.B., B.Ch., 1914 *Awarded Military Cross. Mentioned in Despatches.* Lieut., Royal Army Medical Corps. Promoted Captain and acting Major. *Wounded.*

Carroll, James F. (Entered 1910). Sec.-Lieutenant.

Carroll, John Donal, B.Sc., M.B., B.Ch., 1913. *Awarded Military Cross. Mentioned in Despatches.* Lieut., Royal Army Medical Corps. Promoted Captain.

Carroll, Patrick E. M.B., B.Ch., Lieut., Royal Army Medical Corps.

Carroll, Joseph J. (Entered 1902). Capt., Roy. Dublin Fusiliers. *Wounded.*

Casey, Leo. (Entered 1914). Cadet Company, Leinster Regiment. Promoted Sec.-Lieut., Royal Munster Fusiliers. *Wounded.*

Charles, David A., B.A., LL.B., 1914, Univ. Dub. O.T.C.

Chance, Arthur, B.A., M.D. (Univ. Dub.), 1912, Lieut., Royal Army Medical Corps.

†Christian, William F. (Entered 1899). Major, Royal Artillery.

Clanchy, Arthur D., L.R.C.P.&S.I., 1911, Lieut., Royal Army Medical Corps. Promoted Captain.

Clarke, Herbert E., L.R.C.P.&S.I., 1912, Lieut., Royal Army Medical Corps.

Clarke, James K., M.B., B.Ch., 1909, Lieut., Royal Army Medical Corps. (T.F.)

Coffey, Thomas M. (Entered 1912). Sec.-Lieut., Royal Field Artillery. *Wounded.*

Coghlan, John A. (Entered 1913). *Mentioned in Despatches. Awarded Military Cross.* Sec.-Lieut., 3rd Batt. Royal Irish Regiment. Lieut., Tank Corps. *Wounded.*

Coghlan, Joseph P., M.Sc., 1914. *Awarded Military Cross.* Entered Woolwich 1915. Sec.-Lieut., Royal Engineers. *Killed.*

Colahan, Arthur A., M.B., B.Ch., 1913, Lieut., Royal Army Medical Corps. Promoted Captain.

Collins, Thomas F., L.A.H., 1914, Lieut., Royal Army Medical Corps. Promoted Captain.

Collins, Geoffrey, L.R.C.P.&S.I., 1908, Lieut., Royal Army Medical Corps. Promoted Captain.

Conan, Alan. (Entered 1912). Sergeant, Army Service Corps.

†Connolly, Edward P., L.R.C.P.&S.I., 1898, Lt.-Col., Royal Army Medical Corps.

Connolly, John J. (Entered 1914). *Awarded Military Medal and Parchment Certificate.* Sergeant, 7th Batt. Leinster Regiment. Promoted, now Cadet, 7th Officers' Cadet Batt.

Connor, Victor F., L.R.C.P.&S.I., 1902, Capt., Canadian Army Medical Corps, Militia.

†Coppinger, Walter, B.A., M.B. (Univ. Dub.), 1897. *Awarded D.S.O. Mentioned in Despatches.* Major, Indian Medical Service.

Corbet, William, M.B., B.Ch., 1915, Lieut., Royal Army Medical Corps. Promoted Captain.

Corcoran, John P. (Entered 1913). Sec.-Lieut., 3rd Batt. Royal Irish Regiment. *Wounded. Prisoner of War—repatriated*

Costello, Christopher, M.B., B.Ch., 1916, Lieut. Royal Army Medical Corps.

Costello, Joseph M.A. M.B., B.Ch., 1907. *Awarded the Military Cross. Mentioned in Despatches.* Lieut., Royal Army Medical Corps. Promoted Captain (T.F.) and Lieut.-Col.

Costello, Thomas J., B.Sc., M.B., B.Ch., 1913. *Awarded Military Cross. Mentioned in Despatches.* Lieut., Royal Army Medical Corps. Promoted Captain (T.F.)

Cox, Vincent A., B.A., Sec.-Lieut., Royal Field Artillery *Wounded.*

Coyle, Cecil D., M.B., B.Ch., 1916. *Mentioned in Despatches.* Lieut., Royal Army Medical Corps. Promoted Captain. *Wounded.*

Coyne, Eugene H., M.B., B.Ch., 1915. *Awarded Military Cross. Mentioned in Despatches.* Lieut., Royal Army Medical Corps. (T.F.) Promoted Captain.

Creagh, Pierce N., L.R.C.P.&S.I., 1902, Lieut., Royal Army Medical Corps.

Cregan, Michael D. (Entered 1910). Lieut., 9th Batt. Royal Dublin Fusiliers.

Culhane, Albert J. C. (Entered 1914). Passed for Sandhurst.

Cusack, Berchmans J., L.R.C.P.S.I., Lieut., Royal Army Medical Corps.

†Daly, James H., L.R.C.P.&S.I., 1881, Col., Army Medical Service.

†Daly, Joseph T., M.B., M.Ch., 1884, Lieut.-Col., Indian Medical Service. Promoted Colonel.

D'Arcy, Richard. (Entered 1911). Royal Flying Corps.

Daly, Peter, L.R.C.P.&S.I., Lieut., Royal Army Medical Corps.

Dargan, Rev. Patrick J., M.A., Army Chaplain.

Davoren, Ambrose J. S., B.A., LL.B., 1914, Sec.-Lieut., Royal Garrison Artillery. *Killed.*

Davys, John H., L.R.C.P.&S.I., 1895, Lieut., Royal Army Medical Corps. Promoted Captain.

Deighan, William J., L.R.C.P.&S.I., Lieut., Royal Army Medical Corps. (T.F.) *Rescued from Troopship "King Edward VII."* Promoted Captain.

†Delany, Thomas H., M.D., 1905, Major, Indian Medical Service. Promoted Lieut.-Col.

Dempsey, Alexander J., M.B., B.Ch., 1912, Lieut., Royal Army Medical Corps. Promoted Captain.

Dempsey, George Alexis, 1915-18, Surgical Probationer, Royal Navy.

Denvir, Joseph C., M.B., B.Ch., 1912, Lieut., Royal Army Medical Corps. (T.F) Promoted Captain.

Delahunt, David J. (Entered 1911). Pte., 3rd Batt. Irish Guards Promoted Second-Lieut. *Wounded.*

Devereux, John. (Entered 1901). Cadet Company, 7th Leinster. Promoted Sec.-Lieut., 7th Royal Irish Rifles.

Devine, James, L.R.C.P.&S.I., Lieut., Royal Army Medical Corps.

Devine, Michael G., M.B., B.Ch., 1912, Lieut., Royal Army Medical Corps.

†Dickinson, Richard F. O'T., L.R.C.P.&S.I., 1905, Capt., Royal Army Medical Corps. Acting Major.

Dillon-Kelly, Cecil F., L.R.C.P.&S.I., 1914. *Awarded Military Cross. Mentioned in Despatches.* Lieut., Royal Army Medical Corps. Promoted Captain. *Wounded.*

Dillon-Kelly, Lomond C., L.R.C.P.&S.I., 1914. *Awarded Military Cross. Mentioned in Despatches.* Lieut., Royal Army Medical Corps. Promoted Captain. *Wounded.*

Donovan, John J. (Entered 1913). Sec.-Lieut., 2nd Batt. Royal Irish Regiment. *Wounded. Prisoner of War.*

Dooley, John L. (Entered 1914). Surgical Probationer, Royal Navy.

Dowdall, John J., M.B., B.Ch., 1913, Lieut., Royal Army Medical Corps.

†Dowling, Francis T., B.A., M.B., B.Ch., 1907. *Mentioned in Despatches.* Capt., Royal Army Medical Corps. Promoted Major.

Dowling, Ignatius A., L.R.C.P.&S.I., 1911, Lieut., Royal Army Medical Corps.

Doyle, John J., 1914-18, Surgical Probationer, Royal Navy.

Downey, Charles S., B.E., 1913, Lieut., Army Ordnance Department.

Doyle, James J., B.A., 1908, Rifleman, 3rd Batt. Royal Irish Rifles.

Doyle, John J. (Entered 1911). Lieut., 6th Batt. Royal Dublin Fusiliers. *Killed.*

Doyle, John P. (1904), Indian Civil Service, Captain on Staff.

Doyle, Joseph S., M.B., B.Ch., 1908. *Mentioned in Despatches.* Lieut., Royal Army Medical Corps. Promoted Captain and Acting-Major.

Doyle, Patrick A., L.R.C.P.&S.I., 1910, Lieut., Royal Army Medical Corps. Promoted Captain. *Wounded.*

Duff, John E., B.Sc., 1914, Trooper, South Irish Horse.

Duggan, Joseph R., B.A., 1912, Sergt.-Major, 10th Batt. R. Dublin Fusiliers. *Wounded.*

Duggan, Thomas A. (Entered 1912). Sec.-Lieut., 10th Batt. Lancashire Fusiliers. *Killed.*

Dundon, James St. John, M.B., B.Ch., 1915, Lieut., Royal Army Medical Corps. *Died on Active Service.*

Dundon, John, L.R.C.P.&S.I., 1901, Lieut., Royal Army Medical Corps.

A 2

Dundon, Michael. (Entered 1912). Private, 10th Batt. Royal Dublin Fusiliers. Promoted Sec.-Lieut., 11th Batt. Royal Dublin Fusiliers. *Wounded.*

Dunlea, Rev. John M., M.Sc., 1914, Chaplain.

Dunne, Frank, B.A., M.B., B.Ch., 1891, Lieut., Royal Army Medical Corps. Promoted Captain.

Dunne, John J., L.R.C.S.E., 1898, Med. Staff, South African Forces.

Dwyer, James Jameson, L.R.C.P.&S.I., 1909. *Awarded D.S.O. Mentioned in Despatches.* Lieut., Royal Army Medical Corps. Promoted Captain.

†Dwyer, Patrick, M.B., B.Ch., 1903. *Awarded the Military Cross. Mentioned in Despatches.* Capt., Royal Army Medical Corps. Promoted Major and acting Lieut.-Col.

Eager, Francis J., L.R.C.P.&S.I., 1912, Lieut., Royal Army Medical Corps.

†Egan, William, M.B., B.Ch., 1904. *Awarded D.S.O. Mentioned in Despatches.* Capt., Royal Army Medical Corps. *Prisoner of War—repatriated.* Promoted Major and acting Lieut.-Col.

Elwood, John Rudolph, L.A.H., 1915, Lieut., Royal Army Medical Corps. *Wounded.*

Enright, James J., B.A., M.B., B.Ch., 1914, Lieut., Royal Army Medical Corps. Promoted Captain.

Enright, Thomas L., L.R.C.P.&S.I., 1914, Lieut., Royal Army Medical Corps. Promoted Captain. *Died on Active Service.*

Fagan, Joseph P., L.R.C.P.&S.I., 1890, Lieut., Royal Army Medical Corps. Late P.M.O. Northern Nigeria.

Farrell, Charles A., L.R.C.P.&S.I., 1910, Lieut., Royal Army Medical Corps. Promoted Captain.

Fagan, George P. (Entered 1911). Sec.-Lieut., Royal Field Artillery.

Fennessy, Edward H., M.B., B.Ch., 1913, Lieut., Royal Army Medical Corps. Promoted Captain.

Fitzgerald, Gerald, M.B., B.Ch., 1911, Lieut., Royal Army Medical Corps.

Flanagan, Stanislaus J., 1915, Sergeant, 3rd Batt. Royal Irish Rifles.

Flanigan, Edmund H., M.B., B.Ch., 1908, Lieut., Royal Army Medical Corps. Promoted Captain. *Died on Active Service.*

Flannery, Arthur H , M.B., B.Ch., 1908, Lieut., Royal Army Medical Corps. Subsequently Surgeon, R.N. *Died on Active Service.*

Flood Edward S. (Entered 1911). New Zealand Forces. *Wounded.*

Fogarty, Gerald J. (Entered 1912). Sec.-Lieut., 3rd Batt. Royal Irish Regiment. Observer, Royal Flying Corps. *Killed.*

Foley, Michael A. (Entered 1914). Lieut., 6th Batt. Leinster Regiment. *Wounded.*

Foley, John, L.R.C.P.&S.I., 1899, Lieut., Royal Army Medical Corps.

Ford, Richard A. W., L.R.C.P.&S.I., Surgeon, Royal Navy.

†Forde, Bernard, M.B., B.Ch., 1886. *Awarded the C.M.G.. Mentioned in Despatches. Serbian Award, Third Class Order of St. Sava.* Lieut.-Col., Royal Army Medical Corps.

Forde, Dudley, M.D., 1908, Lieut., Royal Army Medical Corps Promoted Captain.

Foy, Henry B. (Entered 1911). Lieut., Royal Engineers.

Fraser, George, L.R.C.P.&S.I., 1913, Lieut., Royal Army Medical Corps.

Frengley, Joseph P., B.A., M.D., 1899, Lieut.-Col., Army Medical Corps., New Zealand.

†Frost, George H., B.A., M.B., B.Ch., 1890, Indian Medical Service. Promoted Lieut.-Col.

†Frost, William A., M.B., B.Ch., 1909, Capt., Royal Army Medical Corps.

Furlong, Rev. Laurence J., B.A., 1913, Chaplain.

Furlong, Stanislaus A., L.R.C.P.&S.I., 1907. *Mentioned in Despatches.* Lieut., Royal Army Medical Corps. Promoted Captain.

Gallagher, Michael J., M.B., B.Ch., 1912, Lieut., Royal Army Medical Corps. Promoted Captain.

Gallagher, Gerald Hugh, L.R.C.P.&.S.I., 1905, West African Medical Staff. On Army Service, Africa.

Galvin, Daniel J. (Entered 1912). Lieut., 9th Batt. Royal Dublin Fusiliers. *Wounded.*

†Garland, Frederick, M.B., B.Ch., 1901. *Mentioned in Despatches. Awarded D.S.O.* Capt., Royal Army Medical Corps. Promoted Major and Acting Lieut.-Col.

Gavin, William C., M.B., B.Ch., 1901, Lieut., Royal Army Medical Corps. Promoted Captain.

Gaynor, George C., M.B., B.Ch., 1915. *Awarded the Military Cross. Mentioned in Despatches.* Lieut., Royal Army Medical Corps. Promoted Captain.

Gerrard, Edward. (Entered 1911). Lieut., Royal Field Artillery *Wounded.*

Gibbons, John F., L.R.C.P.&S.I., 1910, Lieut., Royal Army Medical Corps.

†Gill, J. Jeffrey, L.R.C.P.&S.I., 1896. *Mentioned in Despatches. Awarded the D.S.O.* Major, Royal Army Medical Corps. Promoted Lieut.-Colonel and Colonel.

Gill, Henry J., Rev *Awarded Military Cross. Awarded D.S.O. Mentioned in Despatches.* Chaplain.

Gilligan, John Joseph. (Entered 1913). Sec.-Lieut., Royal Field Artillery. *Killed.*

Glynn, Patrick. (Entered 1915). Sec.-Lieut., Royal Field Artillery

Gordon, Reginald E. (Entered 1914). Sergeant, 5th Batt. Leinsters.

Goulding, Patrick J. (Entered 1914). O.T.C.; subsequently Sec.-Lieut. *Wounded.*

Graham, Matthew J., M.B., B.Ch., 1915, Lieut., Royal Army Medical Corps. Promoted Captain.

Graham, William E., M.B., B.Ch., 1911. *Awarded Military Cross. Mentioned in Despatches.* Lieut., Royal Army Medical Corps. Promoted Captain. *Wounded.*

Green, John G. J., M.B., B.Ch., 1914, Lieut., Royal Army Medical Corps. Promoted Captain. Transferred Indian Medical Service.

Griffith, Thomas. (Entered 1911). Private, 5th Lancers.

Gwynn, Denis Rolleston, B.A., 1914, Inns of Court O.T.C. Sec.-Lieut. *Wounded.*

Hackett, Bartholomew, M.B., B.Ch., 1899. *Awarded the Military Cross, With Bar. Mentioned in Despatches.* Lieut., Royal Army Medical Corps. Promoted Captain.

Halligan, Aloysius J., L.R.C.P.&S.I., 1894, Lieut., Royal Army Medical Corps. Promoted Captain.

†Hanafin, John B., F.R.C.S.I., 1907, Capt., Royal Army Medical Corps. Promoted Major.

†Hanafin, Patrick J., L.R.C.P.&S.I., 1901. *Awarded D.S.O., With Bar. Mentioned in Despatches.* Major, Royal Army Medical Corps. Promoted Lieut.-Colonel.

Hannan, William F., 1916-17, Royal Air Force.

Hanratty, Francis V., L.R.C.P.&S.I., Lieut., Royal Army Medical Corps. Promoted Captain.

Hanratty, Patrick A. (Entered 1913). Sec.-Lieut., 3rd Batt. Royal Irish Regiment.

Hannigan, Charles J., B.A., M.B., B.Ch., 1914. *Awarded Military Cross. Mentioned in Despatches., With Bar.* Lieut., Royal Army Medical Corps. Promoted Captain.

Hannigan, Francis, L.R.C.P.&S.I., 1912, Lieut., Royal Army Medical Corps. Promoted Captain.

Hannigan, Henry, M.B., B.Ch., 1912, Lieut., Royal Army Medical Corps. Promoted Captain.

Harbinson, Henry, M.B., B.Ch., 1913. *Awarded the Military Cross. Mentioned in Despatches, With Bar.* Lieut., Royal Army Medical Corps. Promoted Captain.

Harford, John E., M.B., B.Ch., 1913, Lieut., Royal Army Medical Corps.

†Hartigan, James A., M.D. (Durh.). (Session 1897). *Mentioned in Despatches. Awarded D.S.O.* Major, Royal Army Medical Corps.

Hartigan, Timothy J., M.B., B.Ch., 1901, Surgeon, Royal Navy. *Died on Active Service.*

†Hastings, Albert E. F., L.R.C.P.&S.I., 1903, Capt., Royal Army Medical Corps. *Deceased.*

Healy, Dermot. (Entered 1912). Inns of Court O.T.C.; subsequently Sec.-Lieut., Roy. Dublin Fusiliers. *Killed.*

Healy, Joseph, B.A (Entered 1905). Lieut., R.N.R.

Healy, Maurice, B.A., 1907, Sec.-Lieut., 4th Batt. Royal Dublin Fusiliers.

Heffernan, Edward, M.B., B.Ch., 1912., Surgeon, Royal Navy.

Heffernan, John T., L.R.C.P.&S.I., 1910, Lieut., Royal Army Medical Corps. *Wounded.* Promoted Captain.

†Heffernan, Patrick, B.A., M.B., B.Ch., 1901, Capt., Royal Army Medical Corps. Promoted Major.

Hennessy, Richard B., M.B., B.Ch., 1913, Lieut., Royal Army Medical Corps.

Herbert, John F., B.Sc., M.B., B.Ch., 1914, Lieut., Royal Army Medical Corps.

Herlihy, William. (Entered 1912). O.T.C.

Heron, Oscar, 1915, Inns of Court O.T.C.; subsequently Sec.-Lieut., Royal Air Force.

Higgins, Thomas F., L.R.C.P.&S.I. (Entered 1907). Lieut., Royal Army Medical Corps.

Hickey, William, M.B., B.Ch., 1918, Lieut., Royal Army Medical Corps. *Wounded.*

Hickey, William A. E., 1914, Private, Royal Garrison Artillery.

Hughes, John J., M.B., B.Ch., Lieut., Royal Army Medical Corps.

Higgins, Peter M'Loughlin, B.E., 1912, Private, 81st Batt. Canadian Force.

Hodnett, George. (Entered 1908). Sec.-Lieut., Army Service Corps.

Hollywood, James J., M.B., B.Ch., 1906, Capt. with Australian General Hospital No. 1.

Huban, John P., M.B., B.Ch., 1914, Lieut., Royal Army Medical Corps. Promoted Captain.

Humphreys, Francis, M.B., B.Ch., 1915, Lieut., Royal Army Medical Corps. Promoted Captain. *Wounded.*

Humphreys, Joseph, L.R.C.P.&S.I., 1908, Lieut., Royal Army Medical Corps.

Hynes, Bernard P., M.B., B.Ch., 1915, Lieut., Royal Army Medical Corps.

Jackson, George, M.B., B.Ch., 1915, Lieut., Royal Army Medical Corps. Promoted Captain.

Jago. Richard, B.A., 1912. South Irish Horse.

Johnson, John Stafford, B.A., M.B., B.Ch., 1914, Lieut., Royal Army Medical Corps.

Joyce Francis J., M.B., B.Ch., 1917, Lieut., Royal Army Medical Corps.

†Kavanagh, Edward, M.B., B.Ch., 1906. *Awarded the Military Cross. Mentioned in Despatches. Awarded D.S.O.* Capt., Royal Army Medical Corps. Promoted Major, and acting Lieut.-Col.

Kavanagh, Thomas O. (Entered 1913). Sec.-Lieut., 3rd Battalion Royal Irish Fusiliers. *Killed.*

†Keane, Michael, L.R.C.P.&S.I., 1904, Capt., Royal Army Medical Corps. Promoted Major.

Keane, Percival M L.R.C.P.&S.I., Surgeon, Royal Navy.

Kearney, Anthony J., L.R.C.P.&S.I., 1894, Lieut., Royal Army Medical Corps. Promoted Captain. *Wounded.*

Keating, Thomas J. (Entered 1912). Sec.-Lieut., Royal Field Artillery. Promoted Captain. *Killed.*

Kelly, Charles J., L.R.C.P.&S.I., 1912, Lieut., Royal Army Medical Corps. Promoted Captain.

Kelly, John, L.R.C.P.&S.I., 1913, Lieut., Royal Army Medical Corps.

†Kelly, Joseph F., M.B., B.Ch., 1891. *Twice mentioned in Despatches.* Lt.-Col., Royal Army Medical Corps. Promoted Colonel. *Died on Active Service.*

Kelly, Peter B., L.R.C.P.&S.I. *Awarded D.S.O. Mentioned in Despatches.* Surgeon, Royal Navy.

Kelly, Richard Jasper, B.A. (1915), Sub-Lieut., R.N.V.R.

Kelly, Thomas, L.R.C.P.&S.I., 1913, Lieut., Royal Army Medical Corps. Promoted Captain. *Wounded.*

Kenefick, Richard, M.B., B.Ch., 1912. *Awarded Military Cross Mentioned in Despatches.* Lieut., Royal Army Medical Corps. Promoted Captain. *Wounded.*

Kennedy, Alphonsus P. M. (Entered 1914). *Awarded Military Cross.* Private, Royal Army Medical Corps. *Wounded.*

Kennedy, Arthur P., L.R.C.P.&S.I., Lieut., Royal Army Medical Corps Promoted Captain. *Wounded.*

Kennedy, Edward A. (Entered 1903). Army Service Corps. *Wounded.*

Kennedy, Francis, L.R.C.P.&S.I., 1914, Lieut., Royal Army Medical Corps.

Kennedy, Frederick J. M., L.R.C.P.&S.I., 1913, Lieut., Royal Army Medical Corps. Promoted Captain (T.F.).

Kennedy, Gerald L., M.B., B.Ch., 1913, Lieut., Royal Army Medical Corps. Promoted Captain. *Wounded.*

Kennedy, John E. (Entered 1905). Trooper, 2nd King Edward's Horse.

Kenny, Charles A,, L.R.C.P.&S.I., 1898. *Mentioned in Despatches.* Lieut., Royal Army Medical Corps. Promoted Captain.

†Kenny, Edward B., M.B., B.Ch., 1903. *Mentioned in Despatches.* Staff Surgeon, Royal Navy. *Wounded.*

Keogh, Francis de C., M.B., B.Ch., 1914, Lieut., Royal Army Medical Corps. Promoted Captain.

Kilbride, John L., M.B., B.Ch., 1911, Lieut., Royal Army Medical Corps. Promoted Captain.

†Kilbride, Thomas, M.B., B.Ch., 1912, Surgeon, Royal Navy.

King, John Leo. (Entered 1913). Sec.-Lieut., Royal Irish Rifles. 1914.

†Kirwan, Ernest W. O'G., M.B., B.Ch., 1909. *Awarded the Military Cross. Mentioned in Despatches.* Capt., Indian Medical Service. Promoted Major.

Kirwan, J. St. L., B.A., M.B., B.Ch., 1896., Lieut., Royal Army Medical Corps.

Kirwan, John J. (Entered 1910). Private, Garrison Artillery.

Kyne, Thomas J., 1917-18, South Irish Horse.

Kirwan, Richard R., M.B., B.Ch., Lieut., Royal Army Medical Corps.

Lacy, Thomas J. (Entered 1912). Sec.-Lieut., Royal Field Artillery. *Killed.*

†Laffan, Michael, B.A., M.B., B.Ch., 1901, Staff Surgeon, Royal Navy.

†Lalor, Purcell O'G., M.B., B.Ch., 1894, Major, Indian Medical Service. Promoted Lieut.-Colonel.

Lane, Patrick J., M.B., B.Ch., 1915. *Awarded the Military Cross. Mentioned in Despatches.* Lieut., Royal Army Medical Corps. Promoted Captain, and Acting Major. *Wounded.*

Lawlor ,James H. (Entered 1910). Captain, Munster Fusiliers. *Wounded.*

Lee, John P. (Entered 1911). Sergt., 4th Canadian Batt *Wounded.*

Levinston, Asher, F.R.C.S.I., 1894, Major, Indian Medical Service. Promoted Lieut.-Colonel.

Little, Thomas J., M.B., B.Ch., B.A.O., 1900, Captain, Royal Army Medical Corps.

Lloyd. Timothy J., L.R.C.P.&S.I., Lieut., Royal Army Medical Corps. Promoted Captain. *Wounded.*

Loftus, Michael J., L.R.C.P.&S.I., 1915, Lieut., Royal Army Medical Corps. Promoted Captain.

Lucas, George, B.Sc., B.E., 1914, Lieut., Royal Garrison Artillery.

Lydon, Patrick J., B.A., M.B., B.Ch., 1910, Lieut., Royal Army Medical Corps. Promoted Captain.

Lynch, Patrick S. (Entered 1910). *Awarded the Military Cross, With Bar. Mentioned in Despatches.* Lieut., 7th Batt. Leinster Regt. *Killed.*

McAllister, Alister, B.A., Motor Machine Gun Service. Promoted Second Lieut., A.S.C. *Wounded.*

†M'Allister, Edmund J. (Entered 1895). *Awarded the D.S O. Mentioned in Despatches.* Lieut.-Col., Army Service Corps. *Wounded.*

McAllister, Victor J., M.B., B.Ch., 1907, M.A.O. 1913, Lieut., Royal Army Medical Corps. Promoted Captain.

M'Ardle, Robert, *Wounded.*

M'Arevey, John Aloysius, B.A., 1910, Sec.-Lieut., 4th Inniskilling Fusiliers. *Wounded.*

M'Arevey, Joseph B. (Entered 1914). *Awarded Military Cross. Mentioned in Despatches.* Lieut., 3rd Batt. Royal Irish Rifles. Promoted Captain. *Wounded.*

M'Bride, Michael. (Entered 1911)

M'Carthy, Alexander A., B.A., 1911, Lieut., R.N.V.R.

M'Carthy, Charles J., M.B., B.Ch., 1915, Lieut., Royal Army Medical Corps.

†M'Carthy, Denis T., M.B., B.Ch., 1906, Capt., Royal Army Medical Corps. Acting Major.

M'Carthy, Frederick J., L.R.C.P.&S.I., 1913, Lieut., Royal Army Medical Corps. Promoted Captain.

M'Carthy, Michael J., M.B., B.Ch., 1917, Lieut., Royal Army Medical Corps.

M'Crea, Michael J., 1917-18. Private.

M'Carthy, Randal, L.R.C.P.&S., Edin., 1892, Lieut., Royal Army Medical Corps.

M'Clintock, Hugh T. S., M.B., B.Ch., 1912, Surgeon, Royal Navy.

M'Connell, John J., L.R.C.P.&S.I., 1903, Lieut., Royal Army Medical Corps. Promoted Captain.

M'Cormack, Charles P., L.R.C.P.&S.I., 1913, Lieut., Royal Army Medical Corps. Promoted Captain. *Wounded.*

M'Cormack, John D., L.R.C.P.&S.I., 1914. *Awarded Military Cross. Mentioned in Despatches.* Lieut., Royal Army Medical Corps. Promoted Captain. *Wounded.*

McCrea, Michael, 1917, Private.

M'Dermott, Francis P., L.R.C.P.&S.I., 1912, Lieut., Royal Army Medical Corps.

†M'Dermott, Thomas, B.A., M.B., B.Ch., 1889, Major, Royal Army Medical Corps. Promoted Lieut.-Colonel.

M'Donnell, Patrick, M.B., B.Ch., 1913, Lieut., Royal Army Medical Corps. Promoted Captain.

M'Donnell, Robert P., F.R.C.S.I., 1901, Lieut., Royal Army Medical Corps. Promoted Captain.

M'Elligott, Maurice G., F.R.C.S.I., 1892, Lieut., Royal Army Medical Corps.

M'Geehan, Michael, Corporal, N. Lancashire Regt.

M'Gennis, Thomas F. (Entered 1912). Cadet Company, 4th Batt. Leinster Regiment.

M'Gorry, Thomas F. E., Corporal, 10th Batt. Dublin Fusiliers. Promoted Sec.-Lieut., Indian Army.

M'Donald, Terence J., Lieut., Royal Army Medical Corps.

M'Grath, Alphonsus, M.B., B.Ch., 1914, Lieut., Royal Army Medical Corps.

M'Grath, John Niall. (Entered 1914). Tank Corps.

M'Grath, Roger, M.B., B.Ch., 1914. *Awarded Military Cross. Mentioned in Despatches.* Lieut., Royal Army Medical Corps. Promoted Captain. *Died of Wounds.*

M'Hugh, Louis J. E., M.B., B.Ch., 1912, Lieut., Royal Army Medical Corps (T.F.).

M'Keever, Louis, L.R.C.P.&S.I., 1914. *Awarded Military Cross. Mentioned in Despatches.* Lieut., Royal Army Medical Corps. Promoted Captain. *Killed.*

M'Keever, Michael, B.A., M.B., B.Ch., 1914, Lieut., Royal Army Medical Corps. Promoted Captain.

†M'Kenna, Francis J. L. P., M.B., B.Ch., 1896., Fleet-Surgeon, Royal Navy.

M'Kenna, James O'N. (entered 1913), Sec.-Lieut., Royal Dublin Fusiliers.

†M'Loughlin, James P. (entered 1910), Lieut., 4th Batt. Royal Dublin Fusiliers. *Killed.*

M'Mahon, Augustine P., M.B., B.Ch., 1907, Lieut., Royal Army Medical Corps.

M'Mahon, Michael T., M.Sc., M.B., B.Ch., 1914. Mentioned in Despatches. Lieut., Royal Army Medical Corps. Promoted Captain. Acting Major.

M'Manus, Francis J., L.R.C.P. & S.I., 1915, Lieut., Royal Army Medical Corps.

M'Namara, John, L.R.C.P&S.I., Lieut., Royal Army Medical Corps

M'Nally, James V., M.B., B.Ch., 1914, Lieut., Royal Army Medical Corps. Promoted Captain.

M'Polin, James, B.Sc., M.B., B.Ch., 1915. Lieut., Royal Army Medical Corps. Promoted Captain. *Wounded.*

M'Swiney, Stephen A., B.A., M.B., B.Ch., 1910, Lieut., Royal Army Medical Corps. Promoted Captain. *Mentioned in Despatches.*

M'Veigh, William J. (entered 1910), Lieut., Royal Munster Fus. *Killed.*

M'Walter, James C., M.A., 1901 (M.B. Univ., Dub.), Lieut., Royal Army Medical Corps. Promoted Captain.

M'Weeney, Desmond (entered 1915), Sec.-Lieut., 6th Batt. Connaught Rangers. Awarded Military Cross. Mentioned in Despatches.

M'Weeny, E. Theophilus (entered 1913), Sec.-Lieut., Royal Field Artillery. Transfer to Royal Flying Corps.

Maher, George (entered 1911), Cadet Company, Leinster Regiment. Captain.

Maguire, Hugh O'N. (entered 1912), Sec.-Lieut., 3rd Batt. Connaught Rangers. *Killed.*

Maguire, Michael, B.A. (entered 1917), Army Service Corps.

Maguire, Patrick J., L.R.C.P. & S.I., Lieut., Royal Army Medical Corps. Promoted Captain.

Maguire, Thomas J. R., M.B., B.Ch., 1912, Lieut., Royal Army Medical Corps. Promoted Captain.

Mahony, Edmund J. (entered 1908), Lieut., 9th Batt. Munster Fusiliers. *Killed.*

Maguire, George C., B.Sc., M.B., B.Ch., Lieut., Royal Army Medical Corps.

Mallen, William (entered 1915), Lieut., Royal Dublin Fusiliers. *Killed.*

Mallon, Patrick L., 1917-18, Royal Flying Force.

Malone, Francis L., B.Comm., 1917, Inns of Court O.T.C.

Maloney, William J., M.B., B.Ch., 1914, Lieut., Royal Army Medical Corps. Promoted Captain.

Marmion, Joseph, L.R.C.P. & S.I., 1912, Lieut., Royal Army Medical Corps. Promoted Captain.

Marren, John P. (entered 1913), Corp., 11th Batt. Durham L.I.

Marron, Thomas, M.B., B.Ch., 1913, Lieut., Royal Army Medical Corps.

Martin, James Charles, L.R.C.P&S.I., 1894, Lieut., Royal Army Medical Corps.

Matthews, Rev. Joseph, B.A., 1910, Chaplain.

May, John J., 1916-18, Private.

Meagher, Timothy, M.B., B.Ch., 1906, Lieut., Royal Army Medical Corps. Promoted Captain. Mentioned in Despatches. Awarded the Military Cross. French Honours—Croix de Guerre.

Mellon, Bagenal H. (entered 1912), Captain, Army Vet. Corps.

†Meredith, Richard G., M.B., B.Ch., 1904, Capt., Royal Army Medical Corps. Promoted Major.

Milner, Arthur P., 1916, Sec.-Lieut.

Minch, John B., M.B., B.Ch., 1914, Lieut., Royal Army Medical Corps. Promoted Captain.

Molloy, William F., M.A., 1915, Sergt.-Major, Royal Flying Corps.

Moore, Gerald J. (entered 1914), Surgical Probationer, Royal Navy.

Moran, John P., M.B., B.Ch., 1916, Lieut., Royal Army Medical Corps.

Moran, Louis A., L.R.C.P. & S.I., 1910, Lieut., Royal Army Medical Corps. Promoted Captain.

Moriarty, James J. P., M.B., B.Ch., 1915, Lieut., Royal Army Medical Corps.

Morrin, Francis J., M.B., B.Ch., 1915, Lieut., Royal Army Medical Corps.

Morris, William M., M.B., B.Ch., Lieut., Royal Army Medical Corps.

Morrissey, Joseph M., F.R.C.S.I., 1895, Lieut., Royal Army Medical Corps. Promoted Captain.

Moynihan, Michael J., London Rifles. *Killed.*

Mulholland, Henry C., M.B., B.Ch., 1910, Lieut., Royal Army Medical Corps. Promoted Captain. *Wounded.*

Mulderry, Rev. John, B.A., 1911, Chaplain.

Murphy, Bernard, L.R.C.P. & S.I., 1913, Lieut., Royal Army Medical Corps. Promoted Captain.

Murphy, John J. C., Lieut., 2nd Royal Dublin Fusiliers, now Indian Army.

Murphy, Oswald J., M.B., B.Ch., 1914, Colonial Medical Service.

Murphy, Philip, M.B., B.Ch., 1916, Lieut., Royal Army Medical Corps.

Murphy, Richard V., L.R.C.P. & S.I., 1906, Lieut., Royal Army Medical Corps.

Murphy, William L., B.A., M.B. (Cantab.), 1907, Lieut., Royal Army Medical Corps. Promoted Captain. French Honours—Croix de Guerre. Serbian—4th Class Order of Sava.

Murray, Patrick J., M.B., B.Ch., 1903. Lieut., Royal Army Medical Corps.

Naish, Redmond J., B.L. (entered 1908), Sec.-Lieut., Leinster Regiment.

Neary, John F., M.B., B.Ch., 1908, Lieut., Royal Army Medical Corps (T.F.) Promoted Captain.

Neligan, John M.B., B.Ch., 1915, Lieut., Royal Army Medical Corps. Promoted Captain. Mentioned in Despatches. Died on Active Service.

Neilan, Alan, L.R.C.P. & S.I., 1916, Lieut., Royal Army Medical Corps. Promoted Captain. *Wounded.*

†Nixon, Sir C. W., Bart. (entered 1896), Major, Royal Artillery. Wounded. Awarded D.S.O. Mentioned in Despatches.

Nolan, James J. (entered 1913), Surgical Probationer, Royal Navy. *Killed.*

O'Boyle, John T., L.R.C.P. & S.I., Lieut., Royal Army Medical Corps. Promoted Captain.

O'Brien, Cornelius F. (entered 1912), Machine Gun Section, 7th Batt. Leinster Regiment. *Wounded.*

O'Brien, Michael, L.R.C.P. & S.I., 1910, Lieut., Royal Army Medical Corps. Promoted Captain.

O'Brien, Sidney J. (entered 1912), Univ. Dub. O.T.C.

O'Brien, William, M.B., B.Ch., 1911, Lieut., Royal Army Medical Corps. Promoted Captain. Prisoner of War.

O'Callaghan, Maurice A., L.R.C.P. & S.I., 1911, Lieut., Royal Army Medical Corps. Promoted Captain.

†O'Carroll, Arthur D., M.B., B.Ch., 1904. Captain, Royal Army Medical Corps. Promoted Major and Lieut.-Col. Awarded the D.S.O. Mentioned in Despatches. Prisoner of War—repatriated.

O'Carroll, Charles J. (entered 1912), Sec.-Lieut., 8th Batt. Royal Dublin Fusiliers. *Wounded.*

O'Carroll, Francis B. E. (entered 1913), Sec.-Lieut., 6th Batt. Royal Dublin Fusiliers. *Killed.*

O'Carroll, Thomas P. (entered 1911), Sergt., New Zealand Force. *Wounded.*

O'Connor, Arthur (1916), Surgical Probationer, R.N.

†O'Connor, Arthur P., B.A., M.B., B.Ch., 1908, Capt., Royal Army Medical Corps. Acting Major. Mentioned in Despatches.

O'Connor, Fergus L. (entered 1915), Cadet Batt.

O'Connor, James (entered 1916), Artist Rifle Corps.

O'Connor, James, M.B., B.Ch., 1914, Lieut., Royal Army Medical Corps.

O'Connor, John J. P., B.A., M.B., B.Ch., 1910, Lieut., Royal Army Medical Corps. Promoted Captain.

O'Connor, Roderick, L.R.C.P. & S.I., Lieut., Royal Army Medical Corps (T.F.)

O'Connor, Michael A., 1917-18, Royal Flying Force.

O'Dea, Joseph A., M.B., B.Ch., 1912, Lieut., Royal Army Medical Corps. Promoted Captain.

O'Donnell, Gerald P., M.B., B.Ch., 1914, Surgeon, Royal Navy.

†O'Donoghue, Denis J., L.R.C.P. & S.I., 1900, late Captain, R.A.M.C. Medical Officer, West African Service.

O'Donoghue, James F. C., M.B., B.Ch., 1915, Lieut., Royal Army Medical Corps. Promoted Captain.

O'Donoghue, Thomas, L.R.C.P. & S.I., 1914, Lieut., Royal Army Medical Corps.

O'Dowd, Patrick (entered 1910), Lance-Corpl., Motor Transport.

O'Driscoll, John A., L.R.C.P. & S.I. (entered 1908), Lieut., Royal Army Medical Corps. Promoted Captain. *Wounded.* Mentioned in Despatches.

O'Farrell, Joseph C., L.R.C.P. & S.I., 1912, Lieut., Royal Army Medical Corps. Promoted Captain.

O'Farrell, Patrick T., L.R.C.P. & S.I., Lieut., Royal Army Medical Corps.

†O'Farrell, William R., L.R.C.P. & S.I., 1907, Capt., Royal Army Medical Corps. Prisoner of War.

O'Flaherty, William (entered 1913), Pte., Irish Guards. *Wounded.*

†O'Gorman, Charles, L.R.C.P. & S.I., 1894, Lt.-Col., Royal Army Medical Corps. Awarded D.S.O. Mentioned in Despatches.

O'Gorman, Joseph Mervyn Pius, 1891-3, Director of Aeronautics, Lieut.-Colonel.

O'Grady, Patrick J., M.B., B.Ch., 1913, Lieut., Royal Army Medical Corps.

O'Hagan, John Joseph, L.R.C.P. & S.I., 1882, M.B. (Vict.), Lt.-Col., Royal Army Medical Corps (T.F.) Mentioned in Despatches.

O'Keeffe, Ignatius, M.B., B.Ch., 1916, Lieut., Royal Army Medical Corps. Promoted Captain.

O'Kelly, Edward (entered 1912), Lieut.

O'Kelly, John J., L.R.C.P. & S.I., 1912, Lieut., Royal Army Medical Corps. Promoted Captain.

†O'Kelly, Robert, L.R.C.P. & S.I., 1907, Capt., Royal Army Medical Corps. *Wounded.*

O'Malley, David V., M.B., B.Ch., Lieut., Royal Army Medical Corps. Promoted Captain.

†O'Meagher, Kevin (entered 1883), Lieut.-Col., Munster Fusiliers.

†O'Neill, Edward M., M.B., B.Ch., 1905, Capt., Royal Army Medical Corps. Promoted Major and Acting Lieut.-Col. Mentioned in Despatches. Awarded D.S.O.

O'Neill, Hugh, B.A., M.B., B.Ch., 1911, Lieut., Royal Army Medical Corps. Promoted Captain.

O'Neill, William L., M.B., B.Ch., 1915, Lieut., Royal Army Medical Corps. Promoted Captain.

O'Reilly, Edward, M.B., B.Ch., 1909, Lieut., Royal Army Medical Corps.

O'Reilly, James M., M.B. (Belf.), 1911, Lieut., Royal Army Medical Corps.

O'Reilly, James Vincent, B.E., 1915, Sec.-Lieut., Royal Field Artillery.

O'Reilly, John M., M.B., B.Ch., 1915, Lieut., Royal Army Medical Corps. Promoted Captain.

O'Reilly, Joseph P. (entered 1914), Sec.-Lieut., 1st Batt. Royal Munster Fusiliers. Awarded Military Cross. Mentioned in Despatches.

O'Reilly, Patrick J., L.R.C.P. & S.I., 1914, Lieut., Royal Army Medical Corps. Promoted Captain. Awarded the Military Cross. Mentioned in Despatches. Wounded.

O'Rourke, Thomas L. (entered 1914), Private, London-Irish Rifles. *Wounded.*

Osburne, John C., M.B., B.Ch., 1914, Lieut., Royal Army Medical Corps. Promoted Captain.

O'Sullivan, Gerald (entered 1913), Lieut., Royal Dublin Fusiliers.

O'Sullivan, Joseph E., M.B., B.Ch., 1913, Colonial Medical Service, Solomon Islands.

†Petit, Gerard, L.R.C.P. & S.I., 1906, Capt., Royal Army Medical Corps. Mentioned in Despatches. Awarded Military Cross.

Pierse, John A., M.B., B.Ch., 1914, Lieut., Royal Army Medical Corps. Promoted Captain.

Phillips, Harold J. (entered 1914), Surgical Probationer, Royal Navy.

Power, James, B.Sc., B.E., 1914, Lieut., Royal Engineers. Awarded the Military Cross. Mentioned in Despatches.

Power, Maurice A., M.B., B.Ch., 1906, Lieut., Royal Army Medical Corps. Promoted Captain. Awarded Military Cross. Mentioned in Despatches. Wounded.

Power, Michael, L.R.C.P. & S.I., 1908, Major, South African Medical Corps. Awarded D.S.O. Mentioned in Despatches.

Power, Richard, M.B., B.Ch., 1909, Lieut., Royal Army Medical Corps. Promoted Captain.

†Potter, Thomas J., L.R.C.P. & S.I., 1897. Lieut.-Col., Royal Army Medical Corps. Mentioned in Despatches.

Purcell, Edward, L.R.C.P. & S.I., 1904, Lieut., Royal Army Medical Corps.

Purcell, Herbert K., M.A., 1908, Lieut., 7th Batt. Leinster Regiment. *Wounded.*

Purcell, John, L.R.C.P. & S.I., 1914, Lieut., Royal Army Medical Corps. Promoted Captain.

Rearden, James T., L.R.C.P. & S.I., 1907, Lieut., Royal Army Medical Corps.

Redmond, William A., M.P., B.A., 1907, Lieut., 7th Inniskilling Fusiliers. Awarded D.S.O. Mentioned in Despatches.

Reid, Bernard, B.A., 1911, Cadet Company, Leinster Regiment. Promoted Sec.-Lieut., 9th Batt. R. Dublin Fusiliers. *Killed.*

Reynolds, John J., M.B., B.Ch., 1914, Lieut., Royal Army Medical Corps. Promoted Captain.

Reynolds, Richard J., M.B., B.Ch., Lieut., Royal Army Medical Corps. Promoted Captain.

Richardson, Thomas J., M.B., B.Ch., Lieut., Royal Army Medical Corps.

Rishworth, James N., M.B., B.Ch., 1911, Lieut., Royal Army Medical Corps. Promoted Captain.

Rishworth, Walter N., M.B., B.Ch., 1911. Lieut., Royal Army Medical Corps. Promoted Captain. Awarded Military Cross. Mentioned in Despatches.

Roantree, Daniel J., M.B., B.Ch., 1903, Lieut., Royal Army Medical Corps.

Roche, Charles, L.R.C.P. & S.I., 1914, Lieut., Royal Army Medical Corps. Promoted Captain and acting Major. Awarded Military Cross, with Bar. Mentioned in Despatches. *Wounded.*

Roche, Redmond, B.A., 1883, Major, Royal Army Medical Corps (T.F.)

Roche, William, L.R.C.P. & S.I., 1906, Lieut., Royal Army Medical Corps. Promoted Captain.

Roche-Kelly, J., L.R.C.P. & S.I. (entered 1912), Lieut., Royal Army Medical Corps.

†Rooney, Gerald C. (entered 1893), Major, Royal Marine L. I. (H.M.S. "Queen Mary"). Died in Action.

Rooney, Henry J. (entered 1911), Wireless Service.

†Rooney, John, L.R.C.P. & S., Edin., 1901, Staff Surgeon, Royal Navy.

Roe, Patrick J. (entered 1911), Sec.-Lieut., 6th Batt. Leinster Regiment.

Rorke, Laurence C., L.R.C.P. & S.I., 1910, Lieut., Royal Army Medical Corps.

Ross, Angus, B.L. (entered 1902), East African Forces.

Ross, Charles H. G., M.B., B.Ch., 1906. Lieut., Royal Army Medical Corps.

Rowan, Patrick, L.R.C.P. & S.I., 1913, Lieut., Royal Army Medical Corps.

†Rowe, John M., M.B., B.Ch., 1912, Lieut., Royal Army Medical Corps. Promoted Captain. Awarded Military Cross. Mentioned in Despatches.

Ruttledge, Thomas W., M.B., B.Ch., 1910, Lieut., Royal Army Medical Corps. Promoted Captain.

Ryan, Charles O'Beirne, L.R.C.P. & S.I., 1909, Surgeon, Royal Navy.

Ryan, Frederick, M.B., B.Ch., 1899, Lieut., Royal Army Medical Corps. Promoted Captain (T.F.)

Ryan, John C., Lieut., Royal Army Medical Corps.

†Ryan, Peter J., B.A., M.B., B.Ch., 1911, Capt., Royal Army Medical Corps, acting Major. Awarded Military Cross. Mentioned in Despatches.

†Sampson, Francis C., M.B., B.Ch., 1903, Capt., Royal Army Medical Corps. Promoted Major. Mentioned in Despatches. Awarded D.S.O.

Scanlon, Maurice P., M.B., B.Ch., 1906, Lieut., Royal Army Medical Corps. Promoted Captain. Mentioned in Despatches.

Sexton, George J., L.R.C.P. & S.I., 1902, Lieut., Royal Army Medical Corps.

Sharkey, James (entered 1913), Sergt.-Instr., A.G.S., attached 10th Royal Scots.

Sheahan, George P., L.R.C.P. & S.I., 1914, Lieut., Royal Army Medical Corps.

Shelly, James, B.E., 1914, Lieut., Royal Engineers. Promoted Captain and Major. Awarded Military Cross. Mentioned in Despatches.

Sheehy, Eugene, B.A., 1904, Lieut., 9th Batt. R. Dublin Fusiliers.

†Shelley, John P., B.A., 1909, Capt., 2nd Batt. K.O.R. Lancs. Regiment. Staff.

Shiel, George Alex., L.R.C.P. & S.I., 1912, Lieut., Royal Army Medical Corps. Promoted Captain.

Shiel, John W. (entered 1912), Army Medical Corps.

Shuley, George F. (entered 1904), 79th Canadian Batt.

Sheridan, John M., M.Sc., M.B., B.Ch., Lieut., Royal Army Medical Corps.

Slattery, Edmund B. (entered 1906), Sec.-Lieut., 7th Royal Munster Fusiliers. *Wounded.*

Smith, Eugene F. (entered 1914), Private, Royal Army Medical Corps.

Smith, Herbert, M.B., B.Ch., 1915, Lieut., Royal Army Medical Corps. Promoted Captain.

Smyth, Christopher P., B.A., 1914, Sec.-Lieut.

Smyth, James J., M.Sc., 1914, at Woolwich.

Smyth, Patrick J., B.Sc., M.B., B.Ch., 1914, Lieut., Royal Army Medical Corps (T.F.) Promoted Major.

Stephenson, Francis P. (entered 1914), Sec.-Lieut., 7th Batt. Royal Munster Fusiliers.

Stephenson, John, B.A., M.B., B.Ch., 1910, Lieut., Royal Army Medical Corps. Promoted Captain and Acting Major. Awarded Military Cross. Mentioned in Despatches.

Sullivan, Christopher J., F.R.C.S.I., 1900, Lieut., Royal Army Medical Corps. Promoted Captain and Acting Major.

Swan, Andrew T., M.B., B.Ch., 1903, Lieut., Royal Army Medical Corps (T.F.) Promoted Captain.

Swifte-O'Flahertie, Godwin (entered 1913), Sec.-Lieut., 3rd Shropshire Light Infantry. *Killed.*

Tempany, Edward, B.Sc., M.B., B.Ch., 1912, Lieut., Royal Army Medical Corps.

Tierney, Herbert, B.L., B.A., 1908, Sec.-Lieut., 8th Batt. Cheshire Regiment. Missing, and believed killed.

Tighe, McCartan, B.A., 1902, Cadet Company, Leinster Regiment. Promoted Sec.-Lieut., 9th Batt. Royal Dublin Fusiliers. *Wounded.*

Tighe, Rev. Patrick T., B.A., 1890, Chaplain.

Tynan, Edward, F.R.C.S.I., 1901, Medical Officer, West African Medical Service.

Wallace, Bernard, L.R.C.P. & S.I., 1909, Lieut., Royal Army Medical Corps. Promoted Captain.

Wallace, Vivian, L.R.C.P. & S.I., 1911. Lieut., Royal Army Medical Corps. Promoted Captain.

Walsh, Joseph G. (entered 1912), Lce-Corporal, Gunner, Royal Field Artillery. Awarded Military Medal. *Died of Wounds.*

Walsh, John F., L.R.C.P.&S.I., 1908, Lieut., Royal Army Medical Corps.

Walsh, John J., L.R.C.P. & S.I., 1914, Lieut., Royal Army Medical Corps. Promoted Captain.

Walsh, John F., L.R.C.P.&S.I., 1908, Lieut., Royal Army Medical Corps.

Walsh, Stephen B., B.A., M.D., 1905, Lieut., Royal Army Medical Corps. *Killed.*

Walsh, Vincent G. (entered 1914), Captain (general list).

†Ware, George W., M.B., B.Ch., 1905, Capt., Royal Army Medical Corps.

Whelan, Francis (entered 1915), Pte., 10th Batt. Royal Dublin Fusiliers. Promoted Sec.-Lieut., 3rd Batt. Royal Dublin Fusiliers, attached R.A.F.

†Whelan, John, L.R.C.P. & S.I., 1900, Fleet Surgeon, Royal Navy.

†Whelan, Joseph F., M.B., B.Ch., 1896, Major, Royal Army Medical Corps. Acting Lieut.-Col. Awarded D.S.O. Mentioned in Despatches.

†White, Charles F., M.B., B.Ch., 1902, Capt., Royal Army Medical Corps. Promoted Major.

Whyte, George T., F.R.C.S.I., 1892, Lieut., Royal Army Medical Corps. Promoted Captain.

Williams, Samuel E. (entered 1912), Capt., 6th Batt. Royal Irish Regiment. *Wounded.*

AT DUBLIN CASTLE HOSPITAL.

Carew, William K., L.R.C.P. & S.I., L.D.S., Resident Officer, Major.

S.S. "LUSITANIA."

Garry, Joseph, M.B., B.Ch., Assistant Surgeon. *Killed.*

UNIVERSITY COLLEGE, CORK.

Adderley, Major, Royal Army Medical Corps.
Ahern, Capt., Royal Army Medical Corps.
Ahern, David, Lieut.-Col., Royal Army Medical Corps. D.S.O.
Ahern, Michael, Major, Royal Army Medical Corps.
Alcock, H., Capt., Royal Army Medical Corps. *Wounded.*
Allport, C. W., Lieut.-Col., Royal Army Medical Corps.
Andrews, W. P., Lieut., Royal Engineers. Military Cross.
Ashby, W. J., Lieut., Royal Army Medical Corps.
Barry, Donal, Lieut., Royal Army Medical Corps. *Died.*
Barter, G. A., Surgeon-Probationer, Royal Navy.
Bateman, A., Lieut., Royal Army Medical Corps.
Bateman, George, Staff Surgeon, Royal Navy.
Bateman, Nicholas, Australian Forces.
Bateman, O. W., Lieut., Royal Army Medical Corps.
Biggane, F. J., Lieut., Royal Munster Fusiliers. *Killed.*
Boohan, Daniel, Lieut., Royal Army Medical Corps.
Boyle, Michael, Lieut.-Col., Royal Army Medical Corps.
Brind, Walter, Lieut., Royal Flying Corps. D.F.C.
Broderick, W. J., Lieut., Northumberland Fusiliers.
Browne, J. M., Capt., Royal Army Medical Corps.
Buckley, T. J., Lieut., Royal Army Medical Corps.
Bull, Colonel, I.M.S.
Bullen, Lieut.-Col., Royal Army Medical Corps.
Busteed, J., Corporal, Irish Guards. *Wounded.*
Cagney, P., Lieut., Royal Army Medical Corps. Military Cross.
Capps, Fleet-Surgeon, Royal Navy. Killed on H.M.S. "Defence."
Carbery, T. B., Indian Army.
Carr, Col., Royal Army Medical Corps. C.B.
Carroll, J. J., Surgeon, Royal Navy (formerly Surg. Probationer).
Casey, L. J. H., Sec.-Lieut., Royal Engineers.
Clarke, J. W., Lieut., Royal Engineers.
Clerk, J. J., Major, Royal Army Medical Corps.
Coates, Lieut.-Col., Royal Army Medical Corps.
Coleman, T. F., Lieut., North Staffs (retired).
Collins, Lieut.-Col., Royal Army Medical Corps.
Conner, S., Fleet-Surgeon, R.N.
Corcoran, J., Lieut., Royal Army Medical Corps.

Corker, T. M., Surg.-Gen. and King's Honorary Physician. C.B.

Corkery, M. P., Lieut.-Col., Royal Army Medical Corps. Mentioned in Despatches.

Cotter, Edward, Capt., Royal Army Medical Corps.

Cotter, H., Lieut., Royal Army Medical Corps. Military Cross.

Creagh, E. P., Lieut., Royal Army Medical Corps.

Crofts, R., Major, Royal Army Medical Corps. D.S.O. *Died.*

Cronin, J. J., Cadet, Royal Flying Corps.

Crooke-Lawless, Sir Warren C. I. E., Lieut.-Col., Royal Army Medical Corps.

Crowley, J., Lieut., Royal Army Medical Corps (retired).

Crowley, J., Surgeon, R.A.F.

Cummins, A. G., Capt., Royal Army Medical Corps. Military Cross. Fourth Class Order of the Nile.

Cummins, R. C., Lieut., Royal Army Medical Corps.

Cummins, H. A., Major, Royal Army Medical Corps. Commended for valuable services.

Cummins, N. M., Capt., Royal Army Medical Corps. M.C. *Wounded.*

Cummins, S. L., Brevet-Col., A.M.S. Legion of Honour on the Field of Battle. C.M.G. Mentioned in Despatches twice.

Cuppage, Burke, Lieut., Royal Army Medical Corps.

Curtis, Lieut.-Col., Royal Army Medical Corps.

Dee, J. P., Lieut.-Col., I.M.S.

Dennis, Inspector-General, Royal Navy.

Denvir, J., Private, Artists' Rifles.

Dilworth, T. F., Civil Surg., Royal Army Medical Corps.

Dinan, G. A., Lieut., Royal Irish Rifles. *Killed.*

Dixon, A. E., Lieut., Royal Engineers.

Dixon, Wilfred, Civil Surg., Royal Army Medical Corps. *Died.*

Donegan, J. F., Lieut.-Col., Royal Army Medical Corps. C.B.

Donovan, Lieut.-Col., Royal Army Medical Corps.

Donovan, D., Lieut., Royal Navy (retired).

Dorgan, J., Major, Royal Army Medical Corps.

Dowman, Lieut.-Col., Royal Army Medical Corps.

Duggan, C., Lieut., Royal Air Force.

Duggan, Jeremiah, Pte., 3rd Royal Munster Fusiliers.

Duggan, Rev. Thomas, Chaplain to Forces.

Dunlea, J., Surgeon-Probationer, Royal Navy.

Egan, William, Capt., Royal Army Medical Corps.

Evans, G. E. K., Lieut., Royal Munster Fusiliers. *Killed.*

Farrell, E. J.

Fawcett, E. C., Capt., Royal Army Medical Corps.
Fawcett, John, Canadian Infantry.
Fehilly, T., Capt., Royal Army Medical Corps. *Killed.*
Finnegan, G. A., Surgeon, Royal Navy.
FitzGerald, M. P., Surgeon, Royal Navy.
FitzGerald, R., Surgeon, Royal Navy.
Fitzgibbon, D. P., New Zealand Forces.
Fitzmaurice, Frank, Surgeon, Royal Navy.
Flanagin, H. W., B.E., Lieut.
Fleming, A. F., Staff-Surgeon, Royal Navy. Mentioned in Despatches.
Foott, Alex., Capt., Royal Army Medical Corps.
Forbes, E., Capt., Royal Army Medical Corps.
Foxe, V. F. R. B., Training Reserve Brigade.
Fowler, W. H., 11th Batt. Canadian Contingent. *Killed in Ypres.*
Frost, A. T., Major, Royal Army Medical Corps.
Fullin, J. F., Lieut., Royal Munster Fusiliers. M.C. *Killed.*
Galbraith, Capt., Royal Army Medical Corps.
Galbraith, Lieut.
Gallie, J. S., Lieut.-Col., Royal Army Medical Corps. D.S.O.
Gallwey, Sir T., Surg.-Gen., A.M.S., K.C.M.G., C.B.
Garde, Walter H. O., Fleet-Surg., Royal Navy.
Gibbins, R., Lieut., Royal Munster Fusiliers.
Gibson, George, Fleet-Surgeon, Royal Navy.
Gibson, E., West African Medical Service.
Given, David, Surgeon, Royal Navy.
Gloster, T. H., Capt., I.M.S.
Golding, T. J., Capt., Royal Army Medical Corps. Killed in France.
Good, J., Major, I.M.S.
Grier, H., Lieut.-Col., Royal Army Medical Corps.
Griffin, B., 4th King's Dragoon Guards.
Haines, H. A., Lieut.-Col., Royal Army Medical Corps.
Hall, R. H., Lieut.-Col., Royal Army Medical Corps.
Harper, Prof. E. H., Lieut., 10th South Staffs. Regt. *Killed.*
Harrington, C. S., Lieut., Conn. Rangers. *Drowned at Sea.*
Harrison, A. V., Capt., Royal Army Medical Corps.
Harrison, E. W., R.E., Canadian Contingent.
Harty, J. J., Lieut., Royal Army Medical Corps. *Died.*
Harvey, G. S., Surgeon, Royal Navy.
Hawkes, C., Lieut., Royal Army Medical Corps. *Killed.*
Hayes, G. H., Surgeon, Royal Navy.

Hayes, P., Capt., Royal Army Medical Corps.
Hegarty, G. F., Lieut., Royal Army Medical Corps.
Hennessey, J. P., Lieut., Royal Air Force.
Hennessey, Lieut.-Col., Royal Army Medical Corps. C.B.
Herrick, R. De S. B., Lieut., I.M.S.
Herriott, G., Lieut., Royal Army Medical Corps.
Hickey, A. J., Lieut., Royal Army Medical Corps.
Hill, T., Surgeon, Royal Navy.
Hingston, R. W., Capt., I.M.S. Military Cross.
Hobson, E., Capt., Royal Army Medical Corps.
Hodges, R., Capt., Royal Army Medical Corps.
Holmes, Major, Royal Army Medical Corps. *Died in Egypt.*
Holmes, J. G., Lieut., Royal Army Medical Corps.
Horgan, M. J., Lieut., R.A.M.C.
Horan, J. M., Surgeon, Royal Navy.
Hosford, P., Lieut., Royal Air Force.
Howell, H. A. L., Lieut.-Col., Royal Army Medical Corps.
Humphries, F. N., Lieut., Army Service Corps.
Hunt, Barry, Capt., Royal Army Medical Corps.
Jack, C. W. N., Gunner, Royal Garrison Artillery.
Jackson, A., Capt., Royal Garrison Artillery (formerly Private in Agyle and Sutherlands).
Jackson, James, Lieut.-Col., I.M.S.
Jenkins, J. G., Lieut., Royal Engineers (formerly R.D.F.)
Jennings, R. B., Lieut., Royal Engineers. Military Cross.
Johnson, J. C., Capt., New Zealand Medical Service.
Johnston, P. H., Lieut.-Col., Royal Army Medical Corps. C.M.G.
Johnstone, D. P., Major, Royal Army Medical Corps.
Joynt, N. L., Capt., Royal Army Medical Corps. Military Cross.
Julian, F. B., Lieut., Royal Army Medical Corps.
Kearney, Lieut.-Col., Royal Army Medical Corps. Mentioned in Despatches.
Kelleher, T., Surgeon, Royal Navy.
Kennedy, E. G., Capt., I.M.S.
Kennedy, D., Capt., Royal Army Medical Corps. Military Cross.
Kennedy, J., Capt., Royal Army Medical Corps.
Kennedy, R. S., Capt., I.M.S.
Kennedy, T., Capt., Royal Army Medical Corps.
Keogh, J. A., Fleet-Surgeon, Royal Navy.
Keyms, J., Lieut., Royal Army Medical Corps.
Knapp, M. H., Fleet-Surgeon, Royal Navy.
Lapsley, William, Major, I.M.S.

Lapsley, J. B., Capt., I.M.S.
Lane, D. T., Lieut.-Col., I.M.S.
Lanktree, C. J., Capt., Royal Munster Fusiliers.
Leslie, J., Capt., Lincolnshire Regiment.
Levis, J. S., Capt., Royal Army Medical Corps.
Linehan, J. F., Lieut., Royal Engineers. Invalided out.
Liston, J. J., Lieut., I.M.S.
Lucy, D. F., Lieut., Connaught Rangers.
Lucy, D. P., Lieut., Royal Army Medical Corps.
Lucy, D. P., Lieut., Royal Munster Fusiliers.
Lunham, J. L., Capt., I.M.S.
Lynham, B., Lieut., Royal Engineers.
Lynam, G. J., Major, Royal Engineers.
Lynam, E., Lieut., Royal Irish Rifles.
Lynch, D., Lieut., Royal Army Medical Corps.
Lynch, J. P., Major, Royal Army Medical Corps.
McCarthy, Lieut., Royal Munster Fusiliers.
McCarthy, R., Lieut., Royal Air Force.
McDonald, C. J., Col., A.M.S.
McDonnell, E., Major, Royal Army Medical Corps. D.S.O.
McDonnell, G., Lieut.-Col., Royal Army Medical Corps.
McGrath, J. S., Assist.-Surgeon, Royal Navy, previously Surgeon-Probationer. *Wounded in Action.*
McKenna, F. J. L. P., Fleet-Surg., Royal Navy.
McKenna, Sapper, Royal Engineers.
McNamara, Vincent, Lieut., Royal Engineers. *Killed.*
McQueen, Major, Royal Army Medical Corps. Military Cross.
Magner, E. J., Lieut., Leinster Regt. *Twice Wounded.*
Magner, J. J., Lieut., Royal Army Medical Corps.
Magner, W., Lieut., Royal Army Medical Corps. *Wounded and retired.*
Mahony, A., Lieut., Connaught Rangers.
Mahony, G. H., Lieut., I.M.S.
Mahony, M. T., Sub-Lieut., R.N.V.R.
Manley, J. A., Cpl., 1st Indian Cavalry Division.
Mark, E. C., Lieut., Royal Garrison Artillery.
Marks, Lieut.-Col., Royal Army Medical Corps.
Maunsell, Capt. C. M.C.
Moorhead, George, Capt., Royal Garrison Artillery.
Morehead, W., Cadet.
Morehead, F., Lieut., Royal Munster Fusiliers.
Moynihan, E. B., Capt., Royal Army Medical Corps.

Mullane, A., Lieut., Royal Army Medical Corps (retired for ill-health).
Mulvihill, J., Lieut., Royal Air Force.
Murphy, Andrew, Major, I.M.S.
Murphy, Charles, Capt., Royal Army Medical Corps.
Murphy, Denis, Capt., I.M.S.
Murphy, D. V., Lieut., Royal Army Medical Corps.
Murphy, J. N., Surgeon, Royal Navy.
Murphy, J. T., Lieut., Royal Army Medical Corps.
Murphy, J. P. J., Major, Royal Army Medical Corps.
Murphy, J. St. J., Fleet-Surgeon, Royal Navy.
Murphy, Leo, Capt., Royal Army Medical Corps. D.S.O.
Murphy, T. C., Lieut., Royal Army Medical Corps.
Murphy, W. A., Capt., Royal Army Medical Corps.
Murphy, W. O'S., Lieut.-Col., I.M.S.
Murray, P. J., Lieut., Royal Army Medical Corps.
Murray, W. H., Surgeon, Royal Navy.
Nash, C. H., Lieut., Royal Army Medical Corps.
Naylor, G., Lieut., Royal Army Medical Corps. *Died.*
Noonan, J. J. B., Cadet, 7th Leinsters. (Invalided out).
Norgate, F., Lieut., Lincoln Regiment.
Nyhan, C., Lieut., Royal Army Medical Corps.
O'Brien, J., Royal Irish Rifles.
O'Brien, J. W., Lieut., Royal Army Medical Corps. Military Cross.
O'Brien, R. C., Lieut., Royal Engineers. *Wounded and Gassed.*
O'Brien, T. A., Lieut.
O'Brien, T. K., Lieut., Royal Munster Fusiliers. *Killed.*
O'Callaghan, D. M., Colonel, A.M.S.
O'Connor, F. A., Surgeon, Royal Navy.
O'Connor, W. J. M., Lieut., Royal Army Medical Corps.
O'Flynn, Donal Capt., Royal Army Medical Corps.
O'Flynn, J., Lieut., Royal Army Medical Corps.
O'Flynn, Jerome, Lieut., Royal Army Medical Corps.
O'Flynn, J. A., Surgeon, Royal Navy.
O'Gorman, E., Lieut., Royal Air Force.
O'Halloran, Lieut.-Col., Royal Army Medical Corps.
O'Keeffe, M. W., Surg.-Gen., Royal Army Medical Corps. C.B., K.C.M.G.
O'Keeffe, C. W., West African Medical Service.
O'Keeffe, D. S. A., Major, I.M.S.

O'Keeffe, J. J., Capt., R.A.M.C. Military Cross. Legion of Honour.

O'Keeffe, J., Surgeon, Royal Navy.

O'Keeffe, Thomas, Fleet Surgeon.

O'Leary, J., Major, I.M.S. *Killed.*

O'Leary, J., Private, Royal Munster Fusiliers.

O'Mullane, J. J., Lieut., Royal Air Force.

O'Neill, C. T., Surgeon, Royal Navy.

O'Regan, W. F., Lieut., Royal Army Medical Corps.

O'Riordan, T. J., Surgeon, Royal Navy.

O'Riordan, W., Capt., Royal Army Medical Corps.

O'Shea, E. G., Surgeon-Probationer, Royal Navy.

O'Sullivan, D. J., Innis of Court O.T.C.

O'Sullivan, J. I., Lieut., Royal Army Medical Corps.

Oram, A. R., Lieut., Royal Army Medical Corps. M.C. (Formerly Surgeon-Probationer, R.N.) *Wounded.*

Osburne, Lieut.-Col., Royal Army Medical Corps.

Pattison, C. R. M., Capt., Royal Army Medical Corps.

Pearson, C. B., Lieut., Royal Army Medical Corps.

Pearson, D. P. H., Surgeon, Royal Navy.

Pennefather, E. M., Capt., Royal Army Medical Corps.

Perry, H. M. J., Capt., Royal Army Medical Corps.

Phelan, F., Capt., I.M.S.

Pierce, W. H., Lieut., Royal Garrison Artillery.

Popham, C., Capt., Royal Army Medical Corps.

Popham, R. L., Major, Royal Army Medical Corps.

Porter, C. S., Lieut.-Col., Royal Army Medical Corps. Mentioned in Despatches.

Powell, E., Major, Royal Army Medical Corps.

Power, J., Lieut., Royal Army Medical Corps.

Power, P., Capt., Royal Army Medical Corps.

Pratt, J., Surgeon, Royal Navy.

Prendergast, J., Lieut., Royal Air Force.

Punch, Sidney, Surg., Royal Navy. *Drowned on H.M.S. "Indefatigable."*

Quinlan, H. S., Royal Engineers.

Rainsbury, W., 5th Notts. Regiment.

Rea, I., South Irish Horse.

Rearden, R., Royal Irish Rifles.

Reese, A. J., Capt., Royal Field Artillery.

Reynolds, J., Lieut., Royal Army Medical Corps.

Ridge, Arthur, Royal Engineers.

Ridge, P. B., Capt., Royal Army Medical Corps. *Died of Pneumonia.*
Rivers, T., Surgeon, Royal Navy.
Roche, B. E., Royal Engineers, Indian Army.
Roche, Kevin, Surgeon, Royal Navy.
Roche, M. J., Lieut., I.M.S. M.C.
Roche, P. J., Lieut., Royal Engineers. *Died of Enteric.*
Rooney, J. J. F.
Ross, G., Fleet Surgeon, Royal Navy.
Ross, H., Major, I.M.S.
Ryan, Eugene, Major, Royal Army Medical Corps. Legion of Honour. D.S.O.
Ryan, T., Lieut., Royal Army Medical Corps.
Sampson, P., Capt., Royal Army Medical Corps. D.S.O.
Sarsfield, T., Lieut., Royal Army Medical Corps.
Saunders, Lieut.-Col., Royal Army Medical Corps.
Scannell, Rev. Dr., Chaplain to Forces.
Sexton, Col., A.M.S. C.B.
Seymour, S. G., Surgeon, Royal Navy.
Shaw, W. S. J., Capt., I.M.S.
Sheedy, T., Capt., Royal Army Medical Corps.
Sheffield, W. H., Lieut., Royal Army Medical Corps.
Shine, J. M. F., Colonel, A.M.S.
Shipsey, W. J., Corpl., "Tanks."
Shorten, J. A., Capt., I.M.S.
Shorten, J. P., Surgeon, Royal Navy. Dist. Service Cross.
Smith, Lieut.-Col., I.M.S.
Stoker, Stanley P., Capt., Royal Army Medical Corps. M.C.
Stokes, Robert H. C., Lieut., Royal Garrison Artillery.
Stone, C., Lieut.-Col., Royal Army Medical Corps.
Swertz, S. H., Lieut., Royal Army Medical Corps.
Thompson, H. A., Major, Royal Army Medical Corps.
Tinsley, W., Lieut., Indian Army Reserve.
Tivy, C., Lieut., Royal Army Medical Corps.
Tobin, J. A., Major, Royal Army Medical Corps.
Townsend, A., Lieut., Royal Munster Fusiliers. Prisoner of War.
Tuckey, Lieut.-Col., Royal Army Medical Corps.
Twigg, T. J. D., Surgeon, Royal Navy.
Twigg, T. H., Lieut., Royal Army Medical Corps.
Verling, A., Capt., Royal Army Medical Corps.
Wall, William, Private, Royal Flying Corps.
Waller, J. H., Capt., Royal Engineers. D.S.O.

Walsh, J., Lieut., I.M.S.
Walsh, P. J., Lieut., I.M.S. *Killed.*
Ward, E. C., Fleet-Surg., Royal Navy. *Died.*
Ware, E. W W, Major, Royal Army Medical Corps.
Waters, P. F., Lieut., Royal Engineers.
Weakliam, T. F., Lieut., Royal Army Medical Corps.
Whelton, M., Lieut., Royal Air Force.
White, M., Capt., Royal Army Medical Corps.
White, W. W., Brevet-Col., I.M.S. C.B.
Whitelegge, W. A., Fleet-Surgeon, Royal Navy.
Whitty, Lieut.-Col., Royal Army Medical Corps. *Died.*
Wiley, Alan, Capt., Royal Army Medical Corps.
Wiley, Vernon, Capt., Royal Army Medical Corps.
Williams, F., Cadet, Royal Flying Corps.
Wilson, Burkitt.
Wilson, R. F., Lieut., Northumberland Fusiliers.
Wolfe, R. J., Capt., Royal Army Medical Corps.
Woods, S. H., Surgeon, Royal Navy.
Woods, C. G., Major, Royal Army Medical Corps.
Woodley, R. N., Major, Royal Army Medical Corps.
Wren, J., Lieut., Royal Air Force.
Yarr, M. T., Surgeon-Gen., Royal Army Medical Corps. C.B. K.C.M.G.
Yourdi, Lieut.-Col., Royal Army Medical Corps.
Young, C. W., Lieut., Royal Army Medical Corps.
Young, C., Lieut., Royal Air Force.

UNIVERSITY COLLEGE, GALWAY.

Abbot, N., Lieut., Connaught Rangers. Prisoner of War and *Wounded.*

Anderson, Alex., B.Sc. (Honoris Causa), Lieut., Conn. Rangers, attached to R.F.C. Prisoner of War.

Anderson, W., Lieut., Royal Army Medical Corps.

Armour, Rev. J. B. McM., M.A., C.F.

Bell, W., M.A.

Brown, N., M.A., Lieut., Royal Dublin Fusiliers.

Burbridge, H., M.B., Capt., Royal Army Medical Corps.

Carbery, E., M.B., Fleet Surgeon.

Campbell, T., B.E., Lieut., Royal Engineers. *Died of Wounds.*

Compton, A. J. W., B.A., M.D., Capt., Royal Army Medical Corps.

Conroy, M. J., B.E. (Honoris Causa), I.W.T. (Mesopotamia).

Clancy, P. J.

Clarke, N., Lieut., R.N.V.R.

Clements, R. W., B.A., M.B., Lieut.-Colonel, Royal Army Medical Corps. D.S.O., and Mentioned in Despatches.

Cowlishaw, I., B.E., Indian Army.

Costello, J., M.B., Lieut.-Col., R.A.M.C. (M.C.)

Colohan, A. N., M.B., Lieut., R.A.M.C.

Connolly, R., Australian Force.

Devine, G., M.B., Capt., Royal Army Medical Corps.

Donovan, J. T., B.A., I.C.S., Indian Army Reserve.

Dunlop, J. L., B.A., M.B., Capt., Royal Army Medical Corps.

Durdle, R. W., B.Sc. (Assistant), Capt., West Kents. *Killed in Action.*

Fee, W. G., Capt., Royal Army Medical Corps.

Fogarty, M. J., Capt., Connaught Rangers.

Fogarty, P. C., B.A., I.C.S., Indian Army Reserve.

Forde, D., M.B., Capt., Royal Army Medical Corps.

Forde, J. P., Lieut., Royal Dublin Fusiliers. Promoted to Commissioned rank for bravery in the field. *Wounded and Missing.*

Flack, I., M.B., Capt., Royal Army Medical Corps.

Flack, J., M.B., Capt., Royal Army Medical Corps.

Flack, S. H., Hampshire Regiment.

Flack, Rev. W., M.A., C.F.

Freyer, P. J., M.A., M.D., M.Ch., Dip. Obs., Colonel, Royal Army Medical Corps. C.B. and Mentioned in Despatches.

Gannon, P. M., B.E., Cadet, Royal Engineers.

Goff, T., Leinster Regt. D.C.M.

Greene, J.

Gribbon, J.

Haigh, F. F., B.Sc., B.E., Lieut., Royal Engineers. Mentioned in Despatches

Hackett, M. J., M.B., Lieut., Royal Army Medical Corps.

Hare, W. J., M.B., Capt., Royal Army Medical Corps.

Halliday, R. J., B.A., B.E., Major, Royal Engineers (Mesopotamia).

Hardiman, J., B.A., B.E., Royal Munster Fusiliers.

Harvey, C. B. F., Lieut., Connaught Rangers, attached to Staff.

Hay, J. L., Sec.-Lieut., Northumberland Fus., *Killed in Action.*

Hegarty, C.

Heneghan, W. J., Sec.-Lieut., Connaught Rangers.

Hewitt, A. J., M.B., Surgeon, R.N. Mentioned in Despatches.

Hoade, J.

Hughes, J., M.B., Capt., Royal Army Medical Corps.

Joyce, W., Lieut., Irish Guards.

Keane, T. A., Leinster Regiment.

Keane, T. J., B.A., B.E., Lieut.

Keane, W. M. A., B.Sc., Lieut., Royal Irish Fusiliers. *Killed in action.*

Kean, E., M.B., B.Sc. (Honoris Causa).

Kean, M. J. A. F., B.E., South African Infantry.

Kelly, J. J., B.E., Lieut., Royal Irish Rifles.

Kelly, G.

Kerr, R. A., M.B., Capt., Royal Army Medical Corps.

Keegan, J. M., M.B., Capt., Royal Army Medical Corps.

Keogh, Sir A., M.D., M.Ch., Dip. Obs., D.Sc. (Honoris Causa), Director-General, Medical Services. G.C.B.

Kelly, I., M.B., Lieut., Royal Army Medical Corps.

Keegan, W., Lieut., Connaught Rangers.

Kerans, J. C. L., M.B., Major, Indian Medical Service. Mentioned in Despatches. D.S.O.

Kidd, C., M.B., Capt., Royal Army Medical Corps.

Kilkenny, J. C., B.E. (Honoris Causa), Army Ordnance Corps.

Kinkead, G., M.B., Capt., Royal Army Medical Corps. *Killed in action.*

Kinneen, J., B.E., I.P.W., Ind'an Army Reserve.

Killacky, P. A.

Killacky, P. J., Lieut., Royal Dublin Fusiliers.
Kirwan, J. St. L., B.A., M.B., Lieut., Royal Army Medical Corps Died.
Kirwan, F., M.B., Capt., Royal Army Medical Corps.
Lee, G., B.E., Lieut., Royal Engineers.
Lydon, T., M.B., Capt., Royal Army Medical Corps.
Lydon, M., M.B., Capt., Royal Army Medical Corps.
Lindsay, G. E., M.B., B.Sc., Capt., Royal Army Medical Corps. M.C. with Bar.
Lindsay, R. B., T.M.B. *Wounded.*
Macnamara, P. J., M.D., Colonel, Royal Army Medical Corps.
Mahon, Professor R. B., M.D., M.Ch., F.R.S.C.Eng., Capt., Royal Army Medical Corps.
Matthews, W., M.B., Capt., Royal Army Medical Corps. *Died on Service.*
Millar, W., B.E., Lieut., Royal Engineers. Mentioned in Despatches.
Molloy, F., Lieut., Royal Flying Corps.
Morrison, H. N., M.Sc., Naval Instructor.
Morrison, J. A., B.E., Lieut., Royal Dublin Fusiliers.
Mullen, B. J., Capt., Royal Army Medical Corps. M.C.
Mullery, R., B.A., Royal Flying Corps.
Mulligan, M., M.B., Capt., Royal Army Medical Corps. *Wounded.*
Mulholland, H. C., M.B., Capt., Royal Army Medical Corps. *Seriously Wounded.* Mentioned in Despatches.
Murray, T., Capt., Army Service Corps. M.C.
McCausland, J., B.A., M.B., Capt., Royal Army Medical Corps. M.C.
McCausland, S., Capt., Royal Army Medical Corps. M.C.
McClatchie, W. A., B.E., Capt., Royal Flying Corps.
McDonagh, P.
McLachlan, A., Indian Army.
McLachlan, D., B.A., I.C.S., Indian Army Reserve.
McLachlan, J. S., B.A., B.E., Lieut., Royal Engineers. Mentioned in Despatches.
McLachlan, J., B.E., Lieut., Canadian Artillery. M.C
McCrea, R. E., B.E., Naval Service.
McEvilly, D., Connaught Rangers.
Nerney, M., B.E. (Honoris Causa), I.W.T.
Nolan, J. M., Lieut. (M.G.C.)
Nunan, R., B.E., Royal Field Artillery.
O'Brien, T. V., Artists' Rifles.
O'Brien, W., M.B., Capt., Royal Army Medical Corps

B

O'Farrell, A., B.A., B.E., Lieut., Royal Engineers.

O'Malley, C. C., M.B., B.Sc., Lieut., Royal Navy.

O'Malley, Cusack, B.Sc., M.B., Capt., Royal Army Medical Corps. M.C. Prisoner of War.

O'Malley, V., M.B., Capt., Royal Army Medical Corps.

O'Mally, J. F., M.B., Major, Royal Army Medical Corps.

O'Connor, J., Canadians.

O'Sullivan, J., B.E., Major, Royal Engineers. Mentioned in Despatches. Awarded Divisional Parchment for gallantry in the field.

Osburne, J., M.B., Capt., Royal Army Medical Corps.

Paisley, W., M.B., Capt., Royal Army Medical Corps.

Patrick, J., M.B., Capt., Royal Army Medical Corps.

Paul, J., B.E., Canadian Artillery. *Died of Wounds.*

Perry, S., Major, Royal Garrison Artillery.

Peters, A. J. K., Royal Engineers. *Died of Wounds.*

Prendergast, W., B.Sc., B.E., Lieut., Royal Engineers.

Quoyle, J. S.

Roberts, B. R., Lieut., Royal Army Medical Corps. *Died of Wounds.*

Rishworth, W., M.B., Capt., Royal Army Medical Corps. M.C. Mentioned twice in Despatches.

Rishworth, Prof. F. S., B.A., B.E., Lieut., Royal Flying Corps.

Rishworth, J., M.B., Capt., Royal Army Medical Corps.

Rothwell, T., M.B., Capt., Royal Army Medical Corps. Mentioned in Despatches.

Sampy, W., Royal Army Medical Corps.

Sandford, P., Capt., Army Service Corps.

Sheehy, M. J., B.E. (Honoris Causa), I.W.T. (Mesopotamia).

Sheehy, J., B.A., I.C.S., Indian Army Reserve.

Somerville, W., B.E., Major, Royal Engineers. D.S.O. Mentioned in Despatches. *Wounded.*

Smith, H., M.B., Capt., Royal Army Medical Corps.

Smyth, C., B.A., Canadians.

Steinberger, C., Naval Service.

Slattery, F., B.E., Capt., Royal Engineers. M.C. *Died of Wounds.*

Thompson, W. D'Arcy, Naval Service.

Webster, G. D., 2nd Lieut., Leinster Regiment.

Ward, P. F., Lieut., Royal Army Medical Corps. *Died.*

Waller, J. H., M.E., Capt., Royal Engineers. Mentioned twice in Despatches. D.S.O.

Walsh, P. M., B.A. (Honoris Causa), A.S.H. *Discharged Wounded.*

2. *Selected Biographies*

NUI men and the First World War

RONAN MCGREEVY

THE NATIONAL UNIVERSITY of Ireland's Roll of Honour is based on lists compiled by its constituent universities: University College Dublin (UCD), University College Cork (UCC), and University College Galway (UCG).[1] The roll lists 914 men, of whom eighty died in the war. Of the eighty, seventy-six can be found in the Commonwealth War Graves Commission that lists all British and Commonwealth personnel who died in the First World War and/or in the Irish National War Memorial Records (INWMR) first published in 1922, now digitised.[2] In compiling the biographies presented here, I am grateful for the work of Tom Burnell, whose 15 volume series *26 County Casualties of the Great War*, published in 2017, is the most comprehensive and up-to-date list of Irish men who died in the Great War, from what is now the Republic of Ireland.[3] Four men listed in the Roll of Honour, Thomas Lucy (UCD and the Royal Field Artillery); Donal Barry, Wilfred Dixon, and George Naylor (all UCC and the Royal Army Medical Corps) are not documented in either the CWGC or in INWMR. The CWGC only records those who died on 'military service or of causes attributable to service'. It may be the case that these men died of natural causes and not as a consequence of the war. Hence their presence in the Roll of Honour, but not officially among the British or Commonwealth war dead. Forty men from the roll who survived the war are also profiled here. These men distinguished themselves after the war and played a significant part in either the new Irish state and/or states abroad. Biographies of many of these men may be found in the *Dictionary of Irish Biography*. The doctors profiled are also discussed in *Irish Doctors in the First World War* by Patrick Casey, Kevin Cullen, and Joe Duignan, which is a comprehensive chronicle of those who served from the medical profession.[4]

Arthur Chance

Jeremiah Brennan

Joseph Patrick Coghlan

Thomas J. Costello

Ambrose J.S. Davoren

J.J. Donovan

J.J. Doyle

Thomas Louis Enright

Edmund Hughes Flanigan

FIGURE 2.1 *Portraits of NUI students, graduates and staff.*

Gerald Fogerty

John Gilligan

P. Hartigan

T.J. Keating

Hugh Maguire

E.J. Mahony

Louis Lawrence McKeever

James J. Nolan

Arthur O'Carroll

Charles O'Carroll

F.B. O'Carroll

Frank Brendan O'Carroll

R.D. O'Connor

G.C. Rooney

E.B. Slattery

Herbert Tierney

James Hardness de W. Waller

Stephen Barry Walsh

ANDERSON, ALEXANDER (1895–1967), Lieutenant, Connaught Rangers (attached to the Royal Flying Corps). Alexander Jr was the only son of UCG President, Professor Alexander Anderson. He enlisted in the 4th Connaught Rangers as a lieutenant and was attached to the Royal Flying Corps. He was reported missing on 23 November 1916 and ended up as a prisoner of war (POW) until the Armistice. He was awarded an honorary BSc (*Honoris Causa*) in 1917 in his absence. His sister, Emily, was Professor of German in UCG from 1917 until 1920.[5] She left the college to join the Foreign Office as a code breaker and worked in the Middle East specialising in Italian intelligence. She was not only an outstanding codebreaker, but also an excellent linguist and her English translations of the letters of Beethoven and Mozart were bestsellers in their day. Emily Anderson died in 1961 at the age of 71.[6]

BARRETT, JAMES, Staff Surgeon, Royal Navy. Barrett was born in 1880 in Tralee, Co Kerry. He attended Clongowes Wood College in Co Kildare and finished his secondary education at Downside, a Benedictine school in Somerset, favoured by many in the Irish Catholic middle-classes.[7] Barrett qualified as a doctor from UCD in 1907. He joined the Royal Navy a year later, rising to become the surgeon in charge of the Royal Marine barracks in Plymouth.[8] At the beginning of the war, he applied to be sent to sea on active service. Barrett drowned accidentally on 14 December 1914, aged thirty-six, while serving on board *HMS Imperieuse* anchored in the Royal Navy's British Grand Fleet base at Scapa Flow in the Orkney Islands. His accidental death was in mysterious circumstances. He had won several trophies for swimming competitions in his youth. Barrett's family received Christmas greetings from him one day before the telegram came from the War Office announcing his death.[9]

Grave/memorial: Portsmouth Naval Memorial, UK

BARRY, DONAL MOORE, Captain, Royal Army Medical Corps. Born in 1860 in Cork city, Barry was a student at Clongowes Wood College and then graduated from UCC as a doctor. He was working as a police surgeon in Glasgow when war broke out and was commissioned as a temporary captain. He served with the home hospital reserves. He is listed among the UCC war dead in the Roll of Honour but is not documented by the CWGC as a fatality of the war.[10]

BEVERIDGE, JAMES AND ARTHUR O'SHAUGHNESSY, Captains, RAMC. James and his identical twin brother Arthur, from Rathgar in Dublin, served as doctors in the war. Born in March 1893, they were the sons of Dublin's town clerk John Beveridge. They attended Belvedere College and qualified as doctors from UCD in 1915; a year after being commissioned into the Royal Army Medical Corps special reserve in 1914. Prior to that they had both been in the College of Surgeons Officers' Training Corps (OTC), a favoured route for university students into the officer classes. James Beveridge was twenty-four when he died on 22 November 1917 having succumbed to wounds during the Battle of Cambrai; the first great tank battle of the war. In 1918, *The Belvederian*, Belvedere College's annual, reported that James had:

> met his death while bravely doing his duty in one of the biggest battles of the war. He worked unceasingly until he was stricken down with many wounds; in that state he was found by the Catholic chaplain who administered the last rites of the Church to him and he died shortly afterwards. He lived as he died, a fervent and devout Catholic.[11]

His twin was so aggrieved by James's death that he was given three months' compassionate leave from the front. Arthur (1893–1959) remained in the Royal Army Medical Corps and served in the Second World War.[12] He was awarded the Norwegian War Cross for his conduct during the Nazi invasion in 1940. He retired from the British Army in 1953 at the rank of Major General and died in 1959.[13]

Grave / memorial Lebucquiere Communal Cemetery Extension, France

BIGGANE, FRANCIS JOSEPH, Lieutenant, Royal Munster Fusiliers. Biggane was born in 1895 in Cork city.[14] His father John was a well-known businessman who ran the Munster Arcade, a department store in the city. Francis was a first-year student of medicine at UCC in 1914 when he was commissioned as a second lieutenant in the 8th Royal Munster Fusiliers. He went to France with the 16th (Irish) Division in December 1915. At 1am on the morning of 10 May 1916 he was one of two men from the battalion, the other being Lance Corporal Timothy Kemp from Lismore, Co Waterford, who crept across no-man's-land and seized two offending signs which had been left in an unoccupied enemy sap. The signs were erected opposite the trenches of the 8th Munsters in the immediate aftermath of the Easter

Rising by the Germans who had inflicted more than 2,000 casualties on the 16th (Irish) Division including 532 dead during Easter Week 1916. One sign read: 'Irishmen! Heavy Uproar in Ireland. English guns are firing at your wifes (sic) and children'. Another referenced the recent surrender at Kut of 13,000 British troops to the Ottoman Turks in Mesopotamia.[15] For many Irishmen serving at the front, the signs were the first time they heard about the Rising. They were regarded as a provocation and were shot up before being captured by Biggane and Kemp on the instructions of their Commanding Officer, Major Larry Roche, who won a senior football All-Ireland with Limerick in 1896.[16] Biggane later presented the sign to King George V at Buckingham Palace. The signs, which were then the property of Queen Elizabeth II, were lent to Collins Barracks in 2016 to mark the centenary of the Easter Rising.[17] Biggane was killed during the Battle of Langemarck on 16 August 1917, a bloody day for the Irish in which 1,200 men from the 16th (Irish) Division and 36th (Ulster) Division were killed. Major General William Hickie, who commanded the 16th (Irish) Division, wrote to his parents:

> He was one of several young officers in the Munster Fusiliers who throughout the campaign have shown a constant devotion to duty, and on many occasions have proved that the Irish gentleman is a natural soldier and leader of men. I have on several occasions commended him for his cheerfulness and pluck under trying circumstances.[18]

Grave / memorial Tyne Cot Memorial to the Missing, Ypres, Belgium

BLAYNEY, ALEXANDER JOSEPH MCAULEY (1869–1925), Major, Royal Army Medical Corps (RAMC). Blayney, the son of a Belfast shipbuilder, was from Cushendall, Co Antrim. He attended St Malachy's College in Belfast and graduated from UCD [Medical School, Cecilia Street] as a doctor in 1898. Blayney played League of Ireland football for Bohemian FC and was the first chairman of the club.[19] He served in the RAMC during the First World War and was stationed in France. However, it is his activities during the Easter Rising, while he was on home leave, for which he is best remembered. Blayney was on duty in the Mater Hospital during Easter Week 1916. According to one unnamed Sisters of Mercy nun – the order that founded the hospital – Blayney never left the Mater at all during the week. 'He was operating day and night,' the nun told the Bureau of Military

History years later.[20] During the Civil War, he treated the dying Cathal Brugha in the same hospital after Brugha was shot on the streets of Dublin in July 1922.[21] Later Blayney became an Assistant Professor in Surgery at UCD and held various posts as an examiner for the National University of Ireland. His sudden death from a heart attack in 1925 came as a profound shock to his friends.[22]

BRENNAN, GARRETT (1894–1974), Wireless Operator, Merchant Navy. Brennan was a native of Castlecomer, Co Kilkenny.[23] He was born in 1894, the second of ten children of Cornelius Brennan, a shopkeeper, and Margaret Brennan. At UCD, Brennan was taught by Eoin MacNeill, the founder of the Irish Volunteers, and Thomas MacDonagh, one of the seven signatories of the Proclamation. In 1913, Brennan was present at the meeting in the Rotunda when MacNeill launched the Irish Volunteers. Brennan signed a form to join up, but nothing came of it.[24] In 1914, he found himself with an Arts Degree and few options, so he took a radio operator's course in Cork with the Marconi Company. He then joined British troop ships operating in the Mediterranean during the war. Brennan claimed to have got into 'several first-class arguments with the ship's officers over Ireland' and was eventually sent home overland.[25] He returned to Castlecomer in September 1919, joined the local company of the IRA's North Kilkenny Brigade, and was promoted to battalion commandant just before the Truce of July 1921. He narrowly escaped death during the Coolbawn ambush a month earlier when two volunteers were killed during an attempt to lay landmines targeting Crown forces.[26] After serving in the National Army during the Civil War, he joined the newly formed An Garda Síochána. He retired from the force in 1959 as Deputy Commissioner. He was one of the founders of the Garda Technical Bureau and was in charge of investigating the infamous murder of Lavena Ball by her son Edward Ball, a jobbing actor with the Gate Theatre in Dublin. When Ball's mother, a widow with a substantial fortune, refused to give him £60 to tour with the Gate in February 1936, he killed her with an axe. He was found guilty but insane after a six-day trial and spent fourteen years at the Central Criminal Lunatic Asylum in Dundrum.[27]

BRENNAN, JEREMIAH, Second Lieutenant, Lancashire Hussars. Brennan was from Kilbrogan House, Bandon, Co Cork. He attended Clongowes Wood College before going on to study at UCD.[28] He graduated with a

BA and LLB in 1914 and was studying for the bar when he was commissioned into the Inns of Court Officers' Training Corps (OTC) at the Four Courts.[29] Brennan is listed as having been killed accidentally at the age of twenty-six on 8 August 1918, the first day of the Battle of Amiens.[30]

Grave / memorial K1 Cemetery: St Hilaire Cemetery Extension, Frévent, France

BUSTEED, JOHN (1895–1964), Captain, The Irish Guards. Busteed, the son of a ship's steward, was from a modest family in Mayfield, Cork city.[31] After being educated at North Monastery (North Mon) secondary school in Cork, John won a scholarship to UCC in 1913. He joined the Irish Guards and was wounded at the Battle of the Somme in 1916. He spent the rest of the war as a machine gun instructor at Bisley in England, later recalling that his training of thousands of soldiers was of 'great practical educational value'.[32] He returned to UCC as a mature student and graduated with a BComm with first class honours in 1920.[33] Busteed was described by UCC Professor of Economics, Timothy Smiddy, as 'having mathematical knowledge and ability of a high order which are of inestimable value to an economist'.[34] Busteed succeeded Smiddy as Professor of Economics in UCC during 1923, and held the role for forty years. His services were called upon by successive Irish governments who valued his statistical analysis of various aspects of the economy. Busteed was in many ways a public economist, who regularly wrote columns in newspapers arguing, in some cases, against the prevailing economic orthodoxy in Ireland. In the late 1930s, he proposed the break with sterling, an event that would not happen for another four decades. He is also credited with presiding over the merger of the Irish Trade Union Congress and the Congress of Irish Unions to form the Irish Congress of Trade Unions (ICTU) in 1959. Busteed served as a reserve captain in the Irish Army during the Second World War. Fr Paschal Larkin wrote in the *Irish Times* following Busteed's death in August 1964 'He won the respect of all classes not for any conscious cult of popularity, but because of his keen intellect, his easy manner and, above all, his sincerity of purpose,'.[35] Writing his obituary, his fellow former British Army Officer, Denis Gwynn, noted in the *Cork Examiner* that:

> military service in the British Army during those years usually became a handicap for future careers in Ireland, but Busteed has a gift for mixing with all parties, and he soon restored his former popularity when he came back to Cork as a

student ... He was the least pedantic of professors, and his military service had strengthened his naturally bohemian tendencies, besides giving him the self-confidence and the resourcefulness of the old soldier.[36]

BUTLER, JAMES BAYLEY (1884–1964), Major, Royal Army Medical Corps. Butler was born in Secunderabad, India in April 1884.[37] His father was an administrator with the East India Company. A polymath, Butler attended Clongowes Wood College after his family returned to Ireland. He qualified as a doctor from UCD [Medical School. Cecilia Street] in 1909 and stayed on as a lecturer in botany and zoology. In 1915, he joined the RAMC as a lieutenant. He was stationed in France in 1916 at the headquarters of the 48th Division, ended the war at the rank of major and was awarded an MBE for his services. After the war he was appointed Professor of Zoology in UCD and held the position until his retirement in 1956. He became an expert on combating dry rot and was involved in the development of Biotox, an effective treatment for woodworm at the time.[38] He sold his patent for a waterproof map to the United States Army during the Second World War. Perhaps his greatest endeavour was his construction of Glenlion, the Roman-style villa on the Hill of Howth, built with his own hands and with the help of many of his students.[39] Butler used stone from the ruins of the Customs House and Four Courts (badly damaged in the War of Independence and Civil War respectively), and from ancient Rome to construct the 216 square metre house with a Roman garden modelled on the ruins of Pompeii.[40] When he died in 1964, an anonymous contributor to the *Irish Times* stated that, where other men spent their Saturdays on the golf course, 'he played with concrete and stone, moulding them into something permanent'. He was, the contributor added, 'a sort of versatile genius with so many and such varied gifts, some of them exceptionally unusual like his uncanny power of hypnotising almost any type of animal'.[41] He was also renowned for hosting garden parties with snail, cockroach, and frog races.

BYRNE, PATRICK ANTHONY LANGAN, Lieutenant, Royal Flying Corps. Byrne was just twenty-one when he was shot down and killed over France in October 1916. He had already gained a reputation as one of the best-known Irish air aces of the war.[42] Byrne was from Clogherhead, Co Louth where his father, Dr John Byrne, had been the village GP. Patrick Byrne attended Clongowes Wood College and then UCD between 1912 and

1914. He was granted a temporary commission in the Royal Field Artillery in October 1914, and in March 1916 he was transferred to the Royal Flying Corps (RFC). His achievements as a war ace occurred in a three-month span from August to October 1916. He was a notably aggressive fighter – flying into the middle of German formations and scattering them with machine gun fire from his Airco DH2 biplane. Byrne's dauntless bravery won him in short order the Distinguished Service Medal (DSM) and a mention in dispatches.[43] The citation for his DSM stated that Byrne had 'shown great pluck in attacking hostile machines, often against large odds. He has accounted for several downed aircraft. On one occasion, along with two other machines, he attacked 17 enemy machines, shot down one in flames, and forced another to land'. He was killed by Oswald Boelcke, a prolific German war ace, on 16 October 1916.[44] Byrne's squadron leader, Lanoe Hawker, who later won the Victoria Cross, described him as a 'charming Irishman', as 'brave as a lion' and 'the best officer I have ever met'. Byrne's body was never recovered, and his mother clung to the belief that her son was still alive long after the war was over.[45]

Grave / memorial Arras Flying Services Memorial, France

CAMPBELL, THOMAS CALLENDER, Lieutenant, Royal Engineers.[46] Campbell was originally from Ballymoney, Co Antrim. His parents had been Protestant missionaries. He graduated from UCG as an engineer and emigrated to Canada where he was based when war broke out. He served with the Royal Engineers and died during the Gallipoli campaign on 8 October 1915.

Grave / memorial Helles Memorial, Gallipoli, Turkey[47]

CARROLL, JOHN DONAL (J. D) (1890–1928), Captain, Royal Army Medical Corps (RAMC).[48] Carroll was the grandson of P. J. Carroll, the founder of the tobacco dynasty based in Dundalk.[49] J. D., as he was known, was born in 1890 and educated at Clongowes Wood and UCD. He graduated as a doctor in 1913 and joined the RAMC in August 1914. He served in Gibraltar, Malta, Egypt, and France. In June 1917, he won the Military Cross while serving in Flanders with the Royal Warwickshire Regiment after the battalion's observation post had been hit. The citation read: 'He immediately went to the spot and attended the wounded, although the enemy continued to concentrate heavy shell fire on the post'.[50] Carroll was severely shell-shocked when his dugout was blown up during the

Battle of Passchendaele in 1917. After being discharged from the RAMC, he specialised in public health and in 1922 was appointed the chief sanitary officer of the National Army during the Civil War. In 1925, he studied public health medicine in the United States and in 1927 took up the position of medical superintendent in Cork county borough.[51] He died a year later at just the age of thirty-seven after a short illness. The *Irish Times* stated that he had 'completely organised the public health work of the city especially in the directions of child welfare and treatment of tubercular disease'.[52]

Carew, William King (1872–1956), Major, Royal Army Medical Corps
Carew was the doctor in charge of the Red Cross Hospital in Dublin Castle during the Easter Rising and was relieved on 30 April 1916 suffering from exhaustion.[53] Carew was born in Waterford in 1872. He graduated as a doctor from the Royal College of Surgeons in Ireland (RCSI) in 1913 and was promoted to major after the Easter Rising. In later years, he emigrated to New Zealand and worked there and in Fiji as a doctor. He died in Jersey in 1956.

Chance, Sir Arthur Gerald (1859–1928), Lieutenant, RAMC.[54]
Chance was born in Dublin in 1859 into a nationalist family – his brother Patrick was an Irish Parliamentary Party MP representing South Kilkenny. Arthur was educated at Clongowes Wood College. He studied medicine at RCSI and TCD where he graduated as a doctor in 1883. He practiced as a surgeon in the Mater Hospital, Dr Steevens' Hospital, and at the Orthopaedic Hospital of Ireland. His reputation led him to be knighted by King Edward VII in 1905 and he was President of RCSI and a member of the NUI Senate from 1914. During the First World War, he served as a temporary colonel in the RAMC and was the inspector of military surgical hospitals (1917–20) in the Irish Command and an adviser to the War Office. Chance married Eileen Murphy, the daughter of William Martin Murphy, the controversial industrialist and owner of the *Irish Independent*, in 1900. When Murphy died in 1919, Chance became a director of Independent Newspapers.[55] He died in 1928 at the age of sixty-nine.[56] A tribute to him in the *British Medical Journal* stated that 'no complete record could ever be made of the many charitable and devoted acts which Sir Arthur Chance performed ... he might, indeed, be well described as the poor man's surgeon'.[57] Chance's son Neville became friends with Noel Browne who went on to become Minister for Health who successfully tackled the scourge

of tuberculosis in Ireland, and was a significant political figure in Ireland. The Chance family paid for Browne's studies at medical school. Writing in his bestselling autobiography *Against the Tide* in 1986, Browne paid tribute to Neville Chance:

> It transpired that my friendship with him would change the whole direction and purpose of my life, Lady Chance (Sir Arthur's wife) and her remarkable family agreed that I should live with them at their home, Nullamore, just outside Dublin, until my qualification as a doctor. It was an extraordinary selfless decision to make.[58]

COGHLAN, JOSEPH P., Lieutenant, Royal Engineers.[59] Coghlan was from Waltham Terrace, Blackrock. He attended Blackrock College and then UCD where he studied engineering, and won 'numerous prizes, honours, exhibitions and scholarships,' according to the *Weekly Irish Times*.[60] On graduating, he joined the British Army and went to France in September 1916 with the 228th Field Company of the Royal Engineers. Coghlan gained the Military Cross, one of the highest British honours for gallantry, on 31 July 1917, the first day of the Battle of Passchendaele.[61] He continued to erect screen fencing for British troops under heavy machine gun fire. Coghlan was killed while building a pontoon for British infantry on 20 September 1917 during the latter stages of the battle. He was twenty-seven. His family posted a succinct obituary in many of the Irish papers: 'a distinguished scholar: a brave soldier: and a good son'.[62]

Grave / memorial Voormezeele Enclosures No. 1 and No. 2 West-Vlaanderen, Belgium

COLLINGWOOD, BERTRAM (1871–1934), Lieutenant, RAMC. Collingwood is best known for giving his name to the cup which is the most senior intervarsity soccer competition in Ireland and has been run on an all-Ireland basis since 1914.[63] Collingwood played soccer at the University of Oxford and with the famous London amateur club, Corinthians. The first Collingwood Cup competition held in 1914 was won by UCD, but it was not held again until 1920. The Collingwood Cup name survived even after the original trophy was lost in 1940.[64] Collingwood was a nephew of the author Lewis Carroll, the creator of *Alice in Wonderland*. A native of Sunderland in England, he qualified as a doctor from St Mary's Hospital Medical School in London in 1901 and joined the RAMC as a doctor, seeing immediate service in the Boer War.[65] He left the RAMC and worked in the University of London Physiology Research Laboratory, where he did pioneering work to enhance the safety of chloroform as an anaesthetic. In 1912, he was appointed Professor of Physiology at UCD.[66] In 1915, Collingwood re-enlisted in the RAMC and worked in laboratories in Britain and Ireland devising ways to combat gas attacks. He left Ireland in 1920 to take up a post as Professor of Physiology at St Mary's Hospital Medical School. He died in August 1934 of coronary thrombosis at the age of sixty-two.[67]

Colahan, Arthur Nicholas (1884–1952), Captain, RAMC.[68] The Irish neurologist is best remembered for Bing Crosby's 1947 recording of his song 'Galway Bay', which sold six million copies and spawned a host of other covers from such singers as Ruby Murray and Josef Locke (Plate 6). It was referenced too in The Pogues' Christmas classic 'A Fairytale in New York'. The song was inspired by the drowning of Arthur's nineteen-year-old brother Roly in Galway Bay in 1912. Colahan was born in Enniskillen in 1884 but moved to Galway with his family as a child. He came from a long line of west of Ireland doctors. Colahan's father and grandfather had been professors of medicine at Queen's College Galway. Arthur Colahan was educated at St Joseph's College, Galway (The 'Bish') and Mungret College, Limerick. He studied medicine at UCG but was a desultory student and only graduated at the age of twenty-eight in the spring of 1912. One contemporary wrote many years later that, 'Arthur could scarcely be regarded as the model medical student. We prefer to remember him sitting at the piano, strumming out tunes, so that his success with 'Galway Bay' was not unexpected'.[69] He joined the RAMC in February 1916 and a month later was shipped to India. His medical card suggests that he only served in India during the war. In January 1918, he relinquished his temporary captaincy in the RAMC because of ill-health. After the war, Colahan moved to Leicester to work as a neurologist. He wrote dozens of songs about his adopted county, including 'Maccushla Mine', 'Asthoreen Bawn', and 'The Claddagh Ring', but only 'Galway Bay' has endured. When he died in 1952 his body was returned to Ireland, and he was buried in the Colahan family plot at the New Cemetery in Galway in accordance with the last verse of the song: 'I will ask my God to let me make my heaven in that dear land across the Irish Sea'.[70] In 1998, Leicester City Council erected a blue plaque outside 9 Prebend Street where he lived for many years.[71]

COSTELLO, TOM (1890–1945), Lieutenant, RAMC. Costello was the older brother of John A. Costello, Taoiseach between 1948 and 1951 and again from 1954 to 1957. The brothers grew up in Rathdown, Co Dublin. According to John A.'s biographer, David McCullagh, Tom was the more dominant character when the brothers were in UCD and both were members of the Literary and Debating Society.[72] After graduating as a doctor, Tom became a house surgeon in the Mater Hospital and then a temporary doctor in Mountjoy Prison. His younger brother resisted the pressure of his peers in the Law Library to join the war effort, concluding years later that the war had led to the 'sacrifice in vain of many thousands of Irish lives'.[73] It had also taught Ireland the 'unforgettable lesson not to pay for the goods until they are actually and decisively delivered' – a cut at Irish Parliamentary Party leader John Redmond who supported the British war effort unconditionally. Tom, however, joined the RAMC as a lieutenant in the Wessex Field Ambulance. He was awarded the Military Cross in 1918. He emigrated to England in the 1920s and died in 1945 at the age of fifty-five. He had a successful career of his own in politics having been elected as a Liberal Councillor in Darwen, Lancashire in 1927, and served two terms as mayor of the town from 1941 to 1943.

CROFTON, WILLIAM MERVYN, Captain, RAMC.[74] Crofton was born in Dublin in 1879. His father was the clerk of the South Dublin Union; his mother Mary Hayes was the daughter of William Hayes, one of the founders of the Grafton Street pharmacy Hayes, Conyngham & Robinson. Crofton attended St Columba's College in Rathfarnham and then UCD [Medical School, Cecilia Street] where he graduated as a doctor in 1904. His academic achievements were considerable. He received a BA Degree with honours in 1901, followed by a medical degree with a gold medal in 1904, and an MD with honours in 1911. He became an occasional lecturer in Special Pathology in UCD in 1910 and a pathologist to Dr Steevens' Hospital. During Easter Week 1916, his house in Merrion Square was caught in the crossfire and riddled with bullets. He served in the RAMC during the war. He left Ireland afterwards and spent the rest of his life in England. Crofton's theory about the origins of all illnesses – which he ascribed to microbes – was controversial. In 1958, he introduced a paper at the 7th International Cancer Congress in which he said there is 'no cancer ... from which the causative microbe cannot be grown; and that, with a dead antigen of this microbe, by a properly conducted immunisation the tumour can be made to disappear unless the body has gone beyond the capacity of reaction'.[75] His claims were rejected by the American Cancer Society. He was the father of Sir John Crofton (1912–2009), a pioneer in the treatment of tuberculosis and a well-known anti-tobacco campaigner.[76]

CROFTS, RICHARD (1859-1916), Major, RAMC.[77] Crofts was born in Passage West, Co Cork in August 1859. He was educated at Queen's College Cork and graduated as a doctor. He joined the RAMC and served in many colonial campaigns winning the Distinguished Service Order (DSO) during his time in Sierra Leone. He died in Queenstown, now Cobh, Co Cork in February 1916 having spent the duration of the war in Ireland.[78]

Grave / memorial Timoleague Church of Ireland Cemetery, Cork

DAVOREN, AMBROSE J. S., Second Lieutenant, Royal Field Artillery.[79] Davoren was the only surviving son of Richard, a solicitor, and Ina Davoren of Dundrum, Co Dublin. He was a student at Clongowes Wood College and graduated in 1914 from UCD with a BA/LLB.[80] He was killed in Belgium while serving with the Royal Field Artillery on 18 July 1917, aged twenty-seven. The inscription on his grave reads: 'We have loved him in life. Let us not forget him in death RIP'.

Grave / memorial Poperinghe Communal Cemetery, Belgium

DINAN, GEORGE ALBERT (1891-1916), Second Lieutenant, Royal Dublin Fusiliers. Born in 1891, Dinan was the son of John Dinan, a Justice of the Peace and prominent businessman from Cobh, Co Cork.[81] George was educated at the Benedictine College in Ramsgate and UCC where he studied to become a dentist.[82] He was also a very good cricketer and played for UCC against an Australian international XI.[83] He was the first of three Dinan brothers to die in the war. George was killed during the Battle of the Somme at the age of 25 while leading his platoon during the capture of Ginchy on 9 September 1916. According to eyewitnesses, he confronted a German officer, and both fired their revolvers at the same time.[84] Less than a year later, his younger brother Francis was killed while serving with the Royal Field Artillery in Flanders on 31 July 1917, the first day of the Battle of Passchendaele. In September 1917 Captain Fred Dinan, the oldest of the three brothers, died from wounds in France.

Grave / memorial Thiepval Memorial to the Missing, The Somme, France

DIXON, WILFRED STAFFORD, Surgeon, RAMC. Born in 1891 in Galway city, Dixon was the son of Augustus Edward Dixon, Professor of Chemistry in UCG. Wilfred Dixon qualified as a surgeon from UCC. He is listed among the college's war dead but is not listed in either the Commonwealth War Graves Commission database or the digitised version of the Irish National War Memorial records.[85]

DONOVAN, CHARLES (1863–1957), Lieutenant Colonel, RAMC. Donovan was born in Calcutta, India on 19 September 1863. His father, Judge Charles Donovan, was a native of Co Cork. Like many children in the imperial service, Charles Jr was sent 'home' to be educated.[86] He lived with his grandfather, the Rev Charles Donovan, a Church of Ireland clergyman, in Ummera House, Timoleague, Co Cork. Charles Jr studied medicine at Queen's College Cork and at Trinity College Dublin. He graduated as a doctor in 1889. Shortly afterwards he joined the RAMC and rose to the rank of lieutenant colonel. Donovan's most enduring legacy is a parasite that bears his name along with that of another Indian-based doctor, William Leishman. Leishmania donovani is a parasite which causes Leishmaniasis known as *kala-azar* in Hindu or the black fever.[87] The parasite is transmitted through the bite of a female sandfly. *Kala-azar* is the most serious form of Leishmaniasis and attacks the liver, spleen, and bone marrow. The disease is still deadly and claims the lives of 30,000 people worldwide every year. Prior to their separate discoveries of the parasite, doctors did not understand the disease and just thought of it as another form of malaria. Donovan also discovered the bacterial organism that causes Donovanosis, a sexually transmitted disease which still exists in developing countries. He retired from the Indian Medical Service in 1920, aged fifty-seven, and settled in Gloucester, England.[88] UCC's Charles Donovan Prize in Dermatology is named after him.[89]

DOYLE, JOHN JOSEPH, Second Lieutenant, Royal Dublin Fusiliers. Doyle was from Fairview in Dublin. He attended Blackrock College and UCD where he was an engineering student and was a year away from qualifying.[90] Within two days of the outbreak of war in August 1914, Doyle joined the Officers' Training Corps at TCD.[91] He was commissioned into the 6th Royal Dublin Fusiliers as a second lieutenant. Many of the middle-class sons of Dublin joined either the 6th or the 7th battalions of the Royal Dublin Fusiliers (RDF) at the outset of the war. The 6th was generally drawn from the city's merchants; the 7th, which included the famous D

Company of Posh Pals, from the professional classes. Both battalions were sent to Gallipoli as part of the 10th (Irish) Division and suffered terribly during the Suvla Bay landings debacle of August 1915. At the age of twenty-two Doyle was killed on 10 August 1915, two days after landing at Suvla Bay – 'most gallantly leading his platoon', according to his Commanding Officer who wrote to Doyle's parents, Joseph James, a merchant, and Margaret Doyle. 'He was a right good boy, who was always keen, always did his very best'.[92] Another brother, Lieutenant Francis Doyle, died in a hospital in Alexandria, Egypt a year later while serving with the Royal Army Veterinary Corps (RAVC). He was a graduate of the Veterinary College of Ireland, then based in Ballsbridge, Co Dublin.[93]

Grave / memorial Helles Memorial, Gallipoli, Turkey

DUGGAN, THOMAS (TOMMY) ALPHONSUS, Second Lieutenant, East Lancashire Regiment. Duggan was from William Street, Kilkenny. His family owned the Monster House in the town, then its largest department store. Duggan first attended St Kieran's College in Kilkenny, then Clongowes Wood College where he won the Delany Scholarship to study law at UCD in 1912. He was commissioned into the East Lancashire Regiment in March 1915. Severely wounded in France on 17 December 1915, he survived a sniper's bullet which entered his right ear and exited his left eye. Despite the severity of his injuries, Duggan returned to the front, and was killed on 13 November 1916 on the last day of the Battle of the Somme. He was leading two attacking platoons of the 7th East Lancashire Regiment near St Pierre-Divion. His Commanding Officer, Captain Rupert Palmer, wrote to his mother not knowing that she had pre-deceased her son: 'We must be comforted that he died as he would have wished, fighting for his Ireland of which he was so fond'.[94]

Grave / memorial Grandcourt Road Cemetery, France

DUGGAN, THOMAS FRANCIS (TOM) (1890–1961), Captain, Royal Army Chaplains' Department (RAChD).[95] Fr Duggan was born in Ballinhassig, Co Cork into a nationalist family. His grandfather had been a Fenian. He graduated from UCC with a BA in 1911 and was ordained a priest from Maynooth College in 1915. He was a British Army chaplain in both the First and Second World Wars, an active republican in the War of Independence and a peace broker in the Irish Civil War.[96] Duggan joined the British Army as a chaplain in September 1917 and witnessed the horrors of the Battle of Passchendaele. He was captured during the German Spring Offensive of March 1918 and held until the end of the war. In 1919, he returned to Ireland and threw himself into the Irish independence campaign much to the chagrin of the local hierarchy. During the Civil War, Duggan was sent by the Archbishop of Cashel John Harty to guerrilla commander Tom Barry to try and broker a ceasefire between the Free State Government and the anti-Treaty IRA. In peacetime, he was a teacher, parish priest, prison chaplain, and successful fundraiser. At the outbreak of the Second World War, Duggan again volunteered as a chaplain in the British Army though at forty-nine he was well over the age limit for service (forty). He was evacuated from the beaches at Dunkirk, for which he won the Military Cross for bravery, and is reported to have told his adjutant: 'If I shouldn't get back, would you be kind and send these to my mother?' He was awarded the Order of the British Empire (OBE) after the war. At the age of seventy-one, long past the age of retirement for most, Duggan volunteered to become a missionary in Peru and died just two months later from a massive heart attack. He is buried in Peru. His MC and OBE medals were sold at auction in July 2015 for €8,000.[97] The Archdeacon Duggan Bridge over the River Bandon in Kinsale is named after him.[98]

Dundon, James St John, Lieutenant, Royal Army Medical Corps (RAMC). Dundon was from O'Connell Street, Limerick. He was the fourth son of the late John Dundon, formerly the solicitor to Limerick Corporation, and his wife Annie. James attended Crescent College in Limerick, followed by Clongowes Wood College, and then graduated as a doctor from UCD in March 1916. A month later he was shipped to Mesopotamia.[99] He died at the age of twenty-four from contaminated water at his base in Basra (now part of modern-day Iraq) on 17 June 1916. Limerick Corporation unanimously passed a vote of sympathy to the Dundon family on hearing of his death.[100]

Grave / memorial Basra War Cemetery, Iraq

Durdle, Reginald William, Captain, East Kent Buffs. Durdle was from Blandford in Devon.[101] He was academically gifted and before leaving school, he passed the Oxford Senior Local Examination and also matriculated at London University. He graduated from Hartley University College, Southampton with an honour's degree in geology. At the age of just twenty-five he was appointed a temporary professor in UCG in geology and geography and as a science examiner for the National University of Ireland. He gave up his post in 1915 to join the British Army. He was killed on 18 September 1918 on the Western Front.

Grave / memorial Épehy Wood Farm Cemetery, France

DWYER, JAMES JAMESON, Captain, RAMC. Dwyer died of pleurisy three months after the war ended. He graduated from UCD [Medical School, Cecilia Street] as a doctor in 1909 and was commissioned as a temporary lieutenant in the RAMC in December 1914. He spent twenty-one months at the front and was awarded the Distinguished Service Order in June 1917. He died while on active service at a field hospital in Calais on 19 February 1919, aged forty-one.[102]

Grave / memorial Les Baraques Military Cemetery, France

ENRIGHT, THOMAS, Captain, RAMC. Thomas Enright, known as Tod, was from Church Street, Listowel, Co Kerry. He was educated at Castleknock College and then trained to be a doctor at UCD and RCSI. Fifteen of the twenty-one graduates from his class volunteered for the war effort.[103] He served as a house surgeon at the West Kent General Hospital at Maidstone and as a clinical assistant at the Chelsea Hospital for Women before joining the RAMC on 15 February 1915. After service in France, he was shipped to Salonika in December 1915, and remained there for over a year. At the age of twenty-nine, he was killed in a car crash in the Greek mountains on 19 March 1918.[104] His brother Ignatius also served in the war as a doctor. He survived and had a practice as a doctor in Dalkey after the war.[105]

Grave / memorial Salonika (Lembet Road) Military Cemetery, Greece

EVANS, GEORGE ERNEST KNIGHTLY, Second Lieutenant, Leinster Regiment.[106] Evans was the son of George Knightly Evans, the founder of the well-known Tower Hotel in Glenbeigh, Co Kerry, which has hosted many prominent guests over the years, including Charles de Gaulle and the actor Omar Sharif. George Jr studied at University College Cork and was killed during the Battle of the Somme while serving with the 2nd Leinsters at Guillemont on 3 September 1916. He was twenty-six.

Grave / memorial Delville Wood Cemetery, Longueval, France

FEHILY, THOMAS J. (1885–1918), Captain, RAMC. Fehily was the son of Patrick and Margaret Fehily from Ballineen in west Cork. They were prosperous landowners and shopkeepers.[107] Thomas was born in 1885 and studied medicine at UCC and later at RCSI. He was working in England when he enlisted in the RAMC at the outset of war. He was posted to Gallipoli and was involved in the initial disastrous landings in April 1915. Thomas was killed in the German Spring Offensive of April 1918. His body was never found. He is remembered with a stained-glass window at the Church of the Immaculate Conception in Enniskeane, Co Cork.[108] His brother Joseph also served in the RAMC as a doctor in both world wars. Joseph was captured by the Japanese in Hong Kong in 1942, but was released because of his Irish citizenship and eventually escaped to Britain. He returned to Hong Kong after the war and in 1947 received an OBE.

Grave / memorial Ploegsteert Memorial, Flanders

FLANIGAN, EDMUND H. (1883–1916), Lieutenant, RAMC. Flanigan was from a Catholic merchant family in Belfast, which suffered terrible losses in the First World War. Flanigan was born in 1883. His late father Patrick owned the Crown Hotel in Great Victoria Street, Belfast, which exists to this day.[109] Edmund attended Clongowes Wood College and graduated as a doctor from UCD [Medical School, Cecilia Street] in 1908. He emigrated to Zimbabwe (then Rhodesia) to work but returned to Europe to join the RAMC in 1915. He was invalided home from the front with pneumonia and died at his widowed mother's residence in Belfast on 17 June 1916 aged thirty-three. He left behind a widow Mary.[110] Edmund was the third of four Flanigan brothers to die between 1914 and 1917. William died of natural causes in 1914 before the war broke out.[111] Gerald was killed while serving with the Canadian Expeditionary Force in April 1916 just two months before Edmund died. Private Dominic Flanigan, the youngest son, was killed in action a year later in November 1917 while serving with the Leinster Regiment.

Grave / memorial Banbridge Roman Catholic Cemetery, Co Down

FLANNERY, ARTHUR HERBERT (BERTIE) (1890–1916), Surgeon, Royal Navy. Flannery was born in Ballaghadereen, Co Roscommon in 1890.[112] He attended The Bower School in Athlone, then Belvedere College and finally Castleknock College. He studied medicine at UCD and graduated with honours as a doctor in 1915. Flannery was granted a commission in the RAMC in June of that year, and he was immediately posted to Gallipoli.[113] He was invalided out of the peninsula and transferred to the Royal Navy where he worked at its hospital in Gosport outside Portsmouth. The strain of his experiences in Gallipoli may have contributed to his premature death at the age of twenty-seven on New Year's Eve 1916 from a massive heart attack. His body was repatriated to Ireland for burial.

Grave / memorial Glasnevin Cemetery, Dublin

FOGARTY, GERALD, Second Lieutenant, Royal Irish Regiment and Royal Flying Corps (RFC). Fogarty was from Mountjoy Street in Dublin.[114] His father was the *Irish Catholic* journalist and sub-editor Patrick J. Fogarty. Gerald went to O'Connell School in Dublin's North Richmond Street, a school that later produced another famous Irish airman of the Second World War, Brendan 'Paddy' Finucane. While a student at UCD in the autumn of 1915, Gerald volunteered to join the 2nd Royal Irish Regiment. He transferred to the Royal Flying Corps and was shot down and killed during the Battle of Passchendaele on 28 August 1917 aged twenty-two.

Grave / memorial Mendinghem Military Cemetery, Belgium

FOOTT, ALEXANDER BOYD, Captain, RAMC. Foott was born in England, but brought up in Bishopstown, Co Cork where his father was a doctor.[115] He graduated in medicine from UCC in 1914, and became resident surgeon at the Cork Eye, Ear, and Throat Hospital. He resigned in August 1914 to join the RAMC. He was severely wounded at the Battle of Loos on 18 October 1915. He continued with his war service but was struck by many illnesses and finally succumbed to malaria in Egypt in June 1918.

Grave/memorial Jerusalem War Cemetery, Israel

FORDE, JOHN PATRICK, Lieutenant, Royal Dublin Fusiliers.[116] Forde, from Wood Quay in Galway city, was educated at the Jesuit College (the Jes). He enrolled as a medical student in UCG, but left university to join the 9th Royal Dublin Fusiliers (RDF). He was killed on 16 August 1917 during the Battle of Passchendaele.

Grave/memorial Tyne Cot Memorial to the Missing, Belgium

FOWLER, WILLIAM (1893-1915), Lieutenant, Canadian Contingent. Fowler, born in 1893, was the son of John Busteed Fowler of Bellevue Park, Cork, a member of the Cork Stock Exchange and an insurance agent.[117] William attended Cork Grammar School and UCC before the family emigrated to Calgary, Alberta in 1912. William and his three brothers, Richard, John, and Frank, all served in the Canadian Expeditionary Force (CEF). Three of them were working for the Canadian Bank of Commerce when war was declared, and the bank gave them leave of absence to fight overseas. Fowler was killed, aged twenty-one, during the Second Battle of Ypres in April 1915 when the Germans introduced poison gas into the First World War. Frank Fowler died in October 1916 in France while serving with the Leinster Regiment. The unionist *Cork Constitution* newspaper expressed sympathies with their father on his double loss.

Grave / memorial New Menin Gate memorial to the missing, Ypres, Belgium

FREYER, SIR PETER JOHNSON (1851–1921), Colonel, RAMC. Freyer was born in Connemara in 1851. He attended Galway Grammar School and then Queen's College Galway. He had an outstanding academic career at QCG gaining a first-class honours BA in science followed by a senior scholarship in chemistry. He graduated as a doctor in 1875 and won first place in the Indian Medical School (IMS) examinations, a prized posting at the time.[118] In India, he was the subject of considerable public controversy after receiving a payment of 100,000 rupees (€10,000) by the Nawab of Rampur for treatment received for services rendered in removing a painful bladder stone. Freyer was ordered by the British administration in India to return the money, but he refused and was barred from promotion in India. He returned to Britain and had a brilliant career as a surgeon, pioneering a new method of bladder stone removal which reduced mortality dramatically. In later life, he pioneered an operation in prostatectomy (removal of the prostate). He rejoined the medical service of the British Army during the First World War, acting as a consulting surgeon to the Indian soldiers at the Brighton Military Hospital and finished the war at the rank of colonel. In October 1919, the National University of Ireland conferred on him an honorary degree of Doctor of Law. Though he spent much of his life in the service of the British Empire, Freyer had nationalist sympathies. He frequently corresponded with Irish Parliamentary Party leader, John Redmond, his brother Willie (who died in the war), and with the party's British-based MP, T.P. O'Connor. Freyer was the surgeon who operated on John Redmond before his death on 6 March 1918.[119] Ireland's largest surgical conference, the Sir Peter Freyer Memorial Lecture and Surgical Symposium, is hosted in his honour every year by the University of Galway since 1976.

FULLIN, JOHN FRANCIS (1894-1918), Second Lieutenant, Royal Munster Fusiliers.[120] Fullin was the son of a Royal Irish Constabulary Officer from

Co Donegal who was transferred to Cork, where he was born in 1894. He attended Christian Brothers College, Cork. In 1912, he won the *Irish Independent* poetry competition for his poem 'The Dawn of Christianity'. He was awarded a scholarship to study engineering at University College Cork. In 1916, he was gazetted into the 5th Royal Munster Fusiliers and afterwards posted to the 8th Royal Munster Fusiliers. In November 1917, he won the Military Cross at Bullecourt in northern France having cleared a tunnel in the enemy's lines, with 'courage, coolness and judgment'. He was killed during the German Spring Offensive on 22 March 1918. Fullin's Commanding Officer later wrote to his parents: 'He was beloved by all his brother officers, and was the best platoon commander in the battalion, and always a very gallant soldier. The battalion loses a very fine officer and a great friend'.[121] Fullin's brother Arthur was a journalist with the *Drogheda Independent* and corresponded with the poet Francis Ledwidge who was a regular contributor to the newspaper. Arthur died in 1920 of pneumonia.

Grave / memorial Pozières Memorial, France

Garry, Joseph (1890–1915), Ship's Surgeon, Royal Navy.[122] Garry was born in 1890 in Ennis, Co Clare. His father Patrick was a justice of the peace and a member of Clare County Council. Garry qualified as a doctor after attending UCD, as did his two other brothers, Michael and Dickie. Joseph was practicing as a doctor in Preston, Lancashire when he signed on as an assistant ship's surgeon on the *RMS Lusitania*. When the ship left Liverpool on 15 April 1915, it turned out to be its penultimate journey. On 7 May 1915, a German submarine, the U-20, fired three torpedoes into the ship off the Old Head of Kinsale, Co Cork. Of the 1,959 people aboard, 1,198 were killed. The dead included 140 Irish people – seventy passengers and seventy crew. Among them were Garry and the ship's surgeon, Dr James McDermott from Cork city. After the sinking Michael Garry spent four days in Cobh hoping against hope that his brother's body would be found or that he might turn up alive. On hearing confirmation of the ship surgeon's death, the County Clare Committee of Agriculture passed a resolution in sympathy with the Garry family.[123] There were a number of accounts of Garry's death.[124] One, published in the *British Medical Journal*, quoted a steward on the Lusitania recalling that Garry gave his lifebelt to a female passenger. A passenger eyewitness wrote to Garry's mother Mary saying that he had seen a young doctor attending to a woman on a raft, but the doctor seemed to disappear. His mother later wrote to another bereaved Lusitania mother: 'As mothers we have only to console ourselves with this thought, that God knows what is best for all'.[125]

Grave / memorial Tower Hill Memorial, London, UK

GILL, FR HENRY (1872–1945), Colonel, Royal Army Chaplains' Department (RAChD).[126] Fr Gill was from the famous Dublin publishing family of the same name. He was educated at Clongowes Wood College, and then entered the Society of Jesus as a novitiate at St Stanislaus College, Tullamore, in April 1890. After two years in Tullamore, Gill continued his training in Milltown Park, Dublin. He taught there while also attending lectures in mathematics and science at University College Dublin. In 1895, he spent three years at the Irish College in the University of Louvain. Outraged after the Germans burnt down the library at Louvain in August 1914, Gill volunteered for military chaplain service.[127] He wrote to a friend: 'Louvain is destroyed – destroyed by an act of ruthless soldiery. Could any cause, could any excuse, we ask ourselves, justify such a deed? We are proud to stand by the side of Belgium in her struggle against an unjust aggression which Ireland can but too well sympathise with'. During the war, Gill served with the 2nd Royal Irish Rifles, a mixed battalion of both unionist and nationalist regulars. Gill's letters home from the front reflected his growing ambivalence about the Easter Rising. 'We cannot think of anything else than the terrible things which have been going on in Dublin. Please God it is now over and that the authorities will use – as I am sure they will – tact in dealing with it', he wrote to his superior. He was later dismayed by the execution of the leaders of the Rising. 'I think everyone must admit, no matter what their sympathies are, that England has asked for trouble'. Having witnessed the horrors of the Battle of the Somme, Gill wrote to his Fr Provisional:

> the past two years have been a great strain and I am really tired out body and spirit. I find it an effort to get about – a person of 30 is more fitted for this work than one of 43–44. The Somme mud is white chalk and in the process of drying became a thick putty which made walking very fatiguing. When the battalion came back to rest for a few days, there was only half the original number that went into the trenches.[128]

Gill received the Military Cross, the Distinguished Service Order, and was mentioned twice in dispatches during the war. After the war, he taught in Belvedere College for most of the rest of his life and died in 1945 from liver cancer at the age of seventy-three.

GILLIGAN, JOHN JOSEPH, Second Lieutenant, Royal Field Artillery (RFA).[129] Gilligan, from North Circular Road in Dublin, was a graduate of both Clongowes Wood College and UCD. He was studying mathematics when the war broke out. He entered the Royal Military Academy in Woolwich and had nearly two years active service before he was killed while on observation duty in France, aged just twenty-one on 25 April 1918.[130] His Commanding Officer told his parents: 'Though he had been so short a time with us he had endeared himself to all he came in contact with, and was universally popular and esteemed'.[131]

Grave / memorial Couin New British Cemetery, France

GODWIN, SWIFTE O'FLAHERTIE, Second Lieutenant, Royal Flying Corps. Swifte O'Flahertie was from Rathfarnham, Co Dublin.[132] A distant relative of both Jonathan Swift and Oscar Wilde, his family had served in various British colonial campaigns. He joined the Shropshire Light Infantry and was posted to Egypt in December 1915. While stationed in Egypt, he transferred to the Royal Flying Corps and was killed while on a training mission on 4 March 1918. Swifte O'Flahertie was twenty-one.

Grave / memorial Cairo War Memorial Cemetery, Egypt

GOLDING, THOMAS JOSEPH (1879–1917), Captain, RAMC. Golding was the son of a well-known Cork doctor Dr James Golding. Born in 1879, Thomas was educated at Prior Park College, Bath and graduated as a doctor from Queen's University Cork in 1906. He was working as a GP in Cork when war broke out. He was posted to Gallipoli and attended to Australian troops. Golding was serving with the South Staffordshire Regiment when he was killed during the Battle of Passchendaele on 24 September 1917. Golding was thirty-eight when he died. The *Cork Examiner* reported:

> He possessed a host of acquaintances, and it can be truly said of him that he never made an enemy. His death will be deplored and to his bereaved mother, Mrs Golding, as well as members of the family, will go forth sincere and heartfelt regret and sympathy in their great affliction.[133]

Grave / memorial Belgian Battery Corner Cemetery, West Flanders, Belgium

GWYNN, DENIS ROLLESTON (1893–1971), Second Lieutenant, Royal Munster Fusiliers.[134] Gwynn was the third son of the Irish Parliamentary Party MP and Protestant nationalist Stephen Gwynn. Both father, who was forty-nine when the war broke out, and son served in the First World War. Stephen enlisted in the 7th Leinster Regiment and was later commissioned as a captain in the 6th Connaught Rangers. Denis Gwynn was a second lieutenant in the Royal Munster Fusiliers in 1916.[135] In a 1971 obituary, it was stated that he was 'probably the only pupil of (Patrick) Pearse's school to have enlisted in the British Army'. He was taught at Pearse's St Enda's College in Rathfarnham and by another signatory to the Proclamation, Thomas MacDonagh, at UCD.[136] Gwynn, who was received into the Catholic Church in 1902, graduated from UCD with a BA in 1914 and an MA in 1915. Gwynn, like his father, was a constitutional nationalist who joined the British Army. He was injured during an assault on the Hindenburg Line in 1917 and invalided out. He spent the rest of the war in the British Ministry of Information. After the war, both father and son pursued careers as journalists and authors. Denis Gwynn was a prolific writer producing biographies of Sir Roger Casement, Daniel O'Connell, and Éamon de Valera, and other books on Irish history and Catholicism. Most notably, both father and son sought to rehabilitate the reputation of the Irish Parliamentary Party leader, John Redmond, with successive biographies. Stephen Gwynn's *The Lost Years of Redmond*, published in 1919 portrayed him as a tragic figure.[137] Denis Gwynn's *The Life of John Redmond* was published in 1932. In that book, Gwynn made an impassioned defence of Redmond's support for the British war effort at the outbreak in August 1914.[138] He argued that Redmond had 'interpreted faithfully the instincts of the vast majority of Irishmen', but was let down by British politicians. From 1946 to 1963, Gwynn was Professor of Modern Irish History at UCC and a popular columnist with the *Cork Examiner*. At the age of seventy he married Alice McEnery, a daughter of Lady Lavery. He died eight years later.[139]

GWYNN, JOHN (1866–1915), Captain, Royal Army Chaplains' Department (RAChD). Catholic chaplains in the First World War were noted for their bravery. Of the thirty-two Jesuits of the Irish Province who volunteered as chaplains, eight (one quarter) were killed.[140] The first to die was Gwynn (forty-nine) whose life from a young age had been with the Society as a student, teacher, and then professor. Gwynn was born in Youghal, Co Cork in June 1866. At the time of the outbreak of war in 1914, he was forty-eight.

He suffered from an undiagnosed mental illness, and was, according to some contemporary diagnosis, probably bipolar. In July 1914, he wrote: 'My superiors do not know or guess the broken state I am in. The other day I sat and I trembled from head to foot'.[141] Like the better-known Jesuit chaplain colleague Fr Willie Doyle, he was physically and mentally unfit for frontline service but joined up anyway. Gwynn was posted to the 1st Battalion of the Irish Guards. He quickly gained a reputation for selfless courage, splashing through waterlogged trenches and running the gauntlet of German shells to get to his men. When the fighting was at its worst, Gwynn shared the medical officer's dugout to be near stricken men in their last moments. On 11 October 1915, he was injured when a bomb landed on the door of the regimental headquarters. He died the following morning and was buried in the cemetery in Béthune (Plate 8). Gwynn had been assiduous in writing to the relatives of men killed in battle. His Commanding Officer, Lord Desmond Fitzgerald, wrote to the former President of UCD William Delany SJ:

> It is certainly no exaggeration to say that he was loved by every officer, NCO (non-commissioned officer) and man in the battalion. The Irish Guards owe him a deep and lasting debt of gratitude, and as long as any of us are left who saw him out here, we shall never forget his wonderful life, and shall strive to lead a better life by following his example.[142]

Perhaps, the greatest tribute paid to him was by the Nobel prize-winning author Rudyard Kipling, the official historian of the Irish Guards in the war. Kipling's only son John was killed at the Battle of Loos in September 1915 while serving with the Irish Guards. He wrote of Gwynn: 'He feared nothing, despised no one, betrayed no confidence nor used it to his own advantage; upheld authority, softened asperities, and cheered and comforted every man within his reach'.[143] A plaque to Gwynn is located in the Sacred Heart parish in Caterham, Surrey near Caterham Barracks, where the Irish Guards trained before embarking for the front.

Grave / memorial Bèthune Town Cemetery, France

HARTIGAN, TIMOTHY, J. (T.J.) (1879–1918), Surgeon, Royal Navy.[144] Hartigan, graduated as a doctor from UCD [Medical School, Cecilia Street] in 1901, and had a busy medical practice in Croom, Co Limerick.[145] In 1916, he relinquished his role as the medical officer of the Croom Union and

Dispensary District to join the Royal Navy. In doing so he became the fourth Hartigan brother to serve in the war. Hartigan was evidently a popular doctor at the time given the reception he received while home on furlough in March 1918 when he visited Croom races. 'He had a busy time at the races, shaking hands. He certainly appeared to enjoy the old surroundings. Good luck to him was everybody's wish', the *Limerick Leader* reported. Hartigan died of pneumonia in a hospital in Port Said, Egypt on 30 May 1918 at the age of thirty-nine. He had been a member of the Croom Ancient Order of Hibernians (OAH). He was, according to the branch chairman, Brother Malone, 'a consistent nationalist ever ready to subscribe to and support the national cause.[146] His brother, Fr John Hartigan SJ predeceased him. He died of jaundice while chaplain with the 1st Connaught Rangers in Mesopotamia in July 1916.

Grave / memorial Port Said War Memorial Cemetery, Egypt

HARPER, EDGAR HENRY (1880–1916), Lieutenant, Royal Staffordshire Regiment.[147] In 1913, Edgar Harper was appointed as Professor of Mathematics at UCC, having beaten out the other finalist, Éamon de Valera for the post.[148] Though de Valera had a better teaching portfolio and was doing high-end research in Dublin, Harper had an MA, which de Valera did not have. Harper's book, *Aerial Locomotion*, published in 1911, was one of the most popular science books on the phenomenon of powered flight.[149] He also provided the mathematical calculations for George Hartley Bryan's *Stability in Aviation*, a book that sought to provide a theoretical framework to stable flight at a time when so many early pioneers were dying unnecessarily in accidents.[150] Harper, born in 1880, was from a unionist family in Dungannon, Co Tyrone. He attended the Royal School in the town and then Queen's University Belfast followed by TCD. He was working as a lecturer in Bangor University when he was appointed to UCC. In May 1915, he obtained a commission in the 7th Royal Munster Fusiliers and was later posted to the South Staffordshire Regiment. In August 1915, his younger brother, Ernest, was killed serving with the same regiment in Gallipoli.[151] A year later, Edgar died on 20 July 1916 during the Battle of the Somme. He was thirty-six. In 2018, his contribution to mathematics was remembered with the unveiling of a blue plaque at his old family home in 3 Northland Place, Dungannon, Co Tyrone.

Grave / memorial Thiepval Memorial to the Missing, France

Harty James Johnson (J.J.) (1879–1917), Lieutenant, RAMC. Harty was born in Rochestown, Co Cork in 1879.[152] He received his medical education at Queen's College Cork and graduated as a doctor in 1902.[153] After serving in Bombay, India as the resident surgeon of Cork County Hospital, he went into practice in Colne, Lancashire. He was gazetted as a temporary lieutenant in the RAMC. Though selected for service in Mesopotamia, he was too ill and died in Sheffield on 5 March 1917 at the age of thirty-seven.

Grave / memorial Douglas (St Luke) Church of Ireland Graveyard, Cork

Hawkes, John Cornock (1885–1915), Lieutenant, RAMC. Hawkes was born in 1885 into a Church of Ireland family in Castletownbere, Co Cork, where his father managed the Munster and Leinster Bank. Hawkes studied at Cork Grammar School, University College Cork, and Edinburgh. He had taken up a medical practice in Nottingham when he joined the RAMC in December 1914. On 30 July 1915, he was killed by a shell near the Hooge crater in Ypres while attending to the wounded. He was thirty-one.[154] His death provoked much sympathy in his hometown. The Commission for the Relief of Distress, of which his father was a member, passed a motion of sympathy as did the Berehaven Regatta Committee. He was 'ever popular because of his unassuming cheerful disposition, his successful college and professional career, and his readiness at all times to co-operate with his fellow townsmen in matters of sport,' the *Skibbereen Eagle* reported.[155] The newspaper concluded that it had been a 'glorious if sad ending to a brilliant young life'.

Grave / memorial Divisional Cemetery, Ypres, Belgium

Hay, James Lyle (1896–1916), Second Lieutenant, Royal Northumberland Fusiliers. Hay was born in 1896.[156] His parents were originally from Belfast but moved to work on the Clonbrock Demesne in Ballinasloe, Co Galway. He was educated at the grammar school in Galway city and studied engineering at UCG. He was a second-year engineering student at the outbreak of war, and his extracurricular activities also kept him busy. He was a member of the college's rugby and hockey teams and participated in the production on campus of Shakespeare's *Twelfth Night*.[157] He was commissioned as a second lieutenant into the 15th Royal Northumberland Fusiliers eventually serving with the 12th. The first day of the Battle of the

Somme was the worst in British military history, and the most affected regiment was the Northumberland Fusiliers in the 34th Division.[158] Despite their colossal losses, the battle continued for the regiment. Hay was killed on the third day of the Battle of the Somme, 3 July 1916, during an attack on some wood outside the village of Fricourt. His grave inscription reads: 'One crowded hour of glorious life is worth an age without a name'.[159]

Grave / memorial Gordon Dump Cemetery, Ovillers-la-Boisselle, France

HAYES, DR MAURICE (1878–1930), Captain, RAMC.[160] The son of a Co Limerick farmer, Hayes was educated at Mungret College in Limerick city. He graduated from the Catholic University School of Medicine in 1906 and became a consultant radiologist in the Mater Hospital.[161] Hayes was honorary secretary of the Irish Medical War Committee, which sought to encourage Ireland's doctors to enlist in the British Army. In 1917, he was gazetted as a captain in the RAMC.[162] During the Irish Civil War, he was appointed major general and afterwards Director General of the Irish Free State Army Medical Corps by his friend Michael Collins. Eligible doctors were in short supply as the National Army expanded rapidly to meet the anti-Treaty threat, and Hayes set about recruiting ex-RAMC men like himself. By the end of the Civil War, eighty-five medical officers and 100 civilian doctors were attached to the medical corps. Hayes died in 1930 at the age of fifty-two from the after-effects of continuous exposure throughout his career to harmful X-rays.[163] His funeral mass at the Church of St Andrew, Westland Row in Dublin, was attended by the President of the Executive Council, William T. Cosgrave, and the former chief of staff of the IRA during the War of Independence, General Richard Mulcahy. In the *Irish Independent*, an admirer, W.M.K wrote: 'Maurice Hayes was not merely a great scientist; he was a great man ... I have seen him positively embarrassed by a reference to the position of pre-eminence which he had attained in the scientific world. To the end he was always the big-hearted schoolboy we loved so well'.[164]

HEALY, DERMOT J, Second Lieutenant, Royal Munster Fusiliers.[165] Healy was from Sandymount Road in Dublin. He attended Blackrock College and played for the school's rugby team. He graduated from UCD in 1912 and was practicing as a barrister when he joined the Inns of Court Officers' Training Corps. He was commissioned into the Royal Munster Fusiliers in December 1916. He went to the front in early 1917 and was killed while attached to the 74th Trench Mortar Battery during the Battle of Passchendaele on 5 August 1917.

Grave/memorial Panel 44, New Menin Gate, Ypres, Belgium

HEALY, MAURICE FRANCIS (1887–1943), Captain, Royal Dublin Fusiliers. Barrister, soldier, author, wine critic, teetotaller turned bon vivant, and finally broadcaster, BBC Maurice Healy was among the most famous Irishmen who fought in the First World War. He is best remembered for his 1939 book *The Old Munster Circuit*, a literary memoir about his time as a barrister in Ireland that went through several reprints.[166] Healy's family was steeped in public service and the law. His father, also called Maurice, was an All-for-Ireland League MP for Cork city, described by Charles Stewart Parnell as the man who 'knows more about the Irish land question than anyone now living'. Maurice Jr's uncle Tim Healy was the first governor-general of the Free State. Maurice Healy was born in Cork in 1888, and educated at Christian Brothers Cork, Clongowes Wood College and UCD.[167] He graduated in 1907 with an honour's degree in history, political economy, and jurisprudence. He was called to the Irish Bar in 1910 and the English Bar in 1914. He practiced on the Munster Circuit until war broke out; he then joined the 1st Royal Dublin Fusiliers. In 1915, he appeared on Irish recruiting platforms before departing for the Western Front.[168] He was a contemporary of Tom Kettle at Clongowes and tried to search for Kettle's body when he was stationed in France. He later served at the headquarters of the 29th Division in France and then in Germany during the occupation that followed the cessation of hostilities on 11 November 1918.[169] About his own war service, he was self-deprecating though he received the Military Cross in 1919.[170] Healy moved to England to practice as a King's Counsel for the rest of his career but is remembered best as a broadcaster and wine critic. He had been a teetotaller and then took to wine with the 'zeal of the convert', publishing several books including the bestselling *Stay me with Flagons*.[171] He began broadcasting for the BBC in 1937 and his soft Cork accent and geniality won him a huge audience.[172] 'The best talk in the world,' he once declared 'is to be heard in Cork, where two or three are gathered together. All speak at once; but there is both art and method in it'.[173] He used his profile in Britain to argue publicly against the imposition of conscription in Northern Ireland in 1939 because of the treatment of Catholics in the North who have been 'deliberately and by permanent legislation deprived of the constitutional liberties which the population of the rest of the United Kingdom enjoys'. He died in 1942 at the early age of fifty-five. He had been suffering from nephritis (inflammation of the kidneys) for a time. An anonymous admirer in the *Cork Examiner* paid tribute to his generosity: 'There is an old saying to the effect that the man who dies rich dies disgraced. Healy evidently believed in this implicitly ... The narrator went to see him one Christmas Day and found round his luncheon table a dozen friends who were in financial difficulties and most of them he has staying with him until they found jobs'.[174]

HENNESSY, JOHN (1867–1954), Lieutenant Colonel, RAMC.[175] John Hennessy, originally from Blarney, Co Cork, was born in 1867. He graduated in 1890 from Queen's College Cork with a degree in medicine, and then served with the Royal Army Medical Corps until his retirement in 1921. Following service in the Boer War,[176] he was captured during the siege of Kut in modern-day Iraq in April 1916.[177] He had been a champion Irish racewalker in his younger days. On his return to Cork after retirement, he became one of the first directors of the Mallow Race Course Company.

HERON, OSCAR ALOYSIUS (1896–1933), Flight Commander, Royal Air Force. Heron was one of the most famous Irish pilots of the First World War, and later played a significant role in the new State as a pilot instructor. Heron was from Banbrook, Co Armagh. His parents were both primary school teachers.[178] He is listed by UCD as having left the university in 1915 to join the Inns of Court Officers' Training Corps. He initially served with the Connaught Rangers before transferring to the Royal Flying Corps (later the Royal Air Force). He shot down thirteen enemy planes, all recorded in 1918 when he was assigned to No. 70 squadron. His first victory came on 30 June and the last on 28 October, two weeks before the war ended. His Distinguished Flying Cross citation read: 'An officer conspicuous for his skill and daring in aerial combats'. He remained with the RAF until 1922 when he joined the Free State Air Corps as an instructor in Baldonnel Aerodrome.[179] He was tragically killed on 5 August 1933, when his Vicker's Vespa two-seater army co-operation aircraft crashed during a demonstration in the Phoenix Park. He and his co-pilot, Private Robert Tobin, died in front of horrified 25,000 spectators, including Heron's wife. Heron was thirty-eight. Among those who attended his funeral was the Minister for Defence, Frank Aiken, and the Minister for Industry and Commerce, Seán Lemass. He is buried in Glasnevin Cemetery.

HEWITT, ALFRED JAMES (1874–1947), Rear-Admiral, Surgeon. Hewitt was born in Tyrone in 1874 and graduated as a doctor from Queen's College Galway and then Edinburgh University in 1900. In September 1914, he was almost killed when the *HMS Pegasus* was sunk by a German destroyer, the Königsberg, at port in Zanzibar. Hewitt continued to tend to the wounded on the deck of the Pegasus as she sank. In 1917, he was gazetted 'for accelerated promotion in recognition of the conspicuous gallantry and very exceptional professional ability which he displayed as medical officer of HMS Pegasus'.[180] He remained in the Royal Navy after the war and was promoted to Surgeon Rear Admiral in 1931. He died in Devon in 1947.

HILLYARD, HUGH BERTIE LANCELOT, Lieutenant, Royal Irish Regiment. Hillyard was born in Passage West, Co Cork in 1885, the son of a British Army chaplain. He was educated at Cork Grammar School and at Queen's College Cork. In August 1914, he was working in the Canada Bank of Commerce, but returned to England to join up.[181] He ended the First World War as a lieutenant in the Royal Irish Regiment. Instead of being demobilised, he volunteered for the Russian front to fight with the White Army in the Russian Civil War against the Bolsheviks. He was employed at various times as officer in charge of communications to the Polish General Józef Haller and then as a cypher officer at Murmansk in northern Russia. He was wounded in action in 1919 for the third time and was evacuated back to Canada. He returned to work with the bank in 1920.

JOYNT, NORMAN LOCKHART (1889–1944), Lieutenant, RAMC.[182] Norman Joynt was born in Co Cork in 1889. He attended Cork Grammar School before graduating as a doctor in 1912 from UCC. He joined the Royal Army Medical Corps in September 1914. Two years later he won the Military Cross for, 'conspicuous gallantry when the enemy exploded a camouflet (countermine) which choked a mine gallery with foul gas'.[183] He at once organised rescue work, going down himself repeatedly with rescue apparatus. Through his cool bravery he succeeded in personally rescuing two men and ensured the quick recovery of others.[184] After the war, he worked as a doctor in the British Virgin Islands in the Caribbean. In 1930, he was appointed by King George V as an official member of the Executive Council of the Islands. In north London, on 25 November 1944 he was killed when a V2 German bomb struck 63 King Henry's Road. Having survived the First World War, he was one of the last V2 casualties of the Second World War.

JOYNT, RICHARD LANE (1867–1928), Lieutenant Colonel, RAMC. Joynt was from a well-known Limerick family.[185] His father William, a barrister, was Mayor of Limerick and later Lord Mayor of Dublin. Joynt was educated at TCD and then RCSI. Before the war, he had a successful orthopaedic practice in the Meath Hospital and an international reputation for designing replacement limbs for amputees. He put his skills to good use during the First World War as the general inspector for orthopaedic factories in Great Britain and Ireland. He came to the attention of his fellow orthopaedic surgeon, Sir Robert Jones, who had been given the mammoth task of overseeing the treatment of Britain's injured soldiers.[186] Joynt's contemporary, Sir Thomas Myles, said that many maimed victims of war 'had their lives made tolerable, and their capacity for useful work increased a hundredfold by the apparatus designed and, in many cases, actually made by this modest Irish surgeon'. He was promoted to the rank of lieutenant colonel during the war and awarded an OBE in 1920. Joynt was an early pioneer of X-rays and operated the first one in Ireland just two years after their discovery by the German scientist Wilhelm Roentgen in 1896. In his later years, he was one of the external examiners of the Royal College of Surgeons in Ireland. He died, aged sixty-one, from pneumonia.

KAVANAGH, THOMAS OSBORNE JOSEPH, Lieutenant, Royal Irish Fusiliers.[187] Kavanagh was from Monacurragh House, Co Carlow. Kavanagh graduated from UCD in 1913. He was an apprentice solicitor in Dublin when he joined the British Army. He was killed aged twenty-six on 24 August 1918 during the Hundred Days Offensive which ended the war.

Grave / memorial Bertenacre Military Cemetery, France

KEANE, WILLIAM MARY AUGUSTINE (1892–1916), Lieutenant, Royal Irish Fusiliers. Born in 1892, William Keane was the son of Thomas Keane, a well-known draper based in Shop Street, Galway.[188] Keane was a talented student who won a scholarship to UCG to study arts and engineering. He was studying for the Indian Civil Service examination in England when war was declared. He was killed fighting with the 3rd Royal Irish Fusiliers in November 1916.

Grave / memorial Kemmel Chateau Cemetery, Ypres, Belgium

KEATING, THOMAS JOSEPH (1894–1918), Captain, RAF.[189] Keating was from Ballinamult, Co Waterford. He was a student at UCD between 1912 and 1914. He was serving with the Royal Air Force when he was killed in Mesopotamia on 14 June 1918 at the age of twent-four.

Grave / memorial Baghdad (North Gate) War Cemetery, Iraq

KELLY, JOSEPH FRANCIS MARY (1869–1916), Lieutenant Colonel, RAMC. Kelly, from Athlone, Co Westmeath, was born in 1869.[190] The son of a barrister, he attended Clongowes Wood College and then UCD [Medical School, Cecilia Street] where he obtained his medical degree in 1891. The next year he joined the British Army and was mentioned in dispatches during the Chitral Exhibition of 1895 in northern India. He was decorated for his actions during the North-West Frontier campaign of 1897–1898 and during the Boer War where he received the Queen's Medal with five bars (a bar is given each time you win the same medal again) and the King's Medal with two bars.[191] He was promoted to Lieutenant Colonel on 6 August 1914, and became the Commanding Officer of the 11th Field Ambulance. He was mentioned three times in dispatches during the war. In August 1915, he was sent to Suvla Bay during the Gallipoli landings. Like many, he endured the constant thirst, hunger, and disease of that campaign. He was evacuated from the peninsula in December 1915 suffering from septic poisoning. He was sent back to the front in March 1916, but never fully recovered from his illness and died in a nursing home in Salisbury on 22 August 1916 at the age of forty-seven.[192] He left a widow, Cecilia, and a son Bernard who was born in July 1914.

Grave / memorial Salisbury (London Road) Cemetery, Wiltshire

KEOGH, SIR ALFRED (1857–1936), Lieutenant General, RAMC.[193] When Keogh died in 1936 at the age of seventy-nine, he was the subject of an extraordinary tribute by the journalist and author John Alfred (J.A.) Spender. Keogh was, Spender wrote, 'one of the most remarkable men of his time'. If the worth of a man could be measured by the lives he saved, Keogh deserved the greatest praise: 'For cruel and terrible were the deaths and suffering inflicted by the Great War, scores of thousand are living today who, but for his efforts would have been numbered among the dead'. Keogh was born in Dublin in July 1857, the son of Henry Keogh, a Catholic barrister and magistrate from Co Roscommon. Keogh's family had ambitions for him to become a Catholic priest, but he opted for medicine instead.[194] Keogh's precociousness as a medical student was recognised when he graduated as a doctor from Queen's College Galway at the age of twenty-one and joined the RAMC. Keogh set about devising ways to minimise such deaths and to end the cavalier disregard for sanitation within the British Armed Services at the time.[195] Keogh is credited with having the RAMC ready for the massive casualties that occurred in the First World War. He persuaded the Secretary of State for War, Sir Richard Haldane, to set up a medical reserve available for when major hostilities broke out. Haldane later described Keogh's services as 'irreplaceable'. Spender described Keogh's organisation of medical services during the First World War as 'little less than a work of genius'. A contemporary account in the *Lloyd's Weekly News* stated that Keogh had 'saved more lives in this way than any physician of the most confident optimism would have dared to predict'. Keogh had two stints as Director-General of Army Medical Services (DGAMS) from 1905 to 1910 and during the war from 1914 to 1918. Keogh Barracks in Aldershot is named after him. His picture is in the National Portrait Gallery in London.[196]

KETTLE, TOM (1880–1916), Lieutenant, Royal Dublin Fusiliers. Politician, poet, academic, intellectual, journalist, patriot, and British soldier, Kettle in his short life personified all the contradictions of Irish society before independence. He is probably the most high-profile NUI war casualty and one of the best-known Irish fatalities of the First World War. President Michael D. Higgins, in an address to the Houses of Parliament in 2016, spoke of Kettle as an 'Irish patriot, British soldier, and a true European'. Kettle's wife Mary Sheehy, the daughter of nationalist MP David Sheehy and sister of Eugene, described her husband as an 'internationalist nationalist' in the posthumously published book *The Ways of War*.[197] Kettle was born in Artane, Dublin on 8 February 1880, the seventh of twelve children of the nationalist MP Andrew Kettle, a founder of the Land League. Tom attended Clongowes Wood College and University College Dublin. His academic career at UCD was undistinguished, but his gift for oratory saw him elected as auditor of the college's Literary and Historical Society. He was admitted to King's Inns to read law in 1903 and became a barrister in 1906. In that year, he followed his father into politics by becoming an MP for Tyrone East. In 1908, he was appointed Professor of National Economics in UCD. As a consequence of his academic commitments, he did not seek re-election as an MP in the December 1910 election. He was notably more liberal too than his Irish Parliamentary Party colleagues and was a supporter of the women's suffrage movement.

When the war broke out, Kettle was in Belgium on a clandestine mission for the Irish Parliamentary Party leader, John Redmond, to procure arms in the event that the Home Rule settlement was not implemented. Kettle decided to work in Belgium as a journalist chronicling the occupation of the country by the Germans. 'It is impossible not to be with Belgium in this struggle,' he concluded.[198] Kettle was prone to depression and alcoholism. He hoped by enlisting to triumph over the 'dominion of drink'. He was commissioned as a lieutenant but was kept at home to help in the recruitment campaign. When he proved himself to be sufficiently sober, he was given command of B Company of the 9th Royal Dublin Fusiliers. His final letters home were suffused with a premonition that he was going to die. His last letter to his wife read:

> There was never, in all the world, a dearer woman or a more perfect wife and adorable mother. My heart cries for you and Betty whom I may never see again. I think even that it is perhaps better that I should not see you again. God bless and keep you! If the last sacrifice is ordained think that in the end, I wiped out all the old stains. Tell Betty her Daddy was a soldier and died as one. My love, now at last clean, will find a way to you.[199]

He was killed at Ginchy during the Battle of the Somme on 9 September 1916. His death was witnessed by Second Lieutenant Emmet Dalton, then a teenager, who went on to join the IRA and was with Michael Collins when he was killed at Béal na Bláth. Kettle's body was buried where he fell, but was never recovered from the battlefield. His wife Mary spent years writing letters to those who knew Kettle trying to locate his body. After her husband's death, Mary Kettle became a vocal opponent of the British Government in Ireland and encouraged Irish ex-British servicemen not to join in the victory parade in 1919 because of the British government's failure to honour the victory of Sinn Féin in the 1918 British General Election.[200] Tom Kettle also wrote one of the best-known poems of the First World War, 'To Betty, the Gift of God', which is addressed to his daughter Betty. It concludes:

> And oh! They'll give you rhyme
> And reason: some will call the thing sublime,
> And some decry it in a knowing tone.
> So here, while the mad guns curse overhead,

And tired men sigh with mud for couch and floor,
Know that we fools, now with the foolish dead,
Died not for flag, nor King, nor Emperor,
But for a dream, born in a herdsman's shed,
And for the secret Scripture of the poor.

The poem was read at the commemorations at the Thiepval Memorial in 2016 to mark the centenary of the start of the Battle of the Somme. That centenary was also marked in UCD by an exhibition of Kettle's papers held in the university's archives.

Grave / memorial Thiepval Memorial to the Missing, The Somme, France

KINKEAD, RICHARD CROFTON GEORGE MOORE (1883–1914), Captain, RAMC. Kinkead was born in 1883. He was the son of Thomas Kinkead, Professor of Gynaecology at Galway University from 1876 to March 1928.[201] While at UCG, Richard rowed in the winning crews for the Royal Galway Club. He was also a good shot and a fine horseman.[202] In 1908, he graduated from the college in medicine. He was commissioned into the RAMC a year later and was serving in South Africa when he was called back at the outbreak of the war.[203] While with the 10th Hussars, he was killed on the last day of October 1914 during the First Battle of Ypres at Klein Zillebeke. His father received a letter from him saying he was well on the same day he received a telegram from the War Office stating that he had died. Several officers in the 10th Hussars wrote to Kinkead's father praising his son's courage: 'Over and over again he risked his life in the discharge of his duties in the field'.[204]

Grave / memorial Ypres Town Centre Cemetery, Ypres, Belgium

KIRWAN, DR JAMES ST JOHN (1871–1916), Lieutenant, RAMC.[205] Born in 1871, Kirwan was from a well-known medical family in Tuam, Co Galway and graduated as a doctor from Queen's College Galway in 1896. He was working in the Ballinasloe Asylum as the Resident Medical Superintendent (RMS) when he joined the RAMC in late 1915.[206] He spent six months with the RAMC in Ireland before returning to the asylum in May 1916. His death at home in Ballinasloe in August at the age of forty-four from heat stroke was unexpected. 'To say that Ballinasloe was shocked on Tuesday last would be but faintly to express the feeling created by the news that Dr Kirwan has died,' the *Connaught Tribune* reported.[207]

LUCY, THOMAS JOSEPH, Second Lieutenant, Royal Field Artillery (RFA). Lucy was from Howth, Co Dublin. He was educated at UCD between 1912 and 1915 and at the Royal Military Academy in Woolwich. He was killed in action during the German Spring Offensive on 8 April 1918.

Grave / memorial No information available[208]

LYNCH, PATRICK S. (1891–1916), Lieutenant, Leinster Regiment.[209] Lynch was born in 1891. He was from Grosvenor Terrace in Waterford city, and his father Michael was the manager of the city department store, Robertson, Ledlie and Ferguson. Patrick attended Waterpark College in Waterford and then Clonliffe College in Dublin. He secured an Arts Degree at UCD, winning exhibitions in French, Italian and English. After graduation he joined the National Bank in Cork but gave it up to serve in the First World War. He was an enthusiastic supporter of the war effort and appeared on the same recruiting platform as the Victoria Cross winner Sergeant Michael O'Leary.[210] Lynch was awarded two Military Crosses during the Battle of the Somme. His deed won him the admiration of Brigadier General George Pereira of the 16th (Irish) Division who told Lynch: 'Your leading the attack along the parapet was splendid, but you must be more careful next time'.[211] Lynch won a bar to the Military Cross on 27 July 1916 for 'conspicuous gallantry' during a raid on the enemy's trenches. The *London Gazette* recorded: 'He walked along the parapet directing the bombers in the trench until, after three-quarters of an hour, he was badly wounded'.[212] Lynch died on 27 December 1916 when he and his men were in support trenches in the Loos sector of the Western Front. Lynch and Sergeant Michael McCormack from Dublin were killed from aerial darts (flechettes) known as 'deadly metal rain' dropped from low-flying German aircraft over the British trenches.

Grave / memorial Maroc British Cemetery, Grenay, France

MAGUIRE, HUGH, Second Lieutenant, Connaught Rangers (attached to the Royal Inniskilling Fusiliers). Maguire was from Claremorris, Co Mayo, and the brother of the future Chief Justice of Ireland Conor Maguire. Hugh was an engineering student in UCD during the war and was commissioned into the 3rd Connaught Rangers in January 1916 having previously been in the local volunteer corps in Claremorris.[213] He was attached to the 7th Leinsters and was killed at the age of twenty-four, during the assault on Ginchy by the 16th (Irish) Division on 9 September

1916. Maguire's body was never recovered from the battlefield. He had died nobly leading his men into battle, his Commanding Officer wrote to Maguire's parents after his death, telling them that their son had received communion before he went into battle. There were many expressions of sympathy in the local newspapers.[214]

Grave / memorial Thiepval Memorial to the Missing, France

MAHON, RALPH BODKIN (1862–1943), Colonel, RAMC.[215] Mahon was born in Galway in 1862. He was educated at St Ignatius College Galway (the Jes' now known as Coláiste Iognáid) and at Queen's College Galway. He took first place in his medical examinations in 1885. He continued his studies in London, Berlin, Munich, and Berne and spent most of his medical career as a demonstrator in anatomy first in Queen's College Galway and then Queen's College Cork. He held a temporary commission in the RAMC during the First World War as a surgeon specialist in the Southern Military Hospital in Dartford, Kent. After the war he was appointed Professor of the Practice of Medicine in University College Galway and built up the Galway Central Hospital (now University Hospital Galway). He died in 1943 aged eighty-one.

MAHONY, EDMUND J., Lieutenant, Royal Munster Fusiliers. Mahony was from Raglan Road, Dublin. He was killed on 27 September 1918 near Cambrai when a bullet struck him in the thigh.[216] He was thirty-one. Mahony only joined up to fight at the age of thirty. Previously he worked in the family grain company in Dublin. He was shipped to France in August 1918 just a month before his death. The battalion chaplain, Fr Dominic Devas, wrote to his father to say he had received a general absolution three times before he died, and the priest would remember him in his masses. His sister, Elizabeth (Iza) also served in the war as a Voluntary Aid Detachment (VAD). She served in Dublin's Meath Hospital and then overseas in Malta and in France before being discharged in February 1917. She died of pneumonia in 1919 at the age of thirty just six months after her brother. Both are remembered on the family headstone in Glasnevin Cemetery.[217]

Grave / memorial Hermies Hill British Cemetery, Pas de Calais, France

MALLEN, WILLIAM, Second Lieutenant, Royal Dublin Fusiliers. Mallen was from Grangecon outside Baltinglass in Co Wicklow.[218] He was educated at Rockwell College before entering UCD. At eighteen, he was one of the youngest NUI students to die in the First World War. He had just entered UCD on a Wicklow County Council Scholarship when he joined up to fight. Mallen lost his life on the slopes of Frezenberg Ridge during a joint assault by the 16th (Irish) and 36th (Ulster) divisions on 16 August 1917. Conditions were nearly impossible. Mallen was killed during the assault on the appropriately named Vampir Farm, a heavily fortified German position.

Grave / memorial Tyne Cot Memorial to the Missing, Belgium

MORRIN, FRANCIS JOSEPH (1893–1968), Lieutenant, RAMC. Morrin was from Baltinglass, Co Wicklow.[219] He was educated at Clongowes Wood College and graduated as a doctor from UCD in 1915. He joined the RAMC from medical school. He served first on a hospital ship in the Aegean Sea and then in the trenches in France. For the latter he was awarded the Légion d'honneur by the French Government. He entered the forces of the Free State after independence, serving as the National Army's first director of medical services with the rank of major general from 1922 to 1944. He was Professor of Surgery at UCD between 1953 and 1954. He was also a senior surgeon at St Vincent's Hospital until he retired in 1966 ending a fifty-year relationship with the hospital. His friend Patrick Lynch wrote in an obituary in the *Irish Independent*: 'I have no doubt, myself, that the variety of human suffering with which he had to deal as a young surgeon in the First World War must have played a distinct part in his later development in medicine, in his attitude towards false nationalism and war and in his almost stoical approach to life and death'.[220] Lynch added that Morrin saw the Civil War as a 'disaster' that had long-term consequences for Ireland. He never wavered in his support for the pro-Treaty side, possibly as a consequence of his friendship from his days in Clongowes with Kevin O'Higgins, the Minister for Justice in the Free State Government, who was assassinated in 1927.

MATTHEWS, SAMUEL WAUTHORPE, Captain, RAMC.[221] Matthews died on 15 November,1918, four days after the Armistice in German East Africa (now Tanzania), during the protracted East African campaign in which the redoubtable German General Paul von Lettow-Vorbeck held off a combined Allied force for the whole of the war. Matthews was the son of a Church of Ireland vicar from Belgrave Square in Dublin. He was educated at the Wicklow Academy and studied medicine at UCG as a scholarship student. He was the chairman of the college debating society and captain of the cricket and hockey teams. He spent some time at Temple Street Children's Hospital before joining the Royal Army Medical Corps in 1917. His death on 15 November 1918 came as a result of several bouts of malaria and jaundice which left him weakened. He finally succumbed to typhoid fever.

Grave / memorial Dar Es Salaam War Cemetery, Tanzania

McCormack, John Dillon (J.D.) (1891–1973), Lieutenant, RAMC.[222] McCormack, J.D., as he was universally known, was a remarkable doctor who was almost crippled by the First World War.[223] He graduated as a doctor from UCD in 1914 and joined the RAMC. He was badly wounded twice in the war, once at Ypres in 1915, and then finally in December 1916 where a shell left him shell-shocked and immobile. Yet he was not cowed by his wounds.[224] He became a familiar sight in Dublin in the early years after the war, dragging himself on crutches through the streets. He was saved by a London surgeon who designed a rubber-lined steel corset which allowed him to build the strength back into his legs. Eventually, he recovered enough to walk unaided and then made an astonishing foray into golf, winning three Irish Close Championships in 1923, 1924, and 1927. Only work commitments as a medical inspector at the Department of Local Government prevented him in 1924 from representing Great Britain and Ireland in the Walker Cup, the amateur equivalent of the Ryder Cup. After the war, he became a medical inspector in the Department of Local Government and wrote extensively about dealing with communicable diseases. Dr McCormack died on 21 July 1973. His wife Jean died the following day.

McGrath, Roger (1891–1918), Captain, RAMC. McGrath was born in Clonmel in Co Tipperary in 1891. He graduated from UCD as a doctor and joined the RAMC. He died of wounds on 5 May 1918 aged twenty-seven. In July 1918, he was awarded the Military Medal for:

> conspicuous gallantry and devotion to duty when in charge of the bearers of his field ambulance.During the enemy's advance and while exposed to heavy shell and machine-gun fire, he organised his bearers and evacuated many wounded, who otherwise would have been captured. He set a fine example of energy and courage.[225]

Grave / memorial Boulogne Eastern Cemetery, France

McKeever, Louis Lawrence (1891–1917), Captain, RAMC attached to the Royal Scots Fusiliers. Born in 1891, McKeever was from Killiney, Co Dublin, the son of a pharmacist. He attended Blackrock College and then studied medicine at UCD. He died of wounds, aged twenty-six, in Gaza while serving as a doctor with the Royal Scots Fusiliers. McKeever was killed on 8 November 1917 when the Scots were strongly counterattacked by Ottoman forces during the Battle of Gaza. His posthumous Military Cross citation read: 'Hearing that there was no medical officer in the front line, he went forward at once under an intense bombardment and remained in the front line all attending to the wounded under continuous and violent shell-fire'.[226] Eyewitnesses said he was killed while tending to wounded soldiers in the open instead of behind the lines in a dressing station.

Grave / memorial Gaza War Cemetery, Palestinian Territories

McLoughlin, James Patrick (1881–1915), Lieutenant Royal Dublin Fusiliers (attached to the Royal Irish Regiment). Born in 1881, McLoughlin was from Drumcondra in Dublin. He was a noted student at Belvedere College, acting as secretary of the tennis team and captain of the cricket XI. He studied medicine at Cecilia Street (1906) and Edinburgh (1910) and joined the Royal Army Medical Corps in 1912.[227] A year later, he emigrated to Chile because of a health ailment, but within a year he was recalled to the British Army as a medical captain in the Royal Dublin Fusiliers. He was attached to the 2nd Royal Irish Regiment in France when they became enmeshed in the Second Battle of Ypres. McLoughlin was killed in a terrible gas attack which decimated both the Royal Dublin Fusiliers and the Royal Irish Regiment. He died on 25 May 1915 at Mouse Trap Farm.

Grave / memorial Bailleul Communal Cemetery Extension, France

McNamara, Vincent, Lieutenant, Royal Engineers. McNamara was one of eleven Ireland rugby internationals killed in the First World War. A scrum-half, he won all three caps for Ireland in 1914, scoring a try in the match against Scotland. Born in 1891 in Cork, McNamara attended the Presentation Brothers Cork, then Cork CBC before studying engineering at UCC. During these years he struck up a half-back partnership with out-half Harry Jacks, which lasted through school, university, province, and country. Together they became known as 'Macky and Jacky'.[228] Their last international together was in March 1914 against Wales in what became known as the 'Battle of Balmoral', a brutal encounter distinguished by frequent bouts of fighting. Wales won 11–3. At the outbreak of the war, McNamara secured a commission in the Royal Engineers. He volunteered to work in the tunnelling companies involved in the highly dangerous laying of underground mines under enemy lines. He was serving with the 13th Division in Gallipoli when he died from exposure to poison gas released by his own side on 29 November 1915. McNamara went underground to lay a mine under the Turkish lines and was overcome by fumes. 'It was impossible to reach him to time to save his life,' his commander Officer Major H.W. Laws wrote to his father P.J.: 'He was an officer without a sense of fear and keenly interested in the work and, unfortunately, went down to investigate without allowing sufficient time for the gasses resulting from our countermine to disperse'. 'Mackie was genuine to the core and noted among his fellows for his piety,' his half-back partner wrote: 'I cannot possibly forget those memorable days of our friendship, when we shared the ups and downs of a football career in which he always bore the brunt of attack to make my way easy and to make me conspicuous'. McNamara's Ireland jersey is on display in UCC's sports facility, the Mardyke Pavilion.

Grave / memorial Lancashire Landing Memorial, Gallipoli, Turkey

McPolin, James (1891–1955), Captain, RAMC. The Mother and Child Scheme was a watershed moment in Church and State relations in Ireland. The attempt in 1951 by the inter-party government's Minister for Health, Noel Browne, to bring in a scheme which would allow for free ante- and post-natal care for mothers and their children up to the age of sixteen and without a means test was opposed by the Catholic Church and the medical profession. The Church believed it opened the door to contraception and abortion and undermined the role of the family as the first provider of health care. Doctors objected because the absence of a means test would affect their income. Among the most vocal opponents of the bill was Dr James McPolin, the Chief Medical Officer for Co Limerick.[229] A native of Hilltown, Co Down, he attended St Colman's College in Newry, graduated as a doctor from UCD in 1914 and joined the RAMC. He was wounded at the Battle of the Somme. After the war, he joined the staff of the Mater Hospital in Belfast, before becoming CMO for Co Limerick in 1930. Despite being a state employee, McPolin believed in minimal state interference in health care. A devout Catholic, he opposed the Mother and Child Scheme and was threatened with dismissal after he wrote a long article in the *Limerick Leader* in July 1951 denouncing it as a 'downright denial of the authority of the bishops, a denial of the fact they have received their authority from God made Man and that they alone are competent to decide this issue'.[230] Despite public objections, he remained in his post.[231] In 1939, McPolin was charged with the manslaughter of a woman named Margaret Coffey who he had knocked down and killed while driving. McPolin was acquitted of the charge, but later pleaded guilty to dangerous driving.[232] He was killed in November 1955 when he was hit by a car while crossing the road at O'Connell Street, Limerick. Limerick County Council's monthly meeting was adjourned as a mark of respect.

McVeigh, William J. (1883–1917), Lieutenant, Royal Munster Fusiliers. Born in 1883, McVeigh was from Cookstown, Co Tyrone.[233] He attended St Mary's College and then UCD where he graduated in chemistry. He was working as a chemist's assistant in Bangor, Co Down at the outset of war. Unusually for a university graduate, he joined the British Army as a private, in this case the Leinster Regiment.[234] He was afterwards gazetted as a second lieutenant in March 1915 and assigned to the 9th Royal Munster Fusiliers. He was wounded three times on the Western Front. He was evidently a popular officer, according to a little piece of doggerel published by one of his men in the *Mid-Ulster Mail*: 'Before proceeding further, just a word or two/I'll say in praise of this same officer. Lt J. McVeigh/He never bully-rags his men, or orders them about/He's just a perfect gentleman/a sportsman out and out'. In March 1917, he transferred to the 6th Royal Munster Fusiliers attached to the 10th (Irish) Division. McVeigh was part of General Edmund Allenby's force that captured Jerusalem on 9 December 1917 and pushed the Ottomans out of Palestine. He was killed on 28 December while leading his platoon over the walls of a Palestinian village in the face of heavy rifle and machine gun fire.

Grave / memorial Jerusalem War Cemetery, Israel

McWeeney, Edmond Joseph Theophilus (Theo) (1894–1976), Lieutenant, RAMC.[235] McWeeney was born in 1894, the son of the pathologist Professor Edmond J. McWeeney. He was a childhood friend of Proclamation signatory Joseph Mary Plunkett. Edmond Jr's medical studies at UCD were interrupted by the war when he joined the RAMC.[236] After the war, he returned to Dublin receiving his MB in 1922, after which he spent time in the Irish Free State army medical service and the medical service of the Royal Air Force. He served on the medical staff of the Department of Local Government and Public Health and then the Department of Health. McWeeney received his MD in 1932. Afterwards, he worked for the Public Health Department in Ireland with a special focus on tuberculosis.[237] In 1950, McWeeney moved to the World Health Organization (WHO) providing advice on tuberculosis, becoming the first Irish civil servant employed by the United Nations. He retired in 1964 returning to Dublin, where he wrote and lectured, dying in 1976.[238] His papers are in the Royal College of Physicians of Ireland.

MOYNIHAN, MICHAEL JOHN (1891–1918), Lieutenant, King's Liverpool Regiment. Moynihan was born in Tralee, Co Kerry in February 1891.[239] He was one of the first students at UCD when the National University of Ireland came into being in 1908. An outstanding student, he worked in the Inland Revenue in Ireland before moving to Croydon, south London in 1913. He was enraged by the Curragh crisis of March 1914, when Anglo-Irish officers threatened to resign if deployed against Ulster Unionists. Moynihan joined the Civil Service Rifles, a unit of the Territorials (the British Army's reserve force), believing it would help put down any Ulster resistance in the event of Home Rule being implemented in Ireland. He remained with the Civil Service Rifles until 1916 when he joined the London Regiment as a private – a measure of his desperation to join up as somebody as educated as he was could reasonably expect a commission. Few Irishmen who served in the First World War left such a voluminous correspondence. He wrote to his brother John in Kerry, a republican, about the state of Ireland and also to his mother who hated the idea of him joining up. His letters spoke to the ambivalence of an Irishman from a nationalist background serving in the British forces in the First World War.[240] In April 1918, he wrote to his brother at the height of the conscription crisis: 'It is hard to know what the people can do against the colossal forces against them, but I do not expect they will submit quietly'.[241] On the day he died Moynihan's mother Mary wrote to him saying she was 'praying fervently for your safe return'. On 3 June 1918, at Doullens in the Somme region, Moynihan was accidentally shot dead by a sentry on his return from a trench raid. The correspondence between Michael and John were the subject of a book, *The Moynihan Brothers in Peace and War*, by Deirdre McMahon.[242] His brother John, also known as Séan, became a prominent adviser to Éamon de Valera and secretary to the Government after Fianna Fáil's ascent to power in 1932.[243] Another brother, Maurice, became de Valera's personal secretary and chairman of the committee responsible for drafting the Irish constitution. He was later the governor of the Central Bank of Ireland and his name appeared on Irish banknotes.

Grave / memorial Doullens Communal Cemetery Extension No 2, France

MURPHY, WILLIAM LOMBARD (1876–1943), Lieutenant, RAMC.[244] Murphy was the son of William Martin Murphy and the brother-in-law of Arthur Chance who is also listed here.[245] Murphy forged his own career as a doctor having studied at St John's College in Cambridge, the Jesuit College in Feldkirch, Austria, and UCD. He was an ear, nose, and throat surgeon at St Vincent's Hospital, and also had a private practice in Merrion Square. He gave it up to enlist in the RAMC.[246] In August 1916, he was sent to Salonika and appointed liaison officer between the British, French, and Serbian medical services. His wartime service was awarded with honours from both the French (the Légion d'honneur), the Belgian Croix de Guerre, and the Serbian Order of St Sava. In 1919, after his father died suddenly, he assumed his vast business empire including trams, insurance, Clerys department store, and the *Irish Independent*. When William Lombard died in 1943, the *Sunday Independent* reported that he had inherited his father's business empire with 'some diffidence, for perhaps his outstanding characteristic was his modesty. He had not been trained specially for a business career and he was far too realistic not to realise the difficulties of his task'. He had a wide range of outside interests and was at various times the presidents of the Rathmines and Rathgar Musical Society, the Milltown Golf Club, the Irish Lawn Tennis Association, and Vice-President of the Irish Amateur Boxing Association. When he died suddenly at the age of sixty-seven, the list of tributes was so long that they had to be listed in alphabetical order in the *Irish Independent*.[247]

NAYLOR, GEORGE R, Lieutenant, RAMC. Born in Longford in 1873, Naylor was a medical graduate of UCC. He is listed among the UCC war dead in the Roll of Honour but is not recorded on the Commonwealth War Graves Commission (CWGC) database nor the digitised version of the Irish National War Memorial Records.[248]

NELIGAN, JOHN (1889–1917), Lieutenant, RAMC.[249] Neligan was born in Dingle in 1889. His father Maurice was the master of the local workhouse. Neligan qualified as a doctor in 1915 from UCD and joined the RAMC. He died on active service in Egypt on 13 June 1917.

Grave / memorial Port Said War Memorial Cemetery, Egypt

NOLAN, JAMES J., Surgeon Probationer, Royal Navy. Nolan was the last surviving son of the late Dr Joseph Nolan, the coroner for Co Carlow.[250] He attended Clongowes Wood College and entered UCD as a medical student in 1913. He joined the Royal Navy Volunteer Reserve (RNVR) in February 1916. He served as a temporary surgeon probationer on *HMS Avenger* and then *HMS Candytuft*. He drowned aged twenty-one when *HMS Candytuft* was torpedoed and sunk off the coast of Algeria on 18 November 1917.

Grave / memorial Naval Memorial Plymouth, UK

NYHAN, CHARLES (1884–1958), Major, RAMC.[251] Charles Nyhan was the son of a farmer, Daniel Nyhan, and his wife Mary from Kilnagross Co Cork. Daniel Nyhan had been an ardent Parnellite and a member of the All-for-Ireland League, the main nationalist opposition to the Irish Parliamentary Party prior to independence. Charles Nyhan was a medical student at Queen's University Cork and the University of Edinburgh, graduating in 1907. He was commissioned as a second lieutenant into the RAMC in June 1914.[252] Nyhan went ashore in Gallipoli in August 1915 during the Suvla Bay landings and was evacuated due to illness. He suffered from dysentery during the war. He returned to his native Clonakilty, Co Cork in 1919 and was appointed doctor to the British military in the town. He also gave evidence in a number of cases where members of the Royal Irish Constabulary had been injured. He was targeted during the War of Independence by the IRA who considered him a loyalist. During the Civil War Nyhan was held up by anti-Treaty IRA men and his home in Clonakilty was raided.[253] He applied to the Irish Grants Committee (IGC), set up by the British Government to compensate loyal British citizens who suffered for their loyalty, but his application was refused.[254] The assessors concluded that his loss of business was down to the withdrawal of British Crown forces from Ireland. He remained a dispensary doctor in Clonakilty until his retirement in 1950. He was an early supporter of Cumann na nGaedheal and later served as the chairman of the local Fine Gael branch in Clonakilty for many years.[255]

O'Brien, Cornelius (Conor) Francis (1895–1964), Leinster Regiment.[256] Conor O'Brien and his brother William (see below) were the sons of Michael O'Brien, a veteran of the 1867 Fenian Rising who later served six months in Limerick jail in 1882–1883 for supporting Charles Stewart Parnell. Conor O'Brien grew up on Inis Mór, the largest of the Aran Islands, where his father became the local doctor after leaving Co Clare. Conor went to Blackrock College and then won a scholarship to read Greek and Latin at University College Dublin. He joined the Irish Volunteers at its inception in November 1913, but his life was transformed by a chance car drive with his brother William to Woodenbridge where they witnessed Irish Parliamentary Party leader, John Redmond, make his famous speech encouraging Irish men to go and join the British Army to fight in the First World War. William joined up shortly afterwards; Conor enlisted in April 1915 into the Leinster Regiment. He kept a journal of his time in the trenches while serving with the 7th Leinsters in the 16th (Irish) Division. He missed the Battle of the Somme because of an injury and was posted to the Salonika front. There he went down with malaria, ending his war in April 1918, but evidently his experiences of the First World War did not put him off army life, and he re-enlisted as a private in the Connaught Rangers in 1919. He went on to serve another twenty-six years in the British Army.[257]

O'Brien, Thomas Kevin (T.K.) (1894–1916), Captain, Connaught Rangers. O'Brien was from Mitchelstown, Co Cork and is listed as having attended UCC. His father was the local GP. O'Brien offered his services at the start of the war and was killed on 31 May 1916, aged twenty-two.
Grave/memorial Noeux-les-Mines Communal Cemetery, France

O'Brien, William (1887–1975), Captain, RAMC. The older brother of Conor O'Brien was born in Miltown Malbay, Co Clare in 1887 where his father was the director of the Ennistymon workhouse.[258] William was sent to board in Rockwell College and later to study at UCG, where he qualified as a doctor in 1912. William was a dispensary doctor in 1914 when he joined the RAMC and was sent to the Dardenelles. He served on the Royal Navy hospital ship the *Britannic*, the sister ship of the *Titanic*. His parents assumed he was drowned when the *Britannic* hit a mine and sunk on 21 November 1916. However, William was on leave in Egypt. He survived the sinking of another hospital ship, *Dover Castle*, in 1917. After the war, he settled in Yorkshire and married an Irish teacher Mary Catherine Maher.

William was president of his local chapter of the British Legion in Sheffield. He and his wife retired to Strand Road in Sutton, Co Dublin, where William died on 14 February 1975. He is buried in St Fintan's Cemetery in Sutton.

O'Carroll, Frank Brendan (1895–1915), Second Lieutenant, Royal Dublin Fusiliers. O'Carroll was the son of Dr Joseph and Frances O'Carroll from Merrion Square, Dublin. He attended St Mary's College in Rathmines and Shrewsbury School before entering UCD as a law student in 1913.[259] Having been involved in the Officers' Training Corps in Shrewsbury, at the war's outbreak he was offered a commission in the Royal Dublin Fusiliers. O'Carroll was another Irish victim of the disastrous Gallipoli campaign. He died three days after Irish troops landed at Suvla Bay, at Hill 10, an elevated sand dune overlooking the dried-up lake of Suvla Bay. 'It was just at Hill 10 that I saw Dr O'Carroll's son, Frank,' Lieutenant Owen Gill from Nenagh, Co Tipperary, wrote in a letter to his father.[260] 'He was advancing towards the firing line, and I shook hands with him and wished him luck'.[261] O'Carroll was just twenty when he died in August 1915. His father Dr Joseph O'Carroll (see below) endowed a bed at the children's ward in the Richmond Hospital, North Brunswick Street, in his honour and commissioned a bronze memorial which hung in the foyer of the hospital until its closure in 1987.

Grave / memorial Lancashire Landing Memorial, Gallipoli, Turkey

O'Carroll, Joseph Francis (1855–1940), Colonel, RAMC. O'Carroll, the father of Frank, was educated at the Cecilia Street School of Medicine and afterwards in Vienna. In 1890, he was elected a fellow of the Royal College of Physicians of Ireland. In 1912, he was appointed Professor of Medicine at University College Dublin and from 1916 to 1919 he was President of the RCPI. In 1915, his son Frank was killed in Gallipoli. During the First World War, Joseph Francis was also consultant physician to the British forces in Ireland with the rank of colonel. He was awarded the Order of the British Empire (OBE) in the 1919 honours list. He returned his award a year later in protest at the behaviour of British forces in Ireland during the War of Independence. He wrote to the British Home Secretary Edward Shortt in emphatic terms:

> Now that the Parliament of the British Empire, by the enactment of the so-called Restoration of Order Act and its subsequent administration had deprived

> my country of all the guarantees of public and private liberty which are supposed to be the marks of the British Empire, I feel that I can no longer with any self-respect remain a member of the Order.[262]

The profile of Dr Carroll on the RCPI website states that he lost two sons in the war, but the Commonwealth War Graves Commission (CWGC) lists only one son.[263] However, Charles James O'Carroll, who was born in 1888 and is listed in the 1911 census living in Dr O'Carroll's house in Merrion Square, served in the Royal Dublin Fusiliers during the war. He was dismissed from the British Army by general court-martial (reasons not listed) in March 1919 and died in London aged thirty-two in 1922. His father retired from private practice in 1932 and died in 1942 at the age of eighty-seven.

O'Leary, John (1878-1915), Major, Indian Medical Service. O'Leary was born in Crosshaven, Co Cork on 16 May 1878. He graduated as a doctor from Queen's University Cork in 1901 and entered the Indian Medical Service, the British Army's colonial medical service. He participated in the British invasion of Tibet in 1903 and 1904. During the First World War he served with the British Expeditionary Force in the Middle East. He accidentally drowned in the Suez Canal on 9 September 1915. An obituary in the *Skibbereen Eagle* praised 'his genial and gentle disposition which made him immensely popular'.[264] His brother-in-law, Judge Daniel F. Colahan, a leading Irish American political leader, was vehemently against the Irish serving in the First World War. He advocated for American neutrality until the US declared war in April 1917 when he pledged his support for the Allies.[265] Colahan, who was involved in planning the Easter Rising, married Major O'Leary's sister Hanna in 1899 and, after her death in 1911, married another sister Madge.

Grave / memorial Ismailia War Memorial Cemetery, Egypt

O'Reilly, Patrick, Captain, RAMC. O'Reilly was originally from Strabane, Co Tyrone.[266] He was educated at St Columb's College, Derry and at Blackrock College. He graduated as a doctor from the Royal College of Surgeons in Ireland. He was a ship's surgeon on the Blue Funnel Line, a popular passenger liner at the time, when he obtained a temporary commission in the RAMC in 1914. He was severely injured at Hulluch, northern France, in September 1915 and shortly afterwards was awarded the Military Cross for remaining at his post while wounded. In May 1918, he was so badly gassed that he lost his sight completely for several weeks. Recovering again, he was finally killed while treating the wounded on 11 October 1918 just a month before the war ended. He was posthumously awarded a bar to his Military Cross in December 1918.

Grave / memorial Caudry British Cemetery, France

PAUL, JOHN (1896–1917), Gunner, Canadian Field Artillery.[267] Paul was born in Edinburgh in 1896 and spent his early years in Belfast, before his family moved to Galway. At just the age of fifteen, he won a scholarship to UCG. Later he emigrated to Toronto. He joined the Canadian Field Artillery in August 1915 and was shipped overseas in October of that year. He was wounded at the Battle of Vimy Ridge in April 1917, the great Canadian victory of the war. The circumstances of his death were particularly tragic.[268] He was admitted to Granville Special Hospital in Ramsgate, Kent, on 15 August 1917, suffering from flat feet, a medical condition which often resulted in safe duties for those afflicted. He may have felt safe there, but on 22 August 1917, the hospital was hit by German Gotha bombers that had been continually targeting the coastal town. Paul was killed and was buried three days later in the local cemetery.

Grave / memorial Ramsgate Cemetery, UK

PERRY, HENRY MARRIAN JOSEPH (1884–1955), Major General, RAMC. Perry was born in Cork in 1884. He studied medicine at Queen's University Cork and graduated in 1906. He joined the RAMC a year later. He was captured during the Battle of Mons on 23 August 1914, the first encounter between the Germans and British in the First World War.[269] He was later repatriated in a prisoner swap in 1915.[270] After the war, he remained with the RAMC and became its director of pathology in 1934. He rose to the rank of Major General in 1935. He served as director of pathology at the War Office from 1939 to his retirement in 1941. His research on common communicative diseases most notably dysentery, syphilis, and typhus was well regarded internationally.[271]

PETERS, ARTHUR JOHN KERSHAW (A.J.K.) (1882–1916), Sapper, Royal Engineers. Peters was born in Hucknall, Nottinghamshire in 1882. He was an architect in London and South Africa before he joined the Galway Technical School as an instructor in building construction.[272] In 1913, at the age of thirty-one, he enrolled in UCG as a mature student to study engineering. He passed his first-year engineering examination in the summer of 1914, but did not complete his second year. He enlisted in the Royal Engineers in Galway and landed in France in July 1915. He was hit by shellfire on 18 February 1916 and died of his wounds shortly afterwards in Boulogne. He was thirty-four and left a widow, Amy, and a child. Several of his comrades wrote to his parents after his death. Sgt James Hebden was one of them: 'He was a man upon whose steadiness and intelligence I could safely rely upon in all circumstances'.[273]

Grave / memorial Boulogne Eastern Cemetery, France

PUNCH, SIDNEY EDWARD (1885–1916), Surgeon Lieutenant, Royal Navy. Punch was from Woollahara, a large home in Douglas Road, Cork city.[274] His family were well-known entrepreneurs who owned the Punch brand of shoe polish. He was educated at Clongowes Wood College and UCC. He joined the Royal Navy as a surgeon in 1912 after graduating as a doctor. Punch drowned during the Battle of Jutland, one of 350 Irish sailors perished when the British and German fleets met at Jutland off the coast of Denmark on 31 May 1916. Punch was on board *HMS Indefatigable* when it was sunk by a shell strike, which set off her ammunition magazine, killing all but two of her crew.[275] He was thirty years old.

Grave/memorial Plymouth Naval Memorial, UK

REDMOND, WILLIAM ARCHER (1886–1932), Captain, Royal Dublin Fusiliers and later Irish Guards.[276] Redmond was the son of the Irish Parliamentary Party leader, John Redmond, and the nephew of Major Willie Redmond who was killed at the Battle of Messines Ridge in 1917. William Archer was the third generation of his family to be educated at Clongowes Wood College, followed by the RUI. In 1907, he graduated with a BA degree in political economy and the history of philosophy. He was elected MP for Tyrone East in the December 1910 General Election, succeeding Tom Kettle, and later served as a TD until his death in 1932. William Archer answered his father's call for Irishmen to go 'wherever the firing line extends in defence of right, of freedom and of religion'.[277] He immediately came up against General Lawrence Parsons, the officer commanding the newly formed and mostly nationalist 16th (Irish) Division, who refused to offer a commission to those who without prior military experience or to those who had not served in an Officers' Training Corps before the war. Redmond enlisted instead as a private in the Royal Dublin Fusiliers, but was soon commissioned in the Irish Guards, initially reaching the rank of captain. In September 1917, Billie, as he was known, won the Distinguished Service Order (DSO) at Ney Copse outside Ypres. His citation read: 'When, following a heavy barrage, the enemy attacked in strength and a bomb fell in his post, knocking out half the occupants, he immediately led the survivors out and drove the enemy back, which enabled him to establish a new defensive line and to hold it'.[278] On 29 March 1918, Redmond, campaigning in a British uniform, retained the Waterford city seat held by his father who had died earlier that month. He also managed to avoid the wipeout of the Irish Parliamentary Party in the December 1918 General Election as the only party candidate elected in the south of Ireland. He remained one of the few nationalist voices in the British parliament during the War of Independence. In 1923, he entered the Dáil as an independent, and regularly raised the fate of ex-British servicemen living in the Free State. In 1926, he co-founded the short-lived National League Party. In August 1927, the party held the balance of power and came close to toppling the government, but for a notorious incident in which one of its TDs, John Jinks from Sligo, went missing from the vote in mysterious circumstances. In November 1931, Redmond joined the Cumann na nGaedheal party, which he had previously opposed. He died suddenly in April 1932 at just the age of forty-six. Redmond's widow Bridget won the subsequent by-election and was re-elected at every turn until she died in 1952, ending more than a century of public service by the Redmond family in the south-east of Ireland.[279]

REID, BERNARD (1888–1916), Second Lieutenant, Royal Dublin Fusiliers.[280] Reid was from Tower Hill, Dalkey, Co Dublin. He studied literature at UCD where he was President of the University Literary Society. In 1914, he was taken by the plight of Belgium and tried to join the French Army but was prevented by his British citizenship. He was commissioned as a second lieutenant in the Royal Dublin Fusiliers in September 1915 and went to France with the 16th (Irish) Division in December 1915. He was an Irish nationalist, British soldier, and fluent French speaker whose promising life was cut short by the First World War. He also wrote of the 'malice and crushing cruelty' of being under shell fire: 'You never see a German, you never hear them. There are only a series of scored lines in the ground to tell you that there lie the Germans watching, and here lies you, watching too. There is nothing for you to do except to keep a firm grip over everything and wait till the bombardment stops'. Reid was killed by a German shell while serving with the 16th (Irish) Division in the Loos sector of northern France on 28 June 1916, just three days before the start of the Battle of the Somme. He was twenty-eight. The *Freeman's Journal* lamented a 'brilliant student of University College Dublin, a writer of great promise, and a young man of most upright and sincere character'.[281]

Grave / memorial Vermelles British Cemetery, France

RIDGE, PERCY BREWSTER (1883–1916), Captain, RAMC. A Presbyterian from Sidney Ville, Co Cork, Ridge was born in 1883.[282] He graduated as a doctor from Queen's College Cork in 1906. He served in a number of hospitals in London and became an assistant pathologist and curator of the museum of King's College Hospital. He was also a lecturer on morbid anatomy at the hospital medical school. He contracted pneumonia shortly after joining the 4th London General Hospital unit of the RAMC as a captain, and died on 12 March 1916, aged thirty-three.

Grave / memorial Wandsworth (Streatham) Cemetery, London, UK

ROBERTS, BENJAMIN (1875–1916), Lieutenant, RAMC.[283] Roberts was born in Athlone in 1875. He studied medicine at Queen's College Galway and the Royal College of Surgeons in Edinburgh. He joined the RAMC in 1898 and saw service in the Boer War. He stayed in South Africa as a medical officer in the Central South African Railways. He re-enlisted in the RAMC in 1915 and was killed on 30 July 1916 during the Battle of the Somme while serving with the 98th Field Ambulance.

Grave / memorial Corbie Communal Cemetery Extension, France

ROCHE, PATRICK JOSEPH (P.J.) (1886–1917), Lieutenant, Royal Engineers.[284] Born in 1886, Roche, was from Leitrim Street in Cork city. Paddy, as he was universally known, was one of the finest athletes Ireland produced in the years before independence. In 1908, he represented Great Britain and Ireland at the London Olympics reaching the semi-finals of the 100 and 200 metres. He was unlucky not to qualify for the final of the latter race, stumbling just before the line. Commentators spoke of his elegance as an athlete. He never sprinted, a profile by the sports columnist Carbery in the *Cork Weekly Examiner* stated, he simply glided: 'his limbs were so beautifully straight and graceful that he looked a picture'.[285] His success was most remarkable given a serious injury he sustained as a child when he fell off a horse and damaged his left arm. In 1906, Roche enrolled as an engineering student in Queen's College Cork. In 1907, he won his first Irish championships at 100 and 200 yards and won his 100-yard race while representing Ireland in an international meet against Scotland. After the Olympics of 1908 he retained his Irish championship in the 100 yards for a third year in the row. He graduated from UCC in 1912 with an engineering degree.[286] He served as a lieutenant in the 1st King George's Own Sappers and Miners and was awarded the Military Cross (MC) while stationed in Mesopotamia. He was gazetted on 25 August 1917, the same day he died from Typhoid fever.

Grave / memorial Baghdad (North Gate) War Cemetery, Iraq

ROONEY, GERALD CHRISTOPHER (1876–1916), Major, Royal Marine Light Infantry. Rooney from Monkstown, Co Dublin, was another of the 350 Irishmen lost at sea during the Battle of Jutland.[287] He was born in 1876 in Dublin and entered RUI in 1893. He was commissioned into the Royal Marines, aged twenty, in January 1896. He joined the *HMS Queen Mary* in March 1914 as a gunner and commanded the Marines on board the *Queen Mary*, having control of the fore-turret guns. This battlecruiser was one of the biggest and newest ships in the Royal Navy. During the Battle of Jutland, the crew left explosive propellant lying around the turrets. The ship was hit by two torpedoes from the *SMS Derfflinger*. The explosion was followed by a mushroom cloud that rose hundreds of feet into the air. Just eighteen men out of a crew of 1,284 survived. Rooney was thirty-nine years old.

Grave / memorial Plymouth Naval Memorial, UK

RYAN, EUGENE (1873–1951), Lieutenant Colonel, RAMC. Eugene 'Mickey' Ryan was from Templehill, Co Cork. Ryan was the sixth of eight children born into a well-off farming family. He studied at Queen's University Cork and Edinburgh University and graduated as a doctor in 1898.[288] He was commissioned into the RAMC in 1901 and saw service in the Boer War. He first met Douglas Haig, the future Commander-in-Chief of the British Expeditionary Force (BEF), when Ryan was posted to Aldershot where Haig was stationed. Ryan served as Haig's personal physician throughout the First World War, from the opening days of the Battle of

Mons and the retreat from Mons to the Armistice. Ryan's extraordinary access to Haig was only made apparent when his papers were published by his grandson, Professor Eugene Ryan, in 2013. Haig's wife Dorothy wrote to Ryan in the early stages of the war: 'I think one owes a deep debt of gratitude to you for looking after Douglas so well during the Retreat (from Mons) and after. This has enabled him to stand the strain'. After the war, Ryan remained in the RAMC and was posted to India and finally to Shanghai where he retired in 1930. He moved back to Cork with his wife Sadie in 1942. She predeceased him in 1943 and Ryan died in 1951. *Haig's Medical Officer* was published by Pen & Sword in 2013.[289]

SCANNELL, JOSEPH AUGUSTINE, MONSIGNOR (1881–1961), Lieutenant Colonel, Royal Army Chaplains' Department (RAChD). Born in Co Cork, Monsignor Joseph Scannell was another distinguished army chaplain from the county.[290] Educated at North Monastery Secondary School, he spent several years in Louvain studying for the priesthood and was ordained in 1904. He was thirty-three when he joined the Irish Guards as a chaplain in 1914. Scannell was awarded the Military Cross, the French Croix de Guerre, and the Légion d'honneur for his war service. Denis Gwynn described Scannell as an 'ideal army chaplain with an instinct for soldiering and his gifts of sympathy and generous friendship soon made him seem almost indispensable'. His gifts as an army chaplain were recognised again during the Civil War when he became the first chaplain of the National Army at Collins Barrack in Cork. He presided over the funeral prayers for Michael Collins after Collins' death in August 1922. In 1927, he was invited to unveil the war memorial at the South Mall in Cork dedicated to the more than 3,000 men from the county who died in the First World War. In the post-war years, he held various posts within the diocese of Cork. When he died in 1961 at the age of eighty-three, the band of the Southern Command accompanied his hearse through the streets of Cork.[291]

SHINE, JAMES (1861–1931), Colonel, RAMC. The story of the Shine family is one of the great Irish tragedies of the First World War. James Shine was the son of the workhouse manager in Dungarvan. He studied medicine at Queen's College Cork, graduating in 1886 and joined the RAMC where he served in the Boer War and other colonial campaigns. He served in and survived the First World War; his three sons, John, Hugh, and James Jr, did not.[292] Second Lieutenant John Shine was the first of James Shine's sons to be killed and one of the first Irish fatalities of the war. He died on 25 August 1914 from wounds two days after the Battle of Mons. Hugh died during the Second Battle of Ypres in May 1915 and Captain James Shine, the eldest of the family, died on 16 August 1917 during the Battle of Passchendaele while serving with the Royal Dublin Fusiliers. Their father continued in service throughout the war, was mentioned three times in dispatches and was made a Commander of the Bath (CB) in 1918. He was also injured when a machine gun bullet lodged in his leg.[293] His wife Kathleen died in 1924. He remarried Margaret Coleman and had three more sons, the youngest, another Jim, was born in 1932.[294]

SHEEHY, EUGENE (1883–1958), Lieutenant, Royal Dublin Fusiliers. Sheehy was the son of the Irish Parliamentary Party MP, David Sheehy, and a nephew of Fr Eugene Sheehy who ministered to the GPO garrison during the Easter Rising.[295] Eugene Jr attended Belvedere College with James Joyce, Tom Kettle, and his future brothers-in-law Francis Sheehy-Skeffington and Tom Kettle. He began his studies at the age of sixteen and graduated with a BA in 1903. After serving as a teacher and civil servant, he was called to the Irish Bar in 1910. When the Irish Volunteers split in 1914, Sheehy sided with Irish Parliamentary Party leader, John Redmond, and joined the Royal Dublin Fusiliers. Eugene Sheehy's sisters, Mary and Hanna lost their husbands in 1916. Hanna Sheehy-Skeffington's husband Frank, a pacifist, was infamously executed during the Easter Rising. Mary Sheehy's husband Tom Kettle was killed during the Battle of the Somme.[296] Eugene Sheehy joined the 9th Royal Dublin Fusiliers and served in the trenches. Later he was transferred to counter-battery duties – spotting and then targeting enemy artillery. After the war, he resumed his legal career. In June 1922, Sheehy became legal officer to the National Army and was involved in the winding up of the Dáil courts. In 1928, he became a judge on the northern circuit. In 1954, he was appointed chairman of the board of assessors of military pensions under the Military Service Pensions Act, 1934. Sheehy published a memoir, *May it Please the Court*, in 1951.[297] In it he wrote about the sense of unease felt by many Irish ex-British servicemen after the Rising: 'The threat of conscription in 1918, and the ultimate betrayal of Redmond by the British parliament made those of us who survived feel that the thousands of Irishmen who died in Flanders, France and Gallipoli had their sacrifice in vain'.[298]

SLATTERY, FRANCIS (1892–1919), Captain, Royal Engineers. Slattery was born in 1892 and was from Fergus View in Ennis, Co Clare. He joined the Royal Engineers during the war and was injured fighting in Salonika. He returned to England to recuperate from his wounds but appears to have contracted influenza and died, on 9 January 1919, two months after the war ended.

Grave / memorial Ballynacally (Kilchreest) Cemetery, Co Clare

TIERNEY, HERBERT (1888–1916), Lieutenant, Cheshire Regiment. Tierney was born in 1888 to Christopher and Frances Healy. He was from Rathgar in south Dublin. He studied at Belvedere College, Dublin and UCD.[299] A member of the Irish Bar, Tierney had been on the Munster Circuit when he volunteered to fight in the First World War. He was gazetted as a second lieutenant in the Cheshire Regiment in November 1914. He survived Gallipoli, despite being wounded and hospitalised in Egypt. Promoted to captain, he was involved in the Mesopotamia campaign. Like many Irishmen who found themselves in the Middle East during the war, he marvelled at his proximity to sites that are mentioned in the Bible. From Basra he wrote a letter to his family that he was: 'now on the banks of the Euphrates, not far from the Garden of Eden, but oh! how it has changed'.[300] He died in Mesopotamia during the march to relieve Kut in March 1916. Tierney was reported missing in action after he reached Turkish trenches on the road to Kut. It was another year before the War Office confirmed his death. Tierney was twenty-seven, and his body was never found.

Grave / memorial Basra Memorial, Iraq

WALLER, JAMES HARDNESS DE WARENNE (1884–1968). Waller was the eleventh and youngest child of George Arthur Waller. The family home was in Prior Park near Nenagh. Waller was born in Tasmania in 1884 but came to live in Ireland at a young age.[301] He studied engineering at Queen's College Galway and completed his studies in Cork. During the First World War, he joined the Royal Engineers and spent most of the war in the Eastern theatre. In Gallipoli, he distinguished himself while attached to the 10th (Irish) Division following the landings at Suvla Bay in August 1915. Waller went out under fire several times to rescue three men lying in no-man's-land.[302] General Bryan Cooper, commander of the 10th (Irish) Division, wrote of Waller: 'No sapper officer can ever have shown greater courage and self-sacrifice than Lieutenant Waller did on this occasion'. Waller returned to Ireland in the 1920s and became a significant figure in the new Irish state. He built Loreto Avenue in Rialto, the pier at Foynes, and an extension to the Jacob's biscuit factory in Dublin. His greatest legacy though was his Ctesiphon building technique based on a gigantic arch in the ancient Babylon, which he first viewed while serving in modern-day Iraq after the First World War. The Ctesiphon design became common in the Second World War and even more popular afterwards. Between 1943 and 1953, 500 Ctesiphon-type structures were built worldwide. Waller discovered that a building could be constructed using a catenary arch cross-section made of wood. Hessian fabric is lashed to it, and it is covered in mortar. When the mortar hardens into concrete, the wooden supports can be reused in a similar facility. What it lacked in aesthetic appeal, it made up for in ease of construction. More crucially it did away with the need for reinforced steel which was in short supply after the Second World War.[303] Ctesiphon constructions were used for storage facilities, homes, temporary shelters, aircraft hangers, cow byres, and henhouses. The only surviving example in Ireland is the whiskey storage facility in Kilbeggan distillery known locally as the jellybean because of its shape. Waller patented the Ctesiphon design in 1921 and then sold the patent to Seagrams, the whiskey distillers for whom he had built a large warehouse, in return for a handsome annual pension. Waller retired to Devon and died in 1968 at the age of eighty-three. The company, Delap and Waller, which he co-founded is still in existence today.

WALSH, JOSEPH G., Lance Corporal, Royal Engineers. Walsh was from Cahir, Co Tipperary. He studied engineering at UCD before joining the Royal Engineers. He was awarded the Military Medal before succumbing to a German gas attack on the Western Front on 26 April 1918, aged thirty.

Grave / memorial St Sever Cemetery Extension, Rouen, France

WALSH, PATRICK JOSEPH (1889–1915), Lieutenant, Indian Medical Service. Walsh was born on St Patrick's Day 1889, the son of a draper of the same name in Midleton, Co Cork.[304] He studied medicine at UCC, and won a place in the Indian Medical Service. During the First World War he served with the 59th Scinde Rifles, a British Indian army regiment based in the Punjab. He was killed on 20 September 1915, five days before the start of the Battle of Loos.

Grave / memorial La Gorgue Communal Cemetery, France

WALSH, STEPHEN B. (1881–1915), Lieutenant, RAM. Walsh was born in Kilmallock, Co Limerick in 1881 and was a former student of Clongowes Wood College.[305] He graduated from the Royal University of Ireland in 1905, and then served as a doctor in south Wales, in Kent, and in London. He joined the RAMC in October 1914. He died, aged thirty-four, less than a year later in an accident where his horse fell on top of him while he was serving with the 1st Cavalry Field Ambulance in the French seaside town of St Omar. The *Limerick Leader's* columnist in Kilmallock wrote of his death on 8 September 1915:

> He was endowed with talents of a high order and the spirit and intrepidity that were characteristic of every action of his were fully exemplified when shortly after the outbreak of the war he volunteered for the RAMC and, in the discharge of his duty he has breathed his last in the land of France.[306]

Grave / memorial Calais Southern Cemetery, France

WARD, EDWARD COPLEY (1862–1917), Fleet Surgeon, Royal Navy. Ward was born in Ballyhay, Co Cork on 2 November 1862.[307] He qualified as a surgeon from Queen's College Cork in 1883. He entered the Royal Navy soon after qualifying and attained the rank of fleet surgeon on 21 August 1900. He died of natural causes in England on 7 August 1917.

Grave / memorial Woodlands Naval Cemetery, Kent, UK

WARD, PETER FRANCIS (1887–1915), Lieutenant, RAMC. Ward was born in 1887, the son of Thomas Ward from Headford, Co Galway.[308] He studied medicine at UCG and was the resident surgeon at the Richmond Hospital in Dublin. He later worked in the Isle of Wight. He joined the RAMC in September 1914, and served in France at a base hospital. While home on sick leave during the evening of 12 September 1915 he was driving a car with some friends in Co Clare. He fell out of the car, sustained a fracture of the skull, and died shortly afterwards.[309]

Grave / memorial Cloughanover Graveyard, Co Galway

WHITTY, MICHAEL JOSEPH (1863–1917), Lieutenant Colonel, RAMC. Whitty was born in Carrick-on-Suir, Co Tipperary, in 1863.[310] He was one of several generations of his family who attended the Vincentian Castleknock College in Dublin. He studied medicine at Queen's College Cork and joined the RAMC at the age of 23, seeing service in various colonial campaigns. He spent his First World War service in Liverpool at the Old Haymarket Recruiting Depot inspecting recruits for the Western Front. Four of his sons served in the First World War. John Leo was killed while serving with the Royal Flying Corps (RFC) in 1916. Another son, Patrick Joseph, survived the war and joined the Auxiliary Division of Royal Irish Constabulary tasked with putting down the IRA during the War of Independence. Michael Joseph died of a heart attack aged fifty-three in 1917.

Grave / memorial Liverpool (Yew Tree) Roman Catholic Cemetery, UK

YARR, SIR MICHAEL THOMAS (1862–1937), Major General, RAMC. A native of Cloughjordan, Co Tipperary, Yarr attended Blackrock College and afterward studied medicine at Queen's College Cork.[311] He joined the RAMC in 1886. He was the physician to the Crown Prince of Siam, Mahu Vajiravudh (later King Rama VI) while stationed in the country between 1895 and 1900. He served with the 29th Division during its disastrous Gallipoli landings in April 1915. He was eventually evacuated on Christmas Eve in 1915 and spent the rest of the war in Malta as a director of medical services.[312] Yarr was an ophthalmologist who contributed to the literature on the subject. His Manual of Military Ophthalmology was published in 1902 and widely distributed.[313] He retired in 1921 and died in a London nursing home in 1937, aged seventy-four.

Emily Anderson

Iris Cummins

Mary Josephine Farrell

Mary Hayden

Dr Kathleen Lynn

Agnes O'Farrelly

Alice Perry

Hanna Sheehy-Skeffington

FIGURE 3.1 *Portraits of eight NUI women.*

3. 'What has the war got to with a dance?'

NUI women and the First World War

FIONNUALA WALSH

IN 1962, THE WRITER Kate O'Brien fondly recalled her time at University College Dublin in the early twentieth century as a period of peace, 'restlessly and in confusion at peace'. O'Brien studied at the college on St Stephen's Green from 1916 to 1919, a time of immense turmoil for Dublin and Ireland, but her recollections give little indication of the world beyond the university. Her memories of UCD were of a 'rough-and-tumble place' full of 'learning and eccentricity'.[1] The First World War nevertheless intruded into the cloistered world of UCD, and also of University College Galway and University College Cork. In UCD, the war had the gloomy impact of leading to the cancellation of dances and concerts and other enjoyable social activities of the college. The *National Student*, the UCD student magazine, argued that the war was being used as a pretext for 'abolishing things that were never to their taste', observing that neither Trinity College nor the Royal College of Science had been obliged by the war to forbid 'inaugurals of societies, dances, or such thing'. They quite sensibly asked: 'What has the war got to do with a dance?'[2] In December 1915, the students lamented the prospect of another 'very dull year' and joked that funerals provided the only available public functions.[3] The war was equally lamented among women students in Galway 'whose dream in life since coming to college has been to go out "au pair"'.[4] The War List of the National University of Ireland (NUI) reveals the service of NUI men in the armed forces, but the university's women are absent from this record. This chapter explores the response to the war in the three colleges and examines women's contribution to the war effort.

O'Brien was one of the few women students in UCD at the time of the war. She recalled that amongst the 'hundreds of youths, rowdy and unwashed', there were about twenty girls and wondered whether they were now in 'lost eastern mission, in desolate Donegal townland or in South Dublin kitchenette'.[5] Higher education was still a relatively new phenomenon for Irish women at the time of the outbreak of the war in 1914. In 1878, the Intermediate Examination was established, and girls were allowed to sit it on the same terms as boys. By 1921, girls made up 36% of those who sat the exam. When parents could not afford to send all their children to secondary school or college, they typically prioritised boys, assuming girls would marry and make more limited use of their education.[6] In the late nineteenth century however, concern with the growing number of unmarried women who needed to earn their own living led to increased momentum in the campaign for women's access to education.[7] Under the Royal University of Ireland women could obtain degrees through the constituent colleges. By 1895, all facilities in the Queen's Colleges in Galway, Cork, and Belfast were made available to women (nine years ahead of Trinity College Dublin).[8] When NUI was founded in 1908, women were admitted on equal terms as men. By 1914, 345 women had received degrees from NUI across the three NUI colleges.[9]

On the outbreak of war, hundreds of NUI graduates and current students joined the British military. In University College Cork, several staff members signed up for active service; for example, Professor Edgar Harper, the Chair of Mathematical Physics, joined the 10th Battalion of the South Staffordshire regiment in 1915.[10] The governing body of UCC decided early on in the war that the positions of staff who enlisted in the military would be kept open for them.[11] The President of UCC, Sir Bertram Windle, offered the College to the military and naval authorities as a base hospital, although this was not taken up.[12] The College War Record lists over three hundred past and current students who participated in military forces, many in the medical services.[13]

However, although the War Record only includes men, some of the women graduates also played a notable role in the war effort. These include Iris Cummins. The daughter of a UCC professor, Iris entered UCC in 1912 to study engineering. She was just one of seventy-eight female students at the time, of a total of 420 in the college. She was actively involved in college social life, captaining the hockey team, and editing the journal of the Engineering Society. Following her graduation in 1915, she took up munitions work in the Royal Arsenal at Woolwich in London, a factory which employed many Irish women over the course of the war. Although she initially had difficulty securing suitable employment following her return to Ireland, she later worked for the Land Commission and in 1927, she became the first woman admitted to the Institution of Civil Engineers of Ireland.[14] Her uncle Major Lyle Cummins, a UCC medical graduate, was awarded the Cross of the Legion of Honour by the French government in autumn 1914 for his service with the Royal Army Medical Corps. Her brother Harry Jackson Cummins was killed in action at the Dardanelles in August 1915 and her brother Fenton King Cummins was killed in action while serving with the Connaught Rangers in 1918.[15]

Iris Cummins was awarded an honorary war degree in 1918 (a BSc) in absentia.[16] Another UCC woman student, Ellen Casey, had been awarded a war degree (a BSc) in 1917 as she was serving as a scientific assistant in the Munitions Department.[17] They were the only women among the over one hundred students awarded honorary war degrees by NUI between 1917 and 1919.[18] These honorary bachelors' degrees were conferred on students who had completed their first two years of study but had missed final examinations due to the war. To qualify for these degrees, the students were required to have spent at least nine months on approved war service or have been invalided on such service.[19]

Across Ireland, thousands of Irish women became involved in activities to support the war effort, in a parallel service to that of the 210,000 Irish men in the British military.[20] These activities included nursing wounded soldiers either on the home front in Ireland or overseas, supporting Belgian refugees, collecting sphagnum moss for surgical dressings, fundraising for specific regiments, and preparing parcels of food and clothing to send to Irish soldiers at the front or in prisoner of war camps. NUI women were among those engaged in war relief work on the home front; for example, the President of UCC, Sir Bertram Windle, and his wife Edith sponsored comfort-and-present activities for soldiers at the front. Although John A. Murphy noted that the college committee established to supply books for the Royal Munster Fusiliers and the Royal Irish Regiment was not especially successful.[21] The committee did manage to collect £231 to provide books and newspapers for the soldiers.[22] This was apparently a common endeavour across all the universities and colleges, on the request of the Lord Lieutenant, with each college assigned two regiments for which to provide reading material.[23]

UCC also had a War Work Guild and a Sphagnum Department involving women of the university. The Guild was established in November 1915 with the President's wife, Lady Windle, acting as president. It involved the wives of members of staff and it was reported in March 1916 that 'many of the women students have associated themselves' with it.[24] Over the course of the war, the guild raised £483, collected and despatched 3,894 items for soldiers at the front, prepared 2,790 sphagnum moss dressings and regularly supplied twenty-two prisoners with food parcels.[25] The UCC Sphagnum Moss Department was established in 1916 in connection with the Irish War Hospital Supply Depot and was led by Eileen Duke, the Acting Professor of Botany.[26] The Irish War Hospital Supply Depot was one of the largest organisations in wartime Ireland. There were over 6,000 women workers on the registers of its eighty-four sub-depots spread across Ireland.[27] One of its primary activities was the collection and treatment of sphagnum moss to use as surgical dressings to replace cotton wool, which was in short supply during the war. This was led by the Royal College of Science in Dublin, which in November 1915 became the headquarters for sphagnum moss collecting in Ireland. By February 1919, the Irish War Hospital Supply Depot had produced 967,422 surgical dressings for hospitals at home and abroad.[28]

Other UCC women joined the British Red Cross to undertake nursing work. Una Magner, for example, was a Special Service member of the British Red Cross, volunteering as a nurse in a military hospital in England from 1918 to 1919.[29] She graduated from UCC in 1912 and was mentioned in the *University College Cork Official Gazette* in June 1918 among other graduates who had applied for commissions in the armed forces.[30] Indeed the popularity of the Red Cross was such that it featured in a satirical description in the *UCG College Annual* of a modern girl seeking an elderly husband: 'she is essentially modern being a leading figure in the woman's suffrage movement when it was in vogue and at present busying herself with Red Cross work'.[31] More than 13,000 Irish women across the island of Ireland served from 1914 to1919 under the wartime joint committee of the British Red Cross and St John Ambulance Association[32].

Women in Galway also played a significant role in the war effort. Mary Donovan O'Sullivan, for example, actively supported the war effort and chaired the Galway Ladies Recruitment Committee. She was appointed the first Professor of History at University College Galway in 1914.[33] In 1915, she married Lieutenant Jeremiah O'Sullivan, a UCG engineering graduate. He served at the front with the Royal Engineers.[34] Donovan O'Sullivan was sharply critical of the republicans in the university, asserting in early 1916 that: 'There [is] no doubt that a number of young men here [in UCG] would be better employed at the front'. The recruitment efforts of Galway women were critiqued in the 'Ladies Notes' section of the UCG College Annual in 1916:

> If College cannot furnish a creditable roll of honour it can at least boast of illustrious recruiting sergeants. No place is too sacred for that zealot. From the heights of Parnassus his voice may be heard drowning that of Shakespeare, Chaucer and Milton. Under his direction the great figures of history pass by pointing to the well-known poster 'Your King and Country need you'.[36]

Although Galway was described in the wartime magazine in idyllic terms 'as one of the few places on earth where one may study and remain happy… at once in the world and out of it', Galway students were unable to ignore the war and its effects.[37] Within sight of the university there was a national shell factory, built in 1917 and employing ninety women and twenty-five men.[38] Obituaries for students and graduates killed on active service appeared regularly in the College Annual.[39]

The contribution of women to the war effort throughout the First World War led to greater interest in and support for women's role in the public sphere. Women were increasingly accepted in the workforce and there was stronger acceptance that middle-class girls might need to earn a living before marriage. Concern at the high mortality rate of soldiers in British Army also led to fears surrounding 'superfluous women'. For the women graduates of NUI, the war offered a means of making use of their education and occasionally availing of opportunities for career advancement opened up by the war. These included women such as Alice Perry. She graduated from Queen's College Galway in 1906 with a Bachelor of Engineering, the first woman in Ireland or Britain to qualify as an engineer. Perry spent the war in England and Scotland serving as a factory inspector, a role of increased importance in the pressured and dangerous wartime conditions. In 1916, she married an English soldier, but he was killed serving in the army the following year.[40] Both Perry and Donovan O'Sullivan were active in the Galway suffrage campaign before the war as members of the Connaught Women's Franchise League.[41] Other former members of the League included Emily Anderson. Anderson graduated from Queen's College Galway in 1911 and after several years abroad, returned to Galway in 1917 to take up a position as Professor of German.[42] During the war, she served on the committee of the Galway sub-depot of the Irish War

Hospital Supply Depot and assisted with the Galway War Fund.[43] In 1920, she moved to London to work in the British Foreign Office. She was awarded the OBE in 1944 for her War Office service during the Second World War. She was also a renowned music history scholar.[44] University of Galway has recognised the pioneering careers of these two graduates: in 2017, the university named the concert hall and engineering building in honour of Anderson and Perry, respectively.

In Ireland, as in other combatant countries, the war brought some improved opportunities for career advancement for women medical graduates.[45] For example, Dr Margaret Purse was appointed house surgeon in the Royal Victoria Hospital, Belfast; she was the first woman to receive the position in its history.[46] The proportion of women among the Irish medical students rapidly increased, rising from 10.1% in 1913 to 22.5% in 1918, with female students helping to fill the gaps left by the doctors serving with the army.[47] Before 1918, there were just ninety-seven women medical graduates from Ireland.[48] However, between 1914 and 1918, 384 women matriculated in medicine in Ireland, with the number of women graduates significantly increasing throughout the National University of Ireland.[49] In UCC, for example, there were 113 women in the college in the year 1917–1918 out of a total of 566 overall, with many filling wartime vacancies in the medical school.[50] In Galway, in 1916 the College Annual remarked on the fact that 'so many of the girls have forsaken the gentler faculty of Arts and turned to Medicine'.[51]

During the war itself, women doctors were praised for their contribution to the war effort.[52] Dr C.M. Benson described in 1916 the important work performed by women in the medical services and considered the effect this would have in the post-war period:

> War has had the effect already of levelling many prejudices; not least among them is that against the women members of our profession ... But of one thing there can be no manner of doubt – namely that women doctors will play an increasingly important part in the near future in looking after the health of the nation and that they are preparing to do so is evidenced by the figures in the Students Register.[53]

Some women medical graduates found their wartime experience useful afterwards or that the war had generated lasting employment for them. Eileen Lawlor, for example, first found employment after graduation nursing soldiers in a military hospital. Lawlor, nee Bouchier-Hayes, was born into a prosperous Catholic family in 1891 in Fermanagh.[54] She studied medicine at University College Dublin. Following her graduation, she moved to England to work in a military hospital at Aldershot, returning after the end of the war in 1919. She worked as a general practice doctor in Limerick and England. She was also active in the Second World War, taking care of the patients of doctors who had been called up, and tending to the injured during the Blitz. Described as a 'walking encyclopaedia' by her family, she was a popular doctor known for her devotion to her patients.[55]

The war also brought expanded opportunities for another UCD medical graduate; Mary Josephine Farrell, from Co Longford, graduated with a first-class honour's degree in medicine from UCD in 1916 and received further postgraduate qualifications from 1921 to 1924. In 1918, she volunteered at the Central Military Hospital in Shropshire before being appointed House Officer at the Liverpool Stanley Hospital later that year. Farrell returned to Ireland in 1921. She worked as a medical referee for the Longford War Pensions Committee from 1921 to 1926 and later worked as an examiner medical officer for the Dublin office of the British Ministry of Pensions.[56]

Another prominent wartime doctor was Ella Webb, who graduated with an MD from the Royal University of Ireland in 1906. During the war, she served as the lady district superintendent of the Alexandra Division of the St John Ambulance Brigade, and eventually as the head of the Nursing VAD of the St John Ambulance Brigade, and as joint chief commandant of the British Red Cross and St John Ambulance Brigade Irish district. She was also a member of the Irish Women's VAD Selection Board in Dublin and was involved in various other committees.[57] W.F. Smith, the assistant commissioner to the Joint Committee of the British Red Cross and St John Ambulance Brigade, described Webb as having 'rendered services of the highest order' during the war years.[58] On duty during the Easter Rising, she took command of the temporary hospital at Merrion Square to treat the wounded soldiers, civilians, and rebels. In 1918, she gained a position as assistant physician at the Adelaide hospital in Dublin where she pioneered improvements in child welfare and paediatric treatments. She later worked as physician to St Ultan's Infant Hospital.[59] In St Ultan's, she worked with Dr Kathleen Lynn, a Catholic University medical graduate, who took a different path during the First World War.

Kathleen Lynn declined to support the British war effort and instead served as medical officer to the Irish Citizen Army during the Easter Rising.

She was involved in the wartime campaign against the spread of venereal disease and in 1919 with Madeleine Ffrench-Mullen, she founded St Ultan's Hospital to combat infant mortality in Dublin, and in particular the high number of cases of syphilis among infants.[60] Lynn was a member of the committee of the National University Women Graduates Association UCD branch during the war years, which may have prompted the resignation of two members in 1917, attributed to the 'inclusion on the committee of a member said to be implicated in the recent rebellion'.[61]

It is worth noting that the war rarely intruded into the minutes of the UCD branch of the National University Women Graduates Association. Brief mentions were confined to a vote of sympathy in October 1914 for Dr Isabella Mulvany, whose nephew was killed in action, and a decision to assist the Labour Exchange with the compiling of a war register in April 1915 (Nancy Wyse-Power dissented from this decision).[62] It is difficult to track the response of UCD women students and graduates to the war and to uncover the extent of war relief work undertaken by them. Although the women students of UCD reportedly participated whenever possible in college affairs, their voices were typically absent from the student magazine, the *National Student*.[63] Indeed the *National Student* was criticised in one letter in December 1915 for persistently failing to publish articles 'from your numerous lady contributors'.[64] Unlike the Galway and Cork magazines, there was no Ladies Notes page nor regular reports of their activities.

The *National Student* in any case was unlikely to devote much attention to the war effort in its pages. From the outset, it took an Irish nationalist standpoint. The editors felt in autumn 1914 that that the war had confirmed the necessity of a separate 'Irish university fundamentally different from Trinity College' with the war demonstrating the different ideals espoused by each: 'the one is essentially Protestant and unionist, the other is as distinctly Catholic and national'. They noted the very different atmosphere in UCD compared to Trinity, arguing that in UCD the men who joined the British forces were 'exceptional' and not the norm. They pledged that 'we students of University College will pursue our ordinary work with untroubled consciences though the din of war be heard all over Europe, knowing that Ireland has done all that could be demanded of her'.[65] There was little mention of the service of UCD students and graduates, and the realities of war beyond UCD were alluded to only in satirical terms with the gossip section, for example, parodying recruitment posters in April

1915, observing: 'the supply of subjects for the dissecting room is in danger of extinction. Join the Army today (advert)'.[66] However, the magazine did not necessarily represent the views of all the UCD students. In April 1915, the editor had to defend the magazine against accusations of 'pro-German' sentiment and tone. Around the same time, the UCD Academic Council asked the magazine to remove the words 'Conducted by the students of University College Dublin' from the magazine's title page in an effort to distance the college authorities from the political position of the magazine.[67]

Several UCD women staff found themselves caught up in debates regarding the correct response to the war. Many women in Ireland in autumn 1914 experienced the outbreak of war as a transformative event and were conscious that they were living in momentous times. Women privately grappled with their conflicted emotions about participation in the British war effort, while the suffrage movement and the women's nationalist movement were openly divided on the issue. These women included RUI graduates Mary Hayden, Hanna Sheehy-Skeffington, and Agnes O'Farrelly.

Mary Hayden had been appointed to the first professorship in Irish history in University College Dublin in 1911. She had graduated with a BA and MA in 1885 and 1887 from the Royal University of Ireland following her studies at Alexandra College. Together with Hanna Sheehy-Skeffington, Hayden was an important campaigner for women's education and employment on the same terms as men, serving as President of the National University Women Graduates Association Dublin branch throughout the war.[68] She was a founding member of the Irish Women's Suffrage and Local Government Association in 1911 and was also active in the Irish Women's Franchise League. A moderate nationalist, she supported the British war effort on the outbreak of war in autumn 1914 and felt that suffragists should 'take their share' in the 'enormous amount of social work' generated by the war.[69] She argued that active propaganda for suffrage should be suspended in wartime but that suffragists could continue their work indirectly and would promote the 'cause of suffrage and hasten its coming' through their loyal service alongside men in war relief organisations'. Hayden viewed the war as offering an opportunity for women to demonstrate their capacity to undertake traditionally male occupations and to show 'they were able to do work as well as men'. Although her UCD professorship occupied much of her time, Hayden was involved in war-related activities such as organising a recreation room for soldiers' wives.[70]

Hayden's stance on the suffrage cause and the war effort, however, met with some criticism, including from a fellow Royal University graduate, and founding member of the Irish Association of Women Graduates, Hanna Sheehy-Skeffington (graduated RUI in 1899 and 1902). Sheehy-Skeffinton felt strongly that the war necessitated a strengthening rather than a weakening of the suffrage movement.[71] She decried the calls to 'roll up the map of suffrage', asking her colleagues 'are we women first of all?' She accepted that joining the Red Cross or replacing men as agricultural labourers could be viewed as 'noble tasks' but argued that they all 'end for suffragists in a cul-de-sac. When the war is over, we shall be gently but firmly put back in our place once more – on our pedestals'. In response to a lecture by Hayden, Sheehy-Skeffington condemned the promotion of the knitting ideal and urged the necessity of 'keeping suffrage to the front if women are not to be put back in their places after the war was over'.[72]

Sheehy-Skeffington, a more radical suffragist and nationalist, strongly opposed Irish involvement in the war. She and her husband Francis, both members of the Irish Women's Franchise League, were editors of the *Irish Citizen* in 1914 and were responsible for its notorious front-page response to the outbreak of war: 'Votes for women now! Damn your war!'.[73] The IWFL felt that the hostile treatment of suffragists in peacetime meant that they owed no service to 'war-mongers'.[74] The society instead saw the war as increasing the need for the immediate enfranchisement of women and thus for heightened suffrage propaganda.[75] They criticised the participation of suffragists in war relief work as 'war fever', 'social chatter' and most damningly as a 'criminally stupid disregard of a rich fund of intellectual energy'.[76]

Another Royal University graduate and UCD staff member also found herself in a divided movement following the outbreak of war. Agnes O'Farrelly (BA from the RUI in 1899) was appointed lecturer in modern Irish in UCD in 1909.[77] An influential member of the Gaelic League, O'Farrelly presided over the first meeting of Cumann na mBan in April 1914, supporting the establishment of a women's auxiliary organisation for the Irish National Volunteers. The founding of Cumann na mBan, also known as the Irish Women's Council, was greeted with approval by the *National Student* magazine, which described the organisation as helping to 'quicken the current of the nation's life after the manner of the Irish Volunteers' and which predicted that the body would have a 'great role to play, and one beyond the natural scope of any organisation of men to fill'.[78] Alongside

O'Farrelly, there were several UCD students and graduates among its early membership including Mary M. Colum, BA, and Louise Gavan Duffy, BA, who served as honorary secretaries of the Central Branch in Dublin.[79]

John Redmond's support for the British war effort in 1914 however divided the Volunteer movement. Supporting Redmond, the majority of the Irish National Volunteers, numbering 170,000, left to form the National Volunteers, and in many cases served overseas with the British Army. A further 11,000 remained in the original organisation, now known as the Irish Volunteers. Under the influence of the Irish Republican Brotherhood, the Irish Volunteers became an advanced nationalist body which was committed to taking action against the British authorities if attempts were made to disarm them or in case of the introduction of conscription. The Volunteer split created a dilemma for Cumann na mBan, obliging them to decide to which of the two groups to lend their allegiance.[80]

The immediate response highlighted uncertainty and ambiguity over just who had the right to speak for Cumann na mBan. A statement in their name appeared on 15 August 1914 declaring that their activities and aims are 'solely national'.[81] On 6 October, a meeting was held of the Central Branch where, according to the *Irish Volunteer*, the manifesto of the organisation was 'heartily endorsed by the overwhelmingly majority of the members'. The manifesto clearly outlined Cumann na mBan's opposition to Irish involvement in the war and their support for the Irish Volunteers:

> We feel bound to make the pronouncement that to urge or encourage Irish Volunteers to enlist in the British Army cannot under any circumstances be regarded as consistent with the work we have set ourselves to do ...We call on Irishmen to remain in their own country and join the army of the Irish Volunteers.[82]

At the meeting, eighty-eight members voted in favour of the manifesto and twenty-eight against it.[83] O'Farrelly initially refused to accept the decision of the Central Branch, claiming as late as 21 November that the organisation was taking a neutral stance: 'The women of Cumann na mBan though sharply divided in their political outlook are I think great enough and patriotic enough to refuse to accentuate the present division'.[84] She had been absent from the 6 October meeting which was described by Bridget Dudley Edwards as a 'caucus' with a 'mischievous manifesto' that was 'sprung without notice' by the self-constituted committee of Cumann na mBan. [85] The formal split took place at the December convention. [86] Those opposed to the war kept the name Cumann na mBan, but the vast majority of its branch membership resigned from the organisation, with many branches disappearing completely. [87] Many of the former Cumann na mBan branches formed themselves into auxiliary organisations to support the National Volunteers serving in the British Army and to promote the Home Rule cause. There was no one umbrella organisation, however, with the moderate nationalist women's movement splintering among different groups.

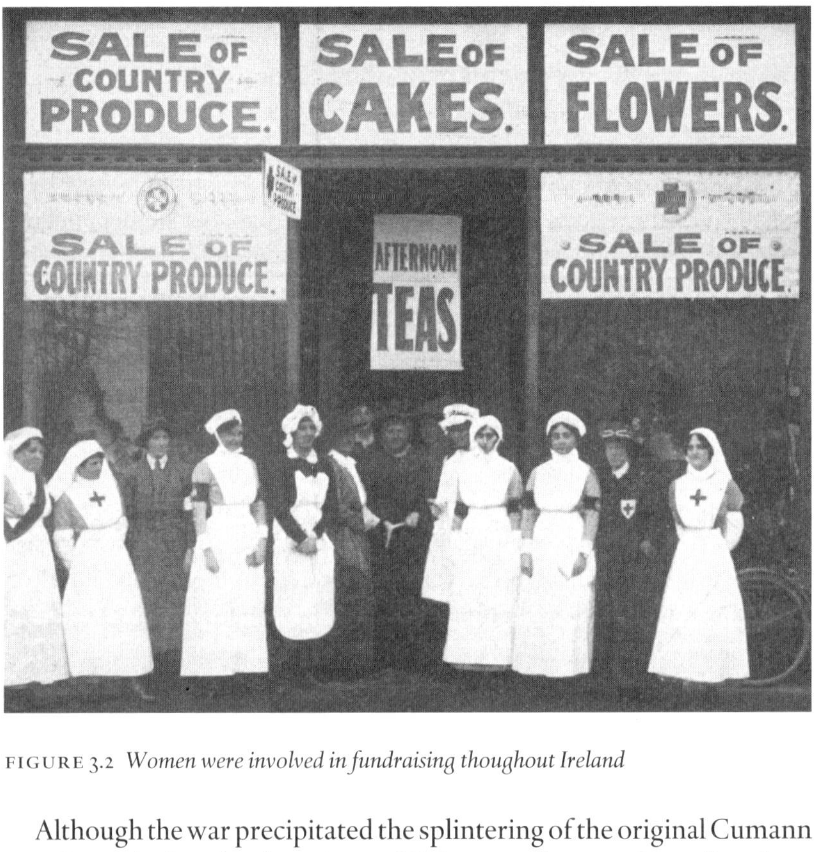

FIGURE 3.2 *Women were involved in fundraising thoughout Ireland*

Although the war precipitated the splintering of the original Cumann na mBan, it is clear that from its establishment a few months earlier, there had been strong differences of opinion within the organisation about their relationship to the Irish National Volunteers and concerning the role of women in the nationalist movement. O'Farrelly was associated with moderate nationalism that was too conservative for some. Áine O'Rahilly recalled her disgust at O'Farrelly's suggestion at their first meeting that they make puttees for the Volunteers.[88] In her vague recollections to the Bureau of Military History decades later, Louise Gavan Duffy believed the split had been caused by the conservatism of O'Farrelly, though she could not quite recall the circumstances: 'I think Agnes O'Farrelly was made President, and then she did something that offended us and we wrote to the papers about it ... We did not think her ideas advanced enough.'[89]

The anti-conscription movement in 1918 however united many of these women again in a common cause. The largest mobilisation of civil society outside of Ulster, it was an 'unprecedented and untypical display of national unity' which in many respects resembled the mass mobilisation of Ulster men and women against Home Rule in 1912.[90] The campaign united republicans and nationalists in a common cause, with opposition to conscription gaining support among those otherwise sympathetic to the war effort. The participation of women was essential to its success. 9 June 1918 became Lá na mBan (Women's Day) and women all over the country participated in demonstrations against conscription. An estimated 8,000 women gathered at City Hall in Dublin that day and signed a pledge to refuse to take conscripted men's jobs.[91] O'Farrelly played an instrumental role in the planning of Lá na mBan, alongside other moderate nationalists such as Alice Stopford Green and Helen Curran, aiming to demonstrate the strength of the opposition to conscription.[92] Invited to participate, Cumann na mBan ultimately took ownership of the event, believing that with their 'widespread organisation we were in a position to arrange a nationwide demonstration'.[93] Diverse factors motivated the participation of women in the campaign, ranging from the personal desire to prevent the conscription of their loved ones, pacifist objection to military service, nationalist belief in Ireland's right to self-determination in such matters, and republican objection to Ireland's participation in the war and to Britain's imposition of such legislation on Ireland. Hayden explained in a letter to the *Irish Citizen* in May 1918, that while she supported the British war effort, she objected to conscription on the grounds that 'Ireland has always preserved her entity as a nation, looking back to a national past and forward to a national future. Her claim for self-determination is stronger than for example Australia or New Zealand'.[94]

The war expanded the number of women interested in higher education. Between 1915 and 1919, 373 women received degrees and diplomas from

NUI, more than the total number of NUI women graduates between 1908 and 1914. By 1925, 30% of all Irish university students were female, compared to 11% of German students, 17% in Italy and 20% in France. [95] This is especially notable given the costs involved in university education and the restricted financial situation of many middle-class and upper-class families during the war years. Many of these new women students were in the medical faculty, where the war had appeared to expand the opportunities for women doctors. However, there were concerns that the rapid wartime influx of women into medicine would lead to problems in what was described as an 'overcrowded profession' where the 'competition for work was likely to be severe'. [96] In 1922, the *Dublin Medical Press* queried the ability of female doctors to secure employment in post-war Ireland and suggested Irish female doctors consider moving to India. Laura Kelly's research demonstrates that employment opportunities for female doctors declined after the war. She attributes this primarily to the saturation of the profession during the war years.[97] The number of women medical students declined significantly again in the immediate aftermath of the war. [98]

In 1914, women represented a minority among the graduates, students, and staff of the National University of Ireland. These were often exceptional woman who had fought for the right and for the requisite support to attend university. When war broke out in August 1914, many recognised the magnitude of the crisis facing Ireland. They debated and grappled with the question of how best to respond and what women's role in wartime Ireland ought to be. The war affected each individual and each college differently and while some students and staff attempted to ignore 'the din of war heard all over Europe' and remain aloof, it could not be avoided entirely. While the UCD magazine focused its lamentations on the cancellations of social events, the college's students and graduates were among those killed. The university may have been 'restlessly and in confusion at peace' as described by Kate O'Brien decades later but the outside world did nonetheless intrude. Obituaries for the casualties jostled for space with the more typical student magazines fixtures, such as maudlin poetry, satirical gossip columns and political grandstanding in the University College Galway annual magazine. Alongside their male colleagues, fellow students or staff, the women of NUI mobilised for the war effort in diverse ways; some using their engineering qualifications in the munitions industry, others engaging in medical work at home or overseas, and still more supporting the soldiers through comforts funds or provision of hospital supplies. These women were not recorded in the War Lists and although two women received war degrees, their war service has been forgotten. Uncovering this war service yields insight into the experiences of these pioneering women graduates and provides a greater understanding of life in the National University of Ireland during this pivotal period of Irish history.

Arthur J. Beveridge

Arthur Chance

Joseph Garry

P.J. Hanafin

Alfred Keogh

FIGURE 4.1 *Portraits of five NUI doctors*

4. NUI Doctors in the First World War[1]

PATRICK CASEY, KEVIN CULLEN & JOE DUIGNAN

IN 1914, IRELAND WAS and had been for a number of centuries an integral part of the British Empire. As a result, Irish universities and medical schools were part of a single educational system that provided graduates across a range of disciplines to work both at home and throughout the Empire's far-flung colonies.

Thom's Directory for Ireland in 1912 recorded 1,500 registered medical practitioners in the whole of Ireland. Irish medical colleges had, for the latter half of the nineteenth century, conferred between 150 and 200 medical degrees annually; this represented 20% of doctors qualifying annually in Great Britain and Ireland. During this period, the National University of Ireland (NUI) colleges in Dublin (UCD), Cork (UCC), and Galway (UCG) produced around eighty medical graduates annually with the remainder graduating from the Royal College of Surgeons in Ireland (RCSI), Queen's University of Belfast (QUB), and Trinity College (TCD). Medical education across Britain and Ireland was fairly similar in that the first two and a half years were university based and consisted of lectures and practicals; few would forget dissecting frogs and dogfish in pre-med. The next year and a half the human body was dissected giving the student a comprehensive knowledge of anatomy. Physiology and biochemistry were also major subjects. At the end of this the students sat the medical exam. From then on, they went to the hospitals and had most of their teaching there. They followed consultants on rounds and in Outpatients, presented case histories, and went to the operating theatre where they assisted at operations. They rotated from one consultant to another and apart from medicine and surgery they rotated through obstetrics and gynaecology, paediatrics, and psychiatry. At each stage there were written, clinical, and oral exams. When they qualified most doctors went into clinical practice right away. There were few hospital jobs for those who wished to specialise, and these were much coveted.

As Ireland only represented 10% of the population of Britain and Ireland at that time this represented a significant annual oversupply of doctors that were required to practice in Ireland's health service. This meant that many of the graduating doctors had to emigrate from an impoverished Ireland to find employment in Britain, or in its armed forces, on the high seas or in its colonies.

At the turn of the twentieth century, 300 Irish doctors held permanent commissions in the Royal Army Medical Corps (RAMC), the medical unit within the British Army; this represented approximately 30% of the total number of doctors employed by the Army at that time. A similar situation existed in the Royal Navy (RN) with numerous Irish doctors filling the post of Fleet Surgeon on the battleships of the Grand Fleet. The Indian Medical Service (IMS) also provided a useful career path for Irish doctors with 116 Irish graduates holding commissions in the IMS prior to August 1914.

By 1914, the Irish medical profession had a long and respected tradition of serving in both the British Army and Royal Navy. The British Armed Forces offered a valuable and rewarding career path to many of the doctors qualifying from Irish medical schools; this was at a time when Ireland's public health services or private practice could not provide the same level of opportunities and advancement. Alternatively, some Irish doctors emigrated to the United States of America; some plied the high seas as ship's surgeons on cruise ships crossing the Atlantic, such as the *Lusitania*, or on passenger ships sailing to and from British colonies.

The skill and administrative ability of Irish doctors was highly respected within the armed forces and many Irish doctors occupied important positions in both the Army and Royal Navy. Sir Alfred Keogh, a Galway University graduate from 1878, is perhaps the best-known example as he was Director-General of the Army Medical Service (AMS) from 1904 until retirement in 1910. He was so respected by the British political establishment that he was called out of retirement when hostilities broke out with Germany in August 1914 to lead the logistical element of the RAMC and returned as Director-General once more.

It is no surprise then, that the call for medical personnel to enlist in the British Armed Forces at the outbreak of hostilities between Britain and Germany was met with a very positive response by Irish doctors working in Ireland, the UK and in the remote regions of the Empire. Those enlisting were offered temporary commissions in the armed forces, mostly for the duration of the war but also for shorter periods as in the case of some officer ranks in the RN such as Surgeon Probationers who served for a six-month period. Many young doctors and students joined up immediately.

Cork had a long association with the Royal Navy through the British naval base at Haulbowline since the time of the Napoleonic wars and this can be seen in the fifty UCC graduates who served with the RN during the war. Officer Training Corps (OTC) had been established at TCD, QUB and RCSI since 1910. These OTCs provided a basic level of military training to students at these colleges and importantly membership of the OTC's assisted with the application for a commission in the British Armed Forces on graduation. A downside of membership was that on the outbreak of war OTC members were required to report immediately for duty with the result being a large number of students left their studies and served with the armed forces. The absence of OTCs in NUI colleges may explain the low number of NUI students who enlisted (10) compared with the overall number of Irish students who served (323). However, the nationalist leaning of the student bodies at NUI colleges in 1914 must also have been a factor in the low representation of NUI students in the enlisting numbers.[2]

Geography of the First World War

Britain declared war on Germany on 4 August 1914, following an 'unsatisfactory reply' to the British ultimatum that Belgium must be kept neutral. Immediately following the declaration of war, the British Expeditionary Force (BEF) of 90,000 soldiers, including Irish doctors belonging to the RAMC, set off for the continent with many believing that they would be back home for Christmas.

The British Army provided a worthwhile career opportunity to the many doctors graduating annually in Ireland with nearly a third of the RAMC officers with permanent military commissions in 1914 being made up of graduates from Irish Medical schools. Many of these doctors were ordered to accompany the BEF to France in the summer and autumn of 1914 and past graduates of the NUI colleges were well represented in this advance military force as detailed below.

TABLE 1 *Graduates from NUI Colleges who served with the BEF in August–November 1914*

Col. David Ahern	Col. Patrick Hanafin	Lt. Michael O'Flynn
Maj. James Butler	Maj. Richard Hodges	Lt. Col. John O'Keefe
Lt. Col. Robert Cahill	Hon. Maj. Richard Kenefick	Lt. Col. Edward O'Neill
Ho. Lt. Col. Phillip Carney	Lt. Col. Thomas McDermot	Lt. Col. Henry Perry
Lt. Col. Patrick Dwyer	Lt. Col. Edmond McDonnell	Lt. Col. Thomas Potter
Lt. Col. William Egan	Lt. Col. Jeremiah Magner	Lt. Col. John Rowe
Lt. Col. Frederick Garland	Capt. William Maloney	Patrick Simpson
Lt. Col. George Ware	Capt. Richard Kinkead	

Britain, France, Russia, and eventually Italy joined together as the Entente Powers to thwart the aggressive ambitions of the Central Powers which consisted of Germany, the Austro-Hungarian Empire, Bulgaria and later the Ottoman Empire. The Entente Powers were later joined by a secondary group of countries including Japan, Belgium, Serbia, Greece, Montenegro, Romania and eventually the United States.

The First World War was fought wherever the main belligerents came into contact with each other, on land, sea, or air, or where their strategic interests were considered to be at risk. While the main theatres of war, and the bloodiest campaigns of the four years, were the Eastern and Western Fronts on continental Europe, major conflicts were also fought in the Balkans, Gallipoli, Egypt, Palestine, Mesopotamia, Africa, and on the oceans (Plates 6 and 7).

Ireland, being an integral part of the United Kingdom in 1914, played an important role throughout the war, providing volunteer recruits for the British Army and Navy; port facilities for the war at sea; and a safe haven for the care and treatment of wounded allied soldiers and sailors. It is estimated that 250,000 Irishmen fought with the British Armed Forces during the four years of the conflict.

The Western Front 1914–18

British and French forces combined in an effort to counter Germany's advance through Belgium and across the German-French border. While the French Army had been engaging with the enemy since 14 August along its borders to the south of Belgium, the BEF first encountered the advancing German forces on 22 August near Mons in Belgium. Initially the German forces had the upper hand, forcing the French and British to retreat to the River Marne in France where they stopped the German Army's advance towards Paris. The Allied victory at the battle of the River Marne, between 5–12 September 1914, when their counterattack forced the German Army to withdraw eastwards towards the Aisne River and dig in there, established the beginnings of a static front that was to last for the next four years. In the final months of 1914 both the Allies and the German army endeavoured to outflank the other in what was to become known as 'The Race to the Sea'. This was a crucial victory for the Allies preventing the German forces access to the ports along the English Channel.

Eventually, a system of opposing trenches became established, running from the French-Swiss border in the south to the North Sea, a distance of nearly 700kms. The military technology available to both sides in the early years of the war was incapable of breaching the heavily manned and readily reinforced trench system. Between 1914 and the early months of 1918, the Western Front witnessed some of the bloodiest campaigns of the entire war as both sides endeavoured to break through each other's defences. Throughout those four years both the Allies and the Germans tried to break the deadlock with artillery bombardments followed by infantry assaults. Successful advances were measured in tens of metres while the accompanying casualties were counted in tens of thousands dead or wounded. Frequently advances gained in the early hours of an attack were lost the same day as the enemy regrouped and counter attacked. These battles fought along the Western Front became household names and account for hundreds of thousands of dead and injured. Names such as Ypres, The Somme, Arras, Messines, and Passchendaele would soon become bywords in Irish families for lost husbands and sons who had died in the killing zone that was the Western Front from late 1914 until 1918. Irish doctors and medical students were also among these casualties, many dying as they tried to help their wounded comrades under shell and rifle fire.

An early NUI casualty of the First Battle of Ypres was Captain Richard Kinkead from Galway, the only son of Professor Thomas and Emily Kinkead. He had accompanied the BEF to Ostend and advanced to the front in October 1914. He was killed by a high explosive shell while attending to the wounded on the 31 October 1914. He is buried in the Ypres Town Cemetery.

Gallipoli 1915

The primary focus of this campaign was an attack on the Gallipoli Peninsula in an effort to take control of the Dardanelles Straits that separated Asia from Europe. The Dardanelle Straits were then part of the Ottoman Empire and defended by Turkish troops. In addition to defeating Turkey, the proponents of the ill-fated military adventure sought to take pressure off Russia and also open the sea route to southern Russian ports in the Black Sea.

The failure of a British naval attack in March 1915 to destroy the Turkish forts defending the Dardanelle Straits, and to breach the minefields laid across the Narrows, meant that a ground assault was required to break the Turkish control of the Dardanelles. A series of landings were planned for April 1915 by New Zealand and Australia, the ANZAC forces, at beaches on the northwest of the Gallipoli Peninsula. At the same time, British, French and Indian Forces landed at Helles on the extreme southern tip of the peninsula. The objective of the 25 April offensive was for the ANZAC and British forces, which included Irish Regiments, to join up, head inland and take control of the Kalid Bahr Plateau that overlooked the Narrows and the naval minefields. Both British and ANZAC forces met stiff and determined resistance from the defending Turkish forces who were well dug into the mountainous terrain that overlooked the landing beaches. Despite bombardment of the Turkish positions and fierce fighting lasting three days, the ANZAC and British forces remained pinned down by the Turkish forces close to the landing beaches. The stand-off lasted for the next eight months and developed into trench warfare similar to that taking place in Europe on the Western Front.

Fleet Surgeon George Waters from Tramore, Co Waterford, was an NUI casualty of the initial attack on Gallipoli. Fleet Surgeon Waters was serving on the RN battleship HMS *Goliath* when it was attacked by an Ottoman destroyer on the night of 13 May 1915. HMS *Goliath* was struck by three torpedoes in quick succession and sank within minutes with only 180 of the men aboard surviving out of a crew of 750 men. Waters was fifty-two years old and is remembered on the Chatham Naval Memorial.

To break the stalemate that had developed after the April landings, a further Allied offensive was planned for early August 1915. This involved British, French, and Indian forces advancing from their Helles positions, with the ANZAC forces breaking out and joining the Helles forces for a new landing at Suvla Bay to the north of the ANZAC positions. As with the earlier attempts to take the Gallipoli Peninsula, the August offensive ended in failure with huge losses on both sides. While some ground was won by the Allies, the Turks remained in control of the high points from where they could bombard the British, French, Indian and ANZAC trenches, and beach positions.

As autumn set in, the intense heat of the summer months lessened but was replaced by rain, snow, and the fierce cold of winter, leading to widespread flooding of the trenches, frostbite, and hypothermia for the men in the trenches. Finally, the Allies recognised the futility of the situation and evacuated their Anzac Cove and Suvla Bay forces in late December 1915 with the Helles troops finally leaving Gallipoli in early January 1916.

The War at Sea

For over a hundred years the Royal Navy had been the premier maritime force across the oceans of the world. The boast that Britain ruled the waves was very true and none of the other empire nations could remotely match Britain's maritime firepower or her naval resources. However, the launch by the Royal Navy of the revolutionary dreadnought class of warship in 1906 began a naval arms race between Britain and Germany. From that time Germany began to build a modern navy; by 1914, she had established a significant naval power capability which, while still inferior to the Royal Navy, would pose a threat to Allied shipping throughout the war. In particular, Germany had greatly expanded its submarine fleet and ultimately it was this new hidden, but as yet unproven, naval force that was to play such an important role in the disruption of Allied shipping and eventually lead to America entering the war on the side of the Allies. Germany was the first country to operate submarines successfully on a large scale in wartime, with over 300 submarines commissioned by the end of the First World War.

Despite some significant losses in the early part of the war and in the Battle of Jutland in May–June 1915, Britain's Grand Fleet retained its naval supremacy. An NUI graduate, Fleet Surgeon Sidney Punch, son of Phillip and Mary Punch, Woollahra, Cork went down with HMS *Indefatigable* during the Battle of Jutland, the largest naval battle of the war. HMS Indefatigable, a battlecruiser of the RN, was hit several times by the German battlecruiser *Von der Tann* and sank within minutes with only three surviving from a crew of 1,019. Sidney Punch is commemorated on the Naval Monument in Plymouth.

Through its blockade of the German ports, the Royal Navy effectively kept the German High Seas Fleet from contributing to the German war effort for the duration of the conflict. The Imperial German Navy was therefore prepared to use its submarine fleet to attack merchant vessels belonging to the Allies in a declared war zone around Britain and Ireland. Vessels belonging to neutral nations such as America were allowed initially to travel unmolested within the maritime war zone.

Submarine warfare against civilian traffic escalated significantly with the attack on the British cruise liner the *Lusitania* on 7 May 1915 off the south coast of Ireland, with the loss of 1,198 lives. Among the lost was NUI graduate Assistant Surgeon Joseph Garry, a medical officer with the Merchant Navy. Joseph Garry was the son of Patrick and Mary Garry of Shanahea More, Co Clare and he is commemorated on the Tower Hill Memorial in London.

The situation deteriorated further in early 1917 when Germany declared unrestricted warfare against all shipping in a larger declared war zone around Britain and Ireland, stretching many hundreds of miles westward into the Atlantic. This use of unrestricted warfare allowed the German submarine fleet to cause considerable losses to merchant shipping passing from America to Britain and France throughout 1917. It is estimated that there were at least 1,800 shipwrecks in the waters around Ireland dating to the years of the First World War.

A joint British and American destroyer fleet was based in Cobh in the latter years of the war. This combined naval operation was particularly successful in protecting shipping convoys as they carried men and materials from the United States to Britain and France.

The Evacuation Pathway

Medical doctors belonging to the RAMC, while attached to individual regiments, were also to function within a BEF medical strategy that had as its core objective the efficient evacuation of the sick and wounded from the battle zone. This plan, known as the Evacuation Pathway, had been pioneered by Sir Alfred Keogh, after the Boer war in the early years of the twentieth century. While conceived in peacetime, the planned evacuation route was confidently expected to function effectively within the range of military tactics experienced up to 1914. However, recent advances in military weapons, particularly artillery and machine guns, together with more effective defence systems, quickly exposed the Evacuation Pathway to much more challenging conditions than previously conceived or experienced.

Between the First Battle of Ypres in 1914 and the spring offensive in 1918 the Western Front was static with little deviation of the front lines more than thirty kilometres. In spite of this the Allies suffered about 2.25 million casualties, although there are no fully accurate figures. Of these it is thought that 750,000 died and the remainder were either captured or wounded. These enormous casualties necessitated the creation of highly organised structures for the assessment, triage, and evacuation of the sick and wounded.

Plate 7 shows how the evacuation of the sick and wounded from the battlefront would take place. The wounded were to pass through a series of medical posts or stations where their wounds could be evaluated and treated if possible or if not then collected into areas for transport away from the fighting. Ambulances would ferry the wounded away from the front to forward medical centres for initial treatment. Those seriously injured would then be transferred by train to a network of fully equipped and staffed base hospitals removed a safe distance from the war zone. Those requiring further treatment or convalescence could then be transferred by hospital ship to Britain or Ireland.

Field Ambulance Units

The military unit with responsibility for the care of casualties in the battle zones was the Field Ambulance within the RAMC. The Field Ambulance was a mobile front-line medical unit; it was not a vehicle. A Field Ambulance was composed of ten officers and 224 men, and each was ascribed a recognition number, such as the No 56 Field Ambulance RAMC. The field ambulance had a senior medical officer in command since they would have to make very serious triage decisions on who to transport when many were wounded or injured and too few ambulances were available.

Notable NUI men who served in the Field Ambulance were David Ahern, educated in Queen's College Cork and then Edinburgh before he joined the RAMC in 1903, becoming a Lieutenant on 31 January. He was promoted to Major in October 1914, having gone to France a month earlier with the BEF. At first, he was a medical officer with the 2nd Brigade of the Royal Field Artillery. He then became Commanding Officer (CO) of the 49th

Field Ambulance from 1915–19. For this work he was awarded the Distinguished Service Order (DSO) on 4 June 1917 and a Bar on the 1 February 1919.

Edward Kavanagh graduated from UCD in 1906 and became a Lieutenant in the RAMC that year; he served in France as a Captain from 17 October 1914, first with the 4th Cavalry Field Ambulance as a medical officer. He was awarded a Military Cross (MC) on 23 June 1915 for his outstanding bravery there. In 1916, he became the CO of the 63rd Field Ambulance, a position he held until 1919. He received the DSO on 1 January 1918 for this work.

Thomas Eves from Donnybrook in Dublin was the CO of the 36th Field Ambulance from 1916 to 1919; he received the DSO on the same day as Edward Kavanagh. Thomas Fielding from Kildare was the CO of the 7th Field Ambulance from 26 November 1914 to 26 September 1915; he also received the DSO for his role. George Allison from Monaghan and Walter Adam from Dublin were the COs in charge of the 150th and 166th Field Ambulance units, respectively.

FIGURE 4.2 *17th Field Ambulance Unit.* *(Courtesy of the Wellcome Library)*

Evacuation Pathway Treatment Posts

The Field Ambulance was responsible for establishing and operating the station points along the casualty evacuation route from the Regimental

Aid Posts (RAP) to the Advanced Dressing Station (ADS), to the Main Dressing Station (MDS). It also provided a Walking Wounded Collecting Station, as well as various rest areas and local sick rooms.

The closest medical station to the fighting was the RAP where the Regimental Medical Officer (RMO) together with his group of stretcher-bearers worked alongside and were in direct contact with the men at the front. In the early stages of the war there were sixteen stretcher-bearers for each RAP; this was later increased to thirty-two. Due to its proximity to the fighting, the RAP was a hazardous place, as shelling did not differentiate between soldiers and medical personnel. Doctors in the trenches set up RAPs just behind the front line in a dugout or in the communication trenches; during an attack they went forward to the trenches to treat those too injured to move; they applied tourniquets when there was serious haemorrhage but rarely performed any surgery apart from an amputation when a soldier was bleeding massively from a severely damaged limb. This was done under local anaesthesia. They treated minor wounds, cleaning them with antiseptics, applied splints to those with fractures, injecting the soldiers with anti-tetanus vaccination. If the wounds were more serious, the RMOs were responsible for getting them to the next stage of treatment, usually to an ADS. They carried out inspections every day and ran a clinic for those with pains and aches, coughs, sore throats, and headaches among other things. Fevers and cough were taken seriously since that might indicate tuberculosis that might spread in the unit. Venereal disease was very common and since the soldier was out of action for a number of weeks the doctors needed to identify those with infections and start treatment early. As there were no antibiotics, the treatments were somewhat crude and not that effective. RMOs were also responsible for hygiene in their regiment and inspected the latrines and made sure that they minimised the risk of spreading infection.

In addition to staffing the RAP, the RMO ventured beyond the front line into no-man's-land located between the opposing trenches to seek out the wounded where they fell and provided treatment in the open if the casualty could not be easily brought back to the RAP. Numerous Irish doctors were awarded the MC in recognition of their bravery in treating and bringing back wounded while under enemy fire. In 1916, the Army outlawed doctors from going into no-man's-land since they were losing too many to enemy fire.

Above is an ad hoc wounded station where a number of wounded soldiers are waiting to be collected and taken to a Casualty Clearing Station. Some distance behind the RAP was located the ADS where the wounded could be treated or organised for movement away from the front. The walking wounded were directed to collection points where field ambulances would take them further from the front. Stretcher cases brought to the ADS from the RAP were given some basic treatment while they awaited their removal by field ambulance or by stretcher for more intensive treatment in a less dangerous location at the MDS.

FIGURE 4.3 *Wounded collection station.* *(Courtesy of the Wellcome Library)*

Geoffrey Fleming joined the RAMC as a Lieutenant when he qualified in 1914; he first entered a theatre of war in November 1914 when he was sent to Egypt as a doctor to the Indian troops. By the next year he was involved in France with the 26th Field Ambulance. He was killed in action on 16 June 1915 near Givenchy when a shell burst through the roof of an ADS where he was attending the injured.

MDSs were located sufficiently back from the fighting so that they were out of the range of artillery. Ideally the MDS was to be located close to a railway line or where motor ambulances could gain ready access. Here the stretcher cases were evaluated and treated. Those considered to require surgery were collected for onward transport to field hospitals established many miles to the rear of the fighting. Those who could be cared for at the MDS were treated as best as possible and returned to their regiment as soon as they were considered fit again.

The railhead hospital Casualty Clearing Station (CCS) was the place where all casualties collected from MDSs were managed until the moment came for their transport to permanent hospitals in France or home if convalescence or further treatment was required. CCSs were located where there was ready access from the front for motor convoys and ready communication by rail or canal for the onward transport of the wounded

FIGURE 4.4 *Cases awaiting transport to a Casualty Clearing Station lie on the ground outside a dressing station at Blangy, France, April 1917.* (Courtesy of the Wellcome Library)

and injured. That is why the CCSs as a whole were distributed irregularly to the distance from the MDSs they served. Also required was a large area for the necessary tents. Ideally a CCS should be outside the range of any artillery shelling but unfortunately this was not always the case along the Western Front. Originally it was expected that all the major surgery would be carried out in the base or stationary hospitals along the coast, but the severity and number of major injuries required that life-saving surgery would be performed in the CCSs much nearer the front line. As a result, they were moved up to within twelve to sixteen kilometres from the front; sometimes they were as close as six kilometres from the front line. Some CCS were in permanent buildings in towns and villages, some in huts far away from all other buildings; others in huts and tent-marquees, others in tent-marquees alone. The completely tented CCSs were usually found in new parts of the line.

FIGURE 4.5 *Scene outside a Casualty Clearing Station as casualties wait to be loaded onto the Princess Christian Hospital train.* (Courtesy of the Imperial War Museum Collection)

As they settled down, they acquired huts for operating theatres and administrative purposes, and if, later on, the lines moved forward, the sites they occupied were likely to prove suitable for stationary hospitals, with all the tents replaced by huts. During a battle, a CCS might expect to get from 300–500 cases in twenty-four hours with another 200–300 patients sent on to base hospitals. CCSs were usually twinned and when one could no longer take in casualties the other would take over.

A surgeon on the Western Front was expected to perform all types of operations, usually on an emergency basis. During the battle, the surgeons at the CCSs worked in theatre all day and night, performing everything from abdominal procedures, bone settings, amputations to arterial repairs, debridement and even some basic brain surgery. Operating so close to the place of wounding was a medical breakthrough and radically improved survival rates.

Base Hospitals

These were the general and stationary hospitals located further back from the front than the CCSs. They were generally about fifty kilometres from the front lines and in Flanders and northern France they were on the coast.

They needed to be close to a railway line for the casualties to have easy access and also near a port for evacuation of those needing long-term care. Every stationary hospital could accommodate at least 500 patients and every general hospital at least 1,000 in times of pressure. The clinical work was divided into medical and surgical divisions, each in charge of a specialist assisted by ward medical officers.

Medical Practice during the War

This depended on where the doctor was based. Those in the Regimental Aid posts were extremely busy during actual battles but it was rather boring otherwise. Needless to say, it was not for the faint hearted. They did get to know their patients well and indeed played the role of advisor much of the time. The big advances in medical care at the front were the use of anti-tetanus vaccination for all the soldiers as well as vaccinations against typhoid. The anti-typhoid vaccine was developed by an Irish graduate Almroth Wright. In the Boer War 7,500 soldiers died in action while 8,250 died from typhoid. Professor Wright developed a vaccine for typhoid and most soldiers who were recruited for the First World War were inoculated. As a result, there were very few cases on the Allies side. On the German side there were 60,000 cases in the first six months of the war until typhoid vaccination became compulsory.

In the early part of the war, fractures of the femur were splinted with a Lee-Enfield rifle that was strapped at the abdomen, the thigh, and below the knee. The aim was to stabilise the fracture, but it simply was not up to the task. When the injured soldier was moved this did not prevent the bony parts from moving and the jagged ends of the shattered bones was agonisingly painful, and frequently increased blood loss by shearing the nearby blood vessels. In contrast, the early application of the simple but effective Thomas splint greatly reduced the mortality rate from badly fractured legs from 80% to 15% in less than two years. The Thomas splint consisted of a padded ring to fit around the top of the thigh with two long lateral bars which met at the heel. An adhesive bandage, which was fixed to the skin with glue, was attached to the leg from mid-thigh level to just above the ankle.

The armaments used in the war had no precedent in history. A direct hit from a high calibre shell could essentially vaporise a body leaving no distinguishing features. The fate of the injured was appalling in spite of huge advances in anaesthesia, surgery, and orthopaedics. Of course, combat violence caused a massive rise in psychological damage much of which was not recognised for some time. Many soldiers were court-martialled, and some were even shot because of this lack of understanding.

Gas gangrene was a very serious infection associated with the richly manured soil of Northern France and Belgium. The clostridial organism responsible thrived in the anaerobic conditions found in this environment. Toxins produced by the organism caused severe pain, swelling and breakdown of muscle and was rapidly fatal. It was recognised that the only effective treatment was wide excision of the affected area with later skin grafting.

When the war started the accepted wisdom was to make the patients with abdominal wounds comfortable and allow them to die. By 1916, a few intrepid surgeons operated on soldiers with abdominal wounds, and they survived. By the end of the war such surgery was routine, although problems did exist. The same was true of chest surgery.

Harvey Cushing, a surgeon from Harvard arrived in France in 1915 and started to operate on patients with brain injuries; to everyone's astonishment they all survived. He initially operated on these patients under local anaesthesia. He removed a wide area of the skull, removed all the dirt and foreign bodies that were amenable to surgery using a magnet to drag out metal bits, cleaned the area with antiseptics and then sewed up the dura (the bag around the brain) carefully. These areas of surgery were a problem because there were no antibiotics available and indeed were only freely available for D-Day in the Second World War. Nevertheless, abdominal surgery, chest surgery, and brain surgery had a survival rate of 70% by the end of the war. This was a result of attention to detail, good control of any bleeding, and the use of antiseptics.

In abdominal surgery the young soldiers were very concerned about a bag, usually a colostomy if there was a large bowel injury. Many became quite depressed later as a result. Intravenous fluid and blood transfusions were another feature of the war which led to the whole area of resuscitation. The principles were all derived from the war. At the start of the war a friend of the injured soldier had blood transfused from a height to the injured one on the ground; when the donor became faint and the injured one became pink the transfusion was discontinued. Sometimes the blood clotted, and the procedure was discontinued. Later in the war the importance of blood groups was recognised, and transfusions were then more successful.

Facial injuries were an area of surgery which blossomed as a result of the war. Harold Gillies, a New Zealand ENT surgeon, pioneered this work along with a dentist Charles Valadier. They preserved the lower teeth in mandibular fractures to allow them to fit a splint. Gillies used full thickness skin grafts to reconstruct the face and produced a fairly presentable result. He started this in the 83rd General hospital in Boulogne, also known as the Dublin hospital since the surgical staff were rotated from Dublin every six months. He later, with the help of Sir Alfred Keogh, set up a 600-bed reconstructive facial unit in Sidcup, Surrey. His major contribution was his holistic care of patients. Apart from the many surgical techniques he developed, he emphasised nutrition and psychological support of his patients and held a multidisciplinary meeting every week for all those involved in a patient's care.

Much of what was learnt in the First World War took time to percolate through the medical community but by the 1930s the standards of care had improved throughout the world.

After the war

When the war was over the doctors dispersed. Many were already in practice in England and returned there. Others had met their North American colleagues and emigrated to the United States, Canada, and Australia. Many liked the Army life and made a career of it. Others stayed in the Royal Navy while quite a few became doctors in the Royal Air Force which only started on 1 April 1918. David Ahern from UCC stayed on in the RAMC and eventually became the Commanding Officer of the Royal Vitoria Hospital in Netley. Henry Alcock, another UCC graduate, also stayed on and travelled extensively as an army doctor including Russia, Mesopotamia, and India in his postings. He also served in the second world war. Arthur Beveridge had a brother James who died on the western front in 1917 while in action at Cambrai. Arthur survived and stayed in the RAMC. He died in Venice in 1959. Recognition of the enormous contribution of Sir Alfred Keogh to the development of the RAMC during the First World War continued after the war with the naming of Keogh Barracks at Mychett in Surrey in his memory and which now houses the RAMC museum. Also, a hall of residence at Imperial College London is named in his honour. He retired and lived in London in good health until he died in 1936.

By the end of the First World War, 3,336 Irish doctors and medical students had served with the British Armed Forces on land and on the High Seas; of these 261 died during the conflict in the various theatres of war. The graduates from NUI colleges are represented in these casualties as; killed in action (8), died of wounds (3), drowned (4), and died on service (16). NUI graduates and students served in all the theatres with NUI casualties recorded from many of the principal events of the war including at the First Battle of Ypres in October 1914, the sinking of the *Lusitania* off the Cork coast in May 1915, in Gallipoli in May 1915, in the major naval engagement at the Battle of Jutland in May 1916 and finally during the German Spring offensive in April 1918.

Royal College of Surgeons in Ireland

ROLL OF HONOUR
1914–1918

REPRODUCTION

Numerous staff and students from RCSI made the trip over to Europe to use their medical skills and training in saving those who were fighting on the front line in First World War. During and after the war, the College continuously compiled the names of these doctors through despatches, newspaper reports, contact with families, and created the RCSI Roll of Honour 1914–1918. The list was produced to remember and celebrate the compassion, medical skill, and unselfish nature of those staff and students, some of whom were not to return home.

CONSILIO MANUQUE

Roll of Honour,

Royal College of Surgeons in Ireland.

GEORGE F. HEALY & Co. Ltd.
Printers, Account Book Makers
Lithographers & Stationers
23, Lower Ormond Quay, DUBLIN.
TELEPHONE No. 1147
No.

Roll of Honour.

ROYAL COLLEGE OF SURGEONS IN IRELAND.

OBITUARY.

Lieut. G. G. C. Adams, L.R.C.P. & S.I.

Surgeon C. E. Addison, L.R.C.P.I.

Temp. Lt.-Col. Sir Charles B. Ball, Bart., F.R.C.S.I.

Lieut.-Col. A. E. J. Barker, F.R.C.S.I.

Capt. J. O. S. Beveridge, R.A.M.C.

Lieut. R. J. Bassett, R.A.M.C.

Private Alfred Henry Boyd, D Company, 7th Batt., Royal Dublin Fusiliers.

Lt.-Col. John Battersby, F.R.C.S.I.

Captain Paget O'Brien Butler, L.R.C.P. & S.I., R.A.M.C.

Guy Beatty, R.C.P. & S.I.

Capt. W. Crymble, L.R.C.P. & S.I., R.A.M.C.

Lt.-Col. Charles D'Alton, L.R.C.P. & S.I., R.A.M.C.

Private F. F. B. Darley, Student.

Capt. Ernest Cotton Deane, L.R.C.P. & S.I., R.A.M.C.

Major J. H. Dauber, F.R.C.S.I., R.A.M.C.

Capt. P. H. Delamere, L.R.C.P. & S.I.

Capt. F. L. Enright, L.R.C.P. & S.I.

Temp. 2nd Lieut. George Evans, Leinster Regt.

Capt. T. J. Fehily, L.R.C.P. & S.I., R.A.M.C., attached Royal Fusiliers.

Surgeon Probationer David H. Ferris, R.N.V.R.

Capt. J. H. C. Gatchell, L.R.C.P. & S.I.

ROYAL COLLEGE OF SURGEONS IN IRELAND.

OBITUARY.

Capt. Benjamin Gibson, L.R.C.P. & S.I.

Capt. T. J. Golding, L.R.C.P. & S.I.

Lieut. Charles C. Iles, D.P.H., R.C.P. & S.I.

Lieut. George G. W. Leary, 10th Gloucesters.

Major Guy F. J. Luther, L.R.C.P. & S.I.

Capt. Michael Joseph Lochrin, L.R.C.P. & S.I.

Lieut. W. T. Mills, L.R.C.P. & S.I.

Lieut.-Col. Henry Moore, *M.C., D.S.O.,* L.R.C.P. & S.I.

Capt. William G. McConnell, L.R.C.P. & S.I.

Lieut. W. T. McCurry, R.A.M.C.

Capt. Louis L. McKeever, *M.C.,* L.R.C.P. & S.I.

Capt. Harry G. Massy-Myles, L.R.C.P. & S.I.

Major John O'Leary, F.R.C.S.I., I.M.S.

Lt. Joseph S. Pegum, L.R.C.P. & S.I.

Lieut. Pierce M. Power, L.R.C.P. & S.I., R.A.M.C.

Private John Power, Student.

Surgeon Probationer Raymond O'Connell Redmond, R.N.V.R.

Capt. Charles G. Sherlock, D.P.H., L.R.C.P. & S.I.

Capt. William F. Smartt, L.R.C.S.I.

Temp. Lieut. P. F. Ward, L.R.C.P. & S.I., R.A.M.C.

Lieut. Peyton T. Warren, L.R.C.P. & S.I., R.A.M.C.

ROYAL COLLEGE OF SURGEONS IN IRELAND.

MENTIONED IN DESPATCHES.

Major W. J. P. Adye-Curran, L.R.C.P. & S.I.

*Major R. B. Ainsworth, D.P.H., R.C.P. & S.I.

Capt. E. G. Annis, L.R.C.P. & S.I.

*Capt. J. H. Barry, *D.S.O.*, *M.C.*, L.R.C.P. & S.I.

Col. A. F. L. Bate, L.R.C.S.I.

Lt.-Col. H. L. Battersby, L.R.C.P. & S.I.

Capt. D. W. Beamish, L.R.C.P. & S.I.

*Lieut.-Col. A. W. Bewley, L.R.C.P. & S.I.

*Lieut.-Col. E. B. Bird, L.R.C.P. & S.I.

*Lt.-Col. Wm. R. Blackwell, L.R.C.P. & S.I.

Col. L. Blandford, A.M.S., D.P.H., R.C.P. & S.I.

*Major E. A. Bourke, L.R.C.P. & S.I.

*Temp. Col. A. W. N. Bowen, L.R.C.P. & S.I.

*Capt. W. W. Boyce, L.R.C.P. & S.I.

Major F. L. Bradish, L.R.C.P. & S.I.

Fleet Surgeon F. Bradshaw, L.R.C.P. & S.I.

Capt. C. H. Brennan, L.R.C.P. & S.I.

*Major R. T. Brown, D.P.H., R.C.P. & S.I.

Col. S. G. Brown, *C.B.*

*Col. E. G. Browne, L.R.C.P. & S.I.

*Capt. T. W. Browne, L.R.C.P. & S.I.

* Mentioned in Despatches more than once.

4

ROYAL COLLEGE OF SURGEONS IN IRELAND.

MENTIONED IN DESPATCHES.

Lt.-Col. A. W. Browne, L.R.C.P. & S.I.

Major B. B. Burke, L.R.C.P. & S.I.

Capt. H. J. Burke, L.R.C.P. & S.I.

Capt. C. P. O'B. Butler, L.R.C.P. & S.I.

Col. E. Butt, F.R.C.S.I.

Capt. L. Cassidy, F.R.C.S.I.

*Temp. Capt. R. Charles, F.R.C.S.I.

Major R. Coffey, L.R.C.P. & S.I.

*Major J. M. H. Conway, F.R.C.S.I.

Capt. T. J. Crean, *V.C.*, L.R.C.P. & S.I

Major W. C. Croly, L.R.C.P. & S.I.

Col. A. E. J. Croly, L.R.C.P. & S.I.

Lieut.-Col. C. D'Alton, L.R.C.P. & S.I.

Col. T. Daly, L.R.C.P. & S.I.

Capt. E. C. Deane, L.R.C.P. & S.I.

Capt. C. F. Dillon-Kelly, L.R.C.P. & S.I.

Capt. T. Duncan, L.R.C.P. & S.I.

Capt. J. S. Dunne, F.R.C.S.I.

*Capt. P. Dwyer, D.P.H., R.C.P. & S.I.

Capt. J. J. Dwyer, L.R.C.P. & S.I.

Lieut.-Col. O. W. A. Elsner, L.R.C.P. & S.I., D.P.H.

* Mentioned in Despatches more than once.

ROYAL COLLEGE OF SURGEONS IN IRELAND.

MENTIONED IN DESPATCHES.

*Capt. P. G. M. Elvery, L.R.C.P. & S.I.

Lt.-Col. E. J. R. Evatt, Professor of Anatomy.

Major M. W. Falkner, L.R.C.P. & S.I.

Temp. Major C. M. Fegen, L.R.C.P. & S.I.

Col. J. D. Ferguson, L.R.C.P. & S.I.

Capt. J. C. Fergusson, L.R.C.P. & S.I.

Col. R. H. J. Fetherston, L.R.C.P. & S.I.

*Col. F. G. Fitzgerald, L.R.C.P. & S.I.

*Capt. D. C. V. Fitzgerald, *M.C.*, L.R.C.P. & S.I.

*Lieut.-Col. B. Forde, D.P.H., R.C.P. & S.I.

Major R. J. Franklin, L.R.C.P. & S.I.

Lieut. F. P. Freeman, L.R.C.P. & S.I.

Col. A. Fullerton, F.R.C.S.I.

Capt. C. E. H. Gater, L.R.C.P. & S.I.

Capt. B. Gibson, L.R.C.P. & S.I.

Lieut.-Col. J. G. Gill, L.R.C.P. & S.I.

Major S. R. Godkin, F.R.C.S.I.

Capt. T. O. Graham, F.R.C.S.I.

Col. F. J. Grieg, L.R.C.P. & S.I.

*Major C. M. Goodbody, *D.S.O.*, F.R.C.S.I.

Major P. J. Hanafin, L.R.C.P. & S.I.

* Mentioned in Despatches more than once.

6

ROYAL COLLEGE OF SURGEONS IN IRELAND.

MENTIONED IN DESPATCHES.

Major D. L. Harding, F.R.C.S.I.

Major G. A. D. Harvey, L.R.C.P. & S.I.

*Lieut.-Col. H. Herrick, L.R.C.P. & S.I.

Capt. R. de S. B. Herrick, L.R.C.P. & S.I.

Capt. F. M. Hewson, L.R.C.P. & S.I.

Lieut.-Col. J. W. Holden, L.R.C.P. & S.I., D.P.H.

Major G. J. Houghton, L.R.C.P. & S.I.

Lieut.-Col. A. E. S. Irvine, L.R.C.P. & S.I.

Lieut.-Col. G. B. Irvine, L.R.C.P. & S.I.

Major A. W. A. Irwin, L.R.C.P. & S.I.

Lieut. H. S. Johnston, L.R.C.P. & S.I.

Fleet Surgeon H. P. Jones, R.N.

Lt.-Col. A. E. C. Kebble, *D.S.O.*, L.R.C.P. & S.I.

Surgeon Peter B. Kelly, L.R.C.P. & S.I.

Temp. Capt. Daniel Kelly, L.R.C.P. & S.I.

*Lieut. C. A. Kenny, L.R.C.P. & S.I.

Major-General W. W. Kenny, L.R.C.P. & S.I.

Capt. J. Kirker, L.R.C.P. & S.I.

Lt.-Col. E. B. Knox, D.P.H., R.C.P. & S.I.

*Lieut.-Col. J. W. Langstaff, L.R.C.P. & S.I.

*Capt. G. Q. Lennane, F.R.C.S.I.

* Mentioned in Despatches more than once.

ROYAL COLLEGE OF SURGEONS IN IRELAND.

MENTIONED IN DESPATCHES.

*Major E. F. L'Estrange, L.R.C.P. & S.I.

Major R. W. D. Leslie, L.R.C.P. & S.I.

Capt. W. F. M. Loughnan, L.R.C.P. & S.I., D.P.H.

*Lieut.-Col. A. J. Luther, L.R.C.P. & S.I.

Major N. S. Manning, F.R.C.S.I.

*Lt.-Col. W. E. P. V. Marriott, L.R.C.P. & S.I.

Capt. McCausland, L.R.C.P. & S.I.

Lieut. W. T. McCurry (Student)

Lt.-Col. H. G. Martin, L.R.C.P. & S.I.

Major C. R. Millar, L.R.C.P. & S.I.

*Lt.-Col. J. R. M'Munn, L.R.C.P. & S.I.

Capt. F. H. Mollan, L.R.C.P. & S.I.

Capt. H. Moore, L.R.C.P. & S.I.

*Temp. Capt. H. Moore, L.R.C.P. & S.I.

*Capt. C. McQueen, L.R.C.P. & S.I.

Major T. B. Moriarty, L.R.C.P. & S.I.

Capt. W. L. Murphy, L.R.C.P. & S.I.

Col. Sir Thomas Myles, F.R.C.S.I.

Lieut.-Col L. T. M. Nash, L.R.C.P. & S.I.

*Col. D. M. O'Callaghan, L.R.C.P. & S.I.

Lt.-Col. M. D. O'Connell, L.R.C.P. & S.I.

* Mentioned in Despatches more than once.

ROYAL COLLEGE OF SURGEONS IN IRELAND.

MENTIONED IN DESPATCHES.

Major W. H. Odlum, L.R.C.P. & S.I.

*Col. T. J. O'Donnell, *D.S.O.*, L.R.C.P. & S.I.

*Capt. J. A. O'Driscoll, L.R.C.P. & S.I.

Capt. L. S. O'Grady, L.R.C.P. & S.I.

Lt.-Col. J. J. O'Hagan, T.D., F.R.C.S.I.

Capt. O. J. O'B. O'Hanlon, F.R.C.S.I.

Major P. S. O'Reilly, L.R.C.P. & S.I.

*Capt. W. H. O'Riordan, L.R.C.P. & S.I.

*Capt. K. L. O'Sullivan, L.R.C.P. & S.I.

Col. D. O'Sullivan, F.R.C.S.I.

Lieut.-Col. F. J. Palmer, F.R.C.S.I.

Capt. A. F. I. Patterson, L.R.C.P. & S.I.

Capt. G. E. Pepper, L.R.C.P. & S.I.

Capt. H. J. Perry, L.R.C.P. & S.I.

*Capt. G. Petit, L.R.C.P. & S.I.

*Temp. Major-General W. W. Pike, F.R.C.S.I.

Temp. Lieut. S. Potter, L.R.C.P. & S.I.

Major T. J. Potter, L.R.C.P. & S.I.

Capt. R. P. Power (Student).

Major W. M. Power, L.R.C.P. & S.I.

Temp.-Surgeon J. Pratt, L.R.C.P. & S.I.

* Mentioned in Despatches more than once.

ROYAL COLLEGE OF SURGEONS IN IRELAND.

MENTIONED IN DESPATCHES.

Major J. J. W. Prescott, *D.S.O.*, L.R.C.P. & S.I.

Capt. W. N. Rishworth, D.P.H., R.C.P. & S.I.

*Col. W. H. B. Robinson, *C.B.* L.R.C.P. & S.I., D.P.H.

Major W. F. Roe, L.R.C.P. & S.I.

Temp. Lieut. L. M. Rowlette, L.R.C.P. & S.I.

Major N. J. C. Rutherford, D.P.H., R.C.P. & S.I.

Capt. P. Sampson, L.R.C.P. & S.I., D.P.H.

*Col. R. H. S. Sawyer, F.R.C.S.I.

*Lieut.-Col. D. D. Shanahan, L.R.C.P. & S.I.

Lieut.-Col. W. S. Sharpe, F.R.C.S.I.

Major G. F. Sheehan, L.R.C.P. & S.I.

Capt. H. B. Sherlock, L.R.C.P. & S.I.

Surgeon J. P. Shorten, R.N., L.R.C.P. & S.I.

Major E. W. Siberry, L.R.C.P. & S.I.

Brevet-Col. F. Smith, *C.M.G.*, *D.S.O.*, L.R.C.P. & S.I.

Col. F. Smith, *D.S.O.*, L.R.C.P. & S.I.

Capt. G. N. Smyth, L.R.C.P. & S.I.

Capt. J. C. Sproule, L.R.C.P. & S.I.

Capt. G. W. Stanley, L.R.C.P. & S.I.

Capt. A. Stokes, F.R.C.S.I.

Lieut.-Col. Sweeny, F.R.C.S.I.

* Mentioned in Despatches more than once.

10

ROYAL COLLEGE OF SURGEONS IN IRELAND.

MENTIONED IN DESPATCHES.

Capt. G. G. Tabuteau, L.R.C.P. & S.I.

Colonel Sir William Taylor, *K.B.E.*, *C.B.*, President, R.C.S.I.

Capt. W. J. Tobin, L.R.C.P. & S.I.

Lt.-Col. G. E. Twiss, L.R.C.P. & S.I.

Major F. S. Walker, F.R.C.S.I.

Capt. N. D. Walker, D.P.H., R.C.P. & S.I

Capt. E. C. Wallace, L.R.C.P. & S.I.

Major J. W. West, D.P.H., R.C.P. & S.I.

Temp. Capt. L. T. Whelan, F.R.C.S.I.

Major W. I. de C. Wheeler, F.R.C.S.I.

Capt. L. D. Woods, L.R.C.P. & S.I.

Lt.-Col. W. A. Woodside, L.R.C.P. & S.I.

*Major W. G. Wright, L.R.C.P. & S.I.

*Lt.-Col. T. J. Wright, L.R.C.P. & S.I.

Surg.-Genl. M. T. Yarr, *C.B.*, F.R.C.S.I.

*Col. C. A. Young, L.R.C.S.I.

* Mentioned in Despatches more than once.

ROYAL COLLEGE OF SURGEONS IN IRELAND.

HONOURS LIST.

To be Major General—	Col. T. J. O'Donnell, *D.S.O.*, L.R.C.P. & S.I.
	Col. William W. Pike, *D.S.O.*, F.R.C.S.I.
	Col. R. H. S. Sawyer, *D.S.O*, F.R.C.S.I.
K. C. M. G.—	Major-Genl. J. D. Bourke, *C.B.* L.R.C.P. & S.I.
	Major-Genl. M. T. Yarr, *C.B.*, F.R.C.S.I.
K. C. B.—	Major-Genl. W. Donovan, L.R.C.P. & S.I.
C. B.—	Col. Edward George Browne, L.R.C.P. & S.I.
	Lieut.-Col. G. B. Irvine, L.R.C.P. & S.I., I.M.S.
	Major-Genl. W. W. Kenny, F.R.C.S.I.
	Lt.-Col. Mawhinny, L.R.C.P. & S.I.
	Lieut.-Col. Sir Thomas Myles, F.R.C.S.I.
	Major-Genl. T. J. O'Donnell, *D.S.O.*, L.R.C.P. & S.I.
	Lieut-Col. W. Henry Banner Robinson, L.R.C.P. & S.I., I.M.S.
	Major-General R. H. S. Sawyer, *C.M.G.*, *D.S.O.*, F.R.C.S.I.
	Col. Sir A. E. Wright, F.R.C.S.
	Col. Michael T. Yarr, F.R.C.S.I.
To be Brevet Lieut.-Colonel—	Lt.-Col. E. B. Bird, *D.S.O.*, L.R.C.P & S.I.
	Major C. M. Goodbody, *D.S.O.*, F.R.C.S.I.
	Lt.-Col. C. W. Holden, *D.S.O.*, L.R.C.P. & S.I
To be Brevet Major—	Capt. R. W. D. Leslie, L.R.C.P. & S.I.

12

ROYAL COLLEGE OF SURGEONS IN IRELAND.

HONOURS LIST.

C. M. G.—

Col. Beeston, V.D., L.R.C.P. & S.I.

Col. A. W. Bewley, L.R.C.P. & S.I.

Lt.-Col. W. R. Blackwell, L.R.C.P. & S.I.

Col. T. Daly, L.R.C.P. & S.I.

Col. J. D. Ferguson, *D.S.O.*, L.R.C.P. & S.I.

Lieut.-Col. B. Forde, D.P.H., R.C.P. & S.I.

Col. A. Fullerton, F.R.C.S.I.

Col. Greig, L.R.C.S.I.

Col. C. W. R. Healy, L.R.C.P. & S.I.

Col. A. E. C. Keble, *D.S.O.*,

Col. H. T. Knaggs, L.R.C.P. & S.I.

Lt.-Col. James Robert McMunn, L.R.C.P. & S.I.

Lieut.-Col. L. T. M. Nash, L.R.C.P. & S.I.

Col. D. M. O'Callaghan, L.R.C.P. & S.I.

Col. D. O'Sullivan, F.R.C.S.I.

Major-Genl. William Watson Pike, *D.S.O.*, F.R.C.S.I.

Col. R. H. S. Sawyer, *D.S.O.*, F.R.C.S.I.

Lt.-Col. D. Shanahan, *D.S.O.*,

Brevet-Col. Frederick Smith, *D.S.O.* L.R.C.P. & S.I.

Lt.-Col. T. H. Sweeny, F.R.C.S.I.

Lieut.-Col. G. E. Twiss, L.R.C.P. & S.I.

Col. Charles Augustus Young, L.R.C.P. & S.I.

ROYAL COLLEGE OF SURGEONS IN IRELAND

HONOURS LIST.

Distinguished Service Cross— Temp.-Surg. JOHN PRATT, R.N., L.R.C.P. & S.I.

G. E. STRAHAN.

D.S.O.—

Major RALPH B. AINSWORTH, D.P.H., R.C.P. & S.I.

Capt. J. H. BARRY, L.R.C.P. & S.I.

Lieut.-Col. W. BENNETT, L.R.C.P. & S.I.

Lieut.-Col. E. B. BIRD, L.R.C.P. & S.I.

Col. R. J. BLACKHAM, Former Student.

Lt.-Col. E. A. BOURKE, L.R.C.P. & S.I.

Lt.-Col. A. W. N. BOWEN, L.R.C.P. & S.I.

Lt.-Col. F. L. BRADISH, L.R.C.P. & S.I.

Major R. T. BROWN, L.R.C.P. & S.I.

Major BERNARD BURKE, L.R.C.P. & S.I.

Major (Temp. Lt.-Col.) R. J. CAHILL, R.A.M.C.

Major R. COFFEY, L.R.C.P. & S.I.

Major J. H. M. CONWAY, F.R.C.S.I.

Capt. T. J. CREAN, *V.C.*, L.R.C.P. & S.I.

Lt.-Col. W. C. CROLY, L.R.C.P. & S.I.

Capt. J. S. DUNNE, F.R.C.S.I.

Capt. J. J. DWYER, L.R.C.P. & S.I.

Lieut.-Col. O. W. A. ELSNER, L.R.C.P. & S.I.

Capt. (Acting Lt.-Col.) P. G. M. ELVERY.

Col. E. J. R. EVATT, Professor of Anatomy, R.C.S.I.

Col. F. G. FITZGERALD, L.R.C.P. & S.I.

Capt. J. G. GILL, L.R.C.P. & S.I.

ROYAL COLLEGE OF SURGEONS IN IRELAND

HONOURS LIST.

D.S.O. (contd.)—

Lt.-Col. (Acting Col.) T. G. Gill, L.R.C.P. & S.I.

Major S. R. Godkin, F.R.C.S.I.

Major C. M. Goodbody, F.R.C.S.I.

Major Patrick J. Hanafin, L.R.C.P. & S.I.

Major Daniel L. Harding, F.R.C.S.I.

Capt. R. de S. B. Herrick, L.R.C.P. & S.I.

Lt.-Col. (Acting Col.) H. Herrick, L.R.C.P. & S.I.

Lieut.-Col. C. W. Holden, L.R.C.P. & S.I.

Major G. J. Houghton, L.R.C.P. & S.I.

Major Arthur E. S. Irvine, L.R.C.P. & S.I.

Lieut.-Col. J. W. Langstaff, L.R.C.P. & S.I.

Lt.-Col. E. W. P. V. Marriott, L.R.C.P. & S.I.

Major C. R. Millar, L.R.C.P. & S.I.

Lt.-Col. Henry Moore, *M.C.*, L.R.C.P. & S.I.

Major William F. Roe, L.R.C.P. & S.I.

Capt. L. M. Rowlette, L.R.C.P. & S.I.

Major N. J. C. Rutherford, D.P.H., R.C.P. & S.I.

Major Francis Sampson, L.R.C.P. & S.I.

Capt. P. Sampson, L.R.C.P. & S.I., D.P.H.

Col. D. D. Shanahan, L.R.C.P. & S.I.

Major G. F. Sheehan, L.R.C.P. & S.I.

Surgeon J. P. Shorten, R.N., L.R.C.P. & S.I.

Col. F. Smith, *C.M.G.*, L.R.C.P. & S.I.

ROYAL COLLEGE OF SURGEONS IN IRELAND.

HONOURS LIST.

D.S.O. (contd.)—

Capt. Adrian Stokes, R.A.M.C., F.R.C.S.I.

Col. G. W. Tate, D.P.H., R.C.P. & S.I.

Lt.-Col. W. A. Woodside, L.R.C.P. & S.I.

Major W. G. Wright, L.R.C.P. & S.I.

Major (Temp. Lt.-Col.) T. J. Wright, L.R.C.P. & S.I.

D. S. O. and Bar—

Lt.-Col. E. J. Hanafin, L.R.C.P. & S.I.

Military Cross—

Capt. J. H. Barry, L.R.C.P. & S.I.

Capt. D. W. Beamish, L.R.C.P. & S.I.

Capt. A. J. Berveridge.

Capt. Frederick W. Brunker, L.R.C.P. & S.I.

Capt. C. H. Brennan, L.R.C.P. & S.I.

Capt. Henry James Burke, L.R.C.P. & S.I.

Capt. Henry J. Cotter, L.R.C.P. & S.I.

Major W. C. Croly, L.R.C.P. & S.I.

Capt. D. E. Crosby, L.R.C.P. & S.I.

Capt. Thomas Dowzer, L.R.C.P. & S.I.

Capt. T. Duncan, L.R.C.P. & S.I.

Capt. E. C. Deane, L.R.C.P. & S.I.

Capt. P. Dwyer, D.P.H., R.C.P. & S.I.

Capt. Philip Gordon Moss Elvery, L.R.C.P. & S.I.

ROYAL COLLEGE OF SURGEONS IN IRELAND.

HONOURS LIST.

Military Cross (contd.)—

Capt. J. C. Fergusson, L.R.C.P. & S.I.

Capt. J. H. C. Gatchell, L.R.C.P. & S.I.

Capt. J. G. Gill, L.R.C.P. & S.I.

Capt. Frank Percy Feeeman, L.R.C.P. & S.I.

Capt. D. V. C. Fitzgerald, L.R.C.P. & S.I.

2nd Lieut. Samuel F. Hill.

Capt. Richard H. Hodges, L.R.C.P. & S.I.

Capt. W. E. Hopkins, L.R.C.P. & S.I.

Lt.-Col. G. B. Irvine, L.R.C.P. & S.I.

Capt. T. J. Kelly, L.R.C.P. & S.I.

Temp. Capt. D. Kelly, L.R.C.P. & S.I.

Capt. John S. Levis, L.R.C.P. & S.I.

Capt. W. F. M. Loughnan, L.R.C.P. & S.I., D.P.H.

Capt. L. L. McKeever, L.R.C.P. & S.I.

Capt. F. R. H. Mollan, L.R.C.P. & S.I.

Temp. Capt. H. Moore, L.R.C.P. & S.I.

Capt. F. J. Morris, L.R.C.P. & S.I.

Major K. A. P. R. Murray, L.R.C.P. & S.I.

Capt. W. H. O'Riordan, L.R.C.P. & S.I.

Capt. Gerard Petit, L.R.C.P. & S.I.

ROYAL COLLEGE OF SURGEONS IN IRELAND.

HONOURS LIST.

Military Cross (contd.)—

Capt. W. N. Rishworth, D.P.H., R.C.P. & S.I.

Capt. L. M. Rowlette, L.R.C.P. & S.I.

Capt. Henry Bowler Sherlock, L.R.C.P. & S.I., D.P.H.

Major F. M. Taylor, L.R.C.P. & S.I.

Capt. E. C. Wallace, L.R.C.P. & S.I.

Capt. L. T. Whelan, L.R.C.P. & S.I.

Capt. Roger Llewelyn Williams, L.R.C.P. & S.I.

Military Medal—

Private R. A. Scott, R.A.M.C.

Military Cross and Bar—

Capt. A. J. Blake, L.R.C.P. & S.I.

Military Cross with 2 Bars—

Capt. J. S. Levis, L.R.C.P. & S.I

Italian Service Medal with Bar—

Sergt. Harry S. Moorhead.

18

ROYAL COLLEGE OF SURGEONS IN IRELAND.

HONOURS LIST—FOREIGN DECORATIONS.

BY THE KING OF SERBIA.

Order of the White Eagle, 3rd Class (with Swords)— Col. A. E. C. Keble, *C.M.G., D.S.O.* L.R.C.P. & S.I.

Order of St. Sava—

(3rd Class) Lt. Col. B. Ford, *C.M.G.*, L.R.C.P. & S.I.

(4th Class) Capt. W. L. Murphy, L.R.C.P. & S.I.

Capt. W. L. Woods, L.R.C.P. & S.I.

Croix de Guerre— Capt. R. R. Scott, L.R.C.P. & S.I.

Order de la Couronne—

Grand Officier Awarded to Lt.-General Sir A. Keogh, *G.C.B.*, Director General A.M.S.

Commandeur To Major-General Sir W. Donovan, *K.C.B.*, Maratime Transport.

Order de la Couronne de Belgique— To Capt. Adrian Stokes, F.R.C.S.I.

Legion d'Honneur—

Croix de Chevalier— Awarded to Captain W. L. Murphy.

Croix de Officier— Lt.-Col. W. R. Blackwell.

ROYAL COLLEGE OF SURGEONS IN IRELAND.

EXTRACTS FROM DESPATCHES.

Capt. Patrick Sampson, L.R.C.P. & S.I., R.A.M.C., awarded the Distinguished Service Order "for frequent and conspicuous gallantry when attending wounded under very heavy shell fire."

Capt. James Stewart Dunne, F.R.C.S.I., R.A.M.C., awarded the Distinguished Service Order "for saving many lives by attending wounded men in the trenches."

Capt. W. F. M. Loughnan, L.R.C.P. & S.I., D.P.H., R.A.M.C., awarded the Military Cross "for gallantry on many occasions in Flanders in assisting to rescue the wounded while exposed to heavy fire."

Capt. Ernest Cotton Deane, L.R.C.P. & S.I., R.A.M.C. (attached 2nd Battalion Leicester Regt.), awarded the Military Cross "for conspicuous gallantry on 22nd August, 1915, near Fauquissart. A standing patrol 120 yards in front of our line was bombed by the enemy at about 10 p.m., the only notification being two loud bomb explosions. Capt. Deane, without any knowledge of the enemy's strength, at once got over the parapet and ran by himself to the spot under rifle and machine gun fire. Finding four wounded men he returned for stretchers and got them back into safety. This is not the first time that Capt. Deane's gallantry under fire has been brought to notice."

Surgeon General T. J. O'Donnell, L.R.C.P. & S.I.

In the course of his Despatch Field Marshal Sir John French says:—

"These results are due to the skill and energy which have characterised in a marked degree the work of the Royal Army Medical Corps throughout the campaign under the able supervision of Surgeon-General T. J. O'Donnell, D.S.O., Deputy Director General, Medical Services."

He is mentioned again in the following message:—

"I have already commented upon the number and severity of the casualities in action which have occurred in the period under report. Here once again I have to draw attention to the excellent work done by Surgeon-General O'Donnell and his officers. No organisation could excel the efficiency of the arrangements—whether in regard to time, space, care, and comfort, or transport—which are made for the speedy evacuation of the wounded."

Capt. Frank Percy Freeman, R.A.M.C., Special Reserve attached 23rd Field Ambulance, awarded the Military Cross "for conspicuous gallantry and devotion to duty during operations near Hulloch, from 25th to 28th September, 1915. He brought in and attended to the wounded during four consecutive days and nights, repeatedly going out under heavy fire. By his personal bravery and energy he set a splendid example to his men."

ROYAL COLLEGE OF SURGEONS IN IRELAND.

EXTRACTS FROM DESPATCHES.

Temporary Capt. Henry James Burke, Royal Army Medical Corps (attached 1st-8th Battalion West Yorkshire Regiment, Territorial Force), awarded the Military Cross for conspicuous gallantry on 8th November, 1915, near Turco Farm. A sergeant in the front line had his leg crushed by the blowing in of a dug-out, and Captain Burke found immediate amputation necessary. In order to save time he crawled across the open to get his instruments, while the enemy turned a machine gun on to him. In spite of their fire he returned the same way, and coolly performed the operation in the trench while the enemy were shelling it heavily."

Capt. Roger Llewellyn Williams, R.A.M.C., D.P.H., R.C.P. & S.I. (attached South Staffs. Regt.), awarded the Military Cross "for conspicuous gallantry and devotion to duty. He displayed marked courage and determination in tending the wounded under very heavy fire. He has on many previous occasions done fine work."

Capt. John S. Levis, R.A.M.C., was awarded the Military Cross "for conspicuous gallantry and devotion to duty. He displayed great courage and determination when in charge of stretcher-bearers under heavy fire. He has on many previous occasions done fine work."

Capt. Frederick W. Brunker, R.A.M.C., awarded the Military Cross "for conspicuous gallantry in action. He continually went into the open under very heavy fire and attended to the wounded. He displayed great courage and determination throughout."

Surgeon J. P. Shorten, R.N., received the D.S.O. for continuing to dress and attend to the wounded in the open while under heavy fire."

2nd Lieut. Samuel Frederick Hill, M.C., 1st Battery, Royal Field Artillery, has been awarded the Military Cross "for his exceptional coolness and devotion to duty, controlling his section in a very fine manner, and showing absolute disregard for personal safety, during a very heavy barrage right on the gun position, he walked about giving confidence to the men, by word and example, and when one of the gun detachment became a casualty, he immediately took his place, and kept the gun in action. Later, when the other Section Commander became a casualty, Lieut. Hill took control of both Sections."

Temp. Capt. A. J. M. Blake, R.A.M.C., L R.C.P. & S.I., awarded the Military Cross "for conspicuous gallantry and devotion to duty during operations. He tended wounded men incessantly day and night under most trying conditions. He went into 'No Man's Land,' searching for any wounded men who might still be lying there."

ROYAL COLLEGE OF SURGEONS IN IRELAND.

EXTRACTS FROM DESPATCHES.

Capt. Samuel Brown, R.A.M.C., L.R.C.P. & S.I., awarded the Military Cross "for conspicuous devotion to duty during operations. He was blown up by a shell and so much injured that he had to spend the night in a field ambulance, but, although still suffering, he returned to duty next day. A few days later he was again blown up. He has never spared himself and has displayed the greatest gallantry."

Temp. Capt. R. H. Hodges, R.A.M.C., L.R.C.P. & S.I., awarded the Military Cross. He organised and led parties of stretcher-bearers under heavy fire, displaying great courage and determination."

Temp. Capt. Francis J. Morris, R.A.M.C., L.R.C.P. & S.I., awarded the Military Cross "for conspicuous gallantry and devotion to duty during operations. He led his stretcher-bearers to collect wounded in full view of the enemy's position, and set a fine example to all near him. He has done other similar work."

Temp. Capt. P. J. O'Reilly, R.A.M.C., L.R.C.P. & S.I., awarded the Military Cross. "He tended the wounded under intense fire, displaying great courage and determination. Later, although wounded, he stuck to his post."

Capt. Charles Roche, R.A.M.C., L.R.C.P. & S.I., awarded the Military Cross "for conspicuous courage and skill in the performance of his duties many times under fire. He organised large stretcher parties, and rescued many seriously wounded men from points which were constantly under heavy fire. He has displayed great devotion to duty under distressing circumstances."

Capt. Richard Andrew Austin, R.A.M.C., L.R.C.P. & S.I., awarded the Military Cross "for conspicuous gallantry and devotion to duty. He tended and dressed the wounded under very heavy fire, with great courage and determination. He had previously done very fine work."

Temp. Capt. Thomas Dowser, R.A.M.C. (attached Manchester Regiment), awarded the Military Cross "for conspicuous gallantry and devotion to duty. He showed great personal bravery in moving about in the open under heavy fire, organising his bearers and assisting in the search for the wounded."

Surgeon Peter Burrows Kelly, R.N., L.R.C.P. & S.I., awarded the Distinguished Service Order, "was wounded in the foot on the morning of April 25th in the River Clyde. He remained in the 'River Clyde' until the morning of April 27th, during which time he attended 750 wounded men, although in great pain and unable to walk during the last 24 hours."

22

ROYAL COLLEGE OF SURGEONS IN IRELAND.

EXTRACTS FROM DESPATCHES.

Temp. Capt. James Harding Barry, R.A.M.C. (attached London Regiment), awarded the Military Cross "for conspicuous gallantry and devotion to duty. He showed the utmost coolness and bravery in going out under heavy machine gun fire and assisting to bring in and attend wounded men. Throughout he set a splendid example to all."

Temp. Capt. James Harding Barry, M.C., R.A.M.C., attached London Regiment, awarded the D.S.O. "for conspicuous gallantry and devotion to duty in attending to the wounded under exceptionally trying conditions under very heavy fire he dug out five men who were buried, and amputated two men's legs on the spot. He showed utter disregard of any personal risk, and his example was splendid."

Temp. Capt. Henry Joseph Cotter, R.A.M.C., attached Lincolnshire Regiment, awarded the Military Cross "for conspicuous gallantry and devotion to duty. Although wounded on the previous day, he declined to be relieved, and continued to dress wounded in the open under heavy fire, going through barrage to reach some men lying out in an exposed position."

Capt. Samuel McCausland, awarded the Military Cross "for conspicuous gallantry and devotion to duty. Under very heavy and continuous shell fire he systematically searched from cellar to cellar of a village until he had successfully cleared his part of the villiage of all wounded. These included many who were lying there for days, and who could not be moved owing to the intensity of the enemy barrage. He worked unceasingly amidst conditions of the greatest possible danger for 30 hours."

Major (Temp. Lt.-Col.) Patrick John Hanafin, D.S.O., awarded Bar to D.S.O., "for conspicuous gallantry and devotion to duty. For nine days he was continually under heavy shell fire while supervising the evacuation of the wounded in the most adverse circumstances. Finally, although wounded in passing through a heavy barrage, he continued on duty until the last man had been brought in. The successful evacuation of the wounded was largely due to his gallant conduct."

Capt. Charles Henry Brennan (Special Reserve), awarded Military Cross "for conspicuous gallantry and devotion to duty. He led his bearers fearlessly through heavy shell fire, and made a most valuable reconnasiance beyond the regimental aid post to find out if there were any wounded lying out. Though blown up and gassed, he remained on duty, setting a magnificent example to all."

ROYAL COLLEGE OF SURGEONS IN IRELAND.

EXTRACTS FROM DESPATCHES.

Capt. THOMAS DUNCAN, awarded Military Cross "for conspicuous gallantry and devotion to duty. Though he was wounded on the way up to the line before an attack, he refused to go back, and carried out his duties under most difficult conditions, and though suffering considerable pain, throughout the operations. He was again wounded, but continued to work until ordered to have his wounds attended to."

Temp. Capt. CECIL FRANCIS DILLON-KELLY, R.A.M.C., awarded Military Cross "for conspicuous gallantry and devotion to duty. Establishing his regimental aid post in the captured enemy line, he himself kept in touch with the advanced troops and dressed the wounded under heavy machine gun and rifle fire. He remained in the most advanced positions dressing the wounded until every case had been evacuated, and showed an excellent example of disregard for danger and courageous determination."

Capt. LOUIS LAURENCE McKEEVER, R.A.M.C., awarded Military Cross, "for conspicuous gallantry and devotion to duty during an engagement. Hearing that there was no Medical Officer in the front line, he went forward at once under an intense bombardment, and remained in the front line all night attending to the wounded under continuous and violent shell fire. He set a splendid example of courage and devotion to duty."

Temp. Capt. J. J. REYNOLDS, R.A.M.C., attached 15th Battalion, Hampshire Regiment, for conspicuous gallantry and devotion to duty. He formed an advanced regimental aid-post on the side of the road, thus shortening the stretcher-bearers' journeys. Eventually he was forced to evacuate this position owing to hostile fire. Later he dressed and attended to all the casualties of three battalions, though partially gassed himself. By his untiring energy he undoubtedly saved many lives.

24

ROYAL COLLEGE OF SURGEONS IN IRELAND.

*Acheson, M. K.	D.P.H., R.C.P. & S.I.	Capt., R.A.M.C.
Adams, Albert P.	L.R.C.P. & S.I.	Temp. Lieut., R.A.M.C.
Adams, William J.	L.R.C.P. & S.I.	Temp. Lieut., R.A.M.C.
Adams, R. H.	F.R.C.S.I.	Temp. Lieut., R.A.M.C.
†Adams, G. G. C.	L.R.C.P. & S.I.	Lieut., R.A.M.C.
*Adye-Curran, William J. P.	L.R.C.P. & S.I.	Lt.-Col., R.A.M.C.
Aherne, Richard J.	L.R.C.P. & S.I.	Temp. Lieut., R.A.M.C.
Ahern, Michael J.	L.R.C.P. & S.I.	Temp. Lieut., R.A.M.C.
*Ainsworth, Ralph B.	D.P.H., R.C.P. & S.I.	Major, R.A.M.C.
Aickin, Roland T. G.	D.P.H., R.C.P. & S.I.	Temp. Lieut., R.A.M.C.
Alcorn, Robert M.	L.R.C.P. & S.I.	Temp. Capt., R.A.M.C.
Alcorn, J. M.	L.R.C.P. & S.I.	Major, Australian R.A.M.C.
Alexander, Hugh M.	L.R.C.P. & S.I.	Temp. Capt., R.A.M.C.
Allaun, Israel	L.R.C.P. & S.I.	Temp. Capt., R.A.M.C.
Allen, J. F.	L.R.C.P. & S.I.	Temp. Lieut., R.A.M.C.
Allen, Robert G.	L.R.C.P. & S.I.	Temp. Lieut., R.A.M.C.
Allin, John R. P.	L.R.C.P. & S.I.	Temp. Capt., R.A.M.C.
Allison, George F.	L.R.C.P. & S.I.	Capt., R.A.M.C.
Allison, Robert	L.R.C.P. & S.I.	Recruiting M.O.
Allman, Percy N.	L.R.C.P. & S.I.	Temp. Lieut., R.A.M.C.
Anderson, Louis E.	*C.B.*, L.R.C.P. & S.I.	Surgeon-General, R.A.M.C.
Anderson, William H.	L.R.C.P. & S.I.	Temp. Lieut., R.A.M.C.

* Mentioned in Despatches. † Killed in Action.

ROYAL COLLEGE OF SURGEONS IN IRELAND.

Andrews, Harold E.	Student	Surg. Prob.
Andrews, Leopold A. A.	L.R.C.P. & S.I.	Capt., R.A.M.C.
Andrews, Reginald J.		Cadet, R.A. Force
*Annis, Ernest G.	*D.S.M.*, L.R.C.P. & S.I.	Capt., R.A.M.C.
Anthony, Mark	L.R.C.P. & S.I.	Temp. Lieut., R.A.M.C.
Armitage, Harold G. P.	L.R.C.P. & S.I.	Lieut., R.A.M.C.
Ashe, Patrick	L.R.C.P. & S.I.	Temp. Lieut., R.A.M.C.
Askin, J. G.	Student	Sergt., Munster Fus.
Atkins, Alfred P.		Lieut. R.F.C.
Attridge, James C.	L.R.C.P. & S.I.	Temp. Capt., R.A.M.C.
Aughin, J. H.	L.R.C.P. & S.I.	M.O. I/c. of Troops
*Austin, Richard A.	*M.C.*, L.R.C.P. & S.I.	Capt., R.A.M.C.
Averill, Charles	D.P.H., R.C.P. & S.I.	Lt.-Col., R.A.M.C.
Baker, H. L.	Student	Temp. Lieut., 3rd Royal Irish Rifles
Baker, A. W. W.	F.R.C.S.I.	Temp. Capt., R.A.M.C.
Baker, Richard J.	L.R.C.S.I.	Capt. I.M.S.
†Ball, Sir Charles B., Bart.	F.R.C.S.I.	Temp. Lt.-Col., R.A.M.C.
Ball, Sir C. Arthur K., Bart.	F.R.C.S.I.	Temp. Major, R.A.M.C.
Bannerman, Walter B.	D.P.H., R.C.P. & S.I.	Temp. Lieut., R.A.M.C.
Barcroft, Penrose J.	L.R.C.P. & S.I.	Staff Surg., R.N. (Emergency Officer).
†Barker, Arthur E. J.	F.R.C.S.I.	Temp. Lt.-Col., R.A.M.C.
Barlee, Ronald J.	L.R.C.P. & S.I.	Surgeon, R.N.
Barnett, Kennet B.	F.R.C.S.I.	Lieut.-Col., R.A.M.C.

* Mentioned in Despatches. † Died on Service.

ROYAL COLLEGE OF SURGEONS IN IRELAND.

Barrett, Arthur P.	L.R.C.P. & S.I.	Temp. Surgeon, R.N.
Barrett, Jeremiah	L.R.C.P. & S.I.	Temp. Lieut., R.A.M.C.
Barrett, James H.	L.R.C.P. & S.I.	Temp. Lieut., R.A.M.C.
Barron, S.	L.R.C.P. & S.I.	Temp. Lieut., R.A.M.C.
*Barry, James H.	*D.S.O.*,*M.C.*, L.R.C.P. & S.I.	Temp. Lieut., R.A.M.C.
Barry, Patrick J.	L.R.C.P. & S.I.	Temp. Lieut., R.A.M.C.
Barry, Stephen J.	L.R.C.P. & S.I.	Capt., R.A.M.C.
Barton, T. T.	L.D.S., R.C.S.I.	Civil Dentist, Aldershot Command
Bassett, Robert J.	L.R.C.P. & S.I.	Temp. Lieut., R.A.M.C.
*Bate, L. Albert F.	L.R.C.P. & S.I.	Col., Army Medical Service
Bates, William R.	L.R.C.P. & S.I.	Commandant Ilkley Auxiliary Military Hospital
*Battersby, Henry L.	L.R.C.P. & S.I.	Lieut.-Col., R.A.M.C.
Battersby, John C.	F.R.C.S.I.	Lieut.-Col., R.A.M.C
*Beamish, Benjamin	L.R.C.P. & S.I.	Temp. Lieut., R.A.M.C.
Beamish, Desmond W.	L.R.C.P. & S.I.	Temp. Capt., R.A.M.C.
Beatty, Henry B.	L.R.C.P. & S.I.	Fleet Surgeon, R.N.
Beatty, Martyn C.	D.P.H., R.C.P. & S.I.	Major, R.A.M.C.
Beatty, James	D.P.H.	
*Beeston, J.	L.R.C.P. & S.I.	Col. A.D.M.S., New Zealand and Australian Division
Beeston, W. R. C.	L.R.C.P. & S.I.	Lieut., Z. & A.D.
Beggs, George E.	L.R.C.P. & S.I.	Temp. Capt., R.A.M.C.
*Bell, Harry C.	Student	Sergt.-Major, R.A.M.C.

* Mentioned in Despatches.

ROYAL COLLEGE OF SURGEONS IN IRELAND.

Bennett, Edmund B.	L.R.C.P. & S.I.	Major, R.A.M.C.
Benson, C. M.	F.R.C.S.I.	Temp. Major, R.A.M.C.
Benson, Eric J.	Student	Lieut., Army Service Corps
Bermingham, Hubert J.	Student	Flight Cadet
Bernard, E. A.	L.R.C.P. & S.I.	Temp. Lieut.. R.A.M.C.
Best, Albert J.	L.R.C.P. & S.I.	Temp. Lieut., R.A.M.C.
Best, William H. G. H.	L.R.C.P. & S.I.	Major, R.A.M.C. (Special Reserve)
Beveridge, A. J.	Ex-Student	Capt., R.A.M.C.
Beveridge, J. O'S.	Ex-Student	Capt., R.A.M.C.
Beveridge, W. J.	L.R.C.P. & S.I.	Major, Australian Army Medical Corps
*Bewley, Alfred W.	*C.M.G.*, L.R.C.P. & S.I.	Col., Army Medical Service
*Bird, Elliott B.	*D.S.O.*, L.R.C.P. & S.I.	Temp. Lt.-Col. R.A.M.C. Territorial Force
Black, Bertram D.	L.D.S., R.C.S.I.	Lieut., Leinster Regt.
Black, Desmond G.	Student	Cadet
Black, Charles A. J. A.	D.P.H., R.C.P. & S.I.	Major, R.A.M.C.
*Blackham, Robert J.	*C.M.G., C.I.E., D.S.O.*, Former Student	Col., Army Med. Service
Blackler, Henry J.	D.P.H., R.C.P. & S.I.	Lt. R.A.M.C., Territorial Force
Blackwell, Thomas S.	L.R.C.P. & S.I.	Capt., R.A.M.C.
Blackwell, William R.	L.R.C.P. & S.I.	Lieut.-Col., R.A.M.C.
Blair, Ribton G.	F.R.C.S.I.	Capt., R.A.M.C.
*Blake, A. Maurice J.	*M.C. with Bar*, L.R.C.P. & S.I.	Temp. Capt., R.A.M.C., M.O. 2nd Sth. Wales Borderers

* Mentioned in Despatches.

28

ROYAL COLLEGE OF SURGEONS IN IRELAND.

Blake, S.	L.R.C.P. & S.I.	Temp. Lieut., R.A.M.C.
*Blandford, Lawrence J.	D.P.H., R.C.P. & S.I.	Col., A.M.S.
Blayney, A. J.	F.R.C.S.I.	Temp. Major, R.A.M.C.
Blood, Horace F.	L.R.C.P. & S.I.	Temp. Lieut., R.A.M.C.
Blood, Bagot N.	L.R.C.P. & S.I.	Temp. Lieut., R.A.M.C.
Blood-Smyth, V.	Student	Temp. Lieut., 3rd Royal Irish Rifles
Bogan, James H.	L.R.C.P. & S.I.	Temp. Lieut., R.A.M.C.
Bolger, P. T.	F.R.C.S.I.	Civil Surgeon, French Red Cross
Bonis, Robert J.	L.R.C.P. & S.I.	Temp. Lieut., R.A.M.C.
Boon, J. G.	F.R.C.S.I.	Civil Surgeon.
Bouchier-Hayes, Henry	L.R.C.P. & S.I.	Temp. Lieut., R.A.M.C.
Bourke, Edmond M.	L.R.C.P. & S.I.	Major, R.A.M.C.
*Bourke, Ernest A.	*D.S.O.*, L.R.C.P. & S.I.	Lieut.-Col., R.A.M.C.
Bourke, George D.	*C.B.*, L.R.C.S.I.	Major-Genl., R.A.M.C.
Bourke, James J.	Student	2nd Lieut.
Bourke, James J. F.	L.R.C.P. & S.I.	Temp. Lieut., R.A.M.C.
Bourke, Ulick J.	L.R.C.S.I.	Lieut.-Col., R.A.M.C.
Bourke, Ulick L.	L.R.C.P. & S.I.	Capt. A.A.M.C.
*Bowen, Arthur W. N.	*D.S.O.*, L.R.C.P. & S.I.	Lieut.-Col., R.A.M.C.
Bowen, Robert E.	Student	Capt.
Bowen, Ralph J.	Student	Private, London Regt.
Boyce, William W.	L.R.C.P. & S.I.	Capt., R.A.M.C.

* Mentioned in Despatches.

29

ROYAL COLLEGE OF SURGEONS IN IRELAND.

*Boyd, Alfred H.	Student	Pte. D Compy 7th Battn. Royal Dublin Fusiliers
Boyd, Joseph	F.R.C.S.I.	Civil Surgeon
Boyd, Shepherd	F.R.C.S.I.	Capt., R.A.M.C.
Boyd, Thomas C.	F.R.C.S.I.	Capt., I.M.S.
Boyers, Hedley	L.D.S.I.	Capt.
Bracken, George P. A.	L.R.C.P. & S.I.	Capt., R.A.M.C.
Brackin, R. E. R.	Student	Temp. Lieut. Royal Dublin Fusiliers
*Bradish, Francis L.	*D.S.O.*, L.R.C.P. & S.I.	Capt., R.A.M.C.
Bradshaw, F.	L.R.C.P. & S.I.	Fleet Surgeon, R.N.
*Brennan, Charles H.	*M.C.*, L.R.C.P. & S.I.	Capt., R.A.M.C.
Brennan, John J.	L.R.C.P. & S.I.	Surgeon, R.N.
Briscoe, Arthur J.	Student	2nd Lieut., S. Lancashire Regt.
Briscoe, Moses	L.R.C.P. & S.I.	Temp. Lieut., R.A.M.C.
Broderick, Thomas F.	Student	Surgeon Probationer, R.N.V.R.
Bronte, Robert M.	L.R.C.P. & S.I.	Temp. Capt., R.A.M.C.
Brooke, James S. V. D.	F.R.C.S.I.	Surgeon Lt.-Col. M.O. I/c. of Troops
Brookes, R. J.	L.R.C.P. & S.I.	Temp. Lieut., R.A.M.C.
Brown, Alan P.	Student	Cadet Corpl.
*Brown, Robert T.	*D.S.O.*, D.P.H., R.C.P. & S.I.	Major, R.A.M.C.
Brown, Stephen E.	Student	Private, 9th Lancers
Brown, William J.	L.R.C.S.I.	National Reserve, R.A.M.C., Durham
Brown, Gerard	Student	Temp. Capt., Connaught Rangers

* Mentioned in Despatches.

ROYAL COLLEGE OF SURGEONS IN IRELAND.

*Browne, Abraham W.	L.R.C.P. & S.I.	Lieut.-Col., R.A.M.C.
Browne, Charles H.	D.P.H., R.C.P. & S.I.	Temp. Surgeon, R.N.
Browne, David John	Student	Lieut., R.I. Fusiliers
*Browne, Edward G.	*C.B., D.S.O.* D.P.H., R.C.P. & S.I.	Col., Army Medical Service
*Browne, Thomas W.	L.R.C.P. & S.I.	Capt., R.A.M.C.
Browne, William W.	D.P.H., R.C.P. & S.I.	Major, R.A.M.C.
Browning, Thomas	L.R.C.P. & S.I.	Major, R.A.M.C.
Brunker, Frederick W.	L.R.C.P. & S.I.	Lieut., R.A.M.C., Territorial Force
Bryan, Charles H.	L.R.C.P. & S.I.	Temp. Lieut., R.A.M.C.
Budd, Elizabeth	L.R.C.P. & S.I.	W.A.A.C.
Buchanan, Robert J. B.	D.P.H., R.C.P. & S.I.	Capt., R.A.M.C.
Bullen, John W.	D.P.H., R.C.P. & S.I.	Col., Army Medical Service
Bullen, Walter A.	Student	Lieut., Army Service Corps
*Burke, Bernard B.	L.R.C.P. & S.I.	Major, R.A.M.C.
*Burke, Henry J.	L.R.C.P. & S.I.	Capt., R.A.M.C.
Burke, John	L.R.C.P. & S.I.	Temp. Lieut., R.A.M.C.
Burkitt, John C. S.	D.P.H., R.C.P. & S.I.	Major, R.A.M.C. Territorial Force
Burns, Digby	L.R.C.P. & S.I.	Temp. Lieut., R.A.M.C.
Burton, W. R.	L.R.C.P. & S.I.	Temp. Lieut., R.A.M.C.
Burton, William E.	D.P.H., R.C.P. & S.I.	Capt., Cheshire Regt.
*Butler, C. Paget O'Brien	L.R.C.P. & S.I.	Capt., R.A.M.C.
*Butt, Edward	F.R.C.S.I., D.P.H.	Col., R.A.M.C.

* Mentioned in Despatches.

ROYAL COLLEGE OF SURGEONS IN IRELAND.

Butterly, —	L.R.C.P. & S.I.	M.O. I/c of Transport
Byrne, J. V.	L.D.S., R.C.S.I.	Temp. Lieut., R.A.M.C.
Byrne, F. M. J.	L.R.C.P. & S.I.	Temp. Lieut., R.A.M.C.
Byrne, Leopold F.	Student	Private, R.D.F.
†Byrne, William	Porter, Anatomy Dept.	Corporal, King's Royal Rifles
Byrne, J.	L.R.C.P. & S.I.	Temp. Lieut., R.A.M.C.
Cahill, Robert J.	D.P.H., R.C.P. & S.I.	Capt., R.A.M.C.
Cairns, Thomas	L.R.C.P. & S.I.	Recruiting M.O. 8th Battn Royal Worcester Regt.
Callaghan, James L.	L.R.C.S.I.	Temp. Lieut., R.A.M.C.
Callanan, Francis J.	Student	P.O., R.N.
Campbell Charles M. G.	L.R.C.P. & S.I.	Lieut., R.A.M.C. (Special Reserve)
Campbell, George A.	L.R.C.P. & S.I.	Temp. Lieut., R.A.M.C.
Cane, Edward G. S.	D.P.H., R.C.P. & S.I.	Capt., R.A.M.C.
Cane, R. J.	L.R.C.P. & S.I.	Temp. Lieut., R.A.M.C.
Cannon, Henry C. A. T.	L.R.C.P. & S.I.	Surgeon, R.N.
Carbery, Andrew R. D.	F.R.C.S.I.	Temp. Lieut., R.A.M.C.
Carden, Wilfrid H. W. C.	L.R.C.P. & S.I.	Temp. Lieut., R.A.M.C.
Carew, C. K.	L.R.C.P. & S.I.	Temp. Major, R.A.M.C.
Carrington, George H.	D.P.H., R.C.P. & S.I.	Capt., R.A.M.C., Territorial Force
Carson, William C.	L.R.C.P. & S.I.	Surgeon, R.N.
*Cary, Arthur	*T.D.*, L.R.C.P. & S.I.	Lieut.-Col., R.A.M.C. Territorial Force

* Mentioned in Despatches.

ROYAL COLLEGE OF SURGEONS IN IRELAND.

Carroll, James F.	Student	Second Lieut.
Carson, Robt. G.	Student	Lieut.
Casey, J.	L.R.C.P. & S.I.	M.O. I/c. of Troops
Cashin, J.	L.R.C.P. & S.I.	M.O. 3rd Berkshire Regt.
*Cassidy, Louis L.	F.R.C.S.I.	Temp. Capt., R.A.M.C.
Cathcart, John	D.P.H., R.C.P. & S.I.	Temp. Lieut., R.A.M.C.
Cecil, H. A.	L.R.C.P. & S.I.	Temp. Lieut., R.A.M.C.
Chalmers, Alexander	F.R.C.S.I.	Major, Indian Medical Service
Chambers, James	Student	2nd Lieut., A.S.C.
Chance, Arthur	F.R.C.S.I.	Temp. Capt., R.A.M.C.
Chance, Sir Arthur G.	F.R.C.S.I.	Temp. Col., A.M.S.
*Charles, Richard	F.R.C.S.I.	Temp. Capt., R.A.M.C.
Chatterton, Bernard R.	F.R.C.S.I.	Lt.-Col. Indian Medical Service
Cherry, John D.	L.R.C.P. & S.I.	Temp. Lieut., R.A.M.C.
Cherry, William N. L.	L.R.C.P. & S.I.	Staff Surgeon, R.N.
Clanchy, Arthur D.	L.R.C.P. & S.I.	Temp. Lieut., R.A.M.C.
Clarke, Herbert E.	L.R.C.P. & S.I.	Temp. Lieut., R.A.M.C.
Clarke, Miss Ina M.	F.R.C.S.I.	
Clarke, Isaac	L.R.C.P. & S.I.	Temp. Lieut., R.A.M.C.
Clarke, James J.	L.R.C.P. & S.I.	Temp. Lieut., R.A.M.C.
Clement, Robert H.	L.R.C.P. & S.I.	Major, R.A.M.C.
Clifford, Vernon J. V.	L.R.C.P. & S.I.	Temp. Lieut., R.A.M.C.

* Mentioned in Despatches.

ROYAL COLLEGE OF SURGEONS IN IRELAND.

CLINCH, ANDREW D.	D.P.H., R.C.P. & S.I.	Lieut., R.A.M.C. Territorial Force
*COFFEY, RICHARD	*D.S.O.*, L.R.C.P. & S.I.	Lieut.-Col., R.A.M.C.
COFFEY, T. M.	Student	Temp. Lieut., Royal Field Artillery
COLEMAN, T. C.	Student	Temp. Lieut., Royal Dublin Fusiliers
COLLINS, HUBERT S.		Capt., R.A.M.C.
COLLINS, T. F.	Student	Temp. Lieut., R.A.M.C.
COLLINS, GEOFFREY	L.R.C.P. & S.I.	Temp. Lieut., R.A.M.C.
COLT, MYLES	L.R.C.P. & S.I.	Temp. Capt., R.A.M.C.
CONDELL, W. H.	L.R.C.P. & S.I.	Temp. Capt., R.A.M.C.
CONDON, EDGAR H.	L.R.C.S.I.	Lieut.-Col., R.A.M.C.
CONNELL, O. G.	L.R.C.P. & S.I.	Temp. Lieut., R.A.M.C.
CONNELL, ERNEST	L.R.C.P. & S.I.	Temp. Lieut., R.A.M.C.
CONNOLLY, EDWARD P.	L.R.C.P. & S.I.	Lieut.-Col., R.A.M.C.
CONNOLLY, HUGH F.	Student	2nd Lieut., A.S.C.
CONNOLLY, JAMES J.	Student	Private
CONNOLLY, WILLIAM J.	L.R.C.P. & S.I.	Australian Contingent, Egypt
CONNOLLY, BENJAMIN B.	*C.B.*, F.R.C.S.I.	Col., A.M.S., A.D.M.S., Sussex District
CONNOR, V. F.	L.R.C.P. & S.I.	Capt., Canadian Army Medical Corps
CORMICK, M.	L.D.S.I.	Capt., R.A.M.C.
*CONWAY, JOHN M. H.	F.R.C.S.I.	Major, R.A.M.C.
COOKE, FRANCIS H.	L.R.C.P. & S.I.	Temp. Lieut., R.A.M.C.

* Mentioned in Despatches.

ROYAL COLLEGE OF SURGEONS IN IRELAND.

Cookson, Reginald G.	Student	Lieut., M.G.C.
Cooney, William P.	L.R.C.P. & S.I.	Temp. Lieut., R.A.M.C.
Cooper, Anthony A.	L.R.C.P. & S.I.	Temp. Lieut., R.A.M.C.
Cooper, Charles	L.R.C.P. & S.I.	Temp. Lieut., R.A.M.C.
Cope, Joseph Victor	F.R.C.S.I.	Capt., R.A.M.C.
Coppinger, Walter V.	F.R.C.S.I.	Major, Indian Medical Service
Corbett, William E.	L.R.C.P. & S.I.	Capt., 5th Devon Regt.
*Cotter, Henry J.	L.R.C.P. & S.I.	Temp. Capt., R.A.M.C.
Cotter, Thomas E.	L.R.C.P. & S.I.	Temp. Lieut., R.A.M.C.
Cox, Robert H.	F.R.C.S.I.	Temp. Lieut., R.A.M.C.
Cox, Stafford M.	L.R.C.P. & S.I.	Temp. Major, R.A.M.C.
Coxon, Stephen, A. T.	L.D.S., R.C.S.I.	Major, R.A.M.C.
Craig, Barry A.	L.R.C.P. & S.I.	Major, R.A.M.C.
Craig, Samuel McC.	Student	2nd Lieut., R.I.R.
Craig, John L.	Student	Lieut.
Cramb, Rutherford	D.P.H., R.C.P. & S.I.	Temp. Lieut., R.A.M.C.
Crawford, Alfred N.	F.R.C.S.I.	Capt., R.A.M.C., Lancs. Field Artillery, Territorial Force
Crawford, Herbert deC.	F.R.C.S.I.	Temp. Capt., R.A.M.C.
Crawford, John M. M.	F.R.C.S.I.	Major, R.A.M.C.
Crawford, H. de L.	F.R.C.S.I.	Temp. Lieut., R.A.M.C.
Crawley, Frank C.	F.R.C.S.I.	Temp. Capt., R.A.M.C.
Creagh, P. N.	L.R.C.P. & S.I.	Temp. Lieut., R.A.M.C.

* Mentioned in Despatches.

ROYAL COLLEGE OF SURGEONS IN IRELAND.

*CREAN, THOMAS J.	*V.C.*, L.R.C.P. & S.I.	Capt., R.A.M.C.
†CREAN, A. J.	Student	Private, Motor Transport
*CRIMMIN, JOHN	*V.C.*, *C.B.*, *C.I.E.*, L.R.C.S.I.	Col., Indian Medical Service
*CROLY, ARTHUR E. J.	F.R.C.S.I.	Col., A.M.S.
*CROLY, WILLIAM C.	L.R.C.P. & S.I.	Lt.-Col., R.A.M.C.
CROLY, WILLIAM H.	L.R.C.P. & S.I.	Temp. Lieut., R.A.M.C.
CRONHELM, THEODOREA	Student	Private
CRONYN, JOHN G.	L.R.C.P. & S.I.	Lieutenant
CRONYN, J. G.	L.R.C.P. & S.I.	Temp. Lieut., R.A.M.C.
CROSBIE, DOUGLAS E.	L.R.C.P. & S.I.	Temp. Lieut., R.A.M.C.
CROSBIE PIERCE L.	F.R.C.S.I.	Staff Surgeon, R.N.
CROSSLÉ, HOWARD	D.P.H., R.C.P. & S.I.	Major, Indian Medical Service
CROSTHWAITE, WILLIAM S.	L.R.C.P. & S.I.	Major, R.A.M.C.
†CRYMBLE, WILLIAM	L.R.C.P. & S.I.	Capt., R.A.M.C. (Special Reserve)
CUFFE, ALEXANDER	F.R.C.S.I.	Lieut., R.A.M.C. (Territorial Force)
CUMMINS, ARTHUR D. C.	L.R.C.P. & S.I.	Staff-Surgeon, R.N.
CUNNINGHAM, HERBERT H. B.	F.R.C.S.I.	Lieut.-Col., R.A.M.C.
CUNNINGHAN, WM. A.	Student	Cadet
CURRAN, DOMINIC F.	L.R.C.P. & S.I.	Temp. Capt., R.A.M.C.
CUSACK, B. J.	L.R.C.P. & S.I.	Temp. Lieut., R.A.M.C.

* Mentioned in Despatches. † Killed in Action.

ROYAL COLLEGE OF SURGEONS IN IRELAND.

D'ARCY, SAMUEL A.	L.R.C.P. & S.I.	Temp. Major, R.A.M.C.
D'ARCY, THOMAS N.	Student	Surgeon Probationer, R.N.V.R.
†D'ALTON, CHARLES	L.R.C.P. & S.I.	Lt.-Col. R.A.M.C.
DALY, EDMUND J.	Student	2nd Lieut., R. Munster Fus.
DALY, JAMES H.	L.R.C.P. & S.I.	Col., Army Medical Service
*DALY, PETER	L.R.C.P. & S.I.	Temp. Capt., R.A.M.C.
DALY, THOMAS	L.R.C.P. & S.I.	Col., Army Medical Service
DARLEY, ARTHUR LAT.	L.R.C.P. & S.I.	Staff-Surgeon, R.N.
†DARLEY, F. B.	Student	Pte., Princess Patricia's Canadian Light Infantry.
†DAUBER, JOHN H.	F.R.C.S.I.	Major, R.A.M.C. (Territorial Force)
DAUNT, B. J.	L.R.C.P. & S.I.	Temp. Lieut., R.A.M.C.
DAVIDGE, GEORGE S.	L.R.C.P. & S.I.	Staff-Surgeon, R.N.
DAVIS, JAMES H. E.	L.R.C.P. & S.I.	Temp. Lieut., R.A.M.C.
DAVIS, WILLIAM	L.R.C.P. & S.I.	Major, R.A.M.C.
DAVOREN, VESEY H. W.	L.R.C.P. & S.I.	Retired Major, R.A.M.C. (Reserve of Officers re-employed)
DAVYS, GERALD J.	D.P.H., R.C.P. & S.I.	Major, Indian Medical Service
DAVYS, JOHN H. J. L.	L.R.C.P. & S.I.	Temp. Capt., R.A.M.C.
DAY, JOHN C. L.	L.R.C.P. & S.I.	Temp. Capt., R.A.M.C.
*DEANE, ERNEST C.	L.R.C.P. & S.I.	Capt., R.A.M.C.
DEANE, NORMAN S.	L.R.C.P. & S.I.	Temp. Capt., R.A.M.C.
DEIGHAN, WILLIAM J.	L.R.C.P. & S.I.	Temp. Capt., R.A.M.C.
DE CAESTECKER, MAURICE (of Ypres)	L.R.C.P. & S.I.	Belgian Medical Corps

* Mentioned in Despatches. † Killed in Action.

ROYAL COLLEGE OF SURGEONS IN IRELAND.

De Lacey, Robert C.	L.D.S., R.C.S.I.	Temp. Lieut., R.A.M.C.
Delamere, Percy H.	L.R.C.S.I.	Temp. Capt., R.A.M.C.
Delany, Thomas H.	F.R.C.S.I.	Lt.-Col, Indian Medical Service
Delany, John James	L.R.C.P. & S.I.	Temp. Lieut., R.A.M.C.
Delap, George G.	*C.M.G., D.S.O.,* L.R.C.P. & S.I.	Lieut.-Col., R.A.M.C.
Denham, Charles H.	D.P.H., R.C.P. & S.I.	Temp. Capt., R.A.M.C.
Devine, James	L.R.C.P. & S.I.	Temp. Lieut., R.A.M.C.
Dewar, E. P.	L.R.C.P. & S.I.	Temp. Lieut., R.A.M.C.
Dickinson, Richard F. O'T.	L.R.C.P. & S.I.	Capt., R.A.M.C.
Dickson, James A. N.	Student	2nd Lieut., Royal Inniskillen Fusiliers
Dickson, John W.	Student	Lieut., 1st Garrison Batt. , Royal Irish Rifles
Dickson, Robert Francis Goldrick	Student	Lieut., R.D.F.
Digby, Terence K.	Student	Lieut., R.I. Rifles
Dillon, Eugene E. M.	Student	Lieut., 1st Battn. King's Own Regt., Royal Lancs.
Dickson, Wm. A.	Student	Lieut., R.I.R.
*Dillon-Kelly, Cecil F.	*M.C.*, L.R.C.P. & S.I.	Temp. Capt., R.A.M.C.
*Dillon-Kelly, Lomond C.	L.R.C.P. & S.I.	Temp. Capt., R.A.M.C.
Dimond, William E. R.	L.R.C.P. & S.I.	Temp. Capt., R.A.M.C.
Dobbs, T. E.	L.R.C.P. & S.I.	Temp. Lieut., R.A.M.C.
Dobbyn, Michael G.	F.R.C.S.I.	Temp. Lieut., R.A.M.C.
Dockrell, Maurice	L.R.C.P. & S.I.	Temp. Lieut., R.A.M.C.

* Mentioned in Despatches

ROYAL COLLEGE OF SURGEONS IN IRELAND.

DOLAN, S. C.	Student	Temp Lieut., 5th Royal Irish Fusiliers
DONOVAN, WILLIAM	*C.B.*, L.R.C.S.I.	Surgeon-General, R.A.M.C.
DORGAN, JAMES	D.P.H., R.C.P. & S.I.	Major, R.A.M.C.
DOUGAN, FREDERICK R.		
DOUGAN, GEORGE	D.P.H., R.C.P. & S.I.	Temp. Lieut., R.A.M.C.
DOUGLAS, GERALD S.	L.R.C.P. & S.I.	Temp. Lieut., R.A.M.C.
DOWRIS, VALENTINE A.	Student	Private, King's Liverpool R.
DOWLING, IGNATIUS A.	L.R.C.P. & S.I.	Temp. Lieut., R.A.M.C.
DOWSE, WILLIAM ST. L.	L.R.C.P. & S.I.	Capt., R.A.M.C. (Special Reserve)
DOWZER, J. J. M.	L.R.C.P. & S.I.	Temp. Lieut., R.A.M.C,
*DOWZER, THOMAS	*M.C.*, L.R.C.P. & S.I.	Temp. Lieut., R.A.M.C.
DOYLE, PATRICK A.	L.R.C.P. & S.I.	Temp. Capt., R.A.M.C.
DOYLE, JOSEPH P.	L.R.C.P. & S.I.	Temp. Lieut., R.A.M.C.
DREAPER, GEORGE A.	L.R.C.S.I.	Deputy Surgeon-General, Royal Navy
DUDLEY, HARRY	Student	R.A.M.C.
DUGDALE, WILLIAM	L.R.C.S.I.	Lieut.-Col., R.A.M.C. (Retired, temporarily re-employed)
DUNCAN, ALEXANDER H. R.	L.R.C.P. & S.I.	Temp. Capt., R.A.M.C.
*DUNCAN, THOMAS	*M.C.*, L.R.C.P. & S.I.	Temp. Capt., R.A.M.C.
DUNLOP, WILLIAM J.	L.R.C.P. & S.I.	Temp. Capt., R.A.M.C.
DUNNE, JOHN JOSEPH	Student	Lieut., R.I.R.
*DUNNE, JAMES S.	*D.S.O.*, F.R.C.S.I.	Capt., R.A.M.C.

* Mentioned in Despatches.

ROYAL COLLEGE OF SURGEONS IN IRELAND.

DUNNE, J. S.	Student	Temp. Lieut., 16th Durham Light Infantry
DUNNE, P. J.	Student	Temp. Lieut., Royal Irish Fusiliers
DUNWOODY, WM. O.	Student	Private, S.I.H.
DWYER, F. CONWAY	F.R.C.S.I.	Temp. Lt.-Col., R.A.M.C.
*DWYER, JAMES J.	*D.S.O.*, L.R.C.P. & S.I.	Capt., R.A.M.C.
DWYER, JOSEPH J.	L.R.C.P. & S.I.	Temp. Lieut., R.A.M.C.
*DWYER, PATRICK	D.P.H., R.C.P. & S.I.	Major, R.A.M.C.
EAGER, FRANCIS J.	L.R.C.P. & S.I.	Temp. Capt., R.A.M.C.
EAGLESON, HERBERT J.	Student	2nd Lieut., Leinster Regt.
EARL, CHARLES J. C.	Student	Surgeon Prob., R.N.V.R.
*EDGE, JOHN D.	*C.B.*, F.R.C.S.I.	Surgeon-Genl., R.A.M.C.
EGAN, JAMES D. O'D.	L.R.C.P. & S.I.	Lieut., R.A.M.C.
EGAN, LOUIS E.	L.D.S., R.C.S.I.	Temp. Lieut., R.A.M.C.
EGAN, JOHN P.	L.R.C.P. & S.I.	Temp. Lieut., R.A.M.C.
ELDERTON FREDERICK D.	L.R.C.P. & S.I.	Major, R.A.M.C.
ELLENCOGAN, J.	L.R.C.P. & S.I.	Temp. Lieut., R.A.M.C.
ELLIOTT, BRERETON G.	L.R.C.P. & S.I.	Capt., 4th East Lancs. Regt.
ELLIOTT, JOSEPH JOHN	L.R.C.P. & S.I.	Temp. Lieut., R.A.M.C.
ELLIOTT, ROBERT	Student	Corporal, 44th Field Ambulance.
ELLIOTT, THOMAS R.	L.R.C.P. & S.I.	Temp. Capt., R.A.M.C.
ELLIOTT, GEORGE B.	L.R.C.P. & S.I.	Temp. Capt., R.A.M.C.

* Mentioned in Despatches.

ROYAL COLLEGE OF SURGEONS IN IRELAND.

Elliott, John F.	L.R.C.P. & S.I.	R.A.M.C.
Ellis, Abraham E.	L.R.C.P. & S.I.	Temp. Lieut., R.A.M.C.
Elmes, King	L.R.C.P. & S.I.	Temp. Capt., R.A.M.C.
*Elsner, Otto W. A.	*D.S.O.*, L.R.C.P. & S.I.	Lieut.-Col., R.A.M.C.
*Elvery, Philip G. M.	*D.S.O.*, L.R.C.P. & S.I.	Lieut.-Col., R.A.M.C.
Emerson, Isaac B.	L.R.C.P. & S.I.	Lieut.-Col., R.A.M.C.
England, Robt. H.	Student	Sergt., R.A.M.C.
Enright, George H.	L.R.C.P. & S.I.	Temp. Lieut., R.A.M.C.
*Enright, Thomas L.	L.R.C.P. & S.I.	Temp. Capt., R.A.M.C.
Erskine, R. M.	L.R.C.P. & S.I.	Temp. Capt., R.A.M.C.
Eustace, William N.	L.R.C.P. & S.I.	Temp. Lieut., R.A.M.C.
Evans, Edward	L.R.C.P. & S.I.	Temp. Lieut., R.A.M.C.
†Evans, George E. K.	Student	Temp. 2nd Lieut., Leinster Regt.
Evans, Joseph Austin	L.R.C.P. & S.I.	Temp. Lieut., R.A.M.C.
Evatt, Evelyn John	*D.S.O.*, Prof. of Anatomy, F.R.C.S.I.	Lieut.-Col., R.A.M.C. 1st Welsh Field Ambulance
Evatt, George J. H.	*C.B.*, L.R.C.S.I.	Surg.-Genl., R.A.M.C. (Territorial Force)
Ewing, C. W.	L.R.C.P. & S.I.	Temp. Lieut., R.A.M.C.
Fagan, Joseph P.	L.R.C.P. & S.I.	Temp. Capt., R.A.M.C.
Falkiner, John McI.	F.R.C.S.I.	Temp. Capt., R.A.M.C.
*Falkner, Mervyn W.	L.R.C.P. & S.I.	Major, R.A.M.C.
Falkner, Henry G.	L.R.C.P. & S.I.	Temp. Lieut., R.A.M.C.

* Mentioned in Despatches. † Killed in Action.

ROYAL COLLEGE OF SURGEONS IN IRELAND.

Falkner, Percy H.	L.R.C.P. & S.I.	Lieut.-Col., R.A.M.C.
Farmer, Charles H.	Student	Private, R.A.M.C.
Farrell, Charles A.	L.R.C.P. & S.I.	Temp. Capt., R.A.M.C.
Fawcett, Frederick O'D.	L.R.C.P. & S.I.	Capt. Indian Medical Service
*Fegen, Charles M.	D.P.H., R.C.P. & S.I.	Major, R.A.M.C.
Fehily, Thomas	L.R.C.P. & S.I.	Temp. Lieut., R.A.M.C.
Fenton, Victor E. A.	L.R.C.P. & S.I.	Temp. Lieut., R.A.M.C.
Ferguson, John D.	*D.S.O.* L.R.C.P. & S.I.	Lieut.-Col., R.A.M.C.
*Fergusson, John C.	*M.C.*, L.R.C.P. & S.I.	Temp. Capt., R.A.M.C.
*Ferguson, Hugh R. M.	D.P.H., R.C.P. & S.I.	Capt., R.A.M.C.
Ferguson, Malcolm	L.R.C.P. & S.I.	Capt., R.A.M.C.
Ferguson, Percy	Student	Sergt. A. I. F.
†Ferris, David H.	Student	Surgeon-Probationer, R.N.V.R.
Fetherston, Richard H. J.	L.R.C.P. & S.I.	Temp. Surgeon-General, Australian Medical Corps
Ffrench, William J. L.	L.R.C.P. & S.I.	Red Cross Hospital, Lincs.
Filose, Nicholas A.	L.R.C.P. & S.I.	On the Staff Maharajah of Gwalior
Filose, Patrick J.	L.R.C.P. & S.I.	On the Staff Maharajah of Gwalior
Finegan, George A.	L.R.C.P. & S.I.	Surgeon, R.N.
Fisher, Thomas A.	L.R.C.P. & S.I.	Capt., R.A.M.C.
Fitzgerald, Arthur O.	L.R.C.P. & S.I.	Major, R.A.M.C.
*Fitzgerald, Charles C.	D.P.H., R.C.P. & S.I.	Temp. Lieut., R.A.M.C.
*Fitzgerald, Desmond C. V.	L.R.C.P. & S.I.	Capt. Indian Medical Service

* Mentioned in Despatches. † Killed in Action.

ROYAL COLLEGE OF SURGEONS IN IRELAND.

*FITZGERALD, G. FITZGERALD	L.R.C.P. & S.I.	Major, R.A.M.C.
FITZGERALD, RICHARD L.	L.R.C.S.I.	Surgeon-Captain
FITZMAURICE, FRANCIS E.	L.R.C.P. & S.I.	Surgeon, R.N.
FITZPATRICK, DENIS F.	Student	Private
FITZPATRICK, JAMES P.	L.R.C.P. & S.I.	Temp. Lieut., R.A.M.C.
FLANAGAN, GEORGE B. N.	L.R.C.P. & S.I.	Temp. Lieut., R.A.M.C.
FLANEGAN, HENRY J.	F.R.C.S.I.	Temp. Lieut., R.A.M.C.
FLANNERY, HORACE T.	Student	Lieut., 2nd Leinster Regt.
FLANNERY, J. A. J.	Student	Pte., 7th Leinster Regt.
FLEETWOOD, WILLIAM J.	L.R.C.S.I.	Lieut.-Col. R.A.M.C. (Territorial Force)
FLOOD, PATRICK J.	L.R.C.P. & S.I.	Temp. Lieut., R.A.M.C.
FLYNN, ROBERT A.	L.R.C.P. & S.I.	Temp. Lieut., R.A.M.C.
FLYNN, THOMAS A.	L.R.C.P. & S.I.	Lieut., R.A.M.C. (Territorial Force)
FOLEY, EDWARD G.	L.R.C.P. & S.I.	Capt., R.A.M.C.
FOLEY, JOHN	L.R.C.P. & S.I.	Temp. Lieut., R.A.M.C.
FOLEY, DANIEL H.	L.R.C.P. & S.I.	Temp. Lieut., R.A.M.C.
FOLEY, THOMAS McC.	L.R.C.P. & S.I.	Lieut.-Col (Hon. Col.), R.F.A. (T.F.)
FOOTT, ALEXANDER B.	L.R.C.P. & S.I.	Capt., R.A.M.C. (Special Reserve)
FORD, RICHARD A. W.	L.R.C.P. & S.I.	Temp. Surgeon, R.N.
FORDE, BERNARD	*C.M.G.*, D.P.H., R.C P. & S.I.	Lieut.-Col., R.A.M.C.
FORRESTER, A. W.	L.R.C.P. & S.I.	South Rhodesia
FOWLER, WM. P.		
FOX, WILLIAM A. N.	L.R.C.P. & S.I.	Capt., R.A.M.C. (Special Reserve)

* Mentioned in Despatches.

ROYAL COLLEGE OF SURGEONS IN IRELAND.

Fox, Hugh C.	F.R.C.S.I.	Temp. Lieut., R.A.M.C.
Francis, George A.	L.R.C.P. & S.I.	Temp. Lieut., R.A.M.C.
*Franklin, Robert J.	L.R.C.P. & S.I.	Major, R.A.M.C.
Fraser, George	L.R.C.P. & S.I.	Temp. Lieut., R.A.M.C.
*Freeman, Francis P.	L.R.C.P. & S.I.	Capt., R.A.M.C.
Fretton, John A.	L.R.C.P. & S.I.	Temp. Capt., R.A.M.C.
Friel, Alfred R.	F.R.C.S.I.	Capt., Sth. African Military Service
Friel, Robert	F.R.C.S.I.	
*Fullerton, Andrew	*C.M.G.*, F.R.C.S.I.	Temp. Col., A.M.S.
Furlong, S. A.	L.R.C.P. & S.I.	Temp. Lieut., R.A.M.C.
Garret, George A.	Student	Gunner, R.F.A.
Gage, John M.	L.R.C.P. & S.I.	Temp. Capt., R.A.M.C.
Gailey, S. A.	Student	Surgeon Probationer, R.N.V.R.
Gallagher, G. H.	L.R.C.P. & S.I.	West African Medical Staff
†Gatchell, J. H.	*M.C.* Student	Temp. Capt., R.A.M.C.
Gasteen, Henry D.	L.R.C.P. & S.I.	Temp. Capt., R.A.M.C.
*Gater, Cyril E. H.	L.R.C.P. & S.I.	Capt., R.A.M.C. (Special Reserve)
Gentleman, Benson E.	L.D.S., R.C.S.I.	Temp. Lieut., R.A.M.C.
Gibbons, James B.	L.R.C.P. & S.I.	Lieut.-Col., Indian Medical Service (Retired, temp. re-employed)
Gibbons, John F.	L.R.C.P. & S.I.	Temp. Lieut., R.A.M.C.

* Mentioned in Despatches. † Killed in Action.

ROYAL COLLEGE OF SURGEONS IN IRELAND.

Gibbs, Andrew A.	L.R.C.P. & S.I.	Lieut.-Col., Indian Medical Service
†Gibson, Benjamin	L.R.C.P. & S.I.	Capt., 5th Field Artillery Brigade, 2nd Australian Division
Gibson, James A.	D.P.H., R.C.P. & S.I.	Capt., R.A.M.C., Territorial Force
Gilchrist, Thomas	F.R.C.S.I.	Temp. Capt., R.A.M.C.
Giles, James A.	D.P.H., R.C.P. & S.I.	Temp. Lieut., R.A.M.C.
*Gill, James G.	*D.S.O.*, *M.C.*, L.R.C.P. & S.I.	Lieut.-Col., R.A.M.C.
Gill, N. B.	Student	Temp. Lieut., 11th North Staffs. Regt.
Gillies, David	L.R.C.P. & S.I.	Temp. Lieut., R.A.M.C.
Gilmore, Haldane C.	L.R.C.P. & S.I.	Temp. Lieut., R.A.M.C.
Glasson, Bernard	Student	Temp. Major, Royal Garrison Artillery
Glenny, William C. W.	L.R.C.P. & S.I.	Temp. Lieut., R.A.M.C.
Glynn, Patrick D.	L.R.C.P. & S.I.	Temp. Lieut., R.A.M.C.
*Godkin, Samuel R.	*D.S.O.*, F.R.C.S.I.	Major, Indian Medical Service
Golding, Marks	L.R.C.P. & S.I.	Temp. Lieut., R.A.M.C.
†Golding, Thomas J.	L.R.C.P. & S.I.	Temp. Capt., R.A.M.C.
Goldon, T. M.	Student	Lieut., R.A.F.
Good, Susanna H.	L.R.C.P. & S.I.	Q.M.A.A.C.
*Goodbody, Cecil M.	F.R.C.S.I.	Major, Indian Medical Service
Gordon, S. G.	L.R.C.P. & S.I.	Temp. Lieut., R.A.M.C.
Gordon, Thomas E.	F.R.C.S.I.	Temp. Lt.-Col., R.A.M.C.
Gordon, Reginald E.		
Graham, J. W. E.	L.D.S., R.C.S.I.	Temp. Lieut., R.A.M.C.

* Mentioned in Despatches. † Killed in Action.

ROYAL COLLEGE OF SURGEONS IN IRELAND.

Graham, Herbert	L.R.C.P. & S.I.	Lieut., R.A.M.C.
Graham, M. J.	L.R.C.P. & S.I.	Temp. Lieut., R.A.M.C.
*Graham, Thomas O.	F.R.C.S.I.	Capt., R.A.M.C. (Special Reserve)
Grainger, J. P.	L.R.C.P. & S.I.	Temp. Lieut., R.A.M.C.
Gray, Edwin N. H.	L.R.C.P. & S.I.	Capt., R.A.M.C. (Special Reserve)
Gray, Harold	L.R.C.P. & S.I.	Temp. Lieut., R.A.M.C.
Gray, John McFarlane	Student	Surg. Prob., R.N.
Greehy, William J.	L.R.C.P. & S.I.	Temp. Lieut., R.A.M.C.
Green, John G. J.	F.R.C.S.I.	Capt., R.A.M.C.
Green, Robert	L.R.C.P. & S.I.	Major, R.A.M.C. (Special Reserve)
Greene, Arthur	F.R.C.S.I.	Capt., R.A.M.C.
Greene, G. E. J.	L.R.C.P. & S.I.	Temp. Lieut., R.A.M.C.
Greenwood, Alfred	D.P.H., R.C.P. & S.I.	Lieut.-Col., R.A.M.C.
Greer, William J.	F.R.C.S.I.	Capt., R.A.M.C.
Gregg, Edward A.	L.R.C.P. & S.I.	Capt., R.A.M.C.
*Greig, Frederick J.	L.R.C.S.I.	Lieut.-Col., R.A.M.C.
Griffin, Samuel	Student	Capt., Royal Irish Regt.
Griffin, Reginald E. J. St. J.	L.R.C.P. & S.I.	Temp. Lieut., R.A.M.C.
Griffin, Thomas F.	L.R.C.P. & S.I.	Temp. Capt., R.A.M.C.
Griffith, Thomas F.	Student	Private
Gubbins, Sir William L.	*K.C.B., M.V.O.* Hon. F.R.C.S.I.	
Gunn, K. E. Leveson G.	F.R.C.S.I.	Temp. Major, R.A.M.C.

* Mentioned in Despatches.

46

ROYAL COLLEGE OF SURGEONS IN IRELAND.

Gunn, Michael B.	L.R.C.P. & S.I.	Captain, A.A.M.C.
Gunning, Robert C.	L.R.C.P. & S.I.	Lieut.-Col. R.A.M.C. (Retired temporarily re-employed)
Halligan, A. M. J.	L.R.C.P. & S.I.	Temp. Capt., R.A.M.C.
Hamilton, James A.	D.P.H., R.C.P. & S.I.	Major, R.A.M.C. (Territorial Force)
Hamilton, William R. G.	F.R.C.S.I.	Temp. Lieut., R.A.M.C.
Hamilton, James A.	L.R.C.P. & S.I.	Surgeon, R.N.
Hamilton, John D.	L.R.C.P. & S.I.	Temp. Lieut., R.A.M.C.
Hanafin, John B.	F.R.C.S.I.	Capt. Indian Medical Service
*Hanafin, Patrick J.	*D.S.O.*, L.R.C.P. & S.I.	Major, R.A.M.C.
Hanbury, Samuel B.	L.R.C.P. & S.I.	Temp. Lieut., R.A.M.C.
Hannigan, F.	L.R.C.P. & S.I.	Temp. Lieut., R.A.M.C.
Hanofin, de Courcy	Student	Private, 2nd Batt., Welsh Regt.
Hanratty, Francis V.	L.R.C.P. & S.I.	Temp. Lieut., R.A.M.C.
Harboard, A. F. E.	Student	Temp. Lieut., Connaught Rangers
Harling, Walter Wm.	Student	Private, R.A.M.C.
*Harding, Daniel L.	F.R.C.S.I., D.P.H.	Major, R.A.M.C.
Harding, E. P.	L.R.C.P. & S.I.	Temp. Lieut., R.A.M.C.
Harper, Alexander F.	L.R.C.P. & S.I.	Fleet Surgeon, R.N.
Harding, Sidney W.	Student	2nd Lieut., 3rd Leinster Regt.
Harrison, Henry M.	L.R.C.P. & S.I.	Temp. Lieut., R.A.M.C.

* Mentioned in Despatches.

ROYAL COLLEGE OF SURGEONS IN IRELAND.

HARTE, THOMAS C.	L.R.C.P. & S.I.	Temp. Capt., R.A.M.C.
HARTFORD, A. H. B.	L.R.C.P. & S.I.	Temp. Lieut., R.A.M.C.
HARTY, JAMES J.	F.R.C.S.I.	Temp. Lieut., R.A.M.C.
HARVEY, FRANK N.	L.R.C.P. & S.I.	Temp. Capt., R.A.M.C.
*HARVEY, GEORGE A. D.	*C.M.G.*, L.R.C.P. & S.I.	Major, R.A.M.C.
*HARVEY, J. J. G.	Student	Capt., R.E.
HASTINGS, A. E. F.	L.R.C.P. & S.I.	Capt., R.A.M.C.
HAWKINS, V. H.	Student	Temp. Lieut., Manchester Regt.
HAWES, FRANCIS B.	L.R.C.S.I.	Temp. Capt., R.A.M.C.
HAWTHORNE, ERNEST S.	F.R.C.S.I., D.P.H.	Temp. Capt., R.A.M.C.
HAY, MALCOLM B.	D.P.H., R.C.P. & S.I.	Temp. Surgeon, R.N.
HAYDEN, BERNARD	Student	Lt.-Col., R. Welsh Fusiliers
HAYES, JOHN M.	L.R.C.P. & S.I.	Surgeon, R.N.
HAYES, M. R. J.	F.R.C.S.I.	Temp. Capt., R.A.M.C.
HAYMAN, ALBERT A.	Student.	Capt.
*HEALEY, CORYNDON W. R.	*C.M.G.*, L.R.C.P. & S.I.	Col., A.M.S.
HEALEY, H. J.	L.D.S., R.C.S.I.	Temp. Lieut., R.A.M.C.
HEALY, SYLVESTER J.	L.R.C.P. & S.I.	R.A.M.C.
HEANEY, FRANCIS J. S.	F.R.C.S.I.	Surgeon, R.N.V.R.
HEARN, MICHAEL L.	L.R.C.S.I.	Lieut.-Col., R.A.M.C.
HEGARTY, CECIL F. C.	Student	Lieut., Connaught Rangers
HEFFERNAN, FRANCIS J. C.	F.R.C.S.I.	Lieut.-Col., R.A.M.C.

* Mentioned in Despatches.

ROYAL COLLEGE OF SURGEONS IN IRELAND.

Heffernan, John T.	L.R.C.P. & S.I.	Temp. Lieut., R.A.M.C.
Henderson, Greer A.	Student	Temp. Lieut., Royal Dublin Fusiliers
Henry, H. G.	Student	15th Durham Light Infantry
Henry, Arnold K.	F.R.C.S.I.	Temp. Lieut., R.A.M.C.
Herbert, C. E.	Student	Temp. Lt., 6th Leinster Regt.
Heron, Austin	Student	Corpl., R. Inniskilling Fusiliers
*Herrick, Henry	*D.S.O.*, L.R.C.P. & S.I.	Lieut.-Col., R.A.M.C.
*Herrick, Robert de S. B.	L.R.C.P. & S.I.	Capt. Indian Medical Service
Herron, Robert T.	L.R.C.S.I.	Lieut., R.A.M.C.
Hewetson, J. R.	L.R.C.P. & S.I.	Temp. Lieut., R.A.M.C.
Hewison, G. T.	Student	Temp. Lt., 3rd Royal Munster Fusiliers
*Hewson, Falkiner M.	L.R.C.P. & S.I.	Capt., R.A.M.C.
Hewson, Charles K. T.	L.R.C.P. & S.I.	Temp. Lieut., R.A.M.C.
Heywood T. W.	D.P.H., R.C.P. & S.I.	Temp. Lieut., R.A.M.C.
Higgins, Edwd. J.	Student	Sapper
Higgins, F. F.	L.R.C.P. & S.I.	Temp. Lieut., R.A.M.C.
Hill, J. T.	L.R.C.P. & S.I.	Temp. Lieut., R.A.M.C.
*Hill, Samuel Frederick	Student	2nd Lt., 1st Battery R.F.A.
Hillis, Robert W. H.	L.R.C.P. & S.I.	Temp. Lieut., R.A.M.C.
Hipwell, Abraham	L.R.C.P. & S.I.	Temp. Lieut., R.A.M.C.
Hobbs, John	L.R.C.P. & S.I.	Capt., R.A.M.C., Egyptian E.F.
*Hodges, Richard H.	L.R.C.P. & S.I.	Capt., R.A.M.C. (Special Reserve)

* Mentioned in Despatches.

ROYAL COLLEGE OF SURGEONS IN IRELAND.

*HOLDEN, ARTHUR C.	L.D.S., R.C.S.I.	Temp. Lieut., R.A.M.C.
*HOLDEN, CHARLES W.	*C.M.G., D.S.O.*, L.R.C.P. & S.I.	Temp. Lt.-Col., R.A.M.C.
HOLDEN, ERNEST E.	L.R.C.P. & S.I.	Temp. Lieut., R.A.M.C.
HOLDEN, PERCY	Student	Lieut., A.S.C.
HOLLAND, JAMES K.	L.R.C.P. & S.I.	Temp. Lieut., R.A.M.C.
HOLMES, CHARLES J.	F.R.C.S.I.	Major, R.A.M.C.
HOLMES, JOHN M.	D.P.H., R.C.P. & S.I.	Major, Indian Medical Service
HOLMES, J. F.	Student	Lce.-Cpl., Royal Fusiliers
HOLMES, P. J.	L.R.C.P. & S.I.	Temp. Lieut., R.A.M.C.
*HOPKINS, WILLIAM E.	*M.C.*, F.R.C.S.I.	Temp. Capt., R.A.M.C.
HORAN, JAMES M.	L.R.C.P. & S.I.	Surgeon, R.N.
HORGAN-GAUL, NICHOLAS	Student	Lieut., R.F.A.
HOPTON, WM.	Student	2nd Lt., 4th Batt. N. Riding Regt.
*HOUGHTON, GEORGE J.	*D.S.O.*, L.R.C.P. & S.I.	Major, R.A.M.C.
HOWLEY, HENRY E.	L.R.C.P. & S.I.	Major, R.A.M.C.
HUBAN, JOHN P.	Student	Capt., R.A.M.C.
HUDSON, EDWARD	Museum Porter	Private, R.A.M.C.
HUMFREY, RICHARD E.	L.R.C.P. & S.I.	Capt., R.A.M.C.
HUMPHREYS, CHARLES E.	D.P.H., R.C.P. & S.I.	Major, R.A.M.C.
HUMPHREYS, FRANCIS R.	Student	Lieut., Army Service Corps
HUMPHREYS, JOSEPH	L.R.C.P. & S.I.	Temp. Lieut., R.A.M.C.
HUNT, HENRY	L.R.C.P. & S.I.	Fleet Surgeon, R.N.

* Mentioned in Despatches.

ROYAL COLLEGE OF SURGEONS IN IRELAND.

Hunt, Richard B.	L.R.C.P. & S.I.	Temp. Lieut., R.A.M.C.
Hust, Henry	L.R.C.P. & S.I.	Surgeon, R.N.
Iles, Charles C.	D.P.H., R.C.P. & S.I.	Temp. Lieut., R.A.M.C.
*Irvine, Arthur E. S.	L.R.C.P. & S.I.	Major, Deputy Assist., Director of Medical Services
Irvine, Gerald B.	*M.C.*, L.R.C.P. & S.I.	Lieut.-Col. Indian Medical Service
Irvine, Thomas W.	D.P.H., R.C.P. & S.I.	Lieut.-Col., Indian Medical Service
*Irwin, Alfred W. A.	L.R.C.P. & S.I.	Major, R.A.M.C.
*Irwin, N. L. C.	*D.S.O.*, Student	Temp. Capt., Royal Welsh Fus.
Jacob, Archibald H.	L.R.C.P. & S.I.	Temp. Lieut., R.A.M.C.
Jennings, James W.	*D.S.O.*, L.R.C.P. & S.I.	Major, R.A.M.C.
Jennings, William E.	D.P.H., R.C.P. & S.I.	Lieut.-Col. Indian Medical Service
Johnson, William G. F.	L.R.C.S.I.	Temp. Capt., R.A.M.C.
Johnston, Leslie C.	L.R.C.P. & S.I.	Temp. Lieut., R.A.M.C.
Johnston, William H.	L.R.C.P. & S.I.	Temp. Lieut., R.A.M.C.
Johnston, William V.	L.R.C.P. & S.I.	Temp. Capt., R.A.M.C.
Johnston, G. Jameson	F.R.C.S.I.	Temp. Lt.-Col., R.A.M.C.
Johnston, Robt. Alexander	L.M., 1900, R.C.S.I.	Temp. Lieut
Johnston, H. S.	L.R.C.P. & S.I.	Lieut., R.A.M.C.
Johnstone, David P.	D.P.H., R.C.P. & S.I.	Major, R.A.M.C.

* Mentioned in Despatches.

51

ROYAL COLLEGE OF SURGEONS IN IRELAND.

*JONES, HAROLD P.	L.R.C.P. & S.I.	Fleet Surgeon, R.N.
JONES, JOSIAH H.	L.R.C.S.I.	Lieut.-Col., R.A.M.C. (Territorial Force)
JONES, ARNALLT JOHN	D.P.H., R.C.P. & S.I.	Major, R.A.M.C.
JONES, HERBERT	L.R.C.S.I.	Lieut.-Col., R.A.M.C. (T.F.)
JONES, ROBERT	F.R.C.S.I.	Temp. Col., A.M.S.
JOYNT, CECIL W.	L.R.C.P. & S.I.	Temp. Lieut., R.A.M.C.
JUBB, FRANK	L.R.C.P. & S.I.	Temp. Lieut., R.A.M.C.
KAVANAGH, T. O.	Student	Temp. Lieut., 3rd Royal Irish Fusiliers
KEENAN, JAMES	F.R.C.S.I.	Temp. Capt., R.A.M.C.
KELLY, CHARLES J.	L.R.C.P. & S.I.	Temp. Lieut., R.A.M.C.
KEANE, MICHAEL	L.R.C.P. & S.I.	Capt., R.A.M.C.
KEANE, PERCIVAL M.	L.R.C.P. & S.I.	Temp. Surgeon, R.N.
KEARNEY, JAMES	L.R.C.P. & S.I.	Capt., R.A.M.C., Territorial Force
KEATING, T.	Student	Temp. Lieut., Royal Field Artillery
*KEBLE, ALFRED E. C.	*D.S.O., C.M.G.,* L.R.C.P. & S.I.	Col., A.M.S.
KEEGAN, JAMES M.	F.R.C.S.I., D.P.H.	Temp. Lieut., R.A.M.C.
KELLY, B.	L.R.C.P. & S.I.	Temp. Lieut., R.A.M.C.
KELLY, CHARLES J.	L.R.C.P. & S.I.	Temp. Lieut., R.A.M.C.
*KELLY, DANIEL	*M.C.*, L.R.C.P. & S.I.	Temp. Capt., R.A.M.C.

* Mentioned in Despatches.

ROYAL COLLEGE OF SURGEONS IN IRELAND.

KELLY, JOHN B.	L.R.C.P. & S.I.	Temp. Lieut., R.A.M.C.
KELLY, MICHAEL G.	Student	Sergt., R.D.F.
KELLY, MICHAEL J.	L.R.C.P. & S.I.	Temp. Lieut., R.A.M.C.
*KELLY, PETER B.	*D.S.O.*, L.R.C.P. & S.I.	Temp. Surgeon, R.N.
KELLY, THOMAS	L.R.C.P. & S.I.	Temp. Lieut., R.A.M.C.
KELLY, THOMAS J.	L.R.C.P. & S.I.	Temp. Lieut., R.A.M.C.
KENNEDY, ARTHUR	L.R.C.P. & S.I.	Lt.-Col., R.A.M.C.
KENNEDY, ARTHUR P.	L.R.C.P. & S.I.	Lieut., R.A.M.C. (Special Reserve)
KENNEDY, FRANCIS P.	L.R.C.P. & S.I.	Temp. Lieut., R.A.M.C.
KENNEDY, D.	L.R.C.P. & S.I.	Temp. Lieut., R.A.M.C.
KENNEDY, FREDERICK	L.R.C.P. & S.I.	Temp. Lieut., R.A.M.C.
KENNEDY, D.	F.R.C.S.I.	Temp. Major, R.A.M.C.
*KENNY, CHARLES A.	L.R.C.P. & S.I.	Temp. Lieut., R.A.M.C.
*KENNY, WILLIAM W.	F.R.C.S.I.	Major-Genl., A.M.S.
KENNY, WILLIAM J.	Student	Sergt.
KEOGH, SIR ALFRED H.	*K.C.B.*, Hon. F.R.C.S.I.	Surg.-Genl., Army Medical Service
KEOGH, F. DEC.	F.R.C.S.I.	Temp. Capt., R.A.M.C.
KERANS, GEORGE C. L.	L.R.C.P. & S.I.	Major, Indian Medical Service
KEVIN, H. N. K.		
KEYMES, J. J.	L.R.C.P. & S.I.	Temp. Lieut., R.A.M.C.
KEYS, WALTER G.	L.D.S., R.C.S.I.	Temp. Capt., R.A.M.C.
KIDD, JOHN A. C.	Student	Lieut., R.A.M.C. (Special Reserve)

* Mentioned in Despatches

ROYAL COLLEGE OF SURGEONS IN IRELAND.

Kilkelly, Charles R.	*C.M.G., M.V.O.* L.R.C.S.I.	Col., A.M.S.
King, John Leo	Student	2nd Lt., R.I. Fusiliers
Kinsey, Edward D.	L.R.C.P. & S.I.	Temp. Lieut., R.A.M.C.
*Kirker, James	L.R.C.P. & S.I.	Temp. Lieut., R.A.M.C.
Kirwan, Frederick M.	L.R.C.P. & S.I.	Temp. Lieut., R.A.M.C.
Kirk, Henry	L.D.S., R.C.S.I.	Temp. Capt., R.A.M.C.
Knaggs, Henry T.	L.R.C.P. & S.I.	Col., Army Medical Service
*Knox, Ernest B.	D.P.H., R.C.P. & S.I.	Major, R.A.M.C.
Laird, Wellington J. A.	L.R.C.P. & S.I.	Capt., R.A.M.C. (Special Reserve)
Landon, Edward B.	D.P.H., R.C.P. & S.I.	Temp. Lieut., R.A.M.C.
Lane, Daniel T.	D.P.H., R.C.P. & S.I.	Lieut.-Col. Indian Medical Service
Lane, Thomas J.	Student	Surgeon Probationer, R.N.V.R.
Lane-Joynt, R.	F.R.C.S.I.	Lt.-Col., R.A.M.C.
Langran, Bartholomew	L.R.C.P. & S.I.	Temp. Capt., R.A.M.C.
*Langstaff, James W.	L.R.C.P. & S.I.	Lt.-Col., R.A.M.C.
Lanigan, James	L.R.C.P. & S.I.	Capt., R.A.M.C. (Special Reserve)
Lauder, Thomas C.	L.R.C.P. & S.I.	Lt.-Col., R.A.M.C.
Lavertine, Albert X.	L.R.C.P. & S.I.	Fleet Surgeon, R.N.
Lavertine, Joseph C.	F.R.C.S.I.	Temp. Capt., R.A.M.C.

* Mentioned in Despatches.

ROYAL COLLEGE OF SURGEONS IN IRELAND.

Law, William F.	F.R.C.S.I.	Temp. Major, R.A.M.C.
Law, S. Horace	F.R.C.S.I.	Temp. Capt., R.A.M.C.
Lawless, George R.	F.R.C.S.I.	Temp. Lieut., R.A.M.C.
Lawlor, Joseph H.		
Lawrence, Herbert A.	L.D.S., R.C.S.I.	1st Lieut. & Quartermaster, National Reserve
Leach, E. W. P.	Student	Temp. Lieut., Royal Irish Rifles
Leadbeater, Wm. H. C.	Student	R.A.F.
*Leary, George G. W.	Student	Temp. Lieut, 10th Gloucesters
Lennan, F. J.	L.R.C.P. & S.I.	Temp. Lieut., R.A.M.C.
*Lennane, Gerald Q.	F.R.C.S.I., D.P.H.	Capt., R.A.M.C. (Territorial Force)
*Leslie, Robert W. D.	L.R.C.P. & S.I.	Major, R.A.M.C.
Leslie, Thomas C. C.	L.R.C.P. & S.I.	Capt., R.A.M.C.
*L'Estrange, Edgar F.	L.R.C.P. & S.I.	Major, R.A.M.C.
L'Estrange, Henry R.	L.R.C.P. & S.I.	Capt., R.A.M.C.
Leventon, Asher	F.R.C.S.I., D.P.H.	Lieut.-Col. Indian Medical Service
*Levis, John S. Mc	L.R.C.P. & S.I.	Major, R.A.M.C.
Levis, George S.	L.R.C.P. & S.I.	Capt., R.A.M.C. (Territorial Force)
Lewer, Robt P. S.	Student	Gunner, R.H.A.
Lewis, Richard C.	L.R.C.P. & S.I.	Lt.-Col., R.A.M.C.
Lewis, David	D.P.H., R.C.P. & S.I.	Temp. Lieut., R.A.M.C.
Leyland, Michael A.	Student	L/Sergt.
Lillis, William J. P.	L.R.C.P. & S.I.	Temp. Lieut., R.A.M.C.

* Mentioned in Despatches.

ROYAL COLLEGE OF SURGEONS IN IRELAND.

Lloyd, William H.	*K.H.S.*, F.R.C.S.I.	Inspector-Genl. of Hospitals and Fleets (retired, temporarily re-employed)
Lloyd, Timothy J.	L.R.C.P. & S.I.	Temp. Lieut., R.A.M.C.
Lochrin, Michael J.	L.R.C.P. & S.I.	Capt., R.A.M.C.
*Lochnan, William F. M.	L.R.C.P. & S.I., D.P.H.	Capt., R.A.M.C.
Loftus, M. J.	L.R.C.P. & S.I.	Lieut., R.A.M.C.
Lord-Flood, —	Student	Surgeon Prob., R.N.V.R.
Loughrey, Michael J.	L.R.C.P. & S.I.	Temp. Lieut., R.A.M.C.
Love, William J.	L.R.C.S.I.	Temp. Capt., R.A.M.C.
Lowe, Arthur H.	D.P.H., R.C.P. & S.I.	Capt., R.A.M.C. (Territorial Force)
Lucas, J. E.		
Lumley, William	L.R.C.P. & S.I.	Temp. Capt., R.A.M.C.
Lucey, D. F.	Student	Lieut., R.D.F.
Lunham, John L.	F.R.C.S.I.	Major, Indian Medical Service
*Luther, Anthony J.	L.R.C.P. & S.I.	Col., Army Medical Service
Luther, Guy F. J.	L.R.C.P. & S.I.	
Lyle, Allen A.	L.R.C.S.I.	Lieut.-Col., Army Medical Staff
Lydon, Thomas J.	L.R.C.P. & S.I.	Capt., R.A.M.C.
Lynch, Edmund W.	L.R.C.P. & S.I.	Temp. Lieut., R.A.M.C.
Lynch, John P.	L.R.C.P. & S.I.	Major, R.A.M.C.
Lyons, John F.	L.R.C.P. & S.I.	Capt., R.A.M.C. (Special Reserve)
Lyons, T. J.	L.R.C.P. & S.I.	Temp. Lieut., R.A.M.C.
Lyster, John P.	Student	Private, R.A.M.C.

* Mentioned in Despatches.

ROYAL COLLEGE OF SURGEONS IN IRELAND.

McAlister, Leslie W.	Student	Lieut., R.I.R.
McAllister, Victor J.	F.R.C.S.I.	Temp. Lieut., R.A.M.C.
McArevey, J. B.	Student	Temp. Lieut., 3rd Royal Irish Rifles
McBride, John B.	L.R.C.P. & S.I.	Major, R.A.M.C.
McCall, W. G. D.	L.R.C.P. & S.I.	Temp. Capt., R.A.M.C.
McCarthy, F. J.	L.R.C.P. & S.I.	Temp. Lieut., R.A.M.C.
McCarthy, Valentine	Student	R.N.
* McCausland, Samuel	L.R.C.P. & S.I.	Capt., R.A.M.C.
McCawley, Austin	L.R.C.P. & S.I.	Temp. Capt., R.A.M.C.
McCay, C. A. R.	L.R.C.P. & S.I.	Temp. Capt., R.A.M.C.
McClintock, Wm. J.		
McComiskey, Arthur W. S.	L.R.C.P. & S.I.	Temp. Capt., R.A.M.C.
McConkey, J. T.	L.R.C.P. & S.I.	Temp. Capt., R.A.M.C.
McConnell, Charles	Student	Lieut.
†McConnell, W. G.	L.R.C.P. & S.I.	Temp. Capt., R.A.M.C.
McConnell, Francis	Student	Lieut., R.A.S.C.
McConnell, John J.	L.R.C.P. & S.I.	Temp. Lieut., R.A.M.C.
McCormack, John	School Porter	Sergeant, Leinster Regiment
MacCormack, Charles P. V.	L.R.C.P. & S.I.	Temp. Lieut., R.A.M.C.
MacCormack, James	L.R.C.P. & S.I.	Temp. Lieut., R.A.M.C.
*MacCormack, John D.	L.R.C.P. & S.I.	Capt., R.A.M.C.
McCormack, Daniel	L.R.C.P. & S.I.	Temp. Lieut., R.A.M.C.

* Mentioned in Despatches. † Killed in Action.

ROYAL COLLEGE OF SURGEONS IN IRELAND.

McCormick, Francis H.		
*McCurry, Walter T.	Ex-Student	Temp. Lieut., R.A.M.C.
McDermott, F. P.	L.R.C.P. & S.I.	Temp. Lieut., R.A.M.C.
Macdonald, Arthur	L.D.S., R.C.S.I.	Temp. Lieut., R.A.M.C.
MacDonald, John	L.R.C.P. & S.I.	Temp. Lieut., R.A.M.C.
McDonnell, Robert P.	F.R.C.S.I., D.P.H.	Temp. Capt., R.A.M.C.
MacDowel, Francis L. H.	L.R.C.P. & S.I.	Surgeon, R.N.
McElligott, Maurice G.	F.R.C.S.I., D.P.H.	Temp. Lieut., R.A.M.C.
McEntee, S. Drummond G.		Capt.
McEntire, Samuel D. G.	L.R.C.P. & S.I.	Capt., R.A.M.C. (Special Reserve)
Macewan, Sir William	Hon. F.R.C.S.I.	Temp. Consulting Surgeon, R.N
McGee, John H.	L.R.C.P. & S.I.	Temp. Lieut., R.A.M.C.
McGinn, Patrick J.	L.R.C.P. & S.I.	Capt., R.A.M.C. (Territorial Force)
McGlade, Patrick	Student	Pioneer R.E.
Machado, Leo S.	F.R.C.S.I.	Temp. Lieut., I.M.S.
Magrane, V. J.	F.R.C.S.I.	Civil Surgeon
McIlwaine, Alexander G. J.	L.R.C.P. & S.I.	Capt., R.A.M.C.
*McKeever, Louis L.	*M.C.*, L.R.C.P. & S.I.	Temp. Capt., R.A.M.C.
McKenna, J. O'N.	Student	Temp. Lieut., Royal Dublin Fusiliers
MacKenzie, Thomas C.	*D.S.O.*, L.R.C.P. & S.I.	Lt.-Col., R.A.M.C.
MacKenzie, M.	L.R.C.P. & S.I.	Temp. Lieut., R.A.M.C.
McKinney, F. A.	L.D.S., R.C.S.I.	Temp. Capt., R.A.M.C.

* Mentioned in Despatches.

ROYAL COLLEGE OF SURGEONS IN IRELAND.

MacKinnon, John A.	L.R.C.P. & S.I.	Lieut., R.A.M.C.
McLannahan, James G.	L.R.C.P. & S.I.	Capt., R.A.M.C. (Territorial Force)
McLaughlin, John	F.R.C.S.I.	Lieut.-Col., R.A.M.C. (Retired, temporarily re-employed)
MacMahon, Robert F.	L.R.C.P. & S.I.	Staff-Surgeon, R.N.
MacManus, Francis J.	L.R.C.P. & S.I.	Temp. Lieut., R.A.M.C.
McMullen, Marjorie	L.R.C.P. & S.I.	R.A.M.C., B.E.F.
*McMunn, Andrew	L.R.C.P. & S.I.	Lt.-Col., R.A.M.C.
*McMunn, James R.	L.R.C.P. & S.I.	Lt.-Col., R.A.M.C.
MacNamara, James T.	L.R.C.P. & S.I.	Lt.-Col., R.A.M.C.
MacNamara, John	L.R.C.P. & S.I.	Temp. Lieut., R.A.M.C.
MacNeece, James G.	*C.B.*, L.R.C.P. & S.I.	Surgeon-General, R.A.M.C.
McNulty, James J.	Student	Trooper
McQuaid, E. W.	Student	R.F.C.
*McQueen, Campbell	L.R.C.P. & S.I.	Capt., R.A.M.C.
McRea, D. M.	Student	Temp. Lieut., Royal Enniskillen Fusiliers
McWalter, James C.	D.P.H., R.C.P. & S.I.	Temp. Capt., R.A.M.C.
MacSweeny, John A.	L.R.C.P. & S.I.	Lieut., R.A.M.C.
Macaulay, William	Student	Lieut.
MacSwiney, Victor H. L.	L.R.C.P. & S.I.	Temp. Lieut., R.A.M.C.
McTavish, F. P. B.	L.R.C.P. & S.I.	Temp. Lieut., R.A.M.C.
Mackie, A. J.	Student	Temp. Lt., Liverpool Regt.
Magner, J.	L.R.C.P. & S.I.	Temp. Lieut., R.A.M.C.

* Mentioned in Despatches.

ROYAL COLLEGE OF SURGEONS IN IRELAND.

MAGUIRE, JOSEPH	L.R.C.P. & S.I.	Temp. Capt., R.A.M.C.
MAGUIRE, PATRICK	L.R.C.P. & S.I.	Temp. Lieut., R.A.M.C.
MAGUIRE, HUGH G.	Student	Guardsman
MAHON, FREDERICK F.	L.R.C.P. & S.I.	Fleet Surgeon, R.N.
MAHON, W. A.	L.R.C.P. & S.I.	Temp. Lieut., R.A.M.C.
MAITLAND, VIVIAN G.	D.P.H., R.C.P. & S.I.	Temp. Lieut., R.A.M.C.
MALAHER, BRUCE	L.R.C.P. & S.I.	Temp. Capt., R.A.M.C.
McTERNAN, MICHL. PATRICK	Student	Lieut., R.D.F.
MALONE, GERALD H.	Student	Lieut., R.A.F.
MALONE, WILLIAM A.	L.R.C.P. & S.I.	Temp. Capt., R.A.M.C.
MANLEY, J. S.	Student	Surg. Sub-Lieut.
*MANNING, NATHANIEL S.	F.R.C.S.I.	Temp. Major, R.A.M.C.
MARMION, WILLIAM	L.D.S., R.C.S.I.	Temp. Lieut., R.A.M.C.
MARMION, JOSEPH	L.R.C.P. & S.I.	Temp. Capt., R.A.M.C.
MARRETT, CHARLES A.	D.P.H., R.C.P. & S.I.	Temp. Surgeon, R.N.
*MARRIOTT, W. EDWARD P. V.	*D.S.O.*, L.R.C.P. & S.I.	Lieut.-Col. R.A.M.C.
MARTIN, ALBERT E. S.	F.R.C.S.I.	Temp. Lieut., R.A.M.C.
*MARTIN, HENRY G.	L.R.C.P. & S.I.	Lieut.-Col. R.A.M.C.
MARTIN, JAMES C.	L.R.C.P. & S.I.	Temp. Lieut., R.A.M.C.
MARTIN, RICHARD	L.R.C.P. & S.I.	Temp. Surgeon, R.N.
MARTIN, THOMAS S. G.	L.R.C.P. & S.I.	Temp. Lieut., R.A.M.C.
MARTIN, WILLIAM L.	F.R.C.S.I.	Fleet Surgeon, R.N.

* Mentioned in Despatches.

ROYAL COLLEGE OF SURGEONS IN IRELAND.

MILNES, JOSEPH H.	L.D.S., R.C.S.I.	Lieut., National Reserve
MOFFATT, G. M.	Student	Temp. Capt., Royal Dublin Fusiliers
MOFFATT, HUGH H.	L.R.C.P. & S.I.	Temp. Lieut., R.A.M.C.
MOLAN, CORNELIUS	L.R.C.P. & S.I.	Temp. Lieut., R.A.M.C.
*MOLLAN, FRANCIS R. H.	L.R.C.P. & S.I.	Capt., R.A.M.C. (Special Reserve)
MOLONY, CHARTRES A.	L.R.C.P. & S.I.	Capt., R.A.M.C. (Territorial Force)
MONTGOMERY, EDWIN	F.R.C.S.I.	Temp. Lieut., R.A.M.C.
MONTGOMERY, HUGH H.	L.R.C.S.I.	Capt. Australian Medical Corps
MOONEY, HAROLD L.	Student	Surgeon Probationer, R.N.V.R.
MOORHEAD, GEO. A.	Student	Capt.
*MOORHEAD, HARRY S.	Student	Sergt., R.E.
†*MOORE, HENRY	*M.C., D.S.O.,* L.R.C.P. & S.I.	Temp. Lt.-Col., R.A.M.C.
MOORE, M. S.	Student	Surgeon, R.N.
MOORE, THOMAS	L.R.C.P. & S.I.	Temp. Capt., R.A.M.C.
MOORE, W. B. A.	L.R.C.P. & S.I.	Temp. Lieut., R.A.M.C.
MORAN, LOUIS A.	L.R.C.P. & S.I.	Temp. Lieut., R.A.M.C.
MORAN, THOMAS F.	L.R.C.P. & S.I.	Temp. Lieut., R.A.M.C.
MORAN, MICHAEL	L.R.C.P. & S.I.	Temp. Capt., R.A.M.C.
MORGAN, JOHN P.	Student	Private, C Squad, Queen's Bays
*MORIARTY, THOMAS B.	*D.S.O.,* L.R.C.P. & S.I.	Capt., R.A.M.C.
*MORRIS, FRANCIS J.	L.R.C.P. & S.I.	Temp. Capt., R.A.M.C.
MORRIS, ALFRED	Student	Major, R.G.A.

* Mentioned in Despatches. † Killed in Action.

ROYAL COLLEGE OF SURGEONS IN IRELAND.

Martin, George J. M.	L.R.C.P. & S.I.	Capt., R.A.M.C. (T.F.)
Mason, Henry W.	L.R.C.S.I.	Civil Surgeon, King George V. Hospital
†Massy-Myles, Harry G.	L.R.C.P. & S.I.	Temp. Capt., R.A.M.C.
Matson, J. A.	L.R.C.P. & S.I.	Temp. Capt., R.A.M.C.
Maunsell, R. C. B.	F.R.C.S.I.	Temp. Major, R.A.M.C.
*Mawhinny, Robert J. W.	*C.B.*, L.R.C.P. & S.I.	Lieut.-Col., R.A.M.C.
Maxwell, Euphan	F.R.C.S.I.	Civil Surgeon, R.A.M.C.
Meade, Henry S.	F.R.C.S.I.	Capt., R.A.M.C.
Meehan, Michael	L.R.C.P. & S.I.	Surgeon, R.N.
Meenan, F. J.	Student	Private, Royal Irish Regt.
Meldon, G. H.	F.R.C.S.I.	Temp. Capt., R.A.M.C.
Mellon, B. H.	Student	Capt., A.V.C.
Menton, J.	L.R.C.P. & S.I.	Temp. Lieut., R.A.M.C.
Meredith, William R.	L.R.C.P. & S.I.	Temp. Lieut., R.A.M.C.
Merrick, Augustus A. W.	F.R.C.S.I.	Major, R.A.M.C. (Territorial Force)
Merrin, Alfred	L.R.C.P. & S.I.	Temp. Capt., R.A.M.C.
Mescall, Joseph H.	L.R.C.P. & S.I.	Temp. Lieut., R.A.M.C.
Meyler, John F. C.	L.R.C.P. & S.I.	Temp. Lieut., R.A.M.C.
Miles, G. L. N.	L.R.C.P. & S.I.	Temp. Lieut., R.A.M.C.
*Millar, Cecil R.	L.R.C.P. & S.I.	Major, R.A.M.C.
Miller, Alfred	Registrar, R.C.S.I.	O.C., O.T.C., R.C.S.I. Acting Adjutant (unattached)
Mills, William T.	L.R.C.P. & S.I.	Temp. Lieut., R.A.M.C.

* Mentioned in Despatches. † Died on Service.

ROYAL COLLEGE OF SURGEONS IN IRELAND.

Morrissey, Joseph M.	F.R.C.S.I.	Temp. Lieut., R.A.M.C.
Morrison, F. S.	F.R.C.S.I.	Temp. Capt., R.A.M.C.
Mosse, Charles G. D.	F.R.C.S.I.	Lieut.-Col., R.A.M.C. (Retired, temporarily re-employed)
Mosbery, Richard T.	L.D.S., R.C.S.I.	Royal Engineers
Mouritz, Cecil J. H.	Student	2nd Lt., Leinster Regt.
Moxton, Edwin	D.P.H., R.C.P. & S.I.	Temp. Capt., R.A.M.C. (T.F.)
*Moynihan, Sir Berkeley	*C.B.*, Hon. F.R.C.S.I.	Temp. Major-General, A.M.S.
Moynihan, Edward J. B.	L.R.C.P. & S.I.	Temp. Lieut., R.A.M.C.
Mulcahy, Thomas	L.R.C.P. & S.I.	Temp. Capt., R.A.M.C.
Mulhall, Alexander T.	F.R.C.S.I.	Lieut.-Col., R.A.M.C.
*Mullin, J. E.	L.R.C.P. & S.I.	Temp. Lieut., R.A.M.C.
Mullin, Bartholomew J.	L.R.C.P. & S.I.	Temp. Lieut., R.A.M.C.
Murphy, Bernard	L.R.C.P. & S.I.	Lieut., R.A.M.C. (Special Reserve)
*Murphy, Charles E.	F.R.C.S.I.	Temp. Capt., R.A.M.C.
Murphy, John F.	Student	2nd Lt., R. Berkshire Regt.
Murphy, John C.	L.R.C.P. & S.I.	Capt., W. African Medical Service (Active Service)
Murphy, James C.	Student	2nd Lieut., Worcestershire Regt.
Murphy, Christopher F.	L.R.C.P. & S.I.	Capt., R.A.M.C.
Murphy, Lionel E. C.	L.R.C.P. & S.I.	Temp. Lieut., R.A.M.C.
Murphy, Matthew	L.R.C.P. & S.I.	Temp. Capt., R.A.M.C.
Murphy, Patrick J.	F.R.C.S.I.	Temp. Lieut., R.A.M.C.
Murphy, T. E.	Student	11th North Staffs. Regt.

* Mentioned in Despatches.

ROYAL COLLEGE OF SURGEONS IN IRELAND.

*Murphy, William L.	L.R.C.P. & S.I.	Capt., R.A.M.C. (Territorial Force)
Murphy, William O'S.	D.P.H., R.C.P. & S.I.	Major, Indian Medical Service
Murphy, Richard V.	L.R.C.P. & S.I.	Temp. Lieut., R.A.M.C.
Murphy, Walter	L.R.C.P. & S.I.	Temp. Lieut., R.A.M.C.
*Murray, Kenneth A. P. R.	L.R.C.P. & S.I.	Major, R.A.M.C., Territorial Force
Murray, Thomas	L.R.C.P. & S.I.	Lieut., R.A.M.C., Territorial Force
Murray, William H.	L.R.C.P. & S.I.	Surgeon, R.N.
Murray, Cyril	L.R.C.P. & S.I.	Temp. Lieut., R.A.M.C.
Murray, P. J.	L.R.C.P. & S.I.	Temp. Lieut., R.A.M.C.
Murray, James C.	L.R.C.P. & S.I.	Temp. Lieut., R.A.M.C.
Musgrave, John A.	L.R.C.P. & S.I.	Capt., R.A.M.C., Territorial Force
Myles, John	F.R.C.S.I.	Temp. Capt., R.A.M.C.
Myles, Sir Thomas	*C.B.*, F.R.C.S.I.	Temp. Col., A.M.S.

Nash, Llewellyn T. M.	*C.M.G.*, L.R.C.P. & S.I.	Col., Army Medical Service
Nash, Sir Vincent	L.R.C.S.I.	Temp. Major, R.A.M.C.
Neilan, John A.	L.R.C.P. & S.I.	Temp. Lieut., R.A.M.C.
Neilan, Alan J.	L.R.C.P. & S.I.	Lieut., R.A.M.C.
Neill, Robert G.	Student	Temp. 2nd Lieut., Royal Inniskilling Fusiliers
Nelson, Edwin F.	L.R.C.S.I.	Surgeon-Major, M.O. Troops

* Mentioned in Despatches.

ROYAL COLLEGE OF SURGEONS IN IRELAND.

NEWMAN, THOMAS B.	L.R.C.P. & S.I.	Temp. Lieut., R.A.M.C.
NIBLOCK, WILLIAM J.	F.R.C.S.I.	Major, Indian Medical Service
NICHOLSON, RANALD W. E. H.	D.P.H., R.C.P. & S.I.	Lieut.-Col., R.A.M.C.
NIGHTINGALE, G. O.	Student	Temp. Lt., Manchester Regt.
NOLAN, HERBERT F.	L.R.C.P. & S.I.	Temp. Lieut., R.A.M.C.
NOLAN, E. D.	Student	Temp. 2nd Lieut., Royal Lancashire Regt.
NOLAN, THOMAS I. C.	Student	Cadet

O'BOYLE, JOHN T.	L.R.C.P. & S.I.	Temp. Capt., R.A.M.C.
O'BRIEN, HENRY E.	L.R.C.P. & S.I.	Temp. Lieut., R.A.M.C.
*O'BRIEN, JAMES V.	L.R.C.P. & S.I.	Capt, R.A.M.C.
O'BRIEN, MICHAEL	L.R.C.P. & S.I.	Temp. Lieut., R.A.M.C.
O'BRIEN, DANIEL J.	L.R.C.P. & S.I.	Temp. Lieut., R.A.M.C.
O'BRIEN, WILLIAM		Capt.
*O'CALLAGHAN, DENIS M.	*C.M.G.*, L.R.C.P. & S.I.	Col., Army Medical Service
O'CALLAGHAN, MAURICE A.	L.R.C.P. & S.I.	Lieut., R.A.M.C. (Special Reserve)
O'CARROLL, ARTHUR S. FFRENCH	Student	Lieut., R.A.S.C.
O'CONNELL, CHARLES J.	L.R.C.P. & S.I.	Staff-Surgeon, R.N.
*O'CONNELL, MORGAN D.	L.R.C.P. & S.I.	Lieut.-Col., R.A.M.C.
O'CONNOR, AUBREY A.	L.R.C.P. & S.I.	Temp. Lieut., R.A.M.C.

* Mentioned in Despatches.

ROYAL COLLEGE OF SURGEONS IN IRELAND.

O'Connor, Thomas M.	Student	Sergt., R.A.M.C.
O'Connor, Denis V.	L.R.C.P. & S.I.	Temp. Capt., S.A.M.S.
O'Connor, V. R.	Student	Surgeon Probationer, R.N.V.R.
O'Connor, William M.	D.P.H., R.C.P. & S.I.	Lieut.-Col. R.A.M.C.
O'Connor, A. P.	*C.B.*, F.R.C.S.I.	Col., A.M.S.
O'Connor, Carl	L.R.C.P. & S.I.	Temp. Lieut., R.A.M.C.
O'Donnell, B. J.	L.R.C.P. & S.I.	Temp. Lieut., R.A.M.C.
O'Donnell, Godfrey C.	Student	2nd Lieut., Leinster Regt.
*O'Donnell, Thomas J.	*C.B.*, *D.S.O.*, L.R.C.P. & S.I.	Major-General, A.M.S.
O'Donnell Wm.	L.R.C.P. & S.I.	Temp. Lieut., R.A.M.C.
O'Donnell, Frederick A.	L.R.C.P. & S.I.	Temp. Lieut., R.A.M.C.
O'Donoghue, D. J.	L.R.C.P. & S.I.	Capt., West African Medical Service
O'Donohoe, Francis G.	L.R.C.P. & S.I.	Temp. Capt., R.A.M.C.
O'Donovan, Louis J.	L.R.C.P. & S.I.	Temp. Lieut., R.A.M.C.
*O'Driscoll, John A.	L.R.C.P. & S.I.	Capt., R.A.M.C.
O'Dwyer, J. P.	Student	Private, R.A.M.C.
O'Farrell, Emanuel M. J.	F.R.C.S.I., D.P.H.	Temp. Major, R.A.M.C.
O'Farrell, Joseph Connor	L.R.C.P. & S.I.	Temp. Capt., R.A.M.C.
O'Farrell, William R.	L.R.C.P. & S.I.	Capt., R.A.M.C.
O'Farrell, Patrick J.	L.R.C.P. & S.I.	Lieut., R.A.M.C.
O'Farrell, P. T. J.	L.R.C.P. & S.I.	Temp. Lieut., R.A.M.C.
O'Flynn, Dominick T.	L.R.C.P. & S.I.	Temp. Lieut., R.A.M.C.
*O'Gorman, Charles	*D.S.O.*, L.R.C.P. & S.I.	Lieut.-Col., R.A.M.C.

* Mentioned in Despatches.

66

ROYAL COLLEGE OF SURGEONS IN IRELAND.

O'Grady, Donald de C.	L.R.C.P. & S.I.	Capt., R.A.M.C.
*O'Grady, Luke S.	L.R.C.P. & S.I.	Temp. Capt., R.A.M.C.
*O'Grady, Robert L.	*O.B.E.*, L.D.S., R.C.S.I.	Temp. Capt., R.A.M.C.
*O'Hagan, John J.	F.R.C.S.I.	Lieut.-Col., R.A.M.C. (Territorial Force)
O'Hanlon, O. J. O'B.	F.R.C.S.I.	Capt., R.A.M.C. (Special Reserve)
O'Hare, J. H.	L.D.S., R.C.S.I.	Temp. Lieut., R.A.M.C.
O'Keeffe, Cornelius W.	L.R.C.P. & S.I.	Lt., West African Medical Service
O'Kelly, John J.	L.R.C.P. & S.I.	Temp. Capt., R.A.M.C.
O'Kelly, Robert	L.R.C.P. & S.I.	Capt., R.A.M.C.
O'Leary, John	F.R.C.S.I.	Major, I.M.S.
O'Leary, John J.	Student	Lieut., R.A.F.
O'Loghlen, John E.	L.R.C.P. & S.I.	Temp. Capt., R.A.M.C.
O'Meara, M. P.	Student	Temp. Lieut., Munster Fusiliers
*O'Malley, John F.	L.R.C.P. & S.I.	Temp. Lieut., R.A.M.C.
O'Malley, P. J. D.	L.R.C.P. & S.I.	Temp. Lieut., R.A.M.C.
O'Neill, John H.	L.R.C.P. & S.I.	Temp. Lieut., R.A.M.C.
O'Neill, Alphonsus J.	Student	Private, R.A.S.C.
O'Neill, Patrick L.	D.P.H., R.C.P. & S.I.	Major, Indian Medical Service
O'Reilly, E. F.	Student	Gloucester Regiment
*O'Reilly, Patrick J.	L.R.C.P. & S.I.	Temp. Capt., R.A.M.C.
O'Reilly, Patrick S.	*C.M.G.*, L.R.C.P. & S.I.	Major, R.A.M.C.
O'Reilly, Bernard F.	L.R.C.P. & S.I.	Temp. Lieut., R.A.M.C.

* Mentioned in Despatches.

ROYAL COLLEGE OF SURGEONS IN IRELAND.

*O'RIORDAN, WILLIAM H.	L.R.C.P. & S.I.	Capt., R.A.M.C.
O'SULLIVAN, DANIEL	F.R.C.S.I.	Colonel, A.M.S. (retired temporarily re-employed)
*O'SULLIVAN, KINGSLEY L.	L.R.C.P. & S.I.	Capt., R.A.M.C. (Special Reserve)
O'SULLIVAN, PATRICK	Student	Private
ODLUM, BENJAMIN A.	L.R.C.P. & S.I.	Capt., R.A.M.C.
*ODLUM, WILLIAM H.	L.R.C.P. & S.I.	Major, Indian Medical Service
O'RIOIRDAN, CHARLES A.	Student	Sergt.
OLIVER, RICHARD H.	F.R.C.S.I.	Temp. Lieut., R.A.M.C.
ORMSBY, SIR LAMBERT H.	F.R.C.S.I.	Hon. Consultant Surgeon to New Zealand Expeditionary Force, with the Hon. rank of Lieut.-Col.
OWEN FLOOD, ANTHONY	Student	2nd Lieut., R.I.F.
OWEN FLOOD, JOSEPH	Student	2nd Lieut., Northumberland Fusiliers
ORMSBY, WILLIAM	L.R.C.P. & S.I.	Temp. Lieut., R.A.M.C.
OULTON, R. H. G.	L.R.C.P. & S.I.	Temp. Lieut., R.A.M.C.

*PALMER, FRANCIS J.	F.R.C.S.I.	Lieut.-Col. R.A.M.C.
PALLISER WRAY		
PARKER, JAMES	L.R.C.P. & S.I.	Temp. Lieut., R.A.M.C.
PATTERSON, ALEXANDER J.	L.R.C.P. & S.I.	Surgeon, R.N.
*PATTERSON, ARTHUR F. I.	*D.S.O.*, L.R.C.P. & S.I.	Capt., R.A.M.C.
PATTERSON, HUBERT C.	Student	Cadet, R.I.R.

* Mentioned in Despatches.

ROYAL COLLEGE OF SURGEONS IN IRELAND.

Pattison, C. R. Maitland	L.R.C.P. & S.I.	Temp. Capt., R.A.M.C.
Pearson, Devonshire H. P.	L.R.C.P. & S.I.	Surgeon, R.N.
Peel-Davis, George C.		
Pearson, William	F.R.C.S.I.	Temp. Major, R.A.M.C.
Peart, J. F.	L.R.C.P. & S.I.	Temp. Lieut., R.A.M.C.
†Pegum, J. P.	L.R.C.P. & S.I.	Temp. Lieut., R.A.M.C.
Pegum, James Francis	Student	R.N.T.
Pegum, J. S.	L.R.C.P. & S.I.	Temp. Lieut., R.A.M.C.
Pennefather, Edward M.	L.R.C.P. & S.I.	Major, R.A.M.C.
*Pepper, George E.	L.R.C.P. & S.I.	Capt., R.A.M.C. (Special Reserve)
*Perry, Henry J.	L.R.C.P. & S.I.	Capt., R.A.M.C.
Perry, Samuel J. C. P.	F.R.C.S.I.	Lieut.-Col. R.A.M.C.
Peters, B. H.	L.R.C.P. & S.I.	Temp. Lieut., R.A.M.C.
*Petit, Gerard	*M.C.*, L.R.C.P. & S.I.	Capt., R.A.M.C.
Phelan, Francis	L.R.C.P. & S.I.	Capt., Indian Medical Service
Phelan, Paul J.	Student	Lieut. Russian Army
Pierce, William K.	Student	Temp. Lieut., Royal Garrison Artillery
Pigott, J. G. Glynn	L.R.C.P. & S.I.	Temp. Lieut., R.A.M.C.
Pilkington, James P.	Student	Private, R.D.F.
*Pike, Sir William W.	*K.C.M.G.*, *D.S.O.*, F.R.C.S.I.	Major-General, Army Medical Service
Pollock, Rowland	L.R.C.P. & S.I.	Civil Surgeon.
Pooley, Edward B.	L.R.C.S.I.	Temp. Major, R.A.M.C.

* Mentioned in Despatches. † Killed in Action.

69

ROYAL COLLEGE OF SURGEONS IN IRELAND.

Pope, George W.	L.R.C.P. & S.I.	Temp. Lieut., R.A.M.C.
Potter, R. J.	Student	Temp. Lieut., Royal Dublin Fusiliers
*Potter, Thomas J.	L.R.C.P. & S.I.	Major, R.A.M.C.
Potter, Scott	L.R.C.P. & S.I.	Temp. Lieut., R.A.M.C.
Powell, George M. C.	L.R.C.P. & S.I.	Temp. Lieut., R.A.M.C.
Power, Alfred W.	L.R.C.P. & S.I.	Capt., R.A.M.C. (Territorial Force)
Power, Everard M.	L.R.C.S.I.	Temp. Capt., R.A.M.C.
Power, F. J.	L.R.C.P. & S.I.	Temp. Lieut., R.A.M.C.
Power, John H.	L.R.C.P. & S.I.	Major, R.A.M.C. Household Cavalry Brigade
Power, Pierce M.	L.R.C.P. & S.I.	Temp. Lieut., R.A.M.C.
Power, Robert J.	L.R.C.S.I.	Major, R.A.M.C. (Retired) temporarily re-employed
*Power, R. P.	Student	Capt., Royal Irish Fusiliers
*Power, William M.	L.R.C.P. & S.I.	Major, R.A.M.C.
†Power, John	Student	Private. 10th Batt. R.D. Fus.
*Pratt, John	L.R.C.P. & S.I.	Temp. Surgeon, R.N.
*Pratt, John D.	F.R.C.S.I.	M.O. in charge of the 8th. Dublin Staff
Prescott, John J. W.	*D.S.O.*, L.R.C.P. & S.I.	Lieut.-Col. R.A.M.C.
Price, M.	L.R.C.P. & S.I.	Temp. Lieut., R.A.M.C.
Price, William S. M.	L.R.C.S.I.	Surg.-Genl., R.A.M.C.
Pringle, Harold	F.R.C.S.I.	Temp. Capt., R.A.M.C.
Pringle, Seaton	F.R.C.S.I.	Temp. Lt.-Col., R.A.M.C.
Proctor, J. S.	L.R.C.P. & S.I.	Capt., Australian Medical Corps

* Mentioned in Despatches. † Killed in Action.

70

ROYAL COLLEGE OF SURGEONS IN IRELAND.

Prost, Sidney G.	Student	Private, Canadian Infantry
Punch, Edward P.	L.R.C.P. & S.I.	Royal Naval Volunteer Reserve H.M.S. "Venerable"
Punch, Sidney	L.R.C.P. & S.I.	Surgeon, R.N.
Purcell John	L.R.C.P. & S.I.	Temp. Lieut., R.A.M.C.
Purcell, Edward	L.R.C.P. & S.I.	Temp. Capt., R.A.M.C.
*Purser, Francis C.	L.R.C.S.I.	Temp. Major, R.A.M.C.
Quinlan, F. J.	Student	R.A.F.
Rai, B.	F.R.C.S.I.	Temp. Lieut., I.M.S.
Rainsford, William J. R.	*C.I.E.*, F.R.C.S.I.	Col., A.M.S. (retired temporarily re-employed)
Rainsford, Henry M.	L.R.C.P. & S.I.	Temp. Capt., R.A.M.C.
Rearden, James T.	L.R.C.P. & S.I.	Temp. Lieut., R.A.M.C.
*Redmond, Raymond O'C.	Student	Surgeon Probationer, R.N.V.R.
*Reeves, Thomas S.	L.R.C.P. & S.I.	Temp. Capt., R.A.M.C.
Reilly, Charles W.	D.P.H., R.C.P. & S.I.	Major, R.A.M.C.
Reynolds, J. J.	L.R.C.P. & S.I.	Temp. Lieut., R.A.M.C.
Rice-Oxley, Leonard J.	L.D.S., R.C.S.I.	Capt., K.S.L.I.
Ridgway, William G.	F.R.C.S.I., D.P.H.	Temp. Capt., R.A.M.C.
*Rishworth, Walter N.	*M.C.*, D.P.H., R.C.P. & S.I.	Temp. Lieut., R.A.M.C.
Rishworth, J. M.	L.R.C.P. & S.I.	Temp. Lieut., R.A.M.C.

* Mentioned in Despatches.

71

ROYAL COLLEGE OF SURGEONS IN IRELAND.

ROBERTS, WALTER ALEN	Student	Private, R.A.M.C.
*ROBINSON, WILLIAM H. B.	*C.B.*, L.R.C.P. & S.I. D.P.H.	Lieut.-Col., Indian Medical Service
ROBINSON, GEORGE C.	L.R.C.P. & S.I.	Temp. Lieut., R.A.M.C.
ROBINSON, CECIL W. C.	L.R.C.P. & S.I.	Temp. Capt., R.A.M.C.
ROBINSON, S. H.	L.R.C.P. & S.I.	Temp. Lieut., R.A.M.C.
*ROCHE, CHARLES	*M.C.*, L.R.C.P. & S.I.	Temp. Lieut., R.A.M.C.
ROCHE, WILLIAM	L.R.C.P. & S.I.	Temp. Capt., R.A.M.C.
ROCHE-KELLY, J.	L.R.C.P. & S.I.	Temp. Lieut., R.A.M.C.
ROE, C. D.	Student	Private, R.A.M.C.
*ROE, WILLIAM F.	*D.S.O.*, L.R.C.P. & S.I.	Lieut.-Col., R.A.M.C.
ROE, GEORGE C. F.	L.R.C.P. & S.I.	Temp. Lieut., R.A.M.C.
ROGERS, DANIEL L.	L.D.S., R.C.S.I.	Major, 6th Batt. Gloucestershire Regt.
ROONEY, PATRICK J.	L.R.C.P. & S.I.	Temp. Lieut., R.A.M.C.
RORKE, LAWRENCE C.	L.R.C.P. & S.I.	Temp. Lieut., R.A.M.C.
ROURKE, JOHN ALEX	Student	Lieut., R.A.S.C.
ROWAN, PATRICK	L.R.C.P. & S.I.	Temp. Lieut., R.A.M.C.
*ROWLETTE, LIONEL M.	*D.S.O.*, *M.C.*, L.R.C.P. & S.I.	Temp. Capt., R.A.M.C.
RUSSELL, GEORGE H.	L.R.C.P. & S.I.	Temp. Lieut., R.A.M.C.
RUTHERFORD, GORDON S.	Student	Surg-Prob., R.N.
*RUTHERFORD, NATHANIEL J. C.	*D.S.O.*, D.P.H., R.C.P. & S.I.	Lieut.-Col. R.A.M.C.
RUTHERFORD, WILLIAM G.	L.R.C.P. & S.I.	Temp. Capt., R.A.M.C. (T.F.)
RYAN, CHARLES O'B.	L.R.C.P. & S.I.	Surgeon, Royal Naval Volunteer Reserve

* Mentioned in Despatches.

ROYAL COLLEGE OF SURGEONS IN IRELAND.

Ryan, James D.	L.R.C.P. & S.I.	Temp. Lieut., R.A.M.C.
Ryan, Richard P.	F.R.C.S.I.	Capt., R.A.M.C. (Territorial Force)
Ryan, Charles E.	F.R.C.S.I.	Temp. Capt., R.A.M.C.
Ryan, Thomas J.	L.R.C.P. & S.I.	Temp. Lieut., R.A.M.C.
Ryan, Thomas J.	L.R.C.P. & S.I.	Temp. Lieut., R.A.M.C.
Ryan, William	L.R.C.P. & S.I.	Temp. Capt., R.A.M.C.
Sammon, W. D.	L.R.C.P. & S.I.	Temp. Lieut., R.A.M.C.
Sampey, Alexander W.	L.R.C.P. & S.I.	Bt. Lt.-Col., R.A.M.C.
Sampey, N. E.	L.R.C.P. & S.I.	Temp. Lieut., R.A.M.C.
*Sampson, Patrick	*D.S.O.*, D.P.H. L.R.C.P. & S.I.	Capt., R.A.M.C.
Sarsfield, Thomas H.	L.R.C.P. & S.I.	Temp. Capt., R.A.M.C.
*Sawyer, Richard H. S.	*C.B.*, *C.M.G.*, F.R.C.S.I.	Major General, A.M.S.
Scales, Martin	L.R.C.P. & S.I.	Lieut., R.A.M.C. (Territorial Force)
Scanlan, John J.	D.P.H., R.C.P. & S.I.	Capt., R.A.M.C. (T.F.)
Scher, Louis	Student	
Scott, Harvie	L.R.C.S.I.	Lieut.-Col., R.A.M.C.
*Scott, R. A.	*M.M.*, Student	Private, R.A.M.C.
Scott, R. R.	L.R.C.P. & S.I.	Temp. Lieut., R.A.M.C.
Scott, Samuel J.	L.R.C.P. & S.I.	Capt., C.O. Royal Irish Fusiliers
Scott, William D.	L.R.C.P. & S.I.	Civil Surgeon.

* Mentioned in Despatches.

ROYAL COLLEGE OF SURGEONS IN IRELAND.

Scribner, Bernard R.	L.R.C.P. & S.I.	Staff-Surgeon, R.N.
Seaver, Charles D. K.	L.R.C.P. & S.I.	Capt., R.A.M.C.
Sexton, George J.	L.R.C.P. & S.I.	Temp. Lieut., R.A.M.C.
Seymour, Thomas P.	L.R.C.P. & S.I.	Temp. Lieut., R.A.M.C.
*Shanahan, Daniel D.	*C.M.G., D.S.O.,* L.R.C.P. & S.I.	Col., A.M.S.
Sharpe, Frederick G.	L.R.C.P. & S.I.	Lieut., R.A.M.C. (Territorial Force)
Sharpe, William S.	F.R.C.S.I.	Lieut.-Col. R.A.M.C. (Territorial Force)
Sheedy, Thomas	L.R.C.P. & S.I.	Capt., R.A.M.C. (Special Reserve)
*Sheehan, George F.	*D.S.O.*, L.R.C.P. & S.I.	Major, R.A.M.C.
Sheehan, G. P.	L.R.C.P. & S.I.	Temp. Capt., R.A.M.C.
Shepherd, G. F.	F.R.C.S.I.	Temp. Lieut., R.A.M.C.
Shepherd, A.	Student	Private, R.A.M.C.
Sheppard, J. F.	L.R.C.P. & S.I.	Temp. Lieut., R.A.M.C.
*Sherlock, Charles G.	D.P.H., R.C.P. & S.I.	Capt., R.A.M.C. (died)
*Sherlock, Henry B.	L.R.C.P. & S.I. D.P.H.	Capt., R.A.M.C. (Special Reserve)
Shiel, George A.	L.R.C.P. & S.I.	Temp. Capt., R.A.M.C.
Shipsey, M.	L.R.C.P. & S.I.	Temp. Lieut., R.A.M.C.
*Shorten, James P.	*D.S.O.*, L.R.C.P. & S.I.	Surgeon, R.N.
*Siberry, Edward W.	L.R.C.P. & S.I.	Major, R.A.M.C.
Simons, William	L.D.S., R.C.S.I.	Civil Dental Surgeon
Sinclair, F. H.	L.R.C.P. & S.I.	M.O. on Transport
Skelly, C. A.	L.R.C.P. & S.I.	Temp. Lieut., R.A.M.C.

* Mentioned in Despatches.

74

ROYAL COLLEGE OF SURGEONS IN IRELAND.

SLANEY, ROBERT	L.R.C.P. & S.I.	Temp. Lieut., R.A.M.C.
SLATTERY, R. V.	F.R.C.S.I.	Capt., R.A.M.C.
SMALES, WILLIAM C.	D.P.H., R.C.P. & S.I.	Capt., R.A.M.C.
SMARTT, HENRY W.	L.R.C.S.I.	Temp. Capt., R.A.M.C.
SMARTT, WALTER	F.R.C.S.I.	North Hampshire Yeomanry
*SMARTT, WILLIAM F.	L.R.C.S.I.	Capt., R.A.M.C.
SMITH, FREDERICK	*C.M.G., D.S.O.,* L.R.C.P. & S.I.	Lieut.-Col., R.A.M.C.
SMITH, JOHN S.	L.D.S., R.C.S.I.	Temp. Lieut., R.A.M.C.
SMITH, MICHAEL J.	F.R.C.S.I.	Fleet-Surgeon, R.N.
SMITH, R. TRAVERS	Professor in R.C.S.I.	Temp. Major, R.A.M.C.
*SMYTH, GEOFFREY N.	L.R.C.P. & S.I.	Capt., R.A.M.C. (Special Reserve)
SMYTHE, J. A.	Student	Temp. Lieut., Royal Fusiliers
SMYTH, H. CARSON	L.R.C.P. & S.I.	Temp. Capt., R.A.M.C.
SMYTH, ROBERT M.	F.R.C.S.I.	Major, South African Medical Corps
SMYTH, JAMES C.	L.R.C.P. & S.I.	Temp. Lieut., R.A.F.M.S.
SOADY, WILLIAM H.	L.R.C.P. & S.I.	Temp. Lieut., R.A.M.C.
SOADY, ARTHUR R.	L.R.C.P. & S.I.	Lieut., R.A.M.C.
SPAIGHT, HENRY W.	L.R.C.P. & S.I.	R.A.M.C.
SPARROW, HENRY H. K.	L.R.C.P. & S.I.	Temp. Lieut., R.A.M.C.
SPILLER, WILLIAM M. H.	D.P.H., R.C.P. & S.I.	Major, R.A.M.C.
SPRENT, WILLIAM S.	L.R.C.P. & S.I.	Temp. Capt., R.A.M.C.
SPROULE, CHARLES L.	L.R.C.P. & S.I.	Temp. Lieut., R.A.M.C.

* Mentioned in Despatches.

ROYAL COLLEGE OF SURGEONS IN IRELAND.

*SPROULE, JAMES C.	L.R.C.P. & S.I.	Capt., R.A.M.C.
STACK, EDWARD C.	F.R.C.S.I.	Major, R.A.M.C.
*STANLEY, GEORGE W.	L.R.C.P. & S.I.	Temp. Capt., R.A.M.C.
STEELE, D. J.	L.R.C.P. & S.I.	Lieut., R.A.M.C.
STEPHENS, NORMAN E.	L.D.S., R.C.S.I.	Temp. Capt., R.A.M.C.
STEPHINSON, F. P.	Student	Royal Munster Fusiliers
STEVENS, THOMAS G.	F.R.C.S.I.	Temp. Lieut., R.A.M.C.
STOKER, EDWARD A. G.	Student	Lieut., Army Service Corps
STOKER, ERNEST W.	F.R.C.S.I.	Civil Surgeon
STOKER, GRAVES	F.R.C.S.I.	Temp. Capt., R.A.M.C.
STOKER, HENRY	L.R.C.P. & S.I.	Attached to Australian Forces
*STOKES, ADRIAN	F.R.C.S.I.	Temp. Capt., R.A.M.C.
STOKES, HENRY	F.R.C.S.I.	Capt., R.A.M.C.
STONE, FREDERICK W. S.	L.R.C.P. & S.I.	Temp. Capt., R.A.M.C.
STONEY, RICHARD A.	F.R.C.S.I.	French Croix Rouge
STONEY, ROBERT T.	L.R.C.P. & S.I.	Surgeon, R.N.
STORY, WILLIAM G. T.	L.D.S., R.C.S.I.	Capt., R.A.M.C.
STEVENS, NORMAN E.	L.D.S.I.	Lieut., R.A.M.C.
STRAHAN, GEORGE E.	Student	Surgeon Prob., R.N.V.R.
STEVENS, THOMAS A.	Student	Surg. Prob., R.N.
STREETEN, FRIEND E.	D.P.H., R.C.P. & S.I.	Capt., R.A.M.C. (Territorial Force)
STRINGER, CHARLES H.	L.R.C.P. & S.I.	Lt.-Col, R.A.M.C.

* Mentioned in Despatches.

76

ROYAL COLLEGE OF SURGEONS IN IRELAND.

STUDLEY, D. J.	Student	Private, R.D.F.
STUDLEY, THOMAS C.	Student	Private, R.A.M.C.
SUGRUE, T. E.	Student	Temp. Lieut.; The Welsh Regt.
SULLIVAN, MICHAEL A.	L.D.S., R.C.S.I.	Temp. Lieut., R.A.M.C.
SULLIVAN, C. J.	F.R.C.S.I.	Temp. Capt., R.A.M.C.
SWAIN, JAMES S.	L.R.C.P. & S.I.	Surgeon-Major, R.A.M.C. (Territorial Force)
SWANSON, ALEXANDER P.	L.R.C.S.I.	Lieut.-Col. R.A.M.C. (Territorial Force)
*SWEENY, TERENCE H.	F.R.C.S.I.	Lt.-Col., Indian Medical Service
*SWEETEN, BENJAMIN	*C.M.G.*, D.P.H., R.C.P. & S.I.	Temp. Lieut., R.A.M.C.
TABUTEAU, AUGUSTUS W.	F.R.C.S.I.	Temp. Lieut., R.A.M.C.
*TABUTEAU, GEORGE G.	L.R.C.P. & S.I.	Capt., R.A.M.C.
TATE, GERARD W.	D.P.H., R.C.P. & S.I.	Lieut.-Col., R.A.M.C.
TATE, JOHN J.	L.R.C.P. & S.I.	Temp. Col.
*TAYLOR, FRANCIS M. D.	*M.C.*, L.R.C.P. & S.I.	Major, R.A.M.C. (Special Reserve)
TAYLOR, JAMES D.	Student	2nd Lieut., R.F.C.
TAYLOR, WILLIAM J.	D.P.H., R.C.P. & S.I.	Lieut.-Col., R.A.M.C.
TAYLOR, JOHN C.	Student	Cadet
TAYLOR, WILLIAM K.	L.R.C.S.I.	Temp. Lieut., R.A.M.C.
TAYLOR, E. H.	F.R.C.S.I.	Temp. Lt.-Col., R.A.M.C.

* Mentioned in Despatches.

77

ROYAL COLLEGE OF SURGEONS IN IRELAND.

TAYLOR, ROBERT	Student	Private, Honourable Artillery Comp.
*TAYLOR, SIR WILLIAM	*K.B.E., C.B.,* President, R.C.S.I.	Temp. Col., A.M.S.
THOMAS, EDMUND F.	D.P.H., R.C.P. & S.I.	Temp. Surgeon, R.N.
THOMAS, ROLAND L.	D.P.H., R.C.P. & S.I.	Temp. Capt., R.A.M.C.
THOMPSON, WALTER A.	L.R.C.P. & S.I.	Temp. Lieut., R.A.M.C.
THOMPSON, EDWARD C.	L.R.C.S.I.	Major, R.A.M.C.
THOMPSON, ARTHUR C.	Student	2nd Lieut., R.I.R.
THOMSON, ROBERT P.	L.R.C.P. & S.I.	Temp. Lieut., R.A.M.C.
THOMSON, THOMAS M.	L.R.C.P. & S.I.	Temp. Capt., R.A.M.C.
THURSTON, ARTHUR T.	F.R.C.S.I.	Temp. Lieut., R.A.M.C.
TIGHE, HARMAN R.	F.R.C.S.I.	Temp. Lieut., R.A.M.C.
TIGHE, JOHN W.	Student	Surgeon Prob., R.N.V.R.
*TOBIN, WILLIAM J.	L.R.C.P. & S.I.	Capt., R.A.M.C.
TODD, J.	L.R.C.P. & S.I.	Temp. Lieut., R.A.M.C.
TOWNSEND, EVELYN R.	L.R.C.P. & S.I.	Staff-Surgeon, R.N.
TRANT, DAVID LEO	Student	Corpl., R.I.R.
TRIGG, OSCAR	L.D.S., R.C.S.I.	Dental Surgeon, Royal Naval Barracks, Devonport
TROTTER, WILLIAM J.	L.R.C.S.I.	Major, R.A.M.C.
TUKE, ARTHUR W.	F.R.C.S.I., D.P.H.	Major, Indian Medical Service
TURNER, N. H.	L.R.C.P. & S.I.	Civil Surgeon, City of London Military Hospital
*TWISS, GEORGE E.	L.R.C.S.I.	Lieut.-Col., R.A.M.C.
TYNAN, EDWARD	F.R.C.S.I.	West African Medical Service
TYSON, GEORGE G. M.	L.D.S., R.C.S.I.	Capt., R.A.M.C.

* Mentioned in Despatches.

78

ROYAL COLLEGE OF SURGEONS IN IRELAND.

Ussher, N. R.	L.R.C.P. & S.I.	Temp. Lieut., R.A.M.C.
Vernon, Lawrence P.	L.D.S., R.C.S.I.	Pte., Sth. African Forces
Vernon, Robert C.	L.R.C.P. & S.I.	District Surgeon, Rhodesian Horse, Cape Colony
Villiers, Henry J.	L.R.C.P. & S.I.	Temp. Lieut., R.A.M.C.
Wade, Joseph O'D'.	Student	Lieut., R.D.F.
Waddell, C. H.	L.R.C.P. & S.I.	Temp. Lieut., R.A.M.C.
Wade, George A.	F.R.C.S.I.	Major, R.A.M.C.
*Walker, Francis S.	F.R.C.S.I.	Major, R.A.M.C.
*Walker, Norman D.	D.P.H., R.C.P. & S.I.	Major, R.A.M.C.
Wallace, Bernard	L.R.C.P. & S.I.	Temp. Lieut., R.A.M.C.
Wallace, Cyril R.	L.R.C.P. & S.I.	Lieut. R.A.M.C. (Special Reserve)
*Wallace, Edward C.	*M.C.*, L.R.C.P. & S.I.	Temp. Lieut., R.A.M.C.
Wallace, Vivian	L.R.C.P. & S.I.	Temp. Lieut., R.A.M.C.
Walsh, John J.	L.R.C.P. & S.I.	Temp. Lieut., R.A.M.C.
Walsh, John F.	L.R.C.P. & S.I.	Temp. Lieut., R.A.M.C.
Walsh, Hubert P.	Student	2nd Lieut.
Walsh, Patrick B.	Student	Sergt., The Buffs
Walshe, Patrick W.	L.R.C.P. & S.I.	Temp. Lieut., R.A.M.C.

* Mentioned in Despatches

ROYAL COLLEGE OF SURGEONS IN IRELAND.

WARD, T. R.	Ex-Student	Temp. Lieut., Royal Welsh Fusiliers
*WARREN, PEYTON T.	L.R.C.P. & S.I.	Lieut., R.A.M.C. (Special Reserve)
WARD, PETER F.	L.R.C.P. & S.I.	Lieut., R.A.M.C. (Special Reserve)
WATERFIELD, REGINALD	L.R.C.P. & S.I.	Staff-Surgeon, Royal Navy
WATERS, WILLIAM R. L.	L.R.C.P. & S.I.	Temp. Lieut., R.A.M.C.
WATSON, THOMAS E.	D.P.H., R.C.P. & S.I.	Major, Indian Medical Service
WAUGH, W.	L.R.C.P. & S.I.	Temp. Lieut., R.A.M.C.
WAYLAND, R. S.	Student	Surgeon Probationer, R.N.V.R.
WAYLAND, R. S.	F.R.C.S.I.	Civil Surgeon, W.R.O
WELDON, R. P.	L.R.C.P. & S.I.	Temp. Capt., R.A.M.C.
WELPLY, MARY R. R.	L.R.C.S.I.,	Civil Surgeon
*WEST, JOHN W.	D.P.H., R.C.P. & S.I.	Lt.-Col., R.A.M.C.
WESTCOTT, SINCLAIR	*G.M.C.*, D.P.H., R.C.P. & S.I.	Col., Army Medical Service
WESTROPP, H. G.	L.R.C.P. & S.I.	Temp. Lieut., R.A.M.C.
WHEELER, HENRY G. O.	L.R.C.P. & S.I.	Temp. Lieut., R.A.M.C.
WHEELER, WILLIAM I. DE C.	F.R.C.S.I.	Lt.-Col, R.A.M.C.
WHELAN, JOHN	L.R.C.P. & S.I.	Staff-Surgeon, Royal Navy
*WHELAN LAWDER T.	*M C.*, F.R.C.S.I.	Temp. Capt., R.A.M.C.
WHITE, WILLIAM O'B.	L.R.C.S.I.	Hon. Brigade Surgeon, R.A.M.C.
WHITE, ROBERT S.	F.R.C.S.I.	Capt., R.A.M.C.
WHYTE, GEORGE T.	F.R.C.S.I.	Temp. Capt., R.A.M.C.
WILEY, ALAN	L.R.C.P. & S.I.	Temp. Lieut., R.A.M.C.

* Mentioned in Despatches.

80

ROYAL COLLEGE OF SURGEONS IN IRELAND.

Wilkinson, G. B.	L.R.C.P. & S.I.	Major, S.A.M.C. 5th M.B.F.A.
*Williams, Roger L.	D.P.H., R.C.P. & S.I.	Temp., Capt., R.A.M.C.
Williams, Thomas E. H.	L.R.C.P. & S.I.	Deputy Inspector General, R.N. (Retired), Admiralty Recruiting Service
Williamson, H. N.	Student	8th North Hants. Regt.
Wills, Samuel T.	Student	2nd Lieut., Northamptonshire Regt.
*Wills, Samuel R.	L.R.C.P. & S.I.	Lieut.-Col., R.A.M.C.
Wilson, C. Henry	L.R.C.P. & S.I.	Temp. Lieut., R.A.M.C.
Wilson, T. J.	Student	Temp. Lieut. 6th Royal Dublin Fusiliers
Wilson, Thomas W.	Clerk, Anatomy Dept.	Private, R.A.M.C.
Wilson, W. R.	F.R.C.S.I., D.P.H.	Temp. Lieut., R.A.M.C.
Wilson, Gilbert R.	L.R.C.P. & S.I.	Temp. Lieut., R.A.M.C.
Wilson, Sir William D.	*K.C.M.G.*, L.R.C.S.I.	Surgeon-Genl., A.M.S.
Windmill, W. H.	L.D.S., R.C.S.I.	Civil Dental Surgeon
Wishart, Robert M.	D.P.H., R.C.P. & S.I.	Temp. Lieut., R.A.M.C.
Woodroffe, G. C. L.	L.R.C.P. & S.I.	Capt., R.A.M.C.
Woodroffe, George F.	L.R.C.P. & S.I.	Civil Surgeon.
Woods, Charles R.	F.R.C.S.I.	Lieut.-Col., R.A.M.C.
Woods, Frederick W.	L.R.C.P. & S.I.	Temp. Lieut., R.A.M.C.
*Woods, Lionel D.	L.R.C.P. & S.I.	Temp., Capt., R.A.M.C.
Woodside, William A.	*D.S.O.*, L.R.C.P. & S.I.	Lieut.-Col., R.A.M.C.
Woodwright, Charles S.	L.R.C.S.I.	Fleet-Surgeon, R.N.

* Mentioned in Despatches.

ROYAL COLLEGE OF SURGEONS IN IRELAND.

Woodwright, William H. E.	F.R.C.S.I.	Lt.-Col., Indian Medical Service
Wright, Sir Almroth E.	Hon. F.R.C.S.I.	Temp. Col., Army Medical Service
Wilson, David P.	Student	Lieut., R.A.F.
Wilson, Thomas W.	Student	Pilot Off., R.A.F.
Wilson, Geo. Edwd.	Student	Corpl., Norfolk Regt.
White, Barry Alcorn	Student	Trooper
Wherry, John Holmes	Student	Lieut.
Wright, Robert A.	L.R.C.P. & S.I.	Temp. Lieut., R.A.M.C.
*Wright, Thomas J.	*D.S.O.*, L.R.C.P. & S.I.	Lt.-Col., R.A.M.C.
*Wright, William G.	L.R.C.P. & S.I.	Major, R.A.M.C.
Wright, Hugh R.	L.R.C.P. & S.I.	Temp. Lieut., R.A.M.C.
Wyatt, Claud	L.D.S., R.C.S.I.	Temp. Lieut., R.A.M.C.
Wylie, David T.	L.R.C.P. & S.I.	Civil Surgeon
Wynne, Owen W. J.	L.R.C.P. & S.I.	Capt., R.A.M.C.
Wynne, Albert E.	F.R.C.S.I.	Temp. Capt., R.A.M.C.
Wyse, Thomas F.	L.R.C.P. & S.I.	Temp. Lieut., R.A.M.C.
*Yarr, Michael T.	*K.C.M.G.*, *C.B.*, F.R.C.S.I.	Major-Genl., Army Medical Service
Young, Augustus H. O.	L.R.C.P. & S.I.	Lieut.-Col., R.A.M.C.
Young, B. P.	L.R.C.P. & S.I.	Temp., Capt., R.A.M.C.
Young, Charles A.	*C.M.G.*, L.R.C.P. & S.I.	Col., Army Medical Service
Young, David E.	L.R.C.P. & S.I.	Temp. Lieut., R.A.M.C.
Younge, George H.	F.R.C.S.I.	Lieut.-Col., R.A.M.C.
Ziervogel, Jacob P.	F.R.C.S.I., D.P.H.	Temp. Lieut., R.A.M.C.

* Mentioned in Despatches.

82

ROYAL COLLEGE OF SURGEONS IN IRELAND.

DUBLIN No. 83 GENERAL HOSPITAL, BOULOGNE.

This Hospital was organised and maintained for 12 months by the President of the College, Colonel Sir William Taylor, *K.B.E., C.B.* The following composed the Staff:—

*Col. Sir William Taylor, *K.B.E., C.B.,* Chief of Staff and Organiser.

Temp. Major Sir C. Arthur Ball, Bart.
Temp. Major C. P. Ball.
Temp. Major C. M. Benson.
Temp. Major A. J. Blayney.
Temp. Capt. C. E. Boyce.
Temp. Capt. A. E. Boyd.
Temp. Capt. R. M. Bronte.
Temp. Capt. W. J. Corbett.
Temp. Capt. F. C. Crawley.
Temp. Lt.-Col. H. C. Drury.
Temp. Lt.-Col. T. E. Gordon.
Temp. Major L. G. Gunn.
Temp. Capt. M. R. J. Hayes.
Temp. Lt.-Col. G. J. Johnston.
Temp. Major D. Kennedy.
Temp. Major L. Kidd.
Temp. Capt. J. W. Killen.
Temp. Major S. H. Law.
Temp. Major J. Lumsden.
Temp. Major R. C. B. Maunsell.
Temp. Capt. G. P. Meldon.
Temp. Lt.-Col. T. G. Moorhead.
Temp. Lt.-Col. A. R. Parsons.
Temp. Lt.-Col. R. J. Rowlette.
Temp. Lt.-Col. E. H. Taylor.
Temp Capt. E. J. Watson.
Temp. Major W. A. Winter.

DUBLIN CASTLE RED CROSS HOSPITAL.

The following is the Executive Committee of the Students of the College who organized and equipped a Ward in the above Hospital:—

Chairman—*J. C. Fergusson.

Miss E. Budd.
W. H. Carden.
T. N. D'Arcy.
W. R. Dimond.
M. Dockrell.
K. Elmes.
C. E. H. Gater.
J. F. Lyons.
†W. G. McConnell.
Miss M. McMullen.
†J. O'Brien.
G. C. Woodroffe.

All the foregoing joined His Majesty's Forces, and it is to be regretted that two have been killed in action.

* Mentioned in Despatches. † Killed in Action.

83

ROYAL COLLEGE OF SURGEONS IN IRELAND.

The Officers' Training Corps at present consists of three Officers, one Instructor, 138 Cadets. It is under the control of the Military Education Committee appointed by the Council as follows:—

The President, *Col. Sir William Taylor, *K.B.E., C.B.*,

The Vice-President, John B. Story.

*Col. Sir Thomas Myles, *C.B.*,

Lt.-Col. Sir Lambert H. Ormsby.

Henry G. Sherlock.

Edward H. Taylor.

*Temp. Lt.-Col. Wm. I. de C. Wheeler.

Alexander Blayney

(Ex-Officio Members.)

The Officer Commanding and Acting Adjutant — Lt. Alfred Miller.

Officers.

2nd Lt. C. H. Gick.

2nd Lt. G. A. Henderson.

Instructor.

Sergt.-Major Redding.

Over 150 Members of the Officers Training Corps (other than those with Commissions), are at present serving in various capacities with His Majesty's Forces.

* Mentioned in Despatches.

T.F. Duggan

John Dunlea

Francis Gleeson

John Gwynn

Joseph J. Matthews

FIGURE 5.1 *Portraits of five NUI chaplains.*

5. *Maynooth Chaplains*

St Patrick's College and the First World War

BARBARA MCCORMACK[1]

IRISH CATHOLIC PRIESTS represented at least one in four Catholic chaplains serving with the British Forces in the First World War. Many of these priests trained at Ireland's national Catholic seminary, St Patrick's College, Maynooth, which became a recognised college of the National University of Ireland in 1910, enabling seminarians to complete an accredited undergraduate degree before progressing to a four-year course of theology. Maynooth graduates made up approximately sixty of the total number of Irish Catholic priests to receive commissions as Temporary Chaplains to the Forces, yet very little scholarship has been undertaken on them as a collective. The NUI Roll of Honour, printed in 1919 to commemorate the involvement of over 1,000 staff, students, and graduates who served in the war, does not include a listing from St Patrick's College, Maynooth. This chapter will present the names of Irish Catholic priests who studied at Maynooth and served as military chaplains with the British Forces (see Honorary List). It will provide an overview of the background, military service, post-war experiences of many of these chaplains and will explore the potential impact of the Easter Rising on chaplaincy recruitment through an analysis of commission trends. The role of St Patrick's College, Maynooth in the recruitment of army chaplains will also be discussed.

Although this chapter focuses on Irish Catholic chaplains it is important to remember the significant contribution of other religious denominations to the British Forces in the First World War. Jane Leonard has noted, for instance, that the Church of Ireland contributed at least 109 military chaplains, while the Irish Presbyterian church and Irish Methodist church contributed at least twenty-five and twenty-seven chaplains respectively.[2] It should also be noted that Catholic priests from religious orders were more likely to volunteer for military service than diocesan priests.[3] Current figures suggest that over one hundred priests from orders such as the Society of Jesus, the Congregation of the Passion of Jesus Christ (Passionists), and the Vincentian Order, served as Irish military chaplains in the war. Other chaplains were ordained in diocesan seminaries around Ireland such as St Patrick's College, Carlow and St Peter's College, Wexford, and in the Irish colleges abroad in Salamanca, Rome, and Paris. An analysis of these chaplains is beyond the scope of the current study, which is limited to those graduates from St Patrick's College, Maynooth.

Over the past twenty-five years, research on Catholic chaplains in the British Army during the First World War has increased significantly, particularly during the commemorative period 2014–18, which saw publications like Damien Burke's *Irish Jesuit Chaplains in the First World War*, James Hagerty's *Priests in Uniform*, and Oliver Rafferty's article 'Catholic chaplains to the British Forces in the First World War'.[4] Research on the wider issues of army recruitment and enlistment in Ireland has been conducted by historians such as Patrick Callan and Thomas P. Dooley. Callan has written about army recruitment in Ireland in the First World War and looks at various factors including the age of recruits, differences between rural and urban centres in recruitment, and religious affiliation.[5] Dooley has considered the complexities surrounding the enlistment of Irish Catholic soldiers in the British Army by examining three important areas: social and economic background; immediate reasons for enlistment; and experience of military service.[6] Firstly, an analysis of the socio-economic background of recruits enables the identification of potential factors impacting enlistment, particularly in terms of 'Catholicism and nationalist traditions' and the wider influence of John Redmond's Irish Parliamentary Party.[7] Secondly, Dooley examined what he described as 'more immediate reasons for the man's decision to enlist', which includes the impact of mobilisation, propaganda and recruiting campaigns, familial and community influence, and political beliefs.[8] Finally, Dooley explored the reasons for continued loyalty to the British Army and the impact of military training and service.[9] Some of these factors can also be considered in the context of army-chaplain recruitment and volunteering.

Tom Johnstone and James Hagerty's seminal work on Catholic chaplains in the British Armed Forces from the late eighteenth-century onwards provides an important analysis of the structure and administration of chaplains within the wider army.[10] Edward Madigan's study of Anglican army chaplains in the First World War (2011) also provides an important contextual analysis for this chapter.[11] In 2003, Jérôme aan de Wiel explored the attitudes of the Irish Catholic church during the period 1914–18, adopting a largely thematic rather than strictly chronological approach, which enables an in-depth analysis of seminal events such as the Easter Rising and the conscription crisis against the backdrop of the First World War.[12] De Wiel notes the limitations in a traditional military or commemorative approach to the historiography of the war, instead advocating an analysis of less explored areas such as the attitude of the Catholic Church.[13]

Over 800 Catholic priests served as chaplains with the British Forces during the First World War. However, a comprehensive database of Irish Catholic chaplains does not exist and building such a resource, according to Hugh O'Neill, is fraught with difficulties for a number of reasons, including: a lack of surviving records; the fact that many priests were ordained in Ireland for dioceses in England and elsewhere; and inconsistencies with names across sources.[14] These challenges also made it difficult to compile a comprehensive listing of chaplains who studied at St Patrick's College, Maynooth. A relational database of Irish Catholic army chaplains was created using data extracted from the 'Alphabetical list of the clergy of Ireland' in the *Irish Catholic Directory* for the years 1914–19. These entries were then cross-referenced against Patrick J. Hamell's *Maynooth Students and Ordinations Index* and in some cases, the original matriculation ledgers in the archive of St Patrick's College, Maynooth, to determine possible affiliations with the college.[15] Official information from the *London Gazette* and the surviving military service files for officers in the British Army in the National Archives (UK) provided information on military service, and biographical information was collated from newspaper reports and other primary sources.

Maynooth and the war

At the outbreak of war in 1914, St Patrick's College Maynooth had served as Ireland's national Catholic seminary for nearly 120 years. Established in 1795 by an act of the Irish Parliament, it had experienced a complex relationship with the British Government, which it relied upon for financial support in the form of the annual Maynooth grant. This dependency was effectively ended by the Irish Church Act 1869, which removed state funding and afforded the college greater autonomy over its affairs. The University Education (Ireland) Act 1879 meant that Maynooth students could present themselves for examinations to the Royal University of

Ireland. In 1910, Maynooth was formally recognised as a college of the National University of Ireland, which had been established under the Irish Universities Act, 1908. Students could now matriculate and graduate from NUI, in preparation for their ecclesiastical studies and subsequent ordination.

The course of study at Maynooth took an average of seven years to complete and typically consisted of a three-year philosophy and arts degree followed by four years of theology. Candidates generally matriculated (enrolled) at the Royal University in June and in September entered the class of Rhetoric (first university year) at Maynooth. They sat their first-year arts examinations at the end of the academic year and progressed onto Philosophy I (first-year BA) and then to Philosophy II (second year BA), after which they sat their final degree examinations and generally proceeded directly to the course of theology. However, some students received their undergraduate degrees elsewhere and entered Maynooth for the course of theology.

The socio-economic background of priests was important. According to James O'Shea, the absence of a non-farming Catholic middle-class in the nineteenth century meant that rural priests were typically from farming backgrounds.[16] A randomised sample of fifty-three students at Maynooth College in 1911 indicates that twenty-eight were from farming backgrounds (approximately 53%). A similar study of thirty-nine students at Maynooth in 1901, using matriculation records from the Royal University of Ireland, indicates that twenty-three students were from farming backgrounds (approximately 59%). This is consistent with Oliver Rafferty's assertion that Irish priests in the First World War were generally from the small farmer class rather than the working classes of Irish society.[17]

Not all seminarians studied in Ireland. The closure of the Irish College in Paris, following the outbreak of the First World War, resulted in the admission of an additional forty-five students to Maynooth in October 1914, bringing the total number of students on the college roll to 581. This increase, coupled with poor investments and additional expenditure, affected college finances, a situation that was exacerbated by the loss of £1,000 from the annual Belgian burses, funds that were received from the Malines, Brabant and Hainault Commissions to support Irish Catholic education.[18] The President of Maynooth College, Monsignor John F. Hogan, requested assistance from the (British) Foreign Office to secure this funding and was informed that Foreign Secretary, Sir Edward Grey, would contact the Belgian Government. However, by the third week of October the deteriorating situation in Belgium meant that any intervention on behalf of the college was impossible.[19] The last payment received for the Belgian burse-holders at Maynooth was £190 19*s* 1*d.* in July 1913, which represented six months' payment for fifteen burse-holders.[20] In 1915, a special committee, consisting of three bishops and the finance council of the college, considered the expected deficit arising from, amongst other things, the escalating prices of food, fuel and other supplies caused by the war. The joint committee also speculated on the possibility of an economic depression, noting that 'after the war increased numbers of the helpless and dependent populations will have to be maintained, and the business of the world will be dislocated beyond recognition'.[21] They recommended a continued suspension of thirty free places at the college and a fee increase of £5 per student which would result in an additional £2,600 per year. Moreover, they recommended 'that the connection of the College with the National University be examined by an experienced Committee with a view to curtailment of expenses'.[22]

This complicated an already problematic financial situation whereby students could obtain degrees and leave the college voluntarily before committing to theological studies or before ordination. For instance, five students voluntarily left the college in 1914–15, one of these was a fourth-year divinity student, another was a second-year university student and the remaining three were from the first-year divinity class leading the president to surmise that 'some young men find the road to a University Degree more conveniently and cheaply through Maynooth than they could through any other College, while they have no definite intention of devoting their lives to the Church'.[23]

The war directly impacted the academic curriculum at Maynooth. For instance, Rev Heinrich Bewerunge, Professor of Ecclesiastical Music since 1888, was unable to return to Ireland following a vacation in his native Germany. In September 1914, Bewerunge requested college assistance to secure a passport from the British Government so that he could leave Cologne.[24] The request was ultimately denied by the Home Office which stated:

> The application of Rev H. Bewerunge for permission to return to Ireland was received in September and was very carefully considered at the time. After consulting the Irish Government, the Home Secretary felt unable to give permission asked for. Mr. McKenna has again consulted the Irish Government, and he finds that there are no circumstances which would justify him in revising his decision.[25]

A year later, in September 1915, Bewerunge questioned the nature of Belgian neutrality in a letter to the rector of the Irish College in Salamanca, stating that 'Belgium had ceased to be neutral before the war broke, and that they had binding arrangements with France and England to let their troops through and join them in a campaign against Germany'.[26] The recently appointed Professor of Modern Languages, the Abbé Jean-Louis Rigal, was in Germany at the University of Breslau in 1914 and narrowly avoided internment by travelling to France where he reported to the military authorities. He was later drafted into the auxiliary services in the French Army.[27]

In October 1914, President Hogan publicly deplored the German invasion of neutral Belgium, expressing 'the deep and heartfelt sympathy' of Irish Catholics towards the people of Belgium and noting the strong Christian links between both countries.[28] At the same time, rumours were emerging of a pro-German sentiment at Maynooth, indicative of a wider cultural and political duality between older members of the establishment and the student body. Thomas Gilmartin, Bishop of Clonfert, voiced his concerns about the apparent 'good deal of pro-German feeling in Maynooth' in a letter to the president in March 1915.[29] There is evidence to suggest that Monsignor Hogan was concerned with the optics of such sentiments and was careful to present an outward image of support for the entente powers. This cautionary approach extended to external speakers invited by student societies such as the League of St Columba, founded in 1898 to encourage an appreciation of Irish language and culture at Maynooth, which was forced to abandon its plans to engage an external speaker for its annual lecture in the Aula Maxima 'because the President laid down a rather rigid censorship for an extern lecturer – banning anything in the way of "Pro-German" statements or sentiments'.[30]

In 1966, a Maynooth graduate described the general atmosphere at Maynooth in August 1914 when Britain entered the war:

> I was anxious as to what effect the war would have on the Catholic Church. I was thinking of the war and God. Concentrate as I would on meditation, prayer, and study I had many distractions [...] There I was, thinking of the war and Ireland. That was the way that all the Junior students were thinking – of God and Ireland'.[31]

Additional pressure may have been placed on the college by the British Government. In November 1917, Captain George S. Gordon wrote to Monsignor Hogan in a bid to confirm the number of college staff serving with the forces and to verify an earlier estimate of between eighty and 100.[32] Gordon wrote from Adastral House in Blackfriars, London (formerly De Keyser's Hotel), which in 1916 was occupied by the Air Ministry.[33] If this estimation was correct it suggests that a significant number of staff at the college were actively serving with the forces during the war. Patrick Corish has noted that in 1916 the college received a request from a recruiting officer to interview staff and students.[34] The request was ultimately rejected by the college's Administrative Council, but a compromise was reached so that the officer could approach workmen at the college gates when they left work.

The war's financial and academic disruption at Maynooth College was experienced against a backdrop of increasing pressure to assist with chaplaincy recruitment. There was, to some extent, a tradition of Maynooth graduates serving as military chaplains. In 1877, for instance, Rev Denis Forde, who was ordained as an extern in 1846, died while serving as an army chaplain at St Thomas's Mount, Madras in India.[35] Other graduates served as chaplains in the South African War. Rev Francis Timoney from Co Fermanagh, for instance, studied at Maynooth and at the Irish College in Paris, after which he undertook fourteen-years missionary work in Australia.[36] Timoney left the newly established parish of Mosman and Neutral Bay, North Sydney, and spent thirteen months as Catholic chaplain to the New South Wales Citizens' Bushmen Contingent in South Africa before his death at the age of forty-three.[37] It was also common for Maynooth graduates to serve as chaplains in military barracks around Ireland, such as the Curragh Camp in Co Kildare and the Fermoy Barracks in Co Cork. However, the unprecedented scale and duration of the First World War saw much larger numbers of priests seeking commissions as army chaplains, which created vacancies in parishes around Ireland.

Chaplaincy recruitment

The role of the Catholic army chaplain in the First World War was primarily to address the spiritual needs of sailors and soldiers, which meant that much of their time was spent attending to the dead and dying.[38] Leonard has described the role of the chaplain in the war as 'a combination of undertaker and entertainments officer'. John Hagerty in his work *Priests in Uniform* detailed the role of the average Catholic chaplain which included: administering the last rites to both sides of the conflict, saying mass when possible, hearing confession, giving the Blessed Sacrament, burying the dead, and giving cigarettes, pipes, and other luxuries to the men where possible. He notes however, the difficulties facing new chaplains in the field which included a lack of formal training and mentorship and previous army experience, as well as the loneliness, worry, and fear experienced by both chaplains and soldiers at the front. Senior members of the British Army such as Field Marshall Sir Douglas Haig were keenly aware of the positive impact of religion on soldier's morale and the importance of army chaplains in this regard.[39] Colonel J.E. Nelson, who served in the Irish Guards, the Royal Inniskilling Fusiliers, and the Prince of Wales's Leinster Regiment in the war, would later describe the impact of Catholic chaplains on the troops, noting that 'it was said with justice that a Catholic Chaplain was worth two extra officers to an Irish battalion, so great was this influence on all ranks, both Catholics and Protestants'.[40]

Fifteen Catholic chaplains were serving with the Army Chaplains' Department in the British Army at the outbreak of the war, with a further six acting army chaplains assuming the rank of Temporary Chaplain 4th Class on 30 August 1914.[41] One of these, Rev Peter Bonaventure Bradley OFM, from Draperstown, Co Kerry, had studied in Rome and was ordained at St Isidore's in 1881.[42] Another, Rev William Murphy, studied in Rome and was ordained at St Patrick's College, Carlow.[43] In September 1914, just twelve Catholic chaplains were serving with the British Expeditionary Force (BEF) and by early October it was clear that the priority of the War Office was to supply chaplains to Kitchener's Army rather than at the front.[44] One of the reasons for this was restrictions on the number of non-combatants in the field, which meant that more than two thirds of chaplains were serving with regiments at home.[45]

The Catholic hierarchy described the situation as 'lamentably inadequate' at their annual meeting in October 1914.[46] They noted: 'The dying Catholic is entitled to the last Sacraments, and he needs them. Neither his right nor his need is the less because he dies at war'.[47] The main barrier in terms of chaplaincy recruitment was, according to the bishops, the policy of restricting the transport of Irish priests to the front, which they described as short-sighted. Rafferty has written about the political tensions between the Irish and English Catholic hierarchies that impacted chaplaincy recruitment.[48] In 1906, Francis Bourne, Archbishop of Westminster, assumed responsibility for all Catholic army chaplains in Britain; with local prelates assuming control of chaplains in Ireland and India.[49] This ultimately led to confusion around the role of Cardinal Michael Logue, Archbishop of Armagh and Primate of All Ireland, in the administration of volunteers.

At a visit to the parish of Dundalk in October 1914, Cardinal Logue spoke about the need for Irish Catholic chaplains to accompany Irish regiments at the front, stating that he had been approached to appoint Irish priests to the New Army.[50] In a letter to the editor of the *Irish Independent*, dated 27 October 1914, Cardinal Logue sought to clarify the situation, explaining that although many priests had applied directly to him to serve as army chaplains, he had received no authorisation from the War Office in this regard. Logue quoted an extract from a letter he received from the War Office:

> As you are doubtless aware, the nomination of Roman Catholic priests for military duty is normally in the hands of Cardinal Bourne [Westminster], but having regard to the distinctively national character of the Divisions now in question and the fact that, for the present at least, they will be serving in Ireland, it is considered desirable that the selection of priests for duty with them should be in the hands of the head of the Roman Catholic Church in the country.[51]

This prompted a letter in the *Irish Independent* criticising the War Office and stating that '[t]he request to Cardinal Logue to appoint chaplains to the future Irish Division does not aim at supplying for the soldiers in the field at all'.[52]

Growing pressure on the War Office contributed to the appointment of additional chaplains in November 1914, resulting in over sixty commissioned chaplains serving Catholic troops. Sixteen additional priests, eight of whom were nominated by Cardinal Logue, were given temporary commissions by the 24 November 1914.[53] One of these was Rev Francis Gleeson, a Tipperary-born priest from the diocese of Dublin who studied at Maynooth and was ordained in 1910. Another was Rev Edward Dowling who studied at St Kieran's College, Kilkenny and was ordained at Maynooth in 1908 for the diocese of Ossory. Increased pressure on the War Office meant that, by early December 1914, the number of chaplains serving with the BEF had greatly increased. However, this had a knock-on effect on parishes throughout Ireland, for example Bishop Thomas Gilmartin wrote to Monsignor Hogan seeking additional priests for the diocese of Clonfert to fill vacancies arising from chaplaincy appointments, noting that one of his priests 'is appointed to a Highland regiment and the other to the Irish Brigade'.[54]

The urgent need of navy chaplains in particular was discussed at the Standing Committee of the Irish bishops in January 1915, which passed a resolution that 'as pastors of our brave men, who are so heroic in the service of the State, we will not, and cannot, cease to cry out til their spiritual rights are duly protected'. He later remarked on the difficulties experienced by chaplains in the navy attempting to minister to Catholics on various ships.[55] This pressure would continue throughout the war and in May 1915, Monsignor Hogan wrote to the organisers of an upcoming recruitment meeting for chaplains stating that 'the more men you get, and the more effectively they do their work, the better I shall be pleased'.[56] Four months later, the Archbishop of Westminster, Cardinal Francis Bourne, wrote to members of the Catholic hierarchy appealing 'for their kindly aid in meeting the demand for another large increase in the number of chaplains for the Army and Navy', requesting an additional twenty-five priests to supplement the 270 serving chaplains.[57] Bourne sent the letter to Monsignor Hogan with a personal note lamenting the disappointing response from Ireland: 'In confidence I may say that Westminster has given more secular priests than the whole of Ireland. I know that you will do everything in your power to help'.[58]

Chaplaincy recruitment remained a key concern for the Irish hierarchy at their annual meeting on 12 October 1915 in which they called for applications from members of the secular and regular clergy in order to meet what they deemed 'the spiritual wants of our Catholic sailors and soldiers, at the fronts'.[59] Madigan has noted that by 1916, the military authorities were becoming increasingly aware of the positive impact of chaplains on soldier morale.[60] In February 1916, Cardinal Logue publicly asked Irish priests to apply directly to Cardinal Bourne in Westminster regarding army chaplaincy.[61] Archbishop Walsh also addressed the issue of chaplaincy recruitment in a letter to the *Freeman's Journal* listing the names of twelve priests from the diocese of Dublin, which included Maynooth alumni Francis Gleeson and Laurence Stafford.[62]

Supplying chaplains

In May 1916, the Bishop of Ross, Denis Kelly, declared that 'no doubt, newly ordained priests are not the most suitable army chaplains, but it would be better to have them than to leave the Irish Church under the stigma of deserting her soldiers and sailors.' Eight students from fourth year divinity volunteered as army chaplains in October 1916.[64] Three of these were from the diocese of Dublin, while the remaining five were from Kerry, Tuam, Achonry, Cloyne, and Down and Connor. Despite the willingness of the college to ordain these students, just three of them received permission from their respective bishops.[65] Timothy A. Hurley, Jeremiah Pigott, and Michael J. Mullins were subsequently ordained in December 1916 and were commissioned as chaplains in February 1917.

Hurley, from Portmagee in Co Kerry, was temporarily stationed at the Avington Park Camp before joining the 4th Reserve Battalion at the Hazeley Down Camp, Winchester, where he was nominated for service with the British Salonika Force along with fellow Maynooth alumnus, Rev Matthew Joseph O'Carroll from the diocese of Kilmore, who was with the 14th Training Reserve Battalion at Brockton Camp in Staffordshire.[66] The two priests left Southampton in June 1917. Hurley renewed his contract of service in June 1918 and was attached to the 11th Welsh Regiment in the 84th Infantry Brigade when he relinquished his commission in July 1919. He later taught at St Brendan's Seminary and served as curate in a number of parishes before becoming parish priest of Tuosist in 1945 and Abbeydorney in 1954.[67] He was a supporter of the language movement and was a native Irish speaker.[68]

Rev Michael Joseph Mullins, from Ballinacarrow, Co Sligo also applied for service in January 1917 and was selected for duty with the BEF in March 1917, later serving in the Norfolk War (General) Hospital in Norwich.[69] Mullins went to Los Angeles after the War where he served in the parish of the Good Shepherd and was involved in the Catholic Motion Picture Actors Guild.[70] Rev Jeremiah Pigott of Liscarroll, Co Cork, served as military chaplain with the British Army in the First World War and the Royal Air Force in the Second World war before joining the Maynooth Mission to China.[71] Pigott visited Maynooth in 1917 and encouraged other students to volunteer as army chaplains. One of these students was Thomas Gallagher, a third-year divinity student from the diocese of Cloyne, who wrote to his bishop in April 1917 asking for permission to be ordained with his classmate James Galvin in June 1917.[72] The letter was subsequently referred to Monsignor Hogan with the following note: 'What do you say to this request. Is it advisable to ordain them for Front at end of this scholar year?'[73] The request was discussed at a meeting of the administrative council, which noted that 'such students had not read such important tracts as Justice, Restitution and Contracts and could not be examined on these before ordination'.[74] Gallagher and Galvin were not ordained until 28 April 1918, with Galvin joining the Maynooth Mission to China shortly afterwards.[75] In late 1917, the college adopted a new text on canonical rights, the 'Codex Juris canonical', which contained strict rules on the ordinations process, which meant that sub-deaconship and deaconship could not be conferred on students until they finished third and fourth year divinity respectively.[76]

Casualties

A total of forty-one Catholic priests died while serving as chaplains in the British Army during the First World War.[80] Four of these had studied at Maynooth – the Reverends Donal O'Sullivan, Stephen Clarke, Matthew Prendergast, and John Watters. Donal O'Sullivan was born in Killarney, Co Kerry in the year 1890 and was educated at St Brendan's Seminary in Killarney and at Maynooth College where he was ordained in 1914.[81] He was appointed to the BEF in 1916 and served in the 8th Battalion of the Loyal North Lancashire Regiment, a service battalion of Kitchener's Army. He was killed by a shell on the fifth day of the Battle of the Somme, while ministering to the wounded, less than five months after volunteering.[82] Rev C.T. McGuinness, of the 76th Field Ambulance, BEF, France, wrote to the President of Maynooth College in July 1916 regarding O'Sullivan's death:

> He [O'Sullivan] was quite fearless and faced any danger when it was a question of giving the Sacraments to the wounded and dying. He had a fine character, cheerful and energetic, and was one of the most zealous chaplains I have met.[83]

O'Sullivan was described as 'an enthusiastic Gaelic Leaguer and Irish Irelander' and had spoken on the need to support Irish manufacture.[84] He reportedly received thirty-six converts to Catholicism during his short time in the war.[85] He was later described as having 'passionate and practical patriotism'.[86]

Stephen Clarke was born in Bailieborough, Co Cavan in 1888. He studied at St Patrick's College, Cavan and at Maynooth where he was ordained in 1912.[87] Clarke was curate of Ballintemple when he volunteered with the BEF in March 1916, serving with the Shropshire Light Infantry and later the 7th Battalion of the Lancashire Fusiliers.[88] Clarke was killed in action on 4 October 1917 and is commemorated on the Tyne Cot Memorial; his body was never found.[89] His name appears next to that of Rev Willie Doyle who died at the Battle of Langemarck on 16 August 1917. A report in the *Tablet* newspaper later stated that Clarke's 'unsparing devotion to duty had gained for him the grateful admiration of both officers and men'.[90] An inventory of Clarke's effects, compiled by the BEF on his death, included a cigarette case, broken spectacles, photographs, letters, postcards, and a German book.[91]

Rev Matthew Vincent Prendergast, from Lismore, Co Waterford, studied at St John's College before Maynooth and was ordained in 1908.[92] He applied for service with the Expeditionary Force in 1915 while at the Presbytery, Hebburn-on-Tyne. Prendergast was appointed Acting Chaplain to the 7th and 4th Reserve Infantry Brigades at Purfleet.[93] He joined the Egyptian Expeditionary Force (EEF) in September 1916. In March 1917, he was posted to the 31st General Hospital in Salonika. He renewed his contract of service with the Expeditionary Force in July 1917, but was later admitted to the Nasrieh Hospital in Cairo while 'dangerously ill', dying four days later on 16 September 1918 at the age of thirty-seven.[94] The last Maynooth graduate to die in the war was the Rev John Watters, ordained in 1917 for the diocese of Tuam, who had served for four months before he died of natural causes at the age of twenty-six while on active service with the 115th Infantry Brigade in France. He is buried in the Awoingt British Cemetery.

Military service

Many Maynooth graduates served in the British Expeditionary Force on the Western Front, which experienced some of the bloodiest battles of the war including the Battle of the Somme and the Third Battle of Ypres (also known as Passchendaele) while others served with the 10th (Irish) Division in Gallipoli, Salonika, and Palestine. They were also attached to the Egyptian Expeditionary Force, the Mesopotamia Expeditionary Force, the British Salonika Force, and on home service

Volunteering

Edward Madigan and Michael Snape have noted that the day-to-day role and experience of the British Army chaplain was underpinned by the support of their respective religious bodies for the war effort which they viewed as 'not only legitimate but morally righteous'.[95] This is in contrast to the Irish Catholic hierarchy which, as noted by John Brennan, was largely ambivalent towards the issue of army chaplaincy recruitment.[96] Patrick

Callan has shown that general recruitment in Ireland declined almost continuously during the war, dropping from 50,107 recruits in the first six months to just 9,845 in the last three months of the conflict.[97] Although Callan's figures excluded commissioned officers they still provide a useful benchmark to discuss trends in chaplaincy recruitment. For instance, Callan has shown that recruitment numbers dropped significantly in the period from February to August 1916, noting that this decline 'had been set in train before the Easter Rising'.[98] In contrast, the number of Maynooth graduates commissioned in the period March to August 1916 represented about 32% of the total number appointed. The highest number of commissions per month occurred in March 1916, when twelve Maynooth graduates were commissioned as chaplains. It is difficult to determine if the Easter Rising impacted on chaplaincy recruitment, nevertheless it is remarkable that 20% of the Maynooth cohort received commissions in March 1916.

Maynooth graduates in this research population were ordained over a twenty-four-year period from 1893 to 1917. Approximately 40% of graduates received their first commission within four years of their ordination, which suggests that most graduates were relatively young and inexperienced. An analysis of birth counties indicates that most of the Maynooth chaplains were from Cork, which had more than double the number of chaplains than any other county (see Table 2). These priests came from twenty-four counties, the exceptions being counties Armagh, Derry, Kildare, Louth, Roscommon, Tyrone Wexford, and Wicklow. Census records and other sources indicate that many of these priests came from farming backgrounds. Others were the sons of shopkeepers, publicans, and national schoolteachers.

TABLE 1 *Chaplains by birth county*

Province	*No.**	*Breakdown by county*
Connacht	11	Galway 4, Leitrim 2, Mayo 4, Sligo 1
Leinster	16	Carlow 1, Dublin 2, Kilkenny 3, Laois 2, Longford 2, Meath 2, Offaly 1, Westmeath 3
Munster	19	Clare 1, Cork 9, Kerry 3, Limerick 1, Tipperary 2, Waterford 3
Ulster	14	Antrim 1, Cavan 4, Donegal 3, Down 2, Fermanagh 2, Monaghan 2
TOTAL	60	

**of chaplains*

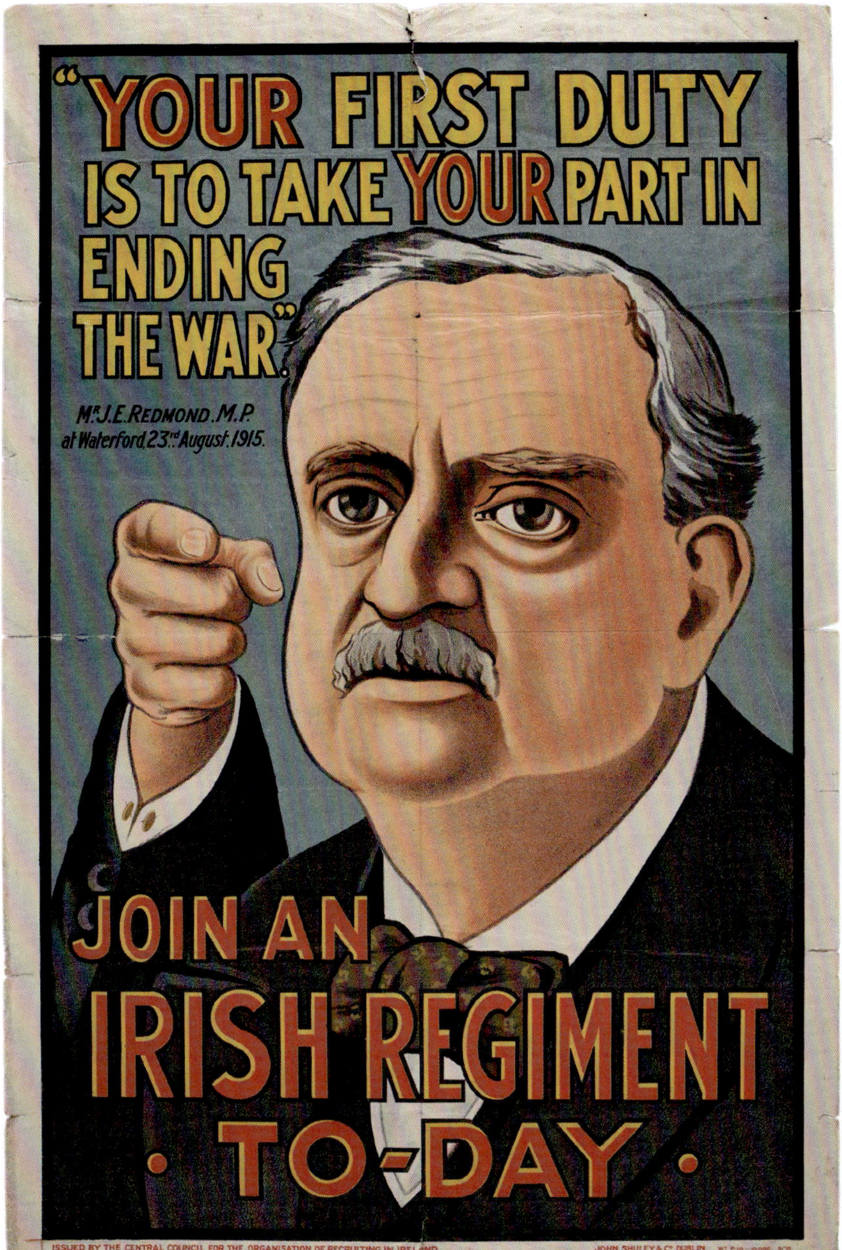

PLATE I

'Your first duty is to take your part in ending the war', John E. Redmond, MP at Waterford, 23rd August, 1915: Join an Irish Regiment to-day. *(Courtesy of the National Library of Ireland)*

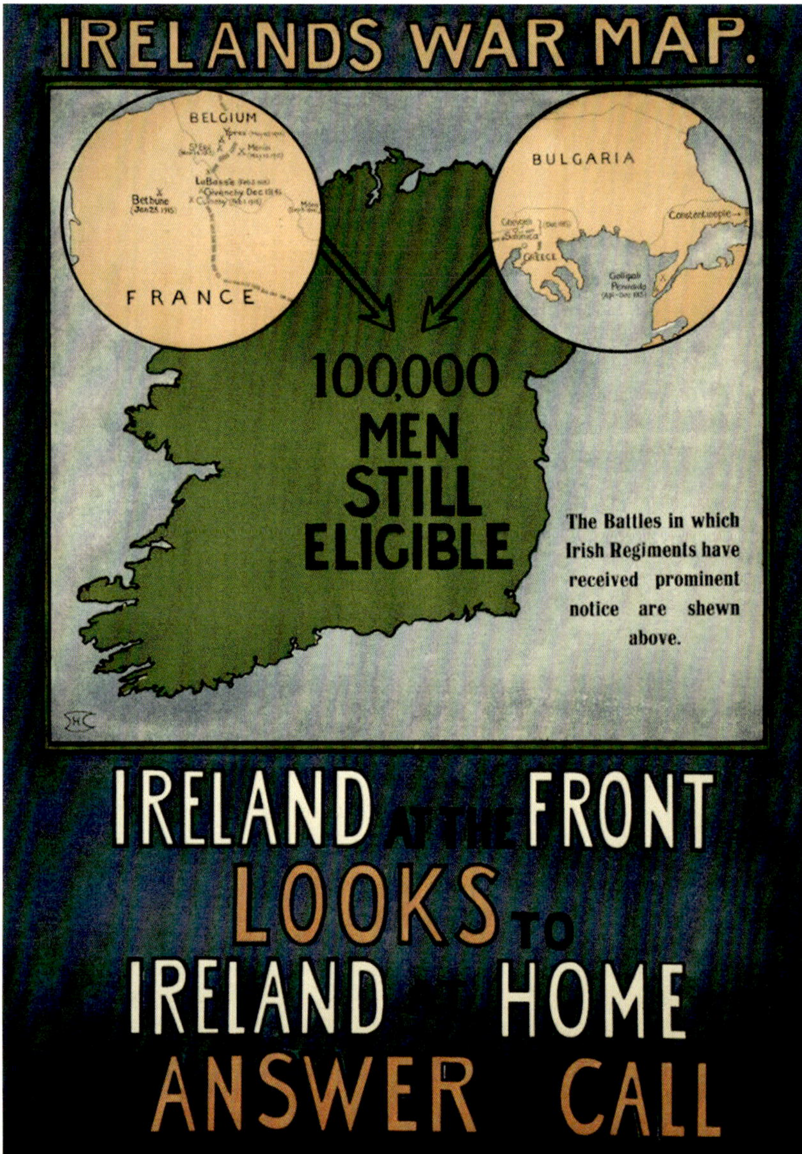

PLATE 2

Recruitment poster showing Irish Regiments

(Courtesy of the Library of Congress, Prints and Photographs Division, Washington)

PLATE 3
Poster advertising Bing Crosby singing 'Galway Bay', a song written by Arthur Colahan.

PLATE 4
(top) *Tom Kettle on the Thiepval War Memorial, France.* (©Ronan McGreevy)
(below) *Memorial to the Missing, Tyne Cot Cemetery, Belgium.* (©Cora Lenihan)

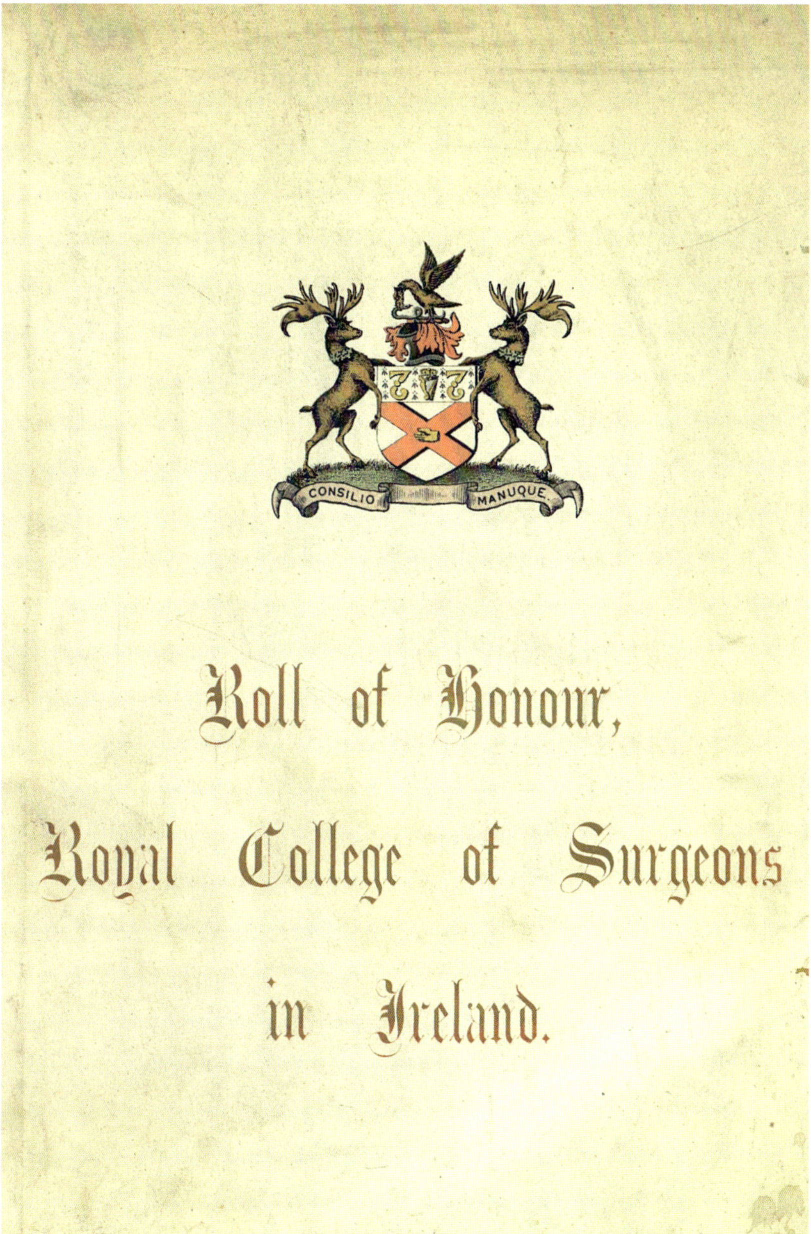

PLATE 5
Cover Page of RCSI Roll of Honour

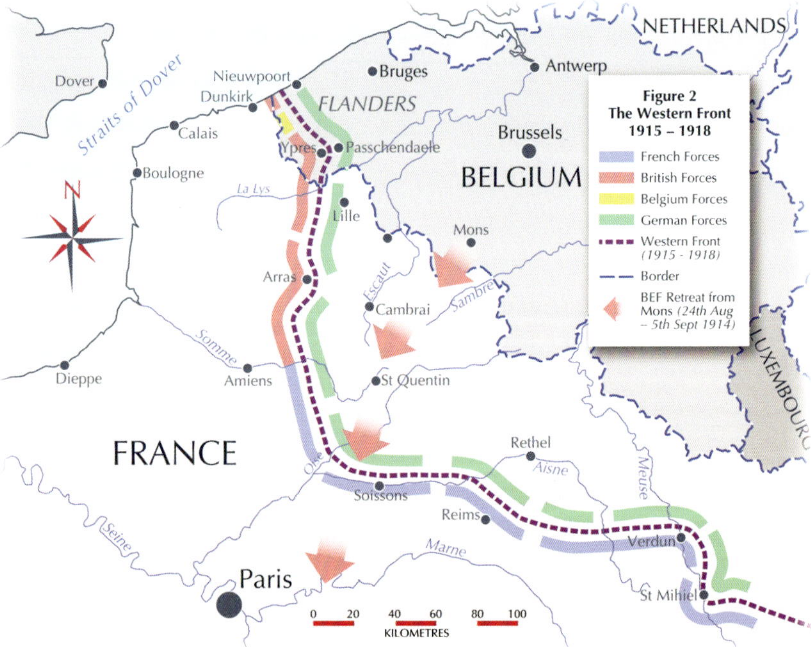

PLATE 6
(top) *Main Theatres of War 1914–1918*
(above) *The Western Front 1915–18*

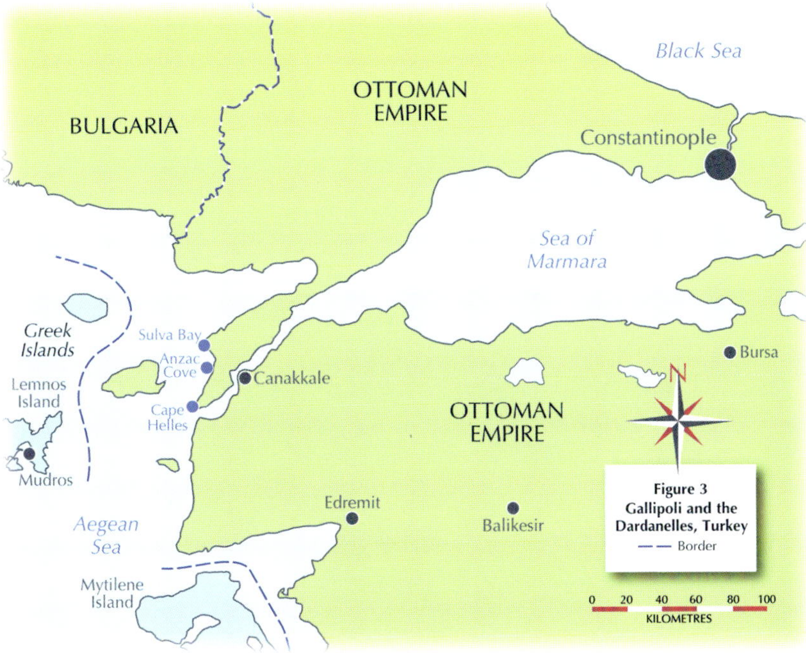

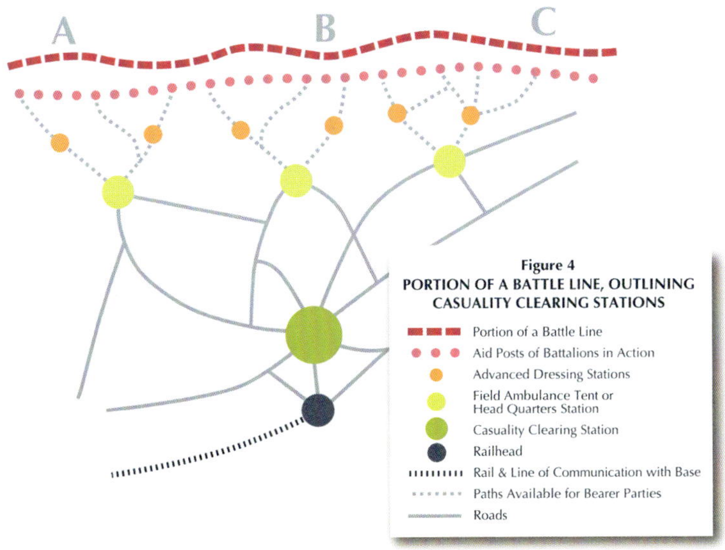

PLATE 7

(top) *Gallipoli and the Dardanelles, Turkey*

(above) *Portion of Battle Line, Outlining Casualty Clearing Stations*

PLATE 8

The Death of Father John Gwynn, Béthune, Northern France, October 11–12 1915.

(Courtesy of the National Library of Ireland)

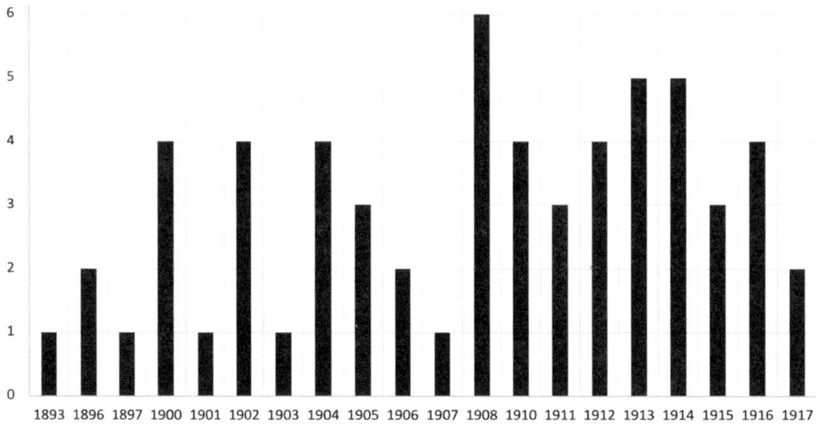

FIGURE 5.2 *Maynooth chaplains by year of ordination, 1893–1917*

Conclusion

The topic of Irish Catholic army chaplains in the First World War is both complex and multi-faceted, which can be seen through this analysis of Maynooth College's contribution to the war effort. The college did not feature in the original Roll of Honour produced by NUI in 1919, despite its formal affiliation since 1910. Even now, over 100 years later, it is difficult to ascertain the exact number of Maynooth graduates who served in the war. Based on current research I would estimate at least sixty graduates.

Forty-one Catholic priests died while serving as chaplains in the British Army and four of these studied at St Patrick's College, Maynooth: Stephen Clarke, Donal O'Sullivan, John Watters, and Matthew Prendergast. The same number of former students from St Cuthbert's College, Ushaw, the largest Catholic seminary in the North of England, died in the war: Charles Watson, William Finn, Matthew Burdess, and Thomas Baines.[99] The overall number of chaplains from each college is also comparable, with sixty from Maynooth and seventy-six from Ushaw. Although, Maynooth priests had served as chaplains in other conflicts, the unprecedented scale and duration of the First World War saw much larger numbers of graduates seeking commissions as army chaplains.

Some Maynooth chaplains, like Rev Henry Beauchamp and Rev Laurence Stafford, had very successful military careers and were appointed senior chaplains. Others went on to serve in the Second World War. Rev John Coghlan, who studied at St Finian's College, Navan and at Maynooth, served in both world wars and was appointed Vicar General to the British Army in 1940.[100] Coghlan, from Castlepollard, Co Westmeath, served in France, Flanders, Egypt, and Mesopotamia during the First World War.[101] Rev Christopher Sheehan, who studied at St Colman's College, Fermoy and Maynooth College, also served in both wars, as did Rev Joseph P. Stapleton, from Callan in Co Kilkenny who received his BA degree in 1911.[102]

Irish priests working in Commonwealth countries also joined local regiments during the war.[103] Rev William Devine, for instance, who was ordained at Maynooth, was serving as a curate in Australia when he volunteered as an army chaplain with the Australian Imperial Force, serving with the 48th Battalion in Egypt and France.[104] He was awarded the Military Cross in November 1918 for assisting the wounded and remaining with troops under enemy fire, rescuing a man during a bombing attack.[105] Very few Maynooth chaplains served in the navy during the First World War. Rev John Hughes, from Daingean, Co Offaly, who was transferred to Bermuda in 1914 and appointed Acting Chaplain (For Seamen and Marines at Bermuda) on 2 August 1918.[106] He later served as chaplain to the Saorstát Army based at the Curragh.[107] Rev John Callanan, ordained in 1903, was serving as curate in Spike Island on the outbreak of war and subsequently acted as chaplain to British and American navy ships stationed in Cork Harbour.[108]

In 2014, Brian Heffernan explored the political opinions and attitudes of Irish Catholic priests during the War of Independence (1919–21) and noted that some republican priests had served as military chaplains in the war.[109] Roy Foster has described the Irish revolutionary generation as 'those born, roughly, between the 1870s and the 1890s', which represents the great majority of the Catholic chaplains discussed in this study.[110] Annette Becker's research on war and religion in France during the period 1914–30 explored how military chaplains sought to meet the emerging spiritual needs of soldiers, noting that they 'always connected and combined faith in the nation with religious faith'.[111] This concept of faith and nationhood is perhaps also applicable to those Catholic chaplains from Maynooth, who may have combined their faith in the Irish nation with their faith in Catholicism when they volunteered for military service.

The chaplains analysed for this study indicate that it was not only the middle-class farming community that supplied Catholic chaplains to the Front. Many of these men were the sons of shopkeepers, publicans, and national schoolteachers. The majority of chaplains were born in Cork, some had extensive clerical experience and others were newly ordained. The highest number of volunteers commissioned in a single month was in March 1916. Many of the chaplains suffered from illness, including influenza, malaria, and dysentery, while others suffered debilitating conditions such as neurasthenia (shell shock) and permanent hearing loss caused by exposure to conditions at the Front. However, this did not stop many of the Maynooth graduates from renewing their contract of service throughout the war. This study has shown that St Patrick's College, Maynooth publicly supported the recruitment of Catholic chaplains by ordaining students early to facilitate volunteering, by making public statements in support of army chaplaincy recruitment and by ordaining students early to fill vacant parishes around Ireland caused by chaplaincy recruitment.

Chaplains of St. Patrick's College Maynooth

FIRST WORLD WAR HONORARY LIST

THIS LIST INCLUDES details of sixty priests who studied or were ordained at St Patrick's College, Maynooth. The majority of these priests were not included in the original 1919 NUI Roll of Honour and were identified by using various primary sources including the *Irish Catholic Directory*, the *London Gazette*, local and national newspaper reports, and other sources. Some priests matriculated at Maynooth but were ordained elsewhere, and others were ordained as 'externs' at Maynooth but studied elsewhere. For the purpose of this study both groups were included..

1. *Beauchamp, Rev Henry*. Studied at St Patrick's College, Carlow and matriculated at St Patrick's College, Maynooth on 29 September 1903, entering Theology I.[112] Ordained 'foris' for the diocese of Kildare and Leighlin on 4 April 1908 in St Patrick's College, Carlow by Bishop Patrick Foley. Appointed Temporary Chaplain to the Forces, 4th Cl. on 28 April 1916.[113] Promoted to Temporary Chaplain to the Forces, 3rd Cl. on 21 June 1918.[114] Awarded the Military Cross.[115] Resigned in June 1919 for transfer to the Royal Air Force.[116] Assumed the rank of Squadron Leader in the Chaplain's Branch of the Royal Air Force, 1920.[117]
2. *Bowen, Rev John Francis.* Studied at Holy Cross College, Clonliffe and matriculated at St Patrick's College, Maynooth on 10 September 1907,

entering Philosophy II.[118] Awarded undergraduate degree in 1909.[119] Ordained on 22 June 1913 for the diocese of Dublin. Appointed Temporary Chaplain to the Forces, 4th Cl on 12 November 1917.[120] Relinquished commission on 4 October 1921.[121] Appointed officiating clergyman on the SS *Derbyshire*.[122]

3. *Bradley, Rev Thomas.* Matriculated at St Patrick's College, Maynooth on 2 September 1898, entering Rhetoric.[123] Ordained in 1906 for the diocese of Kilmore. Appointed Temporary Chaplain to the Forces, 4th Cl. on 8 July 1916.[124] Relinquished commission on 12 November 1919.[125]

4. *Breen, Rev Francis.* Studied at St Brendan's Seminary, Killarney and matriculated at St Patrick's College, Maynooth on 1 September 1901, entering Rhetoric.[126] Ordained in 1908 for the diocese of Kerry. Appointed Temporary Chaplain to the Forces, 4th Cl. on 28 September 1916.[127] Gazetted out of service in June 1919.[128]

5. *Carney, Rev Michael.* Studied at St Jarlath's College, Tuam and matriculated at St Patrick's College, Maynooth on 3 September 1903, entering Rhetoric.[129] Ordained in 1910 for the diocese of Tuam. Appointed Temporary Chaplain to the Forces, 4th Cl. on 21 June 1915.[130] Relinquished commission on 12 December 1918.[131]

6. *Carroll, Rev William.* Matriculated at St Patrick's College, Maynooth on 30 August 1905, entering Rhetoric. Awarded undergraduate degree in 1909.[132] Ordained in 1913 for the diocese of Limerick. Appointed Temporary Chaplain to the Forces, 4th Cl. on 4 January 1916.[133] Awarded Military Cross.[134] Relinquished commission on 16 December 1920.[135]

7. *Casey, Rev Patrick.* Studied at St Finian's College, Navan and matriculated at St Patrick's College, Maynooth on 3 September 1898, entering Philosophy I.[136] Ordained in 1904 for the diocese of Meath. Appointed Temporary Chaplain to the Forces, 4th Cl. on 29 March 1916.[137] Relinquished commission on 13 December 1918.[138]

8. *Clancy, Rev Patrick.* Studied at St Mel's College, Longford and matriculated at St Patrick's College, Maynooth on 1 September 1898, entering Rhetoric.[139] Ordained in 1905 for the diocese of Ardagh. Appointed Temporary Chaplain to the Forces, 4th Cl. on 16 March 1916.[140] Relinquished commission on 6 July 1918.[141]

9. *Clarke, Rev Stephen.* Studied at St Patrick's College, Cavan and matriculated at St Patrick's College, Maynooth on 30 August 1905, entering Rhetoric.[142] Awarded undergraduate degree in 1908.[143] Ordained in 1912 for the diocese of Kilmore. Appointed Temporary Chaplain to the Forces,

4th Cl. on 29 March 1916.[144] Killed while attached to the 9th Battalion Lancashire Fusiliers on 4 October 1917.[145]

10. *Clenaghan, Rev George.* Matriculated at St Patrick's College, Maynooth on 14 September 1909, entering Theology I.[146] Ordained in 1913 for the diocese of Down and Connor. Appointed Temporary Chaplain to the Forces, 4th Cl. on 8 April 1916.[147] Relinquished commission on 7 April 1919.[148]

11. *Coffey, Rev James.*[149] Matriculated at St Patrick's College, Maynooth on 30 September 1895, entering Rhetoric. Ordained in 1902 for the diocese of Dublin. Appointed Temporary Chaplain to the Forces, 4th Cl. on 17 April 1916.[150] Relinquished commission in May 1918.[151]

12. *Coghlan, Rev John.* Matriculated at St Patrick's College, Maynooth in September 1906, entering Rhetoric.[152] Awarded undergraduate degree in 1909.[153] Ordained 'foris' on 29 June 1913 in St Mary's Collinstown by Bishop Patrick Clune (Perth) for the diocese of Meath. Appointed Temporary Chaplain to the Forces, 4th Cl. on 22 May 1915.[154] Promoted to Temporary Chaplain to the Forces, 3rd Cl. on 6 January 1917.[155]

13. *Cohalan, Rev Jeremiah.* Matriculated at St Patrick's College, Maynooth on 31 August 1899, entering Philosophy I. Ordained in 1905 for the diocese of Cork. Appointed Temporary Chaplain to the Forces, 4th Cl. on 13 March 1916.[156]

14. *Cooney, Rev Nicholas.* Matriculated at St Patrick's College, Maynooth on 29 September 1896, entering Philosophy I. Ordained on 22 June 1902 for the diocese of Meath. Appointed Temporary Chaplain to the Forces, 4th Cl. on 29 March 1916.[157] Relinquished commission on 28 March 1917.[158]

15. *Cotter, Rev James A.* Studied at St Colman's College, Fermoy and matriculated at St Patrick's College, Maynooth on 30 August 1905, entering Rhetoric.[159] Awarded undergraduate degree in 1908.[160] Ordained in 1912 for the diocese of Cloyne. Appointed Temporary Chaplain to the Forces, 4th Cl. on 6 January 1915.[161] Relinquished commission on 20 December 1918.[162]

16. *Creed, Rev Cornelius Michael.* Studied at St Finbarr's College, Cork. Awarded undergraduate degree in 1911.[163] and matriculated at St Patrick's College, Maynooth on 11 October 1911, entering Theology I.[164] Ordained in 1915 for the diocese of Cork. Appointed Temporary Chaplain to the Forces, 4th Cl. on 19 February 1917.[165] Relinquished commission on 1 September 1921.[166]

17. *Cullinane, Rev Jeremiah.* Matriculated at St Patrick's College, Maynooth

on 8 September 1908, entering Philosophy I.[167] Awarded undergraduate degree in 1910.[168] Ordained in 1914 for the diocese of Cork. Appointed Temporary Chaplain to the Forces, 4th Cl. on 3 February 1917.[169] Relinquished commission on 6 June 1919.[170]

18. *Daly, Rev Eugene.* Studied at St Finian's College, Navan and matriculated at St Patrick's College, Maynooth on 1 September 1898, entering Philosophy I. Ordained in 1904 for the diocese of Meath. Appointed Temporary Chaplain to the Forces, 4th Cl. on 14 March 1916.[171] Awarded Military Cross.[172] Relinquished commission on 15 May 1919.[173]

19. *Dowling, Rev E.* Studied at St Kieran's College, Kilkenny and matriculated at St Patrick's College, Maynooth on 6 September 1902, entering Philosophy I. Awarded undergraduate degree in 1905.[174] Ordained in 1908 for the diocese of Ossory. Appointed Temporary Chaplain to the Forces, 4th Cl. on 18 November 1914.[175] Promoted to Temporary Chaplain to the Forces, 3rd Cl. on 1 September 1919.[176] Mentioned in Despatches.[177]

20. *Duggan, Rev Thomas Francis.* Studied at University College Cork and awarded undergraduate degree in 1911.[178] Matriculated at St Patrick's College, Maynooth on 11 October 1911, entering Theology I.[179] Ordained on 20 June 1915 for the diocese of Cork. Appointed Temporary Chaplain to the Forces, 4th Cl. on 18 September 1917.[180] Relinquished commission on 1 September 1921.[181]

21. *Farrell, Rev Bernard.* Studied at St Finian's College, Navan and matriculated at St Patrick's College, Maynooth on 28 September 1895, entering Rhetoric.[182] Ordained on 22 June 1902 for the diocese of Meath. Appointed Temporary Chaplain to the Forces, 4th Cl. on 16 March 1916.[183] Appointed Officer of the Military Division of the Order of the British Empire.[184] Relinquished commission on 9 December 1918.[185]

22. *Furlong, Rev Joseph.* Matriculated at St Patrick's College, Maynooth on 15 October 1913, entering Theology I.[186] Ordained for the diocese of Dublin in 1917. Appointed Temporary Chaplain to the Forces, 4th Cl. on 13 November 1917.[187] Relinquished commission on 13 November 1919.[188]

23. *Galvin, Rev Michael.* Matriculated at St Patrick's College, Maynooth on 1 September 1899, entering Rhetoric.[189] Ordained in 1906 for the diocese of Killaloe. Appointed Temporary Chaplain to the Forces, 4th Cl. on 19 April 1916.[190] Relinquished commission on 15 September 1918.[191]

24. *Gleeson, Rev Francis.* Studied at Holy Cross College, Clonliffe and matriculated at St Patrick's College, Maynooth on 3 September 1903, entering Rhetoric. Ordained in 1910 for the diocese of Dublin. Appointed

Temporary Chaplain to the Forces, 4th Cl. on 18 November 1914 and again on 15 May 1917.[192] Relinquished commission on 15 May 1919.[193]

25. *Hughes, Rev John.* Studied at St Patrick's College, Carlow and matriculated at St Patrick's College, Maynooth on 4 September 1898, entering Philosophy I. Ordained 'foris' on 26 June 1904 at St Patrick's College, Carlow for the diocese of Kildare and Leighlin by Bishop Patrick Foley. Appointed Temporary Chaplain to the Forces, 4th Cl. on 1 September 1917.[194] Appointed temporary Acting Chaplain, Admiralty on 2 August 1918.[195]

26. *Hurley, Rev Timothy A.* Ordained for the diocese of Kerry in 1916. Appointed Temporary Chaplain to the Forces, 4th Cl. on 8 February 1917.[196] Relinquished commission on 18 July 1919.[197]

27. *Keenan, Rev Patrick.* Ordained as an extern for the diocese of Dromore in 1912. Appointed Temporary Chaplain to the Forces, 4th Cl. on 24 August 1916.[198] Relinquished commission on 1 September 1921.[199]

28. *Kelly, Rev Edmund.* Studied at St Patrick's College, Thurles and matriculated at St Patrick's College, Maynooth on 5 September 1897, entering Theology II. Ordained for the diocese of Cashel on 17 June 1900. Appointed Temporary Chaplain to the Forces, 4th Cl. on 30 April 1915.[200] Awarded the Military Cross.[201] Relinquished commission on 1 September 1921.[202]

29. *Kerr, Rev Patrick.* Matriculated at St Patrick's College, Maynooth on 10 September 1907, entering Rhetoric. Awarded undergraduate degree in 1910.[203] Appointed Temporary Chaplain to the Forces, 4th Cl. on 14 March 1916.[204] Relinquished commission on 4 June 1919.[205]

30. *McGarvey, Rev Bernard.* Studied at St Macartan's College, Monaghan and matriculated at St Patrick's College, Maynooth in September 1904, entering Rhetoric. Ordained in 1911 for the diocese of Clogher. Appointed Temporary Chaplain to the Forces, 4th Cl. on 23 March 1916.[206] Awarded the Military Cross.[207] Relinquished commission on 1 September 1921.[208]

31. *MacGonigle, Rev Joseph.* Matriculated at St Patrick's College, Maynooth on 14 September 1909, entering Philosophy I.[219] Awarded undergraduate degree in 1911.[210] Ordained 'foris' for the diocese of Raphoe on 19 August 1915 in Letterkenny Cathedral. Appointed Temporary Chaplain to the Forces, 4th Cl. 27 September 1918.[211] Relinquished commission on 25 October 1919.[212]

32. *McMahon, Rev Bernard.* Studied at Rockwell College and Holy Cross College, Clonliffe.[213] Matriculated at St Patrick's College, Maynooth on

29 August 1901, entering Theology I. Ordained in 1905 for the diocese of Dublin. Appointed Temporary Chaplain to the Forces, 4th Cl. on 23 October 1917.[214] Relinquished commission on 23 October 1919.

33. *MacPolin, Rev Owen.* Studied at St Colman's College, Newry and matriculated at St Patrick's College, Maynooth on 10 September 1907, entering Philosophy I.[216] Awarded undergraduate degree in 1909.[217] Ordained in 1913 for the diocese of Dromore. Appointed Temporary Chaplain to the Forces, 4th Cl. on 23 October 1917.[218] Relinquished commission on 12 September 1919.[219]

34. *Maguire, Rev Thomas.* Ordained as an extern on 17 June 1900 for the diocese of Clogher. Appointed Temporary Chaplain to the Forces, 4th Cl. on 1 May 1917.[220] Relinquished commission on 1 September 1921.[221]

35. *Meehan, Rev John F.* Matriculated at St Patrick's College, Maynooth on 10 September1904, entering Rhetoric.[222] Ordained in 1911 for the diocese of Ardagh. Appointed Temporary Chaplain to the Forces, 4th Cl. 13 November 1917.[223] Relinquished commission on 1 September 1921.[224]

36. *Moore, Rev Philip.* Matriculated at St Patrick's College, Maynooth on 6 September 1894, entering Rhetoric.[225] Ordained 'foris' for the diocese of Ossory in June 1901. Appointed Temporary Chaplain to the Forces, 4th Cl. on 13 November 1915.[226] Relinquished commission on 18 December 1917.[227]

37. *Mullins, Rev Michael Joseph.* Studied at St Nathy's College, Ballaghaderreen and matriculated at St Patrick's College, Maynooth in September 1910, entering University I.[228] Ordained in December 1916 for the diocese of Achonry.[229] Appointed Temporary Chaplain to the Forces, 4th Cl. on 9 February 1917. [230] Relinquished commission on 1 September 1921.[231]

38. *Mullins, William.* Matriculated at St Patrick's College, Maynooth on 10 September 1904, entering Rhetoric.[232] Ordained for the diocese of Galway in 1911. Appointed Temporary Chaplain to the Forces, 4th Cl. on 2 September 1916.[233] Officer of the Most Excellent Order of the British Empire.[234] Relinquished commission on 19 November 1918.[235]

39. *Nolan, Rev James.* Matriculated at St Patrick's College, Maynooth on 13 Jan 1906, entering Rhetoric.[236] Awarded undergraduate degree in 1908.[237] Ordained in June 1912 for the diocese of Clogher. Appointed Temporary Chaplain to the Forces, 4th Cl. on 9 August 1916.[238] Relinquished commission on 7 January 1919.[239]

40. *O'Carroll, Rev Matthew Joseph.* Ordained at Maynooth for the diocese

of Kilmore in 1916.[240] Appointed Temporary Chaplain to the Forces, 4th Cl. on 8 February 1917.[241] Mentioned in Despatches.[242]

41. *O'Connell, Rev Maurice.* Matriculated at St Patrick's College, Maynooth on 29 August 1890, entering Rhetoric. Ordained on 20 June 1897 for the diocese of Cloyne. Appointed Temporary Chaplain to the Forces, 4th Cl. on 20 November 1914.[243] Promoted to Temporary Chaplain to the Forces, 3rd Cl. on 12 May 1916.[244] Awarded Distinguished Service Order.[245] Promoted to Temporary Chaplain to the Forces, 2nd Cl. on 12 March 1919.[246] Reverted to Temporary Chaplain to the Forces, 4th Cl. on 6 September 1919.[247]

42. *O'Connor, Rev Thomas J.* Matriculated at St Patrick's College, Maynooth on 31 August 1899, entering Philosophy II. Ordained in 1904 for the diocese of Clonfert. Appointed Temporary Chaplain to the Forces, 4th Cl. on 30 March 1915.[248] Relinquished commission on 1 September 1921.[249]

43. *O'Farrell, Rev Peter.* Studied at St Mel's College, Longford and matriculated at St Patrick's College, Maynooth on 1 September 1901, entering Rhetoric.[250] Ordained in 1908 for the diocese of Ardagh. Appointed Temporary Chaplain to the Forces, 4th Cl. on 23 March 1915.[251] Awarded the Military Cross.[252] Relinquished commission on 7 July 1918.[253]

44. *O'Gorman, Rev Patrick.* Matriculated at St Patrick's College, Maynooth on 9 September1888, entering Philosophy I. Ordained in Rome in 1896.[254] Appointed Temporary Chaplain to the Forces, 4th Cl. on 13 November 1917.[255] Relinquished Commission on 5 December 1918.[256]

45. *O'Hart, Rev Edward.* Studied at St Macartan's, Monaghan and matriculated at St Patrick's College, Maynooth on 27 September 1904, entering Philosophy I. Ordained in 1910 for the diocese of Clogher. Appointed Temporary Chaplain to the Forces, 4th Cl. on 8 May 1917.[257] Relinquished commission on 9 May 1918.[258]

46. *O'Kelly, Rev John T.* Studied at St Joseph's College, Garbally Park in Ballinasloe, Galway.[259] Matriculated at St Patrick's College, Maynooth on 20 September 1900, entering Rhetoric. Ordained in 1907 for the diocese of Galway. Appointed Temporary Chaplain to the Forces, 4th Cl. on 18 March 1916.[260] Relinquished commission on 24 May 1918.[261]

47. *O'Sullivan, Rev Donal.* Studied at St Brendan's Seminary, Killarney and matriculated at St Patrick's College, Maynooth on 10 September 1907, entering Rhetoric.[262] Awarded undergraduate degree in 1910.[263] Ordained in 1914 for the diocese of Kerry. Appointed Temporary Chaplain to the

Forces, 4th Cl. on 3 March1916.[264] Killed on 5 July 1916 while serving with the 8th Battalion, Loyal North Lancashire Regiment.[265]

48. *Owens, Rev Michael J.* Matriculated at St Patrick's College, Maynooth on 16 September 1893, entering Rhetoric.[266] Ordained on 17 June 1900 for the diocese of Tuam.[267] Appointed Temporary Chaplain to the Forces, 4th Cl. on 17 July 1915.[268]

49. *Phelan, Rev William.* Matriculated at St Patrick's College, Maynooth on 38 September 1886, entering Rhetoric.[269] Ordained on 5 March 1893 for the diocese of Kildare. Appointed Temporary Chaplain to the Forces, 4th Cl. on 27 April 1915.[270] Relinquished commission on 9 February 1916.[271]

50. *Pigott, Rev Jeremiah.* Matriculated at St Patrick's College, Maynooth in September1910, entering University I.[272] Awarded undergraduate degree in 1913.[273] Ordained 'foris' on 10 December 1916 for the diocese of Cloyne. Appointed Temporary Chaplain to the Forces, 4th Cl. on 8 February 1917.[274] Awarded the Military Cross.[275] Relinquished commission on 9 August 1919.[276]

51. *Prendergast, Rev Geoffrey J.* Studied at St Jarlath's College, Tuam and matriculated at St Patrick's College, Maynooth on 27 August 1896, entering Rhetoric.[277] Ordained in 1903 for the diocese of Tuam. Appointed Temporary Chaplain to the Forces, 4th Cl. on 26 July 1916.[278] Relinquished Commission on 22 January 1919.[279]

52. *Prendergast, Rev Matthew V.* Matriculated at St Patrick's College, Maynooth on 1 September 1901, entering Rhetoric. Ordained in 1908 for the diocese of Waterford and Lismore. Appointed Temporary Chaplain to the Forces, 4th Cl. on 9 July 1915.[280] Died on Active Service on 16 September 1918.[281]

53. *Rice, Rev William.* Matriculated at St Patrick's College, Maynooth on 31 January 1894, entering Rhetoric. Ordained 'foris' for the diocese of Kildare on 28 January 1900. Appointed Temporary Chaplain to the Forces, 4th Cl. on 8 May 1917.[282] Relinquished commission on 8 May, 1918.[283]

54. *Sheehan, Rev Christopher.* Studied at St Colman's College, Fermoy and matriculated at St Patrick's College, Maynooth on 16 October 1907, entering Rhetoric.[284] Ordained in 1914 for the diocese of Cloyne. Appointed Temporary Chaplain to the Forces, 4th Cl. on 30 July 1915.[285] Promoted to Temporary Chaplain to the Forces, 3rd Cl. on 6 January 1917.[286] Awarded Military Cross.[287] Reverted to Temporary Chaplain to the Forces, 4th Cl. on 29 January 1918.[288] Promoted to Temporary Chaplain to the Forces, 3rd Cl. on 21 May 1918.[289]

55. *Sheridan, Rev James.* Studied at St Patrick's College, Cavan and matriculated at St Patrick's College, Maynooth on 10 September 1907, entering Rhetoric.[290] Awarded undergraduate degree in 1911.[291] Ordained for the diocese of Kilmore in 1914. Appointed Temporary Chaplain to the Forces, 4th Cl. on 11 March 1916.[292] Awarded Military Cross. Relinquished commission on 1 September 1921.[293]

56. *Small, Rev Terence Small.* Matriculated at St Patrick's College, Maynooth on 30 August 1896, entering Philosophy I. Ordained 'foris' on 31 March 1902 for the diocese of Kilmore. Appointed Temporary Chaplain to the Forces, 4th Cl. on 1 June 1917.[294] Relinquished Commission on 20 August 1919.[295]

57. *Smith, Rev Hugh.* Studied at St Columb's College, Derry and matriculated at St Patrick's College, Maynooth on 30 August 1901, entering Rhetoric. Ordained in 1908 for the diocese of Derry. Appointed Temporary Chaplain to the Forces, 4th Cl. on 20 February 1917.[296] Gazetted out of service on 5 March 1919.[297]

58. *Stafford, Rev Laurence.* Studied at Holy Cross College, Clonliffe and matriculated at St Patrick's College, Maynooth on 29 August 1890, entering Philosophy I. Ordained on 21 June 1896 for the diocese of Dublin. Appointed Temporary Chaplain to the Forces, 4th Cl. on 1 February 1915.[298] Promoted to Temporary Chaplain to the Forces, 3rd Cl. on 25 June 1917.[299] Promoted to Temporary Chaplain to the Forces, 2nd Cl. on 16 September 1917.[300] Reverted to Temporary Chaplain to the Forces, 4th Cl. on 21 January 1919.[301]

59. *Stapleton, Rev Joseph.* Studied at St Kieran's College, Kilkenny and matriculated at St Patrick's College, Maynooth on 10 September 1907, entering Rhetoric.[302] Awarded undergraduate degree in 1911.[303] Ordained in 1914 for the diocese of Ossory. Appointed Temporary Chaplain to the Forces, 4th Cl. on 30 May 1916.[304]

60. *Watters, Rev John.* Matriculated at St Patrick's College, Maynooth on 13 September 1910, entering University I.[305] Ordained for the diocese of Tuam in 1917. Appointed Temporary Chaplain to the Forces, 4th Cl. on 2 July 1918.[306] Died on 7 November 1918 on Active Service, while attached to the 115th Infantry Brigade.[307]

MAYNOOTH CHAPLAINS
SELECT BIOGRAPHIES

Henry Beauchamp was born in Rosenallis, Co Laois on 10 June 1884 to Henry and Mary Beauchamp (née Delany).[308] His father was a small merchant farmer.[309] Beauchamp's uncle John Beauchamp, parish priest of Borris, acted as his guardian on the death of his parents.[310] Beauchamp studied at St Patrick's College, Carlow and at Maynooth College and was ordained 'foris' for the diocese of Kildare and Leighlin on 4 April 1908 in St Patrick's College, Carlow.[311] Beauchamp was a curate in Portarlington when he applied for a commission as an army chaplain. He commenced duty at the Ripon Training Centre in Yorkshire in April 1916 and later with the 214th Brigade at Colchester.[312] In October 1917, at the age of thirty-three, he was described by Major General Simpson as '[i]n close touch with the troops and very popular'. Beauchamp embarked for service in France in January 1918 and was appointed Senior Chaplain to the Tank Corps in June 1918. He was awarded the Military Cross in November 1918 for fearlessly performing his duties in the fighting line.[313] In July 1919, he officially left the British Army of the Rhine in order to transfer to the Royal Air Force. In June 1940, Beauchamp was appointed Vicar-General while serving with the British Air Force as staff chaplain.[314] He died in Carlow on 26 April 1948 while serving as Principal Chaplain to the RAF.[315]

John Francis Bowen from Howth in Co Dublin was born on 15 January 1886. His parents Catherine and John Bowen were both national school teachers from Cork.[316] He was educated at the Christian Brothers schools on North Richmond Street, Dublin and at Holy Cross College, Clonliffe before entering Maynooth. He was one of sixty-five seminarians ordained in the College Chapel on 22 June 1913, and one of eight seminarians for the diocese of Dublin.[317] Following his ordination Bowen worked at Clonliffe College, Dublin and in Kingstown and City Quay.[318] Bowen was nominated for service in Mesopotamia in November 1917. He was chaplain to the

Colaba War Hospital in Bombay from January until February 1918 and was attached to the British General Depot in Ashar from March until November 1918. He was then posted to the 41st Field Ambulance, 13th Division, from November 1918 until February 1919.[319] In September 1919 and February 1920, Archbishop William Walsh agreed to the extension of Bowen's military service. In July 1921, Bowen enquired about further service with the Royal Army Chaplain's Department.[320] Although this could not be accommodated Bowen was given the opportunity to act as a civilian priest on a transport vessel to India, which he readily accepted.[321] Described by army officials as a popular chaplain who was 'keen and energetic', he was demobilised on 4 October 1921 and took up the role of officiating clergyman to Catholic troops on the SS *Derbyshire*.[322] After the war, he served in Monkstown, Inchicore, and at the Asylum for the Blind in Dublin.[323] He died at St Columcille's, Merrion Road, in January 1945.[324]

THOMAS J. BRADLEY from Edengora, Bailieborough, Co Cavan, was born in 1879. His father Patrick was a farmer.[325] He was ordained in 1906 for the diocese of Kilmore and later served as curate of Killenkere.[326] Bradley was thirty-seven when he was examined at a recruiting office in Dublin in June 1916, joining the 68th (Welsh) Division at Bedford as Acting Chaplain to the Forces.[327] He applied for service with the BEF in September 1916 and served with the British Troops in France and Flanders, renewing his contract of service in September 1917 and 1918. He was stationed at the No. 2 Rest Camp in Le Havre when he was gazetted out of the service in November 1919, having served for three years and two months.[328] He died in November 1937 while serving as parish priest of Carrigallen, Co Leitrim at the age of fifty-six.[329]

FRANCIS BREEN was born in 1884 in Killarney, Co Kerry. His father, John Breen, was a rate collector in High Street, Killarney.[330] Breen studied at the Presentation Convent and the Presentation Monastery School before entering St Brendan's Seminary and then Maynooth in 1901.[331] He played Gaelic sports while at Maynooth, particularly handball and Gaelic football, and was ordained for the diocese of Kerry in 1908.[332] Breen continued at Maynooth as a Dunboyne scholar (postgraduate student) and was a supporter of Professor Michael O'Hickey's stance on the Irish language for the National University.[333] He served as a chaplain on a ship travelling to Australia in 1916 and volunteered as an army chaplain on his return, in response to an appeal by Cardinal Logue while at St Mary's and St Michael's Church, London.[334] He was appointed to the MEF in September 1916 and arrived in Basra in January where he was attached to the 133rd British General Hospital, Basra, until May 1917 when he joined the 7th Indian Division.[335] In January 1919, Breen was described by Brigadier-General Walter Leslie as 'an efficient chaplain who is popular with the men and zealous in his duties'.[336] He served as curate in various parishes in Kerry on his return from the war, and also served in Westminster.[337] He was involved in the establishment of the Sinn Féin Courts in 1920, later becoming a magistrate in Beaufort.[338]

MICHAEL J. CARNEY, from Belcarra in Co Mayo, was born in 1886 and studied at St Jarlath's College, Tuam before Maynooth and was ordained in 1910.[339] He was a curate in Headford before his commission as an army chaplain.[340] He was first appointed on 21 June 1915 and went on foreign service on 12 October 1915, his contract expired on 11 October 1918 and he was gazetted out of the army on 12 December 1918.[341] He was attached to the EEF, spending three months aboard the hospital ship *Delta* in 1916 and was recommended for home service in early June 1918.[342] In 1916, a Catholic chaplain writing in the *Irish Ecclesiastical Record* described some of the difficulties he experienced while ministering to soldiers on hospital ships in the Eastern Mediterranean, many of which revolved around practicalities such as identifying Catholic soldiers in time to deliver the last sacraments, which he described as 'the sorting of one's sheep'.[343] Carney spent two years and eight months on service in the East. Carney later became parish priest of Aughamore and Cong, Co Mayo.[344] He was transferred from Cong to Inisboffin in 1921'to avoid violence at the hands of the Crown Forces'.[345] In 1958, he led a ceremony for those who died during the War of Independence.[346] The Archbishop of Tuam, Dr Joseph Cunnane, described Carney as suffering from an 'extremely nervous and sensitive disposition' throughout his life.[347] He died in 1969.[348]

JOHN COFFEY, from Newtown, Co Tipperary, studied at Holy Cross College and was a candidate for matriculation at the Royal University of Ireland in 1894 and again in 1895 when he entered Maynooth to begin his undergraduate studies.[349] He volunteered for service while curate at St Nicholas of Myra, leaving Dublin on the day of the Easter Rising, 1916.[350] He relinquished his commission in May 1918 and died two years later at the age of forty. The *Irish Catholic* speculated that 'the hardships he endured undermined his stalwart frame and were ultimately the cause of his untimely decease'.[351]

CORNELIUS CREED, from Ballingeary, Co Cork who was born in 1889. Creed attended St Finbarr's College in Cork before entering Maynooth and was ordained for the diocese of Cork and Ross in 1916.[352] His father, Michael T. Creed, was a farmer in the townland of Illauninagh West.[353] Creed agreed to serve with the 66th (East Lancashire) Division in early February 1917, with the permission of his bishop, the Most Rev Daniel Cohalan. [354] However, just before the 66th Division went overseas it was reported that Creed had vacated his quarters and removed his kit without authority.[355] A month later a letter of enquiry was sent to Creed's father Michael in Cork.[356] On the same day (28 March) Creed wrote from Cork to explain his unauthorised departure, stating that:

> I received an urgent call from home in connection with the serious illness of an *immediate member of my family*. I must state I had *only been in the army a day or two* and had not the remotest conception of military regulations [...] I may say that I should be only too glad to again offer my services, but however on the condition that my leaving shall not in any way prejudice my position, also that I be attached to another division.[357]

This sentiment was shared by his father in a letter to the Army Chaplains' Department in April 1917 in which he states: 'I fear treating him as a criminal will not raise either the army or recruiting or him in any of our estimations around here'.[358] Despite this plea Creed was arrested by the Assistant Provost Marshal, Southern District, Ireland and handed over to the Officer Commanding the Durham Light Infantry in Colchester for safekeeping.[359] Perhaps, unsurprisingly, Creed sought to relinquish his position as Temporary Chaplain to the Forces shortly afterwards.[360] The Adjutant Generals Office (A.G.3.) had decided not to take disciplinary action due to the circumstances of the case and were happy to ignore his absence providing that he stayed away and that his services were not needed.[361] They ordered Creed's release on 18 April 1917.[362] The Army Council decided to give Creed the benefit of the doubt, noting 'that his action in absenting himself without leave was due, to some extent, to ignorance of Military regulations'.[363] Creed reported for duty at Aldershot in May 1917 and was later assigned to the 82nd General Hospital in Salonika, returning to Aldershot and Salisbury Plain after the war ended. He was a curate at Dunmanway and later chaplain at Coláiste Mhuire in Cork and at a residential home in Glanmire.[364] Creed died in August 1958 at the age of sixty-nine.

EDWARD DOWLING from Slieverue, Co Kilkenny, studied at St Kieran's College, Kilkenny before entering Maynooth College, he received his degree from RUI in 1905, and was ordained in 1908 for the diocese of Ossory.[365] Dowling's parents William and Catherine were both national school teachers.[366] Dowling worked on the mission in northern England before becoming Professor of Sacred Scripture and Metaphysics at St Kieran's College.[367] He agreed to serve with the Expeditionary Force on 11 November 1914 and reported for duty seven days later at Rouen.[368] He served with the 2nd Royal Dublin Fusiliers from November 1914 until January 1917, before taking up the post of Assistant Principal Chaplain at Le Havre, and was later awarded the Order of Aviz (Grand Officer) by the Portuguese Government for his service to Portuguese troops in the war.[369] Dowling was promoted in January 1917, spending the next two years at the rank of Temporary 1st Class Chaplain. He was described by Brigadier General A.R. Burrowes, as 'thoroughly efficient from a military point of view'. [370] Dowling went on to become parish priest of Camross, Co Laois in 1941.[371]

THOMAS DUGGAN, from Ballyheeda, Co Cork, had studied at University College Cork and at Maynooth where he was ordained in June 1915.[372] Duggan was serving with the 1st Battalion Royal Munster Fusiliers when he was captured and detained as a prisoner of war in a German camp in Mainz.[373] Duggan would later recall a visit from a German Intelligence Officer from Frankfort in July 1918 seeking a statement for the British press on 'the desirability of peace by negotiation' and describing the chaplain as 'An Irish humbug' on his refusal.[374] Outlining his reasons for becoming an army chaplain Duggan later explained:

> My generation in Maynooth embraced the ideals of Easter Week 1916 with a hundred per cent fervour. That did not prevent us from becoming Chaplains in the British Army. In the First World War there were well over 100,000 Irish Catholics in the fighting ranks. (The casualties alone were 50,000). Everyone

> admitted that these boys were spiritually intractable to anyone save to an Irish priest.[375]

Duggan volunteered to serve as a chaplain again following the outbreak of the Second World War and was safely evacuated from Dunkirk in 1940.[376] He was awarded the Military Cross 'for courage, coolness and outstanding example under shell fire'.[377] Duggan would later note his involvement in three wars in his lifetime – serving as a chaplain in the First and Second World Wars, and as a self-described 'combatant (more or less) against the Black and Tans' in the Irish War of Independence.[378] Duggan's grandfather, also named Thomas Duggan, was a member of the Cork Fenians who was arrested in 1867 and deported to Fremantle.[379] Duggan was at St Finbarr's College, Cork in August 1939[380] and in March 1953, Duggan was President of Farranferris College.[381] In 1961, he left Cork to minister in Peru but died shortly afterwards.[382]

BERNARD FARRELL, from Robertstown, Kilbeg in Co Meath, studied at St Finian's College, Navan and matriculated at Maynooth on 27 September 1895, entering the class of rhetoric.[383] He was ordained on 22 June 1902.[384] Farrell came from a farming background. He was commissioned on 16 March 1916, joining the 59th (North Midland) Division which saw service in Ireland during the Easter Rising, and proceeded on foreign service six months later, arriving in Basra in October 1917 where he joined the 7th Indian Division and was posted to the 133rd General Hospital, Tanooma.[385] He was admitted to hospital in July 1917 and invalided to India where he was struck off the strength of the MEF, re-joining in January 1918 when he left Bombay for Basra and was posted to the 40 British General Hospital.[386] He left Mesopotamia for England on 9 October and formally relinquished his commission on 9 December 1918. Farrell was awarded an OBE in January 1919 'for valuable services rendered in connection with military operations in Mesopotamia'.[387] He died in February 1921 following a fall from the top window of the bishop's palace in Mullingar.[388]

JOSEPH FURLONG, from Rathfarnham, Co Dublin was born in 1892. He was ordained on 17 June 1917 and later undertook parochial work at Terenure. Furlong was twenty-five years old when he applied for an appointment as Chaplain to the Forces. Furlong served with the BEF in France, embarking on foreign service on 11 November 1917. He was nominated by Mgr Bidwell to replace a chaplain appointed as an assistant to the Assistant Principal Chaplain in France.[389] Furlong served with the Munster Fusiliers from 1917-19. He was appointed chaplain to the Royal Hibernian Military School in the Phoenix Park in 1920. Furlong was later known as the Ireland's first 'flying priest' because of his interest in aviation, joining the Dublin Flying Club in 1936.[390] Furlong was appointed parish priest of Kilcullen in 1952 and was made a Canon of the Metropolitan Chapter of the Dublin Archdiocese in 1967.[391] He died in 1971 at the age of seventy-nine.[392]

FRANCIS GLEESON was perhaps one of the most prominent Catholic chaplains in the First World War; he was immortalised in Fortunino Matania's iconic painting *The Last General Absolution of the Munsters at Rue du Bois* while serving with the 2nd Battalion of the Royal Munsters on the eve of the Battle of Aubers Ridge. Gleeson was born in Templemore, Co Tipperary in 1884 and was a student at Clonliffe College before entering Maynooth.[393] He signed a contract of service with the BEF on 11November 1914.[394] He was serving with the Royal Munster Fusiliers in May 1915 when, during a German bombardment, he 'stuck to his post attending to the wounded and the dying Munsters'.[395] Gleeson returned to Dublin but volunteered again in May 1917, renewing this contract twelve months later. [396] In July 1918, John M. Simms, Principal Chaplain to the British Armies in France, described Gleeson's character as excellent, noting that he 'easily gets in touch with his flock'.[397] By August 1918, the Irish Recruiting Council was eager to use Gleeson in its propaganda campaigns but senior Roman Catholic chaplain Stephen Rawlinson disagreed stating that:

> The C.C. of his Irish Regiment begged of me very strongly to take Fr. Gleeson away as he was doing harm to the men from the political point of view. I of course did so. I do not know more about it than this, but with such a record he could hardly be recommended for propaganda purposes.[398]

Despite his desire to serve in Palestine, in February 1919 Gleeson was stationed with the Royal Dublin Fusiliers in Grimsby.[399] He ceased duty on 14 May 1919.[400] Gleeson would later serve as a chaplain with the Dublin Command in the Free State Army.[401]

Gleeson's diaries provide an important insight into the role of the Catholic chaplain at the Front as he recorded information about individual soldiers including when and how they died and the location of their burial, details he would often share with the families of the deceased.[402] He also recorded details of those missing, wounded or taken prisoner. Gleeson, like other Catholic chaplains, anointed the sick, heard confessions and said mass, often in poor conditions. On Sunday, 21 March 1915, for instance, he heard confession in 'kitchens, barns, stables and billets of every description'.[403] On Christmas Day 1917, he heard the confessions of nearly 200 officers and men.[404]

EDMUND KELLY was born in Newtown, New Inn to John and Bridget Kelly in June 1874. He studied at Rockwell College and at St Patricks' College, Thurles.[405] Kelly matriculated for the diocese of Cashel and entered Maynooth College on 1 September 1897. He was ordained sub-deacon by the Archbishop of Dublin in June 1899, and priest in 1900.[406] After his ordination Kelly served for twelve years on the South African Mission.[407] Priests that had previously worked as missionaries were, according to Leonard, the most suited to work at the Front.[408] In 1915, while curate in Mullinahone, he wrote in support of a recruitment meeting at Clonmel, which he was unable to attend due to his commencement as chaplain with the 49th Brigade.

> I heartily wish you success, because never before in the world's history did so much depend on the issue of a war. The freedom of the world is at stake. Right and Justice are trembling for their fate. Of course, the idea of an arrogant Prussian imposing his will on Europe is simply intolerable. But who is to prevent him? Our soldiers; and never did soldiers fight in a holier or more patriotic cause. Irish soldiers at the present crisis are our truest patriots. On them depend the security of all we personally hold dear and our hope for the ideal we cherish for our country.[409]

In June 1917, Kelly was based in the cellar of the chapel at St Antoine Hospice in the village of Locre with Major Willie Redmond, in the nights before the Major died at the Battle of Messines Ridge on 7 June 1917. Three days later Kelly wrote to Monsignor Ryan in Tipperary with an account of Major Redmond's death noting that 'We, the chaplains of the Irish Division, will miss him very much. He used to spend all his spare time with us, and do everything he possibly could to make things comfortable for us'.[410] Described by the *Cork Examiner* as an 'unassuming but fearless Irish priest', Kelly was awarded the MC in 1918 for 'conspicuous gallantry and devotion to duty in tending the wounded and dying of all denominations under the heaviest shell fire' during fighting near Ypres.[411] He continued his role as chaplain after the Armistice of November 1918 and was present at the annual dinner of the 1st Royal Dublin Fusiliers in Berish-Gladback, Germany, on St Patrick's Day 1919.[412] On his return from the war, Kelly was curate in Tipperary and later became parish priest of Cappawhite and then Killenhaule.[413] He died on 11 October 1955 at the age of eighty-one years.

PATRICK KERR, a native Irish speaker from Kindrum, Letterkenny, Co Donegal, was informed of his selection for duty with the 40th Division at Blackdown, Aldershot while a postgraduate student at Maynooth in February 1916 at the age of twenty-seven.[414] He joined the Division in March and later accompanied it to France where he served for three years until he was gazetted out of the army in June 1919 while stationed at Étaples, France. In a letter to *An Crann*, a bilingual quarterly published by the Féis Thir Chonaill Committee in Letterkenny, he described the conditions at the Front:

> Many sleep in unknown graves. The slaying and sepulture of some have been performed in one terrible instance by a single shell. Occasionally the stalwart manly figure of a soldier is scattered, in tiny fragments, for yards around, by the powerful high-explosive. Sometimes the rain and flood, washing away the soft earth, expose the black swollen remains of those who have been buried by shells.[415]

Kerr became a Professor at All Hallows College on his return from the war, spending ten years as a faculty member before becoming President of St Eunan's in Letterkenny and then parish priest of Gortahork.[416]

WILLIAM MULLINS, from William Street in Co Galway, joined the 59th Division in September 1916, when it was based in Ireland following the Easter Rising, and was nominated for service with the Mediterranean Expeditionary Force (MEF) in October 1916.[417] Mullins was attached to a Casualty Clearing Station in the months prior to the Fall of Baghdad. He was later described by the Principal Chaplain, MEF as 'just the type of man we want in the Army'.[418] In February 1919, Mullins was appointed curate in Ennistymon and just three years later parish priest of Roscahill.[419]

JAMES NOLAN was ordained at St Patrick's College, Maynooth in 1912 for the diocese of Clogher.[420] Nolan, from Aghabog, Co Monaghan, later served in the parishes of Cleenish, Coonlan, and Dromore.[421] His father John was a farmer and grocer in Corranewy, Co Monaghan.[422] Nolan was selected for temporary duty as Chaplain to the Forces with the 58th (London) Division in July 1916, reporting for duty at Sutton Veny on 10 August.[423] He embarked for Boulogne from Folkestone on 26 September 1916, having been posted to the 15th Brigade, 5th Division.[424] Nolan was attached to the 25th Field Ambulance Unit of the 8th Division when he was captured at Bouvancourt in Northern France on 27 May 1918.[425] He spent the next five months at the Stralsund-Dänholm POW camp and was repatriated on 2 November 1918. Nolan was thirty-one years old and had served for a total of two years and two months, one month at home and the rest abroad.[426] Nolan later stated that he was searching for a safe way out of the village for the wounded but 'had gone only a very short distance when a party of Germans whom I didn't see at first, but who were I thought about 15 yards from us, shouted on us and we surrendered and were taken prisoners'. A Standing Committee of Enquiry found no blame could be apportioned to Nolan for the incident. Nolan served as a curate in Carrickmacross and Clontibret after the war.[427] He was appointed parish priest of Fivemiletown in 1934.[428] He died in June 1964 at the age of seventy-seven.[429]

EDWARD O'HART was from a farming family in Magheraveely in Co Fermanagh and studied at St Macartan's in Monaghan before he entered Maynooth and was ordained in 1910 for the diocese of Clogher.[430] O'Hart was thirty-three years old when he was selected for duty with the BEF in April 1917, having spent the previous seven years in the parishes of Clones, Ballybay, and Devenish (Garrison).[431] He served with the BEF for twelve months until the expiration of his contract in May 1918. John M. Simms, Principal Army Chaplain with the British Armies in France, later noted that O'Hart was a 'very good worker and does splendidly at Front work. Will be glad to see him back'.[432] O'Hart was 'a great Irish-Irelander' and nationalist supporter with a particular interest in the Irish language and sport.[433] After the war, he was chaplain to the Free State Army in Finner Camp and was later parish priest of Templecarne.[434]

JOHN T. O'KELLY, from Gort, Co Galway, studied at St Joseph's College, Garbally Park in Ballinasloe before entering Maynooth and was ordained in 1907 for the diocese of Galway.[435] His parents Denis and Mary were shopkeepers in Craughwell, Galway.[436] O'Kelly was selected for duty with the 61st (South Midland) Division in February 1916 while at the Church of St Colman. He gave the names of his two brothers, Denis P. O'Kelly, c/o Arnotts and Co., Dublin and Michael J. O'Kelly, RIC John's Street, Kilkenny, and two sisters, Katie and Tessie O'Kelly, both nurses at the County Infirmary Galway as his next of kin on 5 March 1916.[437] He joined the Division in March 1916 at Salisbury Plain and accompanied it to the Western Front in May 1916.[438] O'Kelly renewed his service for a further twelve months in June 1917 and served until his contract expired on 25 May 1918.[439]

PETER O'FARRELL served in several theatres of the war. Born in February 1885, O'Farrell studied at St Mel's College, Longford and was ordained in 1908 for the diocese of Ardagh and Clonmacnois.[440] His father Luke was a farmer and publican.[441] O'Farrell had ten years clerical experience when he applied for service as a Temporary Chaplain to the Forces in March 1915. He was attached to the 5th (Service) Battalion (Pioneers) of the Royal Irish Regiment, which provided support for the 10th Irish Division, serving in Gallipoli, Serbia, Salonika, Egypt, Palestine, and France from July 1915 until July 1918.[442] The 10th Division was to become 'a military and political hot potato' as the war progressed due to the fragmented nature of its deployment in battle and the subsequent disillusion of its senior officers.[443] O'Farrell renewed his contract of service with the Army Chaplains' Department in August 1916, August 1917, and October 1918. He was gazetted out of the Army in September 1920 while stationed at the 37th Casualty Clearing Station in France.

JAMES SHERIDAN was born in Ballyjamesduff, Co Cavan in 1888 and was educated at St Patrick's College, Cavan and then at Maynooth where he received his BA degree from NUI in 1911 and was ordained in 1914. His father Philip was a farmer and merchant in 1901 and a publican in 1911.[444] Sheridan was twenty-nine years old when he joined the 41st Division in March 1916 at Aldershot, going on foreign service shortly thereafter.[445] Sheridan renewed his contract of service on 5 April 1917 for as long as required and in November 1918 he was serving with the 18th Lancashire Fusiliers in France.[446] Principal Chaplain, B.S. Rawlinson described his character as '[e]xcellent', his physical fitness as 'good' and deemed him 'suitable' for army chaplaincy duties.[447]

Terence Small was born in Cavan town in February 1878 and was the only son of Hugh Small, a merchant who ran a shop on Main Street.[448] Small studied at St Patrick's College, Cavan and in Maynooth, and was ordained in 1902. He served in Killinkere and Derrylin before the war. He was forty-one years old in May 1917 when he applied for an appointment as Temporary Chaplain to the Forces.[449] Small noted his proficiency with the French language, stating 'I can read French very well. I have been twice to France. I have some exience [sic.] of hospital work'. However, he was appointed to the Egyptian Expeditionary Force, reporting for temporary duty at Aldershot on 1 June and embarking from Southampton in July 1917 for service in Egypt.[450] He renewed his contract of service on 11 June 1918 for a period of twelve months. Small became parish priest of Kilmainhamwood in 1924 and then Templeport, and was appointed pastor of Knockninny, Derrylin in December 1943.[451] He died in January 1947 at the age of seventy.

Hugh Smith was born in Moville, Co Donegal, in 1884, where his father was a publican.[452] He studied at St Columb's College, Derry and was ordained at Maynooth for the diocese of Derry in 1908.[453] He applied for an appointment as a temporary chaplain on 6 February 1917, stating that he had nearly nine years clerical experience and a 'working knowledge of French'.[454] He joined the 66th (East Lancashire) Division in Colchester on 20 February 1917 at the age of thirty-two, later accompanying it to France.[455] The Division suffered heavy losses during the Battle of Poelcappelle in October 1917 and saw service at the Battle of Cambrai and the Battle of the Selle. Smith officially left the 66th Division on 3 March 1919 and arrived in England the next day.[456] He was deemed 'suitable in every way' for duty as an Army Chaplain.[457]

Laurence Stafford was born in Glen House, Waterford in 1867. His family ran a victualling business on George's Street.[458] He studied at Holy Cross College, Clonliffe and was ordained at Maynooth in 1896. He worked in the parishes of Finglas and Dolphin's Barn before the war. He served with the 10th Division in Gallipoli and was at the landing at Suvla Bay in August 1915.[459] He left the Mediterranean in January 1916 and joined for duty at the prisoner of war camp in Frongoch in July 1916. He received a hostile welcome from nationalist internees at Frongoch because of his khaki uniform, which was considered as 'the full regalia of an officer of the enemy forces'.[460] Michael J. Curran, secretary to Archbishop William Walsh, stated that '[a]t first the prisoners did not like a khaki chaplain but they have settled down'.[461] On one occasion Stafford attempted to end a hunger strike at the camp when authorities began to conscript prisoners into military service.[462] He reportedly threatened the men with damnation because of their intent to commit suicide. [463] He was selected for further duty with the BEF in France in May 1917, embarking for service on 5 June 1917. He was appointed Senior Chaplain to the Forces with the 24th Division in June 1917 and later served in Italy. Stafford appears to have been a divisive character even amongst other Catholic chaplains. Rev William Murphy, for instance, Senior Chaplain to the Forces at the Curragh Camp, wrote to the Army Chaplains' Department in October 1917 in a bid to hinder Stafford's progression, noting that: 'I can honestly say that no chaplain has respect for him.' [464] He suggested a consultation with Lord Granard who had served with Stafford in the Dardanelles and Salonica. Murphy later wrote to Granard (30 January 1918) stating that:

> Fr Stafford is perhaps the best-known priest in Ireland, but the knowledge of him has not commanded the respect of his fellow priests. His extravagances make him known only to be despised and to advance such a man to so responsible a position is calculated to set the whole Irish Church laughing. [...] Am I asking too much of you to use your influence at War Office, with Sir Reginald Brady, to have a Chaplain appointed Principal Chaplain in Italy who will do us credit, and to have Fr. Stafford relegated to a more suitable post? [465]

Granard forwarded Murphy's letter to M.D. Graham, Assistant Military Secretary at the War Office the next day, stating that 'I feel it would be nothing short of a calamity if Father Stafford received a decoration or promotion'. Graham later wrote to the Chaplains' Department in relation to Granard's letter stating that '[p]ossibly you will agree that the waste-paper basket is the best method of disposal – if so kindly destroy'.[466] Stafford was transferred to the EEF on 21 January 1919. After the war, Stafford became a curate in Lucan and was later appointed parish priest of Ballitore in Co Kildare.[467] He died in 1943 at the age of seventy-six.

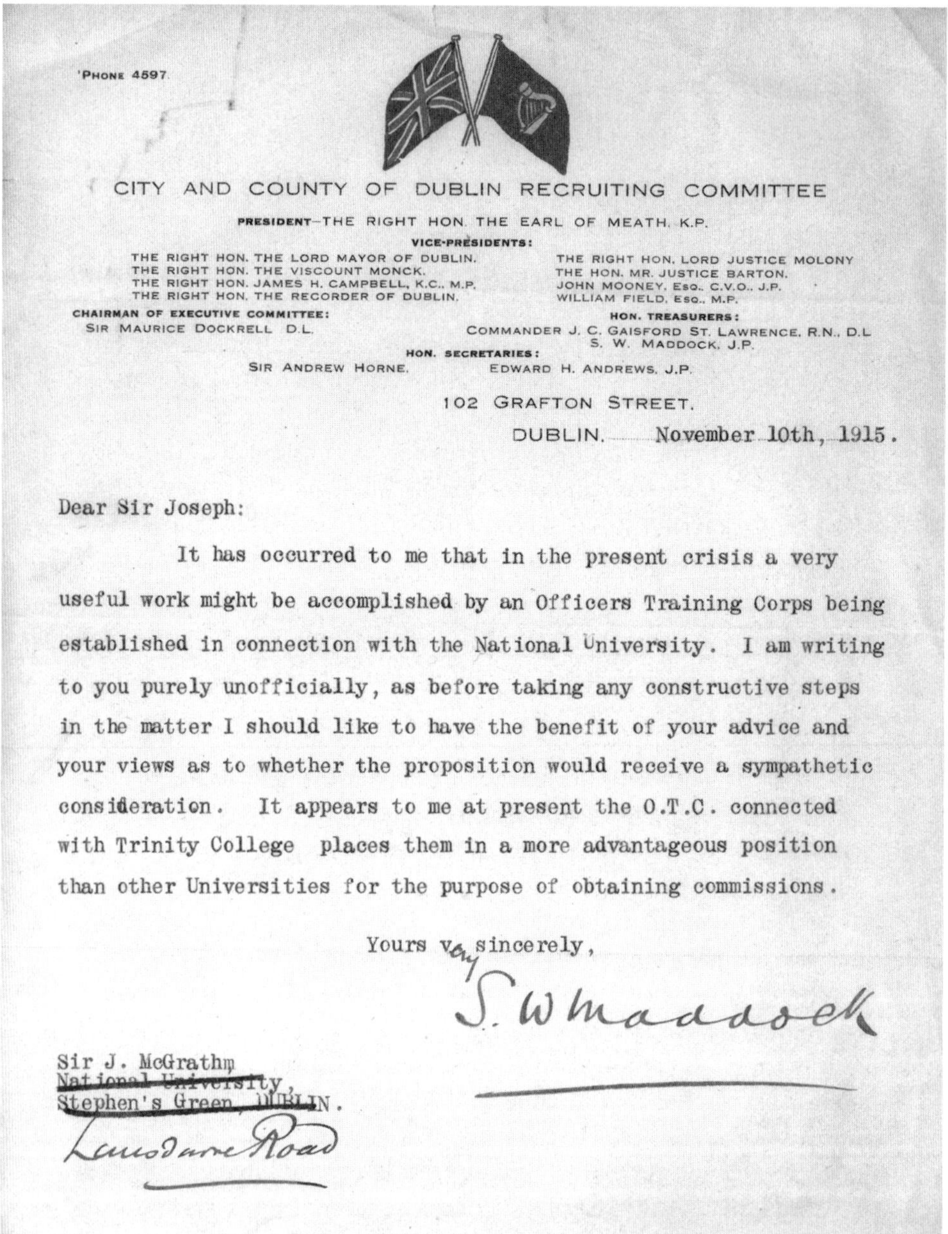

'PHONE 4597.

CITY AND COUNTY OF DUBLIN RECRUITING COMMITTEE

PRESIDENT—THE RIGHT HON. THE EARL OF MEATH, K.P.

VICE-PRESIDENTS:

THE RIGHT HON. THE LORD MAYOR OF DUBLIN.
THE RIGHT HON. THE VISCOUNT MONCK.
THE RIGHT HON. JAMES H. CAMPBELL, K.C., M.P.
THE RIGHT HON. THE RECORDER OF DUBLIN.
THE RIGHT HON. LORD JUSTICE MOLONY
THE HON. MR. JUSTICE BARTON.
JOHN MOONEY, ESQ., C.V.O., J.P.
WILLIAM FIELD, ESQ., M.P.

CHAIRMAN OF EXECUTIVE COMMITTEE:
SIR MAURICE DOCKRELL D.L.

HON. TREASURERS:
COMMANDER J. C. GAISFORD ST. LAWRENCE, R.N., D.L.
S. W. MADDOCK, J.P.

HON. SECRETARIES:
SIR ANDREW HORNE.
EDWARD H. ANDREWS, J.P.

102 GRAFTON STREET.
DUBLIN. November 10th, 1915.

Dear Sir Joseph:

It has occurred to me that in the present crisis a very useful work might be accomplished by an Officers Training Corps being established in connection with the National University. I am writing to you purely unofficially, as before taking any constructive steps in the matter I should like to have the benefit of your advice and your views as to whether the proposition would receive a sympathetic consideration. It appears to me at present the O.T.C. connected with Trinity College places them in a more advantageous position than other Universities for the purpose of obtaining commissions.

Yours very sincerely,

S. W. Maddock

Sir J. McGrath
~~National University,~~
~~Stephen's Green, DUBLIN.~~
Lansdowne Road

1. *Letter from City and County of Dublin Recruiting Committee proposing the establishment of an Officer's Training Camp. 10 November 1915.*

6. *NUI Archival Material*

from the First World War

JOHN FOLEY AND EMER PURCELL

THIS COLLECTION OF MATERIAL is drawn from the work of John Foley, a retired member of NUI staff, who was tasked with looking through the archives to find material relating to the Decade of Centenaries.

1. Letter from City and County of Dublin Recruiting Committee proposing the establishment of an Officer's Training Camp. *10 November 1915.*

2. Letter from W. Kirwan to Joseph McGrath, Registrar of NUI, enquiring about the entrance exam to Surgeon Probationers in the Royal Navy Volunteer Reserve. He details several reasons why he wishes to enter service; amongst them he references his brother who is now home from Gallipoli. *24 May 1916.*

3. Letter from Keating, British Expeditionary Force, to NUI requesting copies of his Matriculation and his Medical Exams certificates. *22 July 1916.*

4. Letter from Alex Anderson, President of University College Galway, to the Registrar of NUI mentioning correspondence with Bertram Windle, President of University College Cork, discussing the passing votes of condolence for Edgar Harper, Professor of Mathematics, UCC, and Tom Kettle, Professor of National Economics, UCD. *8 October 1916.*

5. Letter from J.C. McGrath, Cottonera Military Hospital, Malta, noting that he will be unable to attend Senate and adding 'Several National University men are doing very good work out here'. *19 October 1916.*

6. The Lancet Offices writing to Joseph McGrath, Registrar of NUI, requesting information on Dr Isobel A. Tate, a graduate of the Royal University of Ireland, so that they might write her obituary. *14 March 1917.*

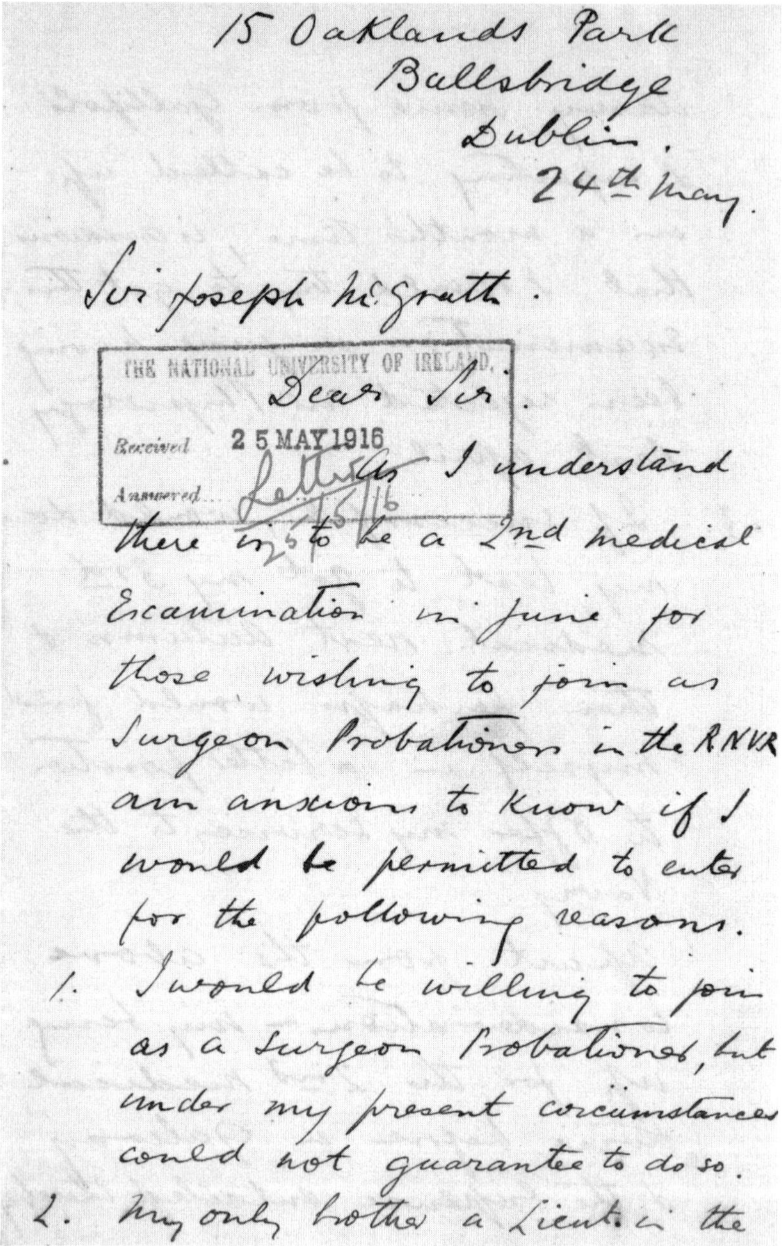

15 Oaklands Park
Ballsbridge
Dublin.
24th May.

Sir Joseph McGrath.

THE NATIONAL UNIVERSITY OF IRELAND.
Received 25 MAY 1916
Answered Letter 25/5/16

Dear Sir.

I understand there is to be a 2nd medical Examination in June for those wishing to join as Surgeon Probationers in the RNVR am anxious to know if I would be permitted to enter for the following reasons.

1. I would be willing to join as a Surgeon Probationer, but under my present circumstances could not guarantee to do so.
2. My only brother a Lieut. in the

[page 1]

2. *Letter from W. Kirwan to Joseph McGrath, NUI Registrar, enquiring about the entrance exam to Surgeon Probationers in the Royal Navy Volunteer Reserve.* [continued opposite]

Army, home from Gallipoli
& expecting to be called up
in a month's time, is anxious
that I should try to get this
Examination in June having
been rejected in Physiology
last April.

3. If successful, would do
my best to get my 3rd
Medical next Autumn &
then perhaps would find
myself in a better position
to offer my services to the
Navy.
Apart from the above
considerations – my being
up for the 2nd medical
twice before in Galway
& the expense entailed thereby

[page 2]

He details several reasons why he wishes to enter service; amongst them he references his brother who is now home from Gallipoli. 24 May 1916.

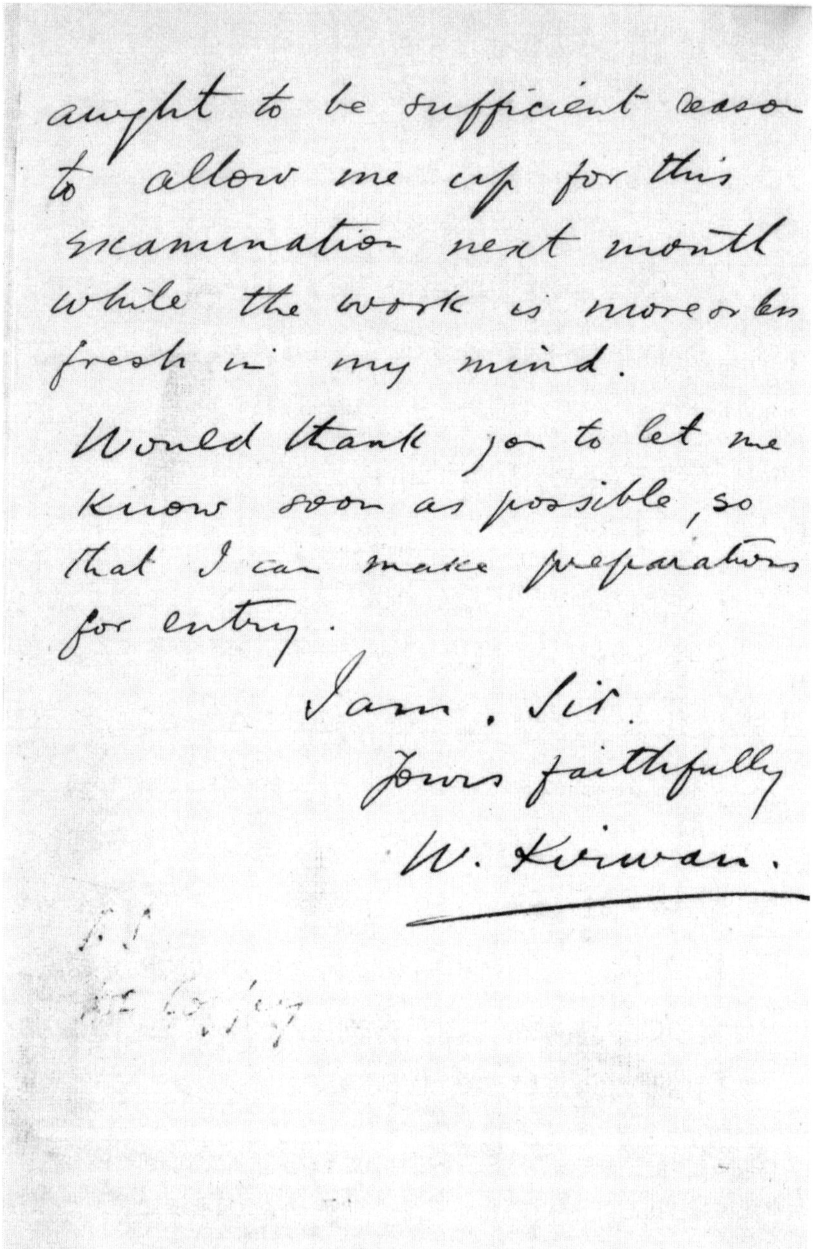

ought to be sufficient reason
to allow me up for this
examination next month
while the work is more or less
fresh in my mind.

Would thank you to let me
know soon as possible, so
that I can make preparations
for entry.

I am, Sir,
Yours faithfully
W. Kirwan.

[page 3]

7. Letter from Robert James Blackham to NUI requesting an Honorary War Degree. Details his military, official, and academic distinctions. *14 June 1917.*

8. Letter from R.W.G. Hingston to NUI, writing from Mesopotamian Expeditionary Force, noting that he had seen a copy of the *Cork Weekly News* [included], reporting that the Senate on 1 June 1917 had approved the recommendation to grant War Degrees. He details his academic qualifications, his military cross, and his military service in France, German East Africa, North West Frontier India, and Mesopotamia. He mentions scientific work for the Government of India in connection with Triangulation Link across the Himalaya between India and Russia. *1 August 1917.*

9. Letter from J.R. Duggan, 'Somewhere in France', noting that he has been granted leave to attend his degree conferring. 19 October 1917.

10. Letter from George T. Phillips to the Registrar of NUI, Joseph McGrath. Writing on behalf of his son Harold J. Phillips, requesting that his degree be conferred in absentia. Harold was onboard his ship when it was torpedoed on 9 September and was recovering 'somewhere in England'. *23 October 1917.*

11. Letter from John J. O'Donovan to Registrar of NUI, writing 'In the field', requesting that his Honorary War Degree be conferred in absentia. *26 October 1917.*

12. Letter from John Ryan to NUI, regarding his Travelling Studentship in Celtic Studies. He plans to study with either Dr Rudolf Thurneysen of the University of Bonn and/or Professor Kuno Meyer of University of Berlin. But owing to the present conditions he is unable to do so. He details a plan of study approved by his professors: Dr [Osborn] Bergin, Dr Douglas Hyde, and [John] Lloyd Jones. *16 October 1919.*

13. Letter from Michael Tierney [later President of UCD and son-in-law of Eoin MacNeill], requesting permission to postpone travel for his Travelling Studentship 'owing to the difficulties caused by the war'. *5 November 1917.*

14. Two letters from Thomas R. Mayne, Salonika Forces, to NUI, looking for the MA syllabus for external students and details of the subjects for the MA

in Latin and Greek, as he is 'doing his best' to get on with his studies. 14 February 1918. He was persistent, writing again when he was back in Ireland in 1919. He askst about War Degrees, and then details his service and his qualifications, mentioning that he was incapacitated by heavy shelling during operations against the Bulgarians and suffered from 'shell shock'. *31 August 1919*

15. University College, Cork, List of Recommendations for (University) Honorary War Distinctions. *Received 1 February 1918.*

16. University College Dublin, Honorary Degrees to Graduates for Distinguished War Service. [*no date*].

17. Letter from D.L. Coughlan to NUI, as he had read in the Cork Examiner of the NUI Senate recommendation that members of the forces may have their service accepted in lieu of Matriculation. He details the history of his service and attempts to obtain qualifications. *6 March 1918.*

18. Letter from J. Walsh to NUI, with regards to his application to have an Honorary War Degree conferred, he details his war service, including time in France at the front, Salonika, and the Jordan Valley in Palestine. *4 November 1918.*

19. Letter from Arthur Beveridge, 135 Field Ambulance, BEF, to the Registrar of NUI, requesting that his name be submitted for the Honorary BSc War Degree. He provides details of qualifications, his military cross for gallantry, and that he was mentioned in dispatches. *21 December 1918.*

20. Letter from A.A. Townsend thanking NUI for granting him matriculation and appealing to them that he might be allowed his first examination, as he had forgotten so much of what he had learned while was 'a prisoner of war in Bulgaria'. *October 1919.*

21. Letter from W. Pegler to the Registrar of NUI, requesting his Honorary War Exemption of two subjects at BA. 'I regret to say that life on board a battleship for 2½ years in a war area was not conducive to study, and … the effects of foreign naval service under trying conditions have rendered it impossible … to further continue serious study'. *22 January 1921.*

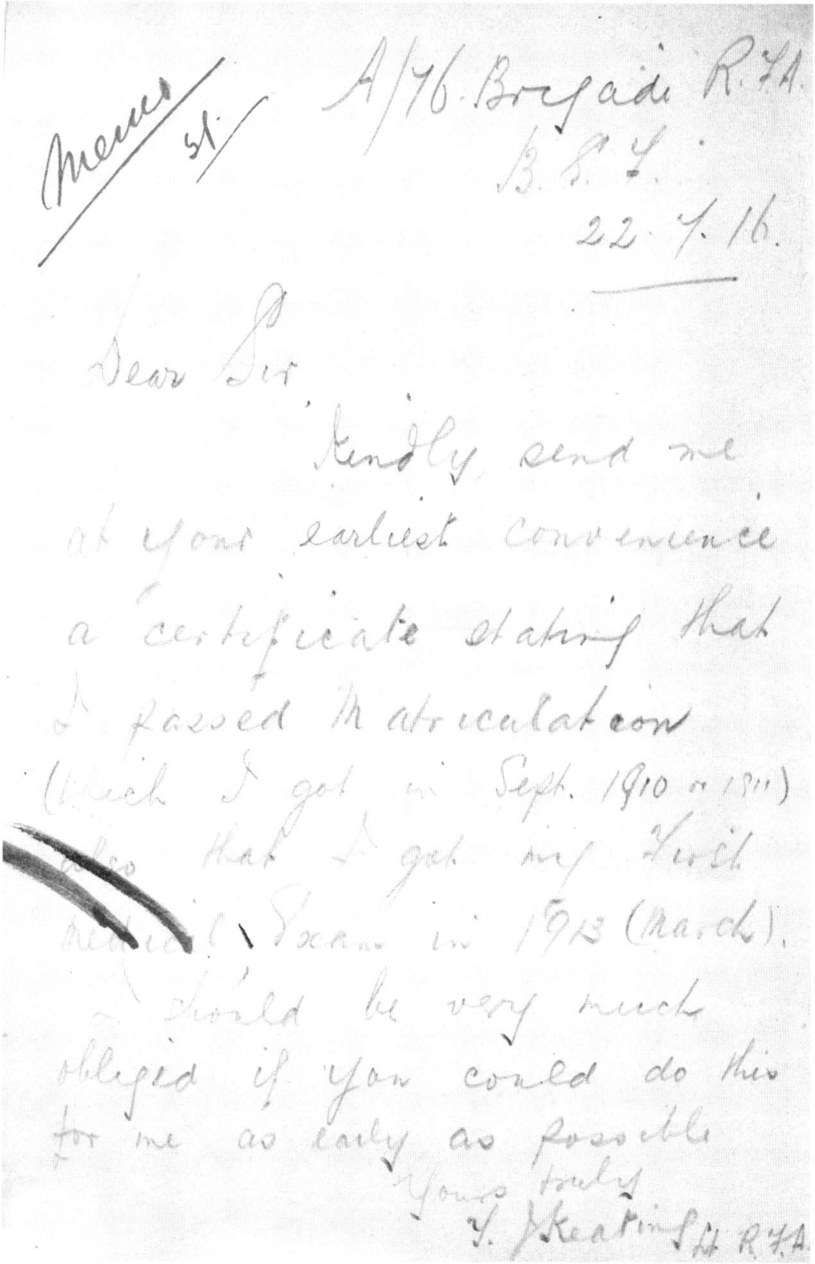

A/76 Brigade R.F.A.
B.E.F.
22.7.16.

Dear Sir,

Kindly send me at your earliest convenience a certificate stating that I passed Matriculation (which I got in Sept. 1910 or 1911) also that I got my First Medical Exam in 1913 (March).

I should be very much obliged if you could do this for me as early as possible

Yours truly

Y. J Keating 2Lt R.F.A.

3. Letter from Keating, British Expeditonary Force, to NUI requesting copies of his Matriculation and his Medical Exams certificates. 22 July 1916.

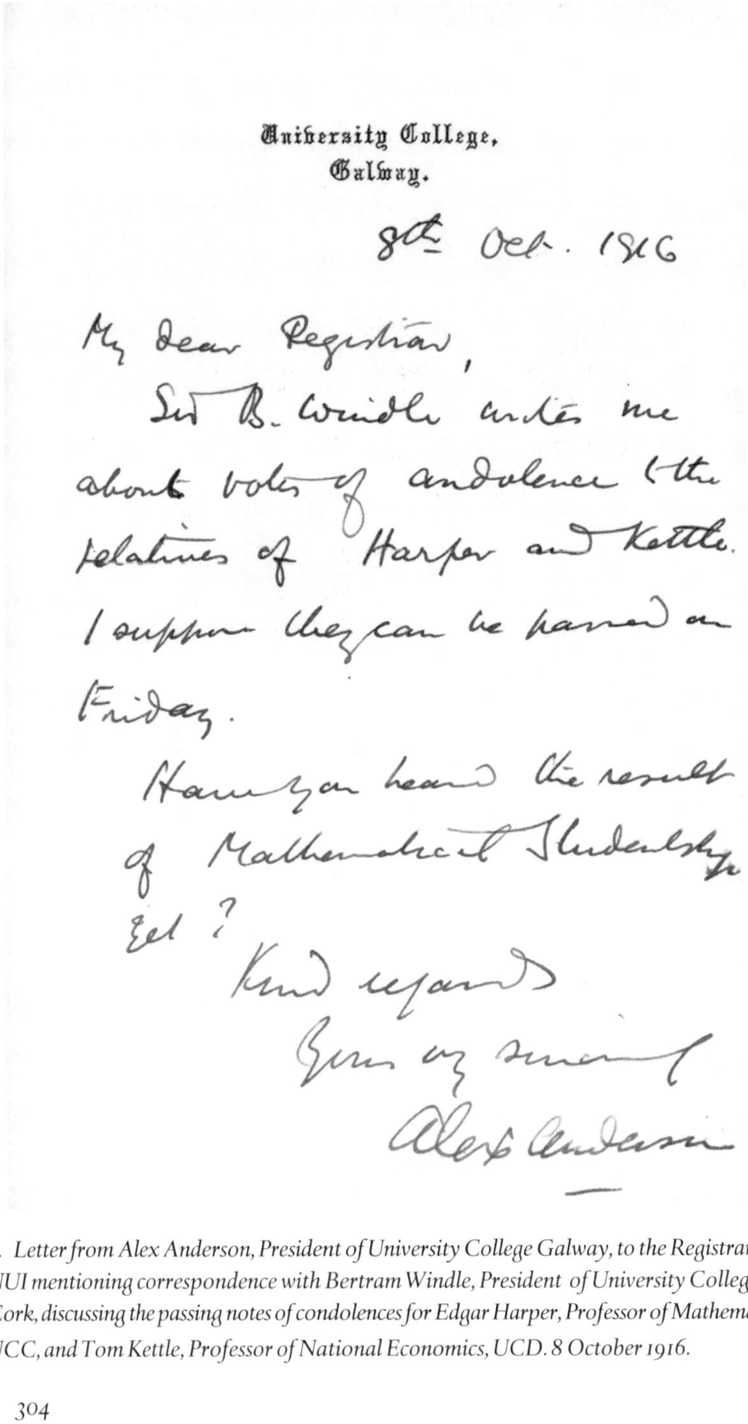

University College,
Galway.

8th Oct. 1916

My dear Registrar,

Sir B. Windle writes me about votes of condolence to the relatives of Harper and Kettle. I suppose they can be passed on Friday.

Have you heard the result of Mathematical Studentship yet?

Kind regards
Yours very sincerely
Alex Anderson

4. *Letter from Alex Anderson, President of University College Galway, to the Registrar of NUI mentioning correspondence with Bertram Windle, President of University College Cork, discussing the passing notes of condolences for Edgar Harper, Professor of Mathematics, UCC, and Tom Kettle, Professor of National Economics, UCD. 8 October 1916.*

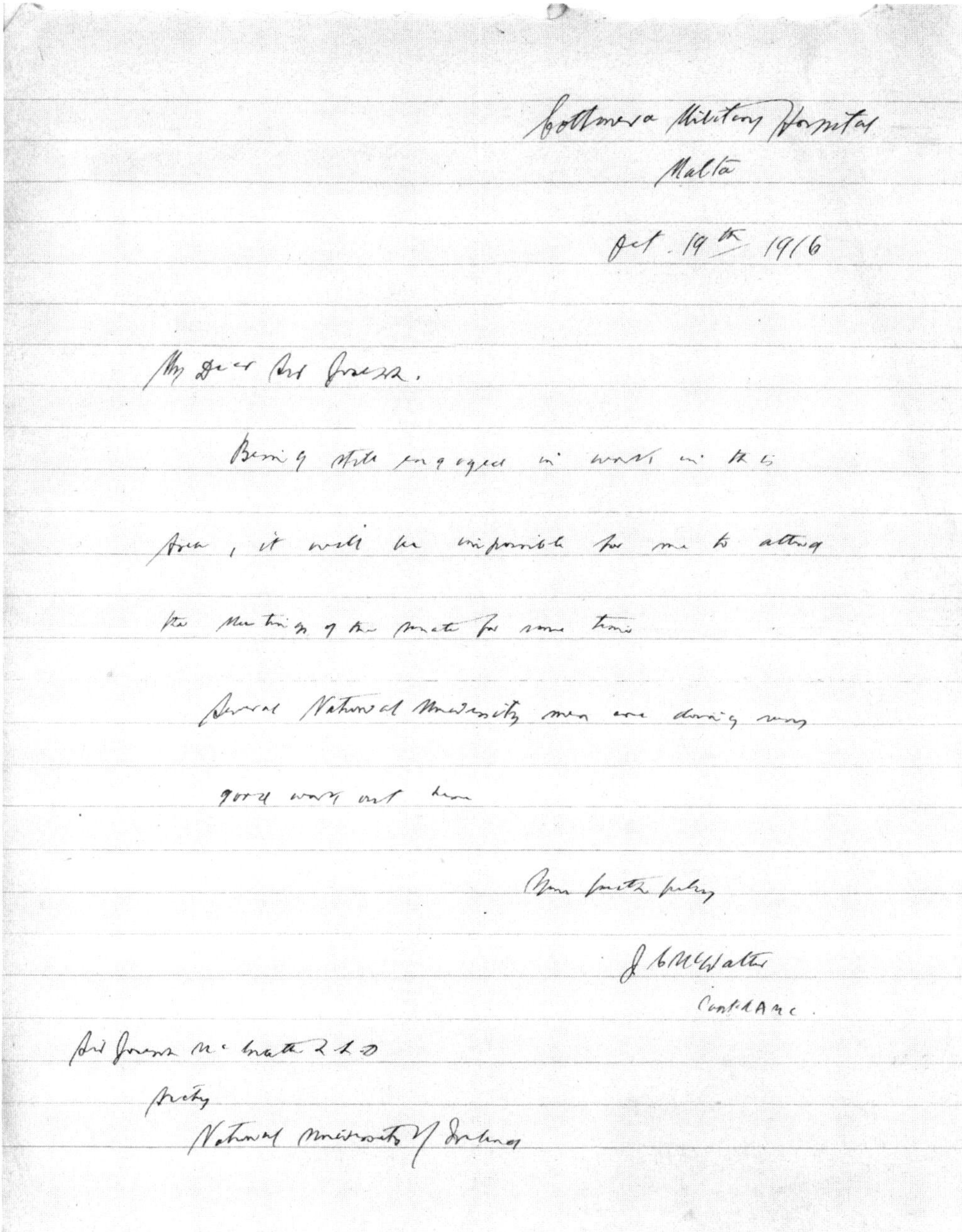

Cottonera Military Hospital
Malta

Oct. 19th 1916

My Dear Sir Joseph,

Being still engaged in work in this Area, it will be impossible for me to attend the meetings of the Senate for some time.

Several National University men are doing very good work out here.

Yours faithfully

J C McGrath
Capt RAMC.

Sir Joseph McGrath LLD
Secty
National University of Ireland

5. Letter from J.C. McGrath, Cottonera Military Hospital, Malta, noting that he will be unable to attend Senate and adding 'Several National University men are doing very good work out here'. 19 October 1916.

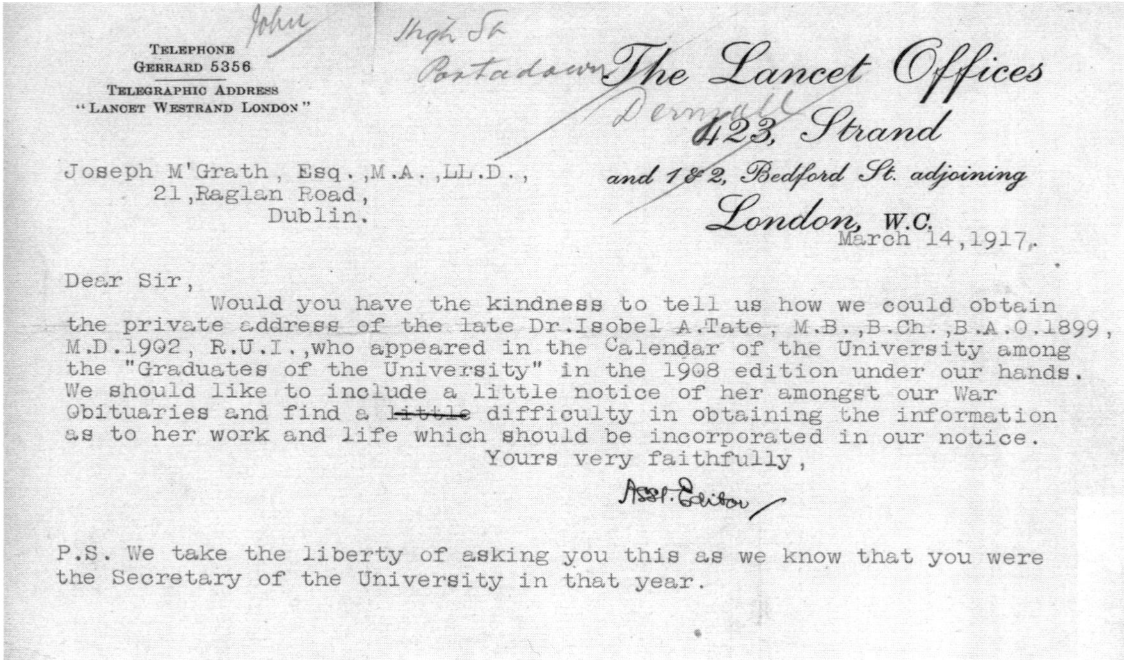

TELEPHONE
GERRARD 5356
TELEGRAPHIC ADDRESS
"LANCET WESTRAND LONDON"

The Lancet Offices
423, Strand
and 1 & 2, Bedford St. adjoining
London, W.C.

March 14, 1917.

Joseph M'Grath, Esq., M.A., LL.D.,
21, Raglan Road,
Dublin.

Dear Sir,

Would you have the kindness to tell us how we could obtain the private address of the late Dr. Isobel A. Tate, M.B., B.Ch., B.A.O. 1899, M.D. 1902, R.U.I., who appeared in the Calendar of the University among the "Graduates of the University" in the 1908 edition under our hands. We should like to include a little notice of her amongst our War Obituaries and find a ~~little~~ difficulty in obtaining the information as to her work and life which should be incorporated in our notice.

Yours very faithfully,

Asst. Editor

P.S. We take the liberty of asking you this as we know that you were the Secretary of the University in that year.

6. *The Lancet Offices writing to Joseph McGrath, Registrar of NUI, requesting information on Dr Isobel A. Tate (inset), a graduate of the Royal University of Ireland, so that they might write her obituary. 14 March 1917.*

PETITION to THE SENATE

of

THE NATIONAL UNIVERSITY OF IRELAND

from

Colonel ROBERT JAMES BLACKHAM, C.I.E., D.S.O.,
ARMY MEDICAL SERVICE

for

an HONORARY WAR DEGREE.

June 14th 1917

Sirs,

I am an undergraduate of the Royal University of Ireland.

I matriculated in 1886, and passed the First Examination in Arts in 1887.

For reasons over which I had no control I did not proceed to a Degree, but completed my medical curriculum in DUBLIN, and qualified as a Physician and Surgeon in 1892. I entered the Army Medical Service and have attained the rank of Colonel.

The following is a brief record of my Military, Official and Academic attainments during the past quarter of a century.

A. MILITARY DISTINCTIONS.

1. Appointed Assistant Director of Medical Services of a Division and temporary full Colonel 1915.

2. Awarded the Distinguished Service Order 1917.

3. Twice Mentioned in Despatches.

4. Served throughout the Present War, and was with TIRAH Expeditionary Force 1897, and KHYBER Brigade 1898.

B. OFFICIAL DISTINCTIONS.

1. Awarded the Companionship of the Most Eminent Order of the Indian Empire (C.I.E) in 1913.

[page 1]

7. Letter from Robert James Blackham to NUI requesting an Honorary War Degree. Details his military, official, and academic distinctions. 14 June 1917.

(2).

2. Awarded the KAISER-I-HIND Medal for Public Service in INDIA in 1911.

3. Gazetted Knight of Grace of the Order of ST. JOHN 1910.

4. Appointed Honorary Surgeon to the VICEROY of INDIA in 1912.

5. Thanked by SECRETARY of STATE and GOVERNMENT of INDIA for Services to VICEROY at State Entry to DELHI 1912.

C. ACADEMIC DISTINCTIONS.

1. Called to the Bar at the Middle Temple 1908.

2. Admitted a Member of the Royal College of Physicians, EDINBURGH 1916.

3. Admitted a Fellow of the Royal Faculty of Physicians and Surgeons 1914.

4. Diploma of Public Health, LONDON, 1905.

5. Author of several monographs which have passed through many editions, and of Tropical Hygiene 3rd Edition. This book was written in conjunction with the Director General of the Indian Medical Service, and issued to Territorial Units arriving in INDIA at the beginning of the present War.

I venture to hope that my record will be considered sufficiently good to merit the honour I ask for from the great University, which has succeeded my alma mater.

I have the honor to be,
Sirs,
Your most obedient servant.

R. J. Blackham

Colonel.
Army Medical Service.

Headquarters
23rd Division
British Expeditionary Force.

[page 2]

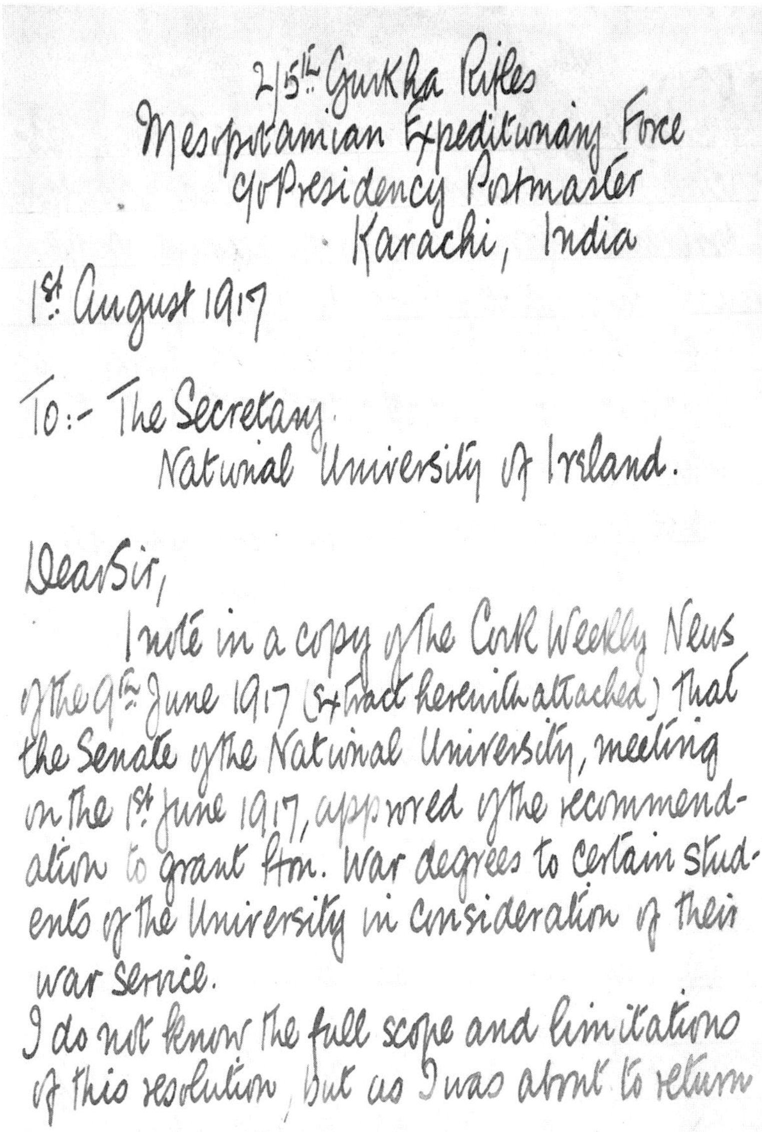

2/5th Gurkha Rifles
Mesopotamian Expeditionary Force
c/o Presidency Postmaster
Karachi, India

1st August 1917

To:- The Secretary
National University of Ireland.

Dear Sir,

I note in a copy of the Cork Weekly News of the 9th June 1917 (extract herewith attached) that the Senate of the National University, meeting on the 1st June 1917, approved of the recommendation to grant Hon. War degrees to certain students of the University in consideration of their war service.

I do not know the full scope and limitations of this resolution, but as I was about to return

[page 1]

8. *Letter from R.W.G. Hingston to NUI, writing from Mesopotamian Expeditionary Force, noting that he had seen a copy of the 'Cork Weekly News'* [included], *reporting that the Senate on 1 June 1917 had approved the recommendation to grant War Degrees. He details his academic qualifications, his military cross, and his military service in* [continued overleaf]

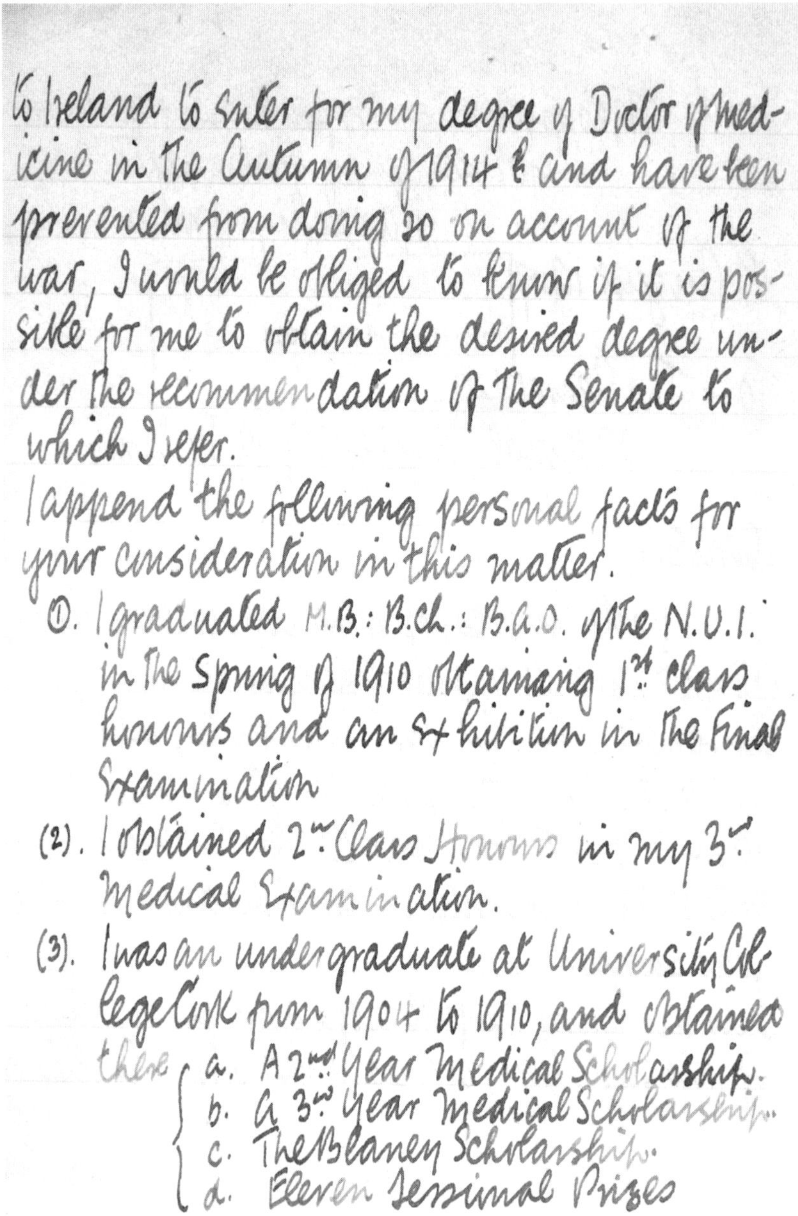
to Ireland to enter for my degree of Doctor of Medicine in the Autumn of 1914 & and have been prevented from doing so on account of the war, I would be obliged to know if it is possible for me to obtain the desired degree under the recommendation of the Senate to which I refer.

I append the following personal facts for your consideration in this matter.

(1). I graduated M.B.: B.Ch.: B.A.O. of the N.U.I. in the Spring of 1910 obtaining 1st class honours and an Exhibition in the Final Examination

(2). I obtained 2nd Class Honours in my 3rd Medical Examination.

(3). I was an undergraduate at University College Cork from 1904 to 1910, and obtained there
- a. A 2nd Year Medical Scholarship.
- b. A 3rd Year Medical Scholarship.
- c. The Blaney Scholarship.
- d. Eleven Sessional Prizes

[page 2]

France, German East Africa, North West Frontier India, and Mesopotamia. He mentions Scientific work for the Government of India in connection with Triangulation Link across the Himalaya between India and Russia. 1 August 1917.

(4). I entered the Indian Medical Service in 1910; obtaining 2nd place.

(5). I have been on war service since September 1914 till the present date and have served, since the outbreak of war, in

- a. France.
- b. German East Africa
- c. North West Frontier India
- d. Mesopotamia

(6). I was awarded the Military Cross for war services in the Field. (Order of the Day. No.38: I.E.F.D.: 23/9/16). (Slip herewith attached).

(7). Since I left for India in 1911 I have had no opportunity of returning to Ireland to present myself for the degree of M.D. nor do I see any prospect of being able to do so for years to come.

(8). In the year 1913 I was engaged in

[page 3]

Scientific work for the Government of India in connection with the Expedition to complete the Triangulation Link across the Himalaya between India and Russia. While thus employed I investigated the changes in the blood at high altitudes (up to 18,500 feet) and the relation of these changes to mountain sickness.

An abstract of these results was published in "Records of Survey of India" Vol. VI prepared under the direction of Sir. S. G. Burrard F.R.S. (Dehra Dun India 1914)

It was my intention to amplify this work with the addition of subsequent observations into a treatise for the M.D. degree but duties connected with the war have prevented this. The abstract is however

[page 4]

published in the Record to which I refer, but
I regret not having any copy on Active
Service which I could send you.

I mention the above facts in order that you
may be able to decide if I am eligible for
an Hon. war degree of M.D. in accordance
with the recommendations of the Senate.

I would remind you that my War Services
have been uninterrupted since the outbreak
of war; that they have been rewarded by
Government; that I have had no oppor-
tunity of presenting myself for the desired
degree nor is there any likelihood of my
being permitted to do so for years to come.

Believe me Sir,

Yours Truly

R.W.G. Hingston Capt. I.M.S.

[page 5]

NATIONAL UNIVERSITY.

The Senate met on Friday, June 1st. 1917, at 10.30 a.m., Sir Bertram C A Windle, M A, M D, D Sc, LL D, F R S, Vice-Chancellor of the University, President University College, Cork, in the chair, and there was a large attendance.

Reports of Standing Committee, Finance Committee, and General Board of Studies were considered, and orders made thereon.

The report of the General Board of Studies included the following recommendations, which were approved by the Senate:—(a) That certain additional exemptions and honorary war degrees should be awarded to certain students of the University in consideration of their war service; (b) that the degree of D.Sc. should be awarded to:—Joseph Algar, M A, M Sc; Henry Kennedy, M A, M Sc; John J Nolan, M A, M Sc., in consideration of the published work submitted by these candidates.

Russell Howard, F R C S, was appointed as Extern Examiner in Surgery for the Autumn Examinations of the year 1917

The following appointments were made:—

University College, Cork.—Alfred J Rahilly, M A, B Sc—Professorship of Mathematical Physics. University College, Galway—W A Byrne, B A, Professorship of English Language and English Literature; Miss Emily Anderson, B A—Professorship of German.

The Senate fixed Friday, June 22nd. 1917, as the date for a meeting of Convocation.

On the motion of the Vice-Chancellor, the following resolution was unanimously adopted:—"That the Senate offers its condolence to the University of Sheffield on the death of their first Chancellor, the Most Noble Henry Fitz-Alan Howard, Duke of Norfolk.'

Other business of a routine character having been transacted, the Senate adjourned.

D. S. O.'S FOR INDIAN ARMY OFFICERS.

The "London Gazette" announces that Distinguished Service Orders have been awarded to the following Indian Army officers: Captain W. G. Harington, who, although severely wounded, commanded and handled his battalion with great courage and ability throughout the action; and Captain W. F. Webb, who, although wounded, handled his battalion with the greatest courage and initiative, and set a splendid example to his men.

A bar to the Distinguished Service Order has been awarded to Major F. A. Maxwell, who led his battalion with the greatest courage and initiative, and later organised three battalions and consolidated the positions under very heavy fire. He had previously done very fine work.

Captain R. W. Hingston is awarded the Military Cross for conspicuous gallantry and devotion to duty. He tended and dressed the wounded continuously under very heavy fire at close range, regardless of his own safety.

Extract from Cork Weekly News
Saturday June 9th 1917

[page 6]

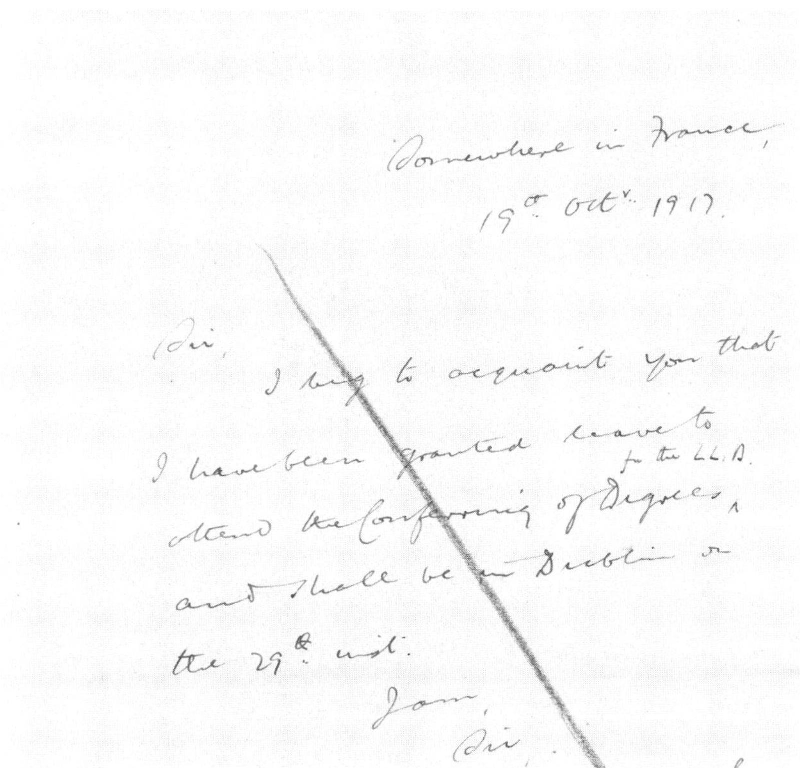

Somewhere in France,
19th Octr. 1917.

Sir,
I beg to acquaint you that I have been granted leave to attend the Conferring of Degrees for the LL.B. and shall be in Dublin on the 29th inst.

I am,
Sir,
Your obedient Servant,
J.R. Duggan, B.A.,
C.Q.M.S.
Acting R.Q.M.S.
9th R.D.F.

To:- The Secretary,
National University of Ireland,
Dublin.

9. Letter from J.R. Duggan, 'Somewhere in France', noting that he has been granted leave to attend his degree conferring. 19 October 1917.

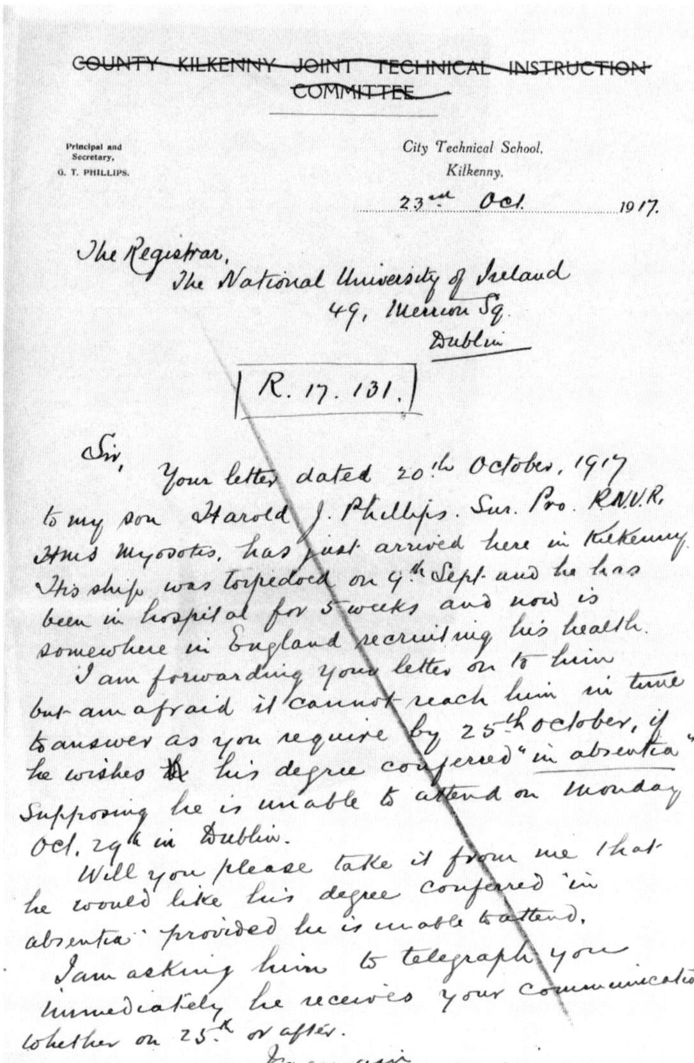

~~COUNTY KILKENNY JOINT TECHNICAL INSTRUCTION COMMITTEE~~

Principal and Secretary, G. T. PHILLIPS.

City Technical School, Kilkenny,

23rd Oct 1917.

The Registrar,
The National University of Ireland
49, Merrion Sq.
Dublin

[R. 17. 131.]

Sir,

Your letter dated 20th October, 1917 to my son Harold J. Phillips. Sur. Pro. R.N.V.R, HMS Myosotis, has just arrived here in Kilkenny. His ship was torpedoed on 9th Sept and he has been in hospital for 5 weeks and now is somewhere in England recruiting his health.

I am forwarding your letter on to him but am afraid it cannot reach him in time to answer as you require by 25th october, if he wishes his degree conferred "in absentia" supposing he is unable to attend on Monday Oct. 29th in Dublin.

Will you please take it from me that he would like his degree conferred "in absentia" provided he is unable to attend.

I am asking him to telegraph you immediately he receives your communication whether on 25th or after.

I remain
Yours faithfully
Geo. T. Phillips

Sir Jos. McGrath
Registrar.

10. *Letter from George T. Phillips to the Registrar of NUI, Joseph McGrath. Writing on behalf of his son Harold J. Phillips, requesting that his degree be conferred in absentia. Harold was onboard his ship when it was torpedoed on 9 September and was recovering 'somewhere in England'. 23 October 1917.*

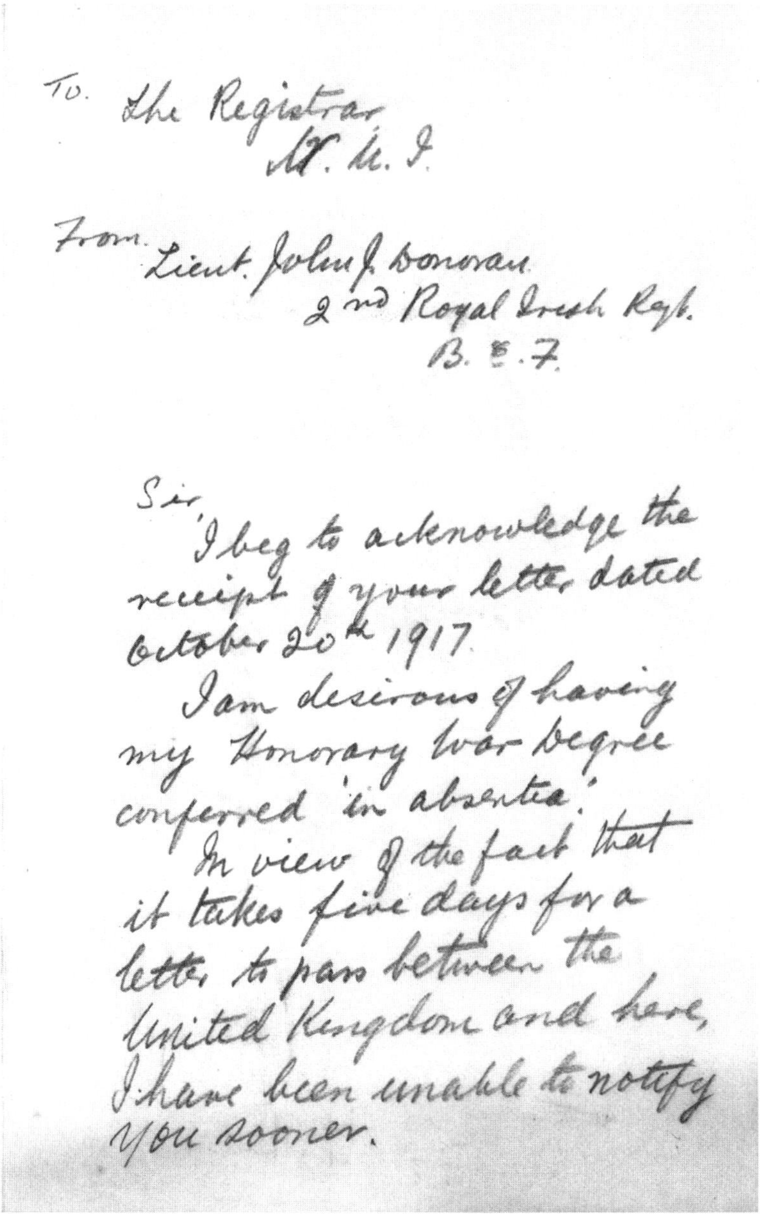

To. The Registrar
N. U. I.

From. Lieut. John J. Donovan
2nd Royal Irish Regt.
B. E. F.

Sir,
I beg to acknowledge the receipt of your letter dated October 20th 1917.
I am desirous of having my Honorary War Degree conferred 'in absentia'.
In view of the fact that it takes five days for a letter to pass between the United Kingdom and here, I have been unable to notify you sooner.

[page 1]

11. Letter from John J. O'Donovan to Registrar of NUI, writing 'In the field', requesting that his Honorary War Degree be conferred in absentia. 26 October 1917.

I am, Sir,
Your obedient Servant,
John Donovan. Lieut.

In the Field
26.10.17.

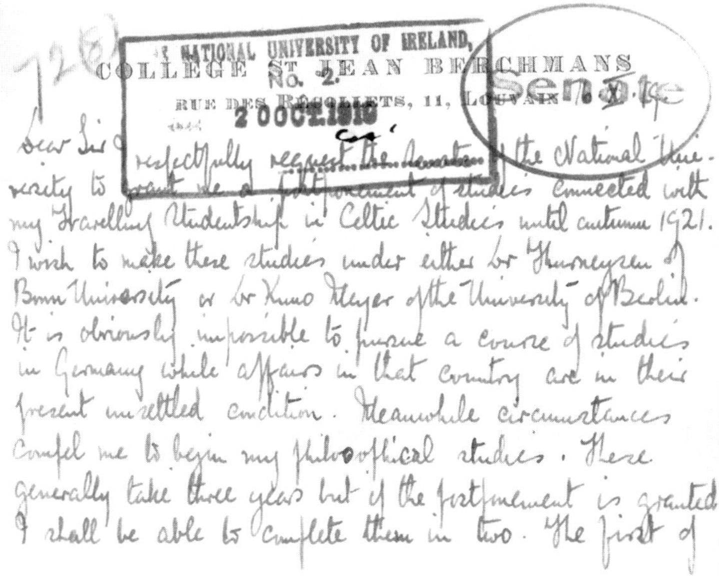

NATIONAL UNIVERSITY OF IRELAND, No. 2. 20 OCT 1919
COLLEGE ST JEAN BERCHMANS
RUE DES RÉCOLLETS, 11, LOUVAIN

Dear Sir I respectfully request the Senate of the National University to grant me a postponement of studies connected with my Travelling Studentship in Celtic Studies until autumn 1921. I wish to make these studies under either Dr Thurneysen of Bonn University or Dr Kuno Meyer of the University of Berlin. It is obviously impossible to pursue a course of studies in Germany while affairs in that country are in their present unsettled condition. Meanwhile circumstances compel me to begin my philosophical studies. These generally take three years but if the postponement is granted I shall be able to complete them in two. The first of

[page 1]

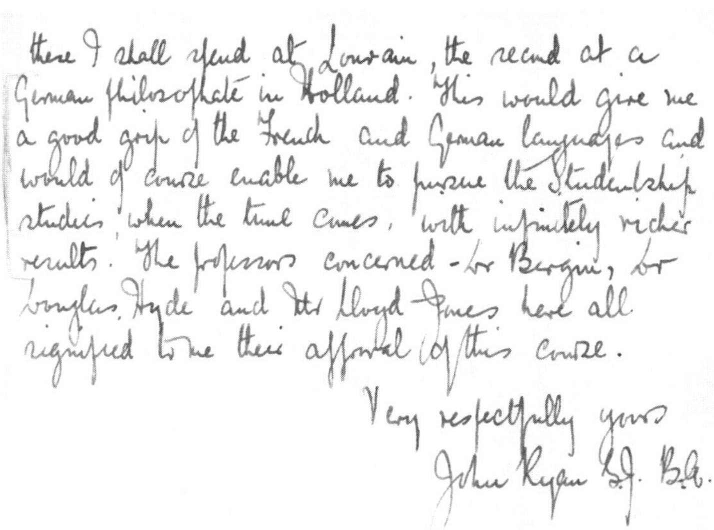

these I shall spend at Louvain, the second at a German philosophate in Holland. This would give me a good grip of the French and German languages and would of course enable me to pursue the Studentship studies, when the time comes, with infinitely richer results. The professors concerned – Dr Bergin, Dr Douglas Hyde and Mr Lloyd Jones have all signified to me their approval of this course.

Very respectfully yours
John Ryan S.J. B.A.

[page 2]

12. Letter from John Ryan to NUI, regarding his Travelling Studentship in Celtic Studies. He plans to study with either Dr Rudolf Thurneysen of the University of Bonn and/or Professor Kuno Meyer of University of Berlin. But owing to the present conditions he is unable to do so. He details a plan of study approved by his professors: Dr [Osborn] Bergin, Dr Douglas Hyde, and [John] Lloyd Jones. 16 October 1919.

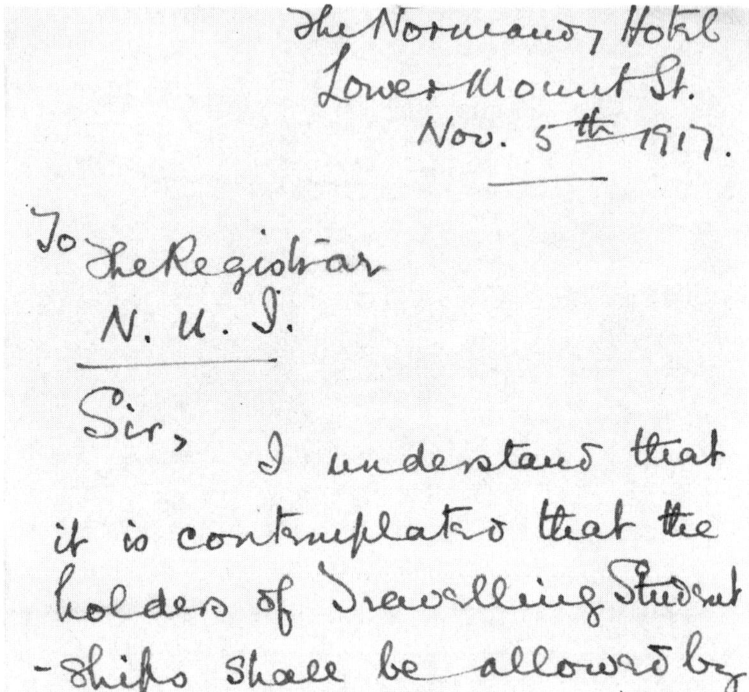

The Normandy Hotel
Lower Mount St.
Nov. 5th 1917.

To The Registrar
N. U. I.

Sir,
I understand that it is contemplated that the holders of Travelling Student-ships shall be allowed by the Senate to postpone travel-ling for the present owing to the difficulties caused by the war, if they so desire.
I beg to ask permission of the Senate to put off the holding of the Travelling

[page 1]

13. *Letter from Michael Tierney* [later President of UCD and son-in-law of Eoin MacNeill], *requesting permission to postpone travel for his Travelling Studentship 'owing to the difficulties caused by the war'. 5 November 1917.*

Studentship in Ancient Classics, till the conclusion of the war, or till the end of the present academic year if the war should conclude during its course.

My reason for doing so is that I contemplated going to Oxford, but have lately got a letter from Mr Lurgan who was a Travelling Student the last year, advising me that it is practically useless to go there at present. He enclosed a statement which he kindly got for me from his tutor, Mr E. Walker,

[page 2]

Fellow & Senior Tutor of Queen's College.

Mr Walker writes that "he has no hesitation in saying very emphatically that any-one who thinks of pursuing a course of advanced studies at Oxford, no matter what his subject may be, had much better wait till the war is over. Very few of the teachers, whether professors or College tutors, will be in regular residence this term; they are for the most part serving in the army, or else doing work in one of the Government Offices... Those few who

[page 3]

are fully resident may be called away at any moment."

Under these circumstances it will be seen that travelling is next to useless at present, and of course conditions can only be expected to become worse for some time. I shall of course pursue my studies to the best of my ability at home till circumstances permit of travelling.

Yours faithfully

M. Tierney

[page 4]

3 - 9 MAR. 1918

10th Hampshire Regt
Salonika Forces
Feb 14 /18

The External Secretary (NUI) Senate
ack
Sir

I am a graduate N.U.I. B.A. 1909, & D.Mus. 1912, and am doing my best to get on with the MA Syllabus for External candidates not attending post-graduate classes.

I have written twice to the NUI to find out the Subjects of Examination & at last have received the Calendar of Univ. College which of course does not apply to my case. Military circumstances necessarily prevent my coming for the exam this Sept, as I had wished to do, & of course may do so next yr. Can you therefore tell me whether the prescribed books for M.A. next year (Latin & Greek), will be the Same as this year? or, if the alterations in this respect happen to be very extensive, will the Senate permit candidates "exiled by fate" to present the books prescribed for 1918. when they attend. I am sure Sir, that you will appreciate my difficulties out here. I am very anxious to get the higher degree, & shall await your reply with considerable interest. Thanking you in anticipation of yr help, Believe me

yrs respectfully
(Capt) Thomas R Mayne

[page 1]

14. Two letters from Thomas R. Mayne, Salonika Forces, to NUI, looking for the MA syllabus for external students and details of the subjects for the MA in Latin and Greek, as he is 'doing his best' to get on with his studies. 14 February 1918. He was persistent, writing again when he was back in Ireland in 1919. He askst about War Degrees, and then details his

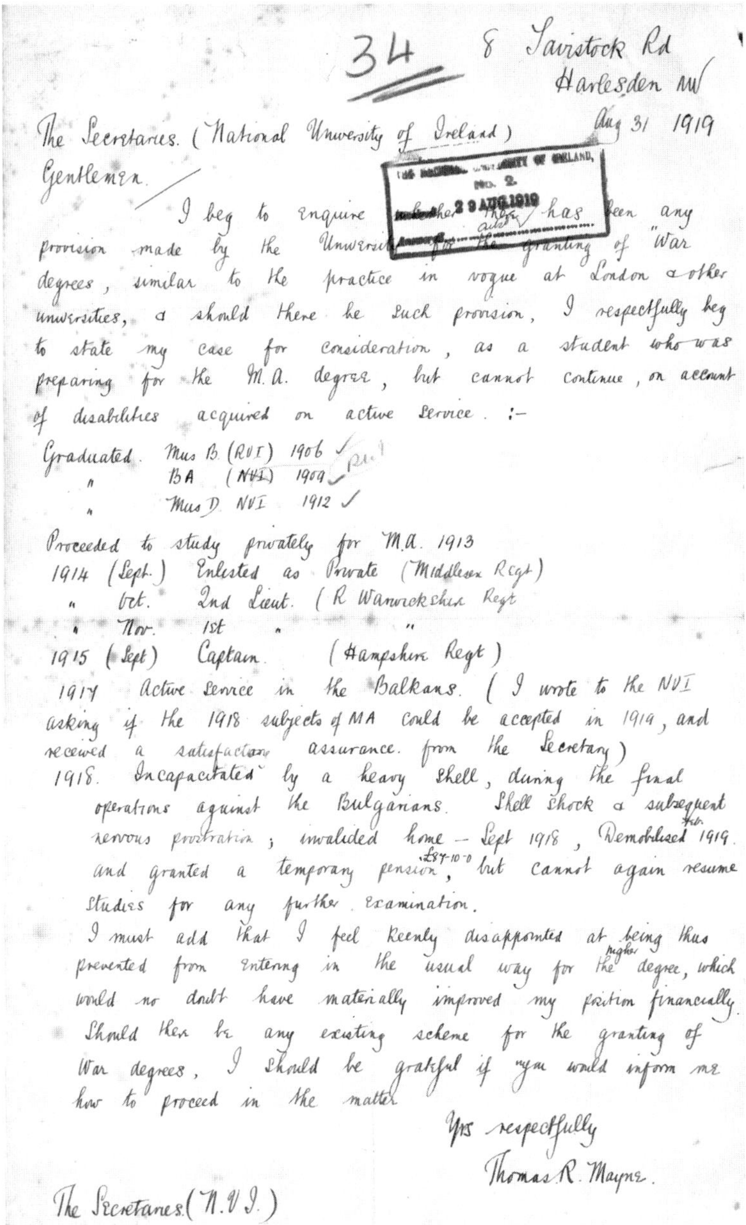

34

8 Sairstock Rd
Harlesden NW
Aug 31 1919

The Secretaries. (National University of Ireland)

Gentlemen

I beg to enquire whether there has been any provision made by the University for the granting of "War degrees", similar to the practice in vogue at London & other universities, & should there be such provision, I respectfully beg to state my case for consideration, as a student who was preparing for the M.A. degree, but cannot continue, on account of disabilities acquired on active service. :-

Graduated. Mus B. (RUI) 1906
" BA (NUI) 1909
" Mus D. NUI 1912

Proceeded to study privately for M.A. 1913
1914 (Sept.) Enlisted as Private (Middlesex Regt)
" Oct. 2nd Lieut. (R Warwickshire Regt
" Nov. 1st " "
1915 (Sept) Captain (Hampshire Regt)
1917 Active service in the Balkans. (I wrote to the NUI asking if the 1918 subjects of MA could be accepted in 1919, and received a satisfactory assurance from the Secretary)
1918. Incapacitated by a heavy shell, during the final operations against the Bulgarians. Shell shock & subsequent nervous prostration; invalided home – Sept 1918, Demobilised Feb. 1919. and granted a temporary pension £87-10-0, but cannot again resume studies for any further examination.

I must add that I feel keenly disappointed at being thus prevented from entering in the usual way for the higher degree, which would no doubt have materially improved my position financially. Should there be any existing scheme for the granting of War degrees, I should be grateful if you would inform me how to proceed in the matter

Yrs respectfully
Thomas R. Mayne.

The Secretaries (N.U.I.)

THE NATIONAL UNIVERSITY OF IRELAND,
No. 2.
29 AUG 1919

[page 2]

service and his qualifications, mentioning that he was incapacitated by heavy shelling during operations against the Bulgarians and suffered from 'shell shock'. 31 August 1919

UNIVERSITY COLLEGE, CORK.

LIST OF RECOMMENDATIONS FOR (UNIVERSITY) HONORARY WAR DISTINCTIONS.

The Academic Council recommends for a higher Degree the following Graduates who have gained military distinction:-

NAME	DISTINCTION	PRESENT DEGREE	RECOMMENDED DEGREE
Andrews, W.P., Lieut., R.E.	M.C.	B.E.	M.E.
Cagney, P., Lieut., R.A.M.C.	M.C.	M.B.	M.D.
Carr, Howard, Col., A.M.S.	C.B.	M.D., M.Ch.	LL.D.
Corker, T. M., Surg. Gen. & Hon. Physician to H.M.	C.B.	M.A., M.D.	LL.D.
Crooke-Lawless, Sir W. R. Lieut.Col., A.M.S.	C.B., C.I.E. Commended for Dist.Ser.	M.D., M.Ch.	LL.D.
Cummins, A.G., Capt., R.A.M.C.	M.C., 4th Class Order of the Nile	M.B.	M.D.
Cummins, Nicholas M., Lieut., R.A.M.C.	M.C.	M.B.	M.D.
Hennessy, J., Lieut.Col., R.A.M.C.	C.B.	M.B.	M.D.
Hingston, R.W.G., Capt., R.A.M.C.	M.C.	M.D.	M.D.
Jennings, R.B., Lieut., R.E.	M.C.	B.E.	M.E.
Johnston, P.H., Lieut.Col., R.A.M.C.	C.M.G.	B.A., M.D., M.Ch.	LL.D.
Joynt, N. L., Capt., R.A.M.C.	M.C.	M.B.	M.D.
Julian, F.B., Capt., R.A.M.C.	D.S.O.	M.B.	M.D.
McDonnell, E., Major, R.A.M.C.	D.S.O.	M.B.	M.D.
O'Brien, J.W., Lieut., R.A.M.C.	M.C.	M.B.	M.D.
O'Keeffe, J.J., Capt., R.A.M.C.	M.C., Legion of Hon.	M.B.	M.D.
O'Keeffe, M. W. Surg.Gen., A.M.S.	C.B., Men. in Desp.	M.D.	LL.D.
O'Sullivan, J.I., Lieut., R.A.M.C.	M.C.	M.B.	M.D.
Roche, M.J., Capt., I.M.S.	M.C.	M.B.	M.D.
Waller, J. H. de W., Capt., R.E.	D.S.O., & Ferro-Concrete Expert at Admiralty	M.E.	D.Sc.
White. W.W., Col., I.M.S.	C.B.	B.A., M.D., M.Ch.	LL.D.

Capt. H. J. Cotter, who took out all his Medical lectures, and passed portion of the Final Examination, but then sat for & obtained the Licence of the Conjoint Board, Ireland, is recommended for the M.B., B.Ch., B.A.O. Degrees, having been granted the Military Cross.

Should the Senate decide to take any action in connection with

[page 1 & 2]

15. University College, Cork, List of Recommendations for (University) Honorary War Distinctions. Received 1 February 1918.

those Mentioned in Despatches, the Academic Council submits the case of P. J. Roche, Lieut., R.E., who obtained the B.E. Degree, was mentioned in despatches, but died on active service, and is of opinion that in all such cases the diplomas might be issued to the nearest relatives of the deceased.

With regard to your letter re T. F. Sheehan, John F. Fullin, and R. W. G. Hingston, the last named is dealt with in above list. The Council feels that nothing can be done for T. F. Sheehan, as those serving in the Navy cannot avail themselves of the concessions lately made by the General Medical Council in the conditions for obtaining the Public Health Diploma. The Council agreed to recommend that John F. Fullin be granted the Second Engineering Examination.

The Council recommends:- (a) that John J. B. Noonan, who has been discharged from the army owing to wounds, and who passed the Professional part of the First Engineering Examination, be granted exemption from the remaining portion. (b) that Thomas A. O'Brien, who matriculated and took out all his First Year lectures in Medicine, passed the Biology part of the Conjoint Board First Examination, and has been discharged from the army through ill-health contracted on active service, be granted the First Medical Examination of the University, as he is now anxious to proceed to a Degree.

I beg to call your attention to the recommendation already made in the case of Major C. J. Lynam, and postponed from last meeting of the General Board of Studies. Major Lynam fulfils all the conditions laid down by the University, having taken out all his Lectures and Practicals and entered the Army before obtaining the B.E. Degree, and the Academic Council recommends him for that Degree. He has attained high rank, and states himself that he beat in competitive examination two students who had obtained the B.E. Degree.

P. J. MERRIMAN.

Registrar.

31st January. 1918.

[page 3]

For Report to Board of Studies:

HONORARY DEGREES TO GRADUATES FOR DISTINGUISHED WAR SERVICE.

Names taken from the list of Graduates of the College serving during the War and students credited with distinctions, viz:-

1. Mention in despatches,
2. Award of Military Cross, M.C.
3. Award of D.S.O.
4. Award of other distinctions.

Asterisked names are those of graduates who were in the Army previous to the War.

	NAME	DEGREE OR QUALIFICATION	RANK	DISTINCTION
X	Adye-Curran, Wm. J.P.	L.R.C.P.S.I., 1898	Lt.Col.	Desp
	~~Barrington~~, Charles	M.D., B.Ch., 1913;	Capt.	M.C. Desp.
	Beveridge, Arthur J.	M.B., B.Ch., 1915,	Capt.	M.C. Desp.
	Blake, Arthur M.J.	L.R.C.P.S.I, 1910	Capt.,	M.C., Desp
X	Cahill, Robert	M.B., B.Ch., 1903	Act.Lt.Col.	Desp. twice.
	Carroll, John D.	B.Sc., M.B., B.Ch., 1913,	Capt.,	M.C. Desp.
	Costello; Joseph M.A.,	M.B., B.Ch., 1907., M.D., 1917	Major	M.C. Desp.
	Costello, ~~Thomas~~ J. -	B.Sc., M.B., B.A., 1913,	Capt.	M.C. Desp.
	Coyle; Cecil D.	M.B., B.Ch., 1916,	Capt.	Wounded Desp.
	Coyne, Eugene H.	M.B., B.Ch., 1915,	Capt.	Desp.
X	Daly, James H.	L.R.C.P.S.I., 1881	Col.A.M.S.	
	Dillon-Kelly, Cecil F.	L.R.C.P.S.I., 1914	Capt.	Wounded. Desp. Prisoner of War
X	Dowling, Francis T.	B.A., M.B., B.Ch., 1907.	Major	Desp.
	Dwyer; James Jameson	L.R.C.P.S.I. 1909	Capt.	D.S.O.- Desp.
X	Dwyer, Patrick	M.B.; B.Ch.; 1903	Capt.	M.C., Desp.
X	Egan, William	M.B.; B.Ch., 1904,	~~Major~~	D.S.O. Desp.
X	Forde, Bernard	M.B.; B.Ch.; 1886	C.M.G	Desp.
X	Garland, Frederick	M.B., B.Ch., 1901	Major	Desp.
	Gaynor, George C.	M.B., B.Ch, 1915,	Capt.,	M.C. Desp.
X	Gill; James Geoffrey	L.R.C.P.S.I. 1896	Col.	D.S.O. Desp.
	Gill, Rev. Henry		Chap.	M.C. Desp.
	Graham, Wm. E.,	M.B., B.Ch.; 1911	Capt.	M.C., Desp.
	Hackett, Bartholomew	M.B., B.Ch.,	Capt.,	M.C. Desp.
X	Hanafin, Patrick J.	L.R.C.P.S.I., 1901	Lt.Col.	D.S.O. with Bar. Desp.
	Hannigan, Charles J.	B.A., M.B., B.Ch., 1914.	Capt.,	M.C., Desp.
	Harbinson, Henry	M.B., B.Ch., 1913,	Capt.,	M.C., with Bar. Desp.
X	Kavanagh, Edward	M.B., B.Ch., 1906,	Major	M.C., D.S.O., Desp. twice,
	Kelly, Peter B.	L.R.C.P.S.I., 1909	Surgeon R.N.	D.S.O. Desp.
	~~Kennedy, Arthur P.~~	~~L.R.C.P.S.I.,~~	~~Capt.~~	~~M.C., Desp. Wounded.~~

[page 1]

16. *University College Dublin, Honorary Degrees to Graduates for Distinguished War Service. [no date].*

	NAME	DEGREE OR QUALIFICATION	RANK	DISTINCTION.
	Kenny, Charles A.	L.R.C.P.S.I., 1898	Capt.	Despatches
X	Kenny, Edward B.	M.B., B.Ch., 1903	Staff Surgeon R.N.	
X	Kirwan, Ernest W.O'L	M.B., B.Ch., 1909	Major M.C.,	Desp. Wounded. Desp. M.C.,
	Lane, Patrick J.	M.B., B.Ch., 1915	Capt.	M.C., Desp.
	McCormack, John D.	L.R.C.P.S.I. 1914	Capt.,	M.C. Desp. Wounded.
	McMahon, Michael T.	M.Sc., M.B., B.Ch., 1914	Capt.	Desp.
	Meagher, Timothy	M.B., B.Ch., 1906	Capt.	M.C. Desp. Croix de Guerre
	Murphy, William L.	B.A., M.B., B.Ch. (Cantab) 1907.		Croix de [illegible] or Croix [illegible] Chevalier Desp
X	O'Carroll, Arthur D.	M.B., B.Ch., 1904	Lt.Col.	D.S.O. Desp.
X	O'Connor, Arthur P.	B.A. M.B., B.Ch., 1908	Capt.	Desp.
X	O'Farrell, William R.	L.R.C.P.S.I. 1907	Capt.	Prisoner of War
X	O'Gorman, Charles	L.R.C.P.S.I. 1894	Lt.Col.	D.S.O. Desp.
	O'Hagan, John J.	L.R.C.P.S.I. 1882 (M.B. Liverpool)	Lt.Col.	Desp.
	O'Hanlon, Oriel O'B.	M.B., B.Ch.,	Capt.	Desp.
X	O'Reilly, Robert	L.R.C.P.S.I., 1907	Capt.	Twice wounded.
X	O'Neill, Edward M.	M.B., B.Ch., 1905	Major	D.S.O. Desp.
	O'Reilly, Patrick J.	L.R.C.P.S.I., 1914	Capt.,	M.C. Desp.
	Power, James	B.Sc., B.E., 1914	Capt. R.E.	M.C. Desp.
X	Petit, Gerald	L.R.C.P.S.I., 1906	Capt.	M.C. Desp.
	Power, Maurice A.	M.B., B.Ch., 1906	Capt.,	M.C. Desp.
X	Potter, Thomas	L.R.C.P.S.I., 1897	Lt.Col.	Desp.
	Redmond, William A.	B.A., 1907	Capt.	D.S.O.
	Rishworth, William W.	M.B., B.Ch., 1911.	Capt.	M.C. Desp.
	Roche, Chas.,	L.R.C.P.S.I. 1914,	Capt.,	M.C. Desp.
	Ryan, Frederick	M.B., B.Ch., 1899	Capt.,	Wounded, Prisoner of War.
X	Ryan, Peter	B.A., M.B., B.Ch., 1911.	Capt.,	Desp.
X	Sampson, Francis C.	M.B., B.Ch., 1905	Major	D.S.O. Desp.
	Scanlon, Maurice P.	M.B., B.Ch., 1906	Capt.	Desp.
	Sheehan, William J.	M.B., B.Ch., 1902	S.African Force,	Desp.
	Shelley, James	B.E. 1914	Capt R.E.	M.C. Desp.

[page 2]

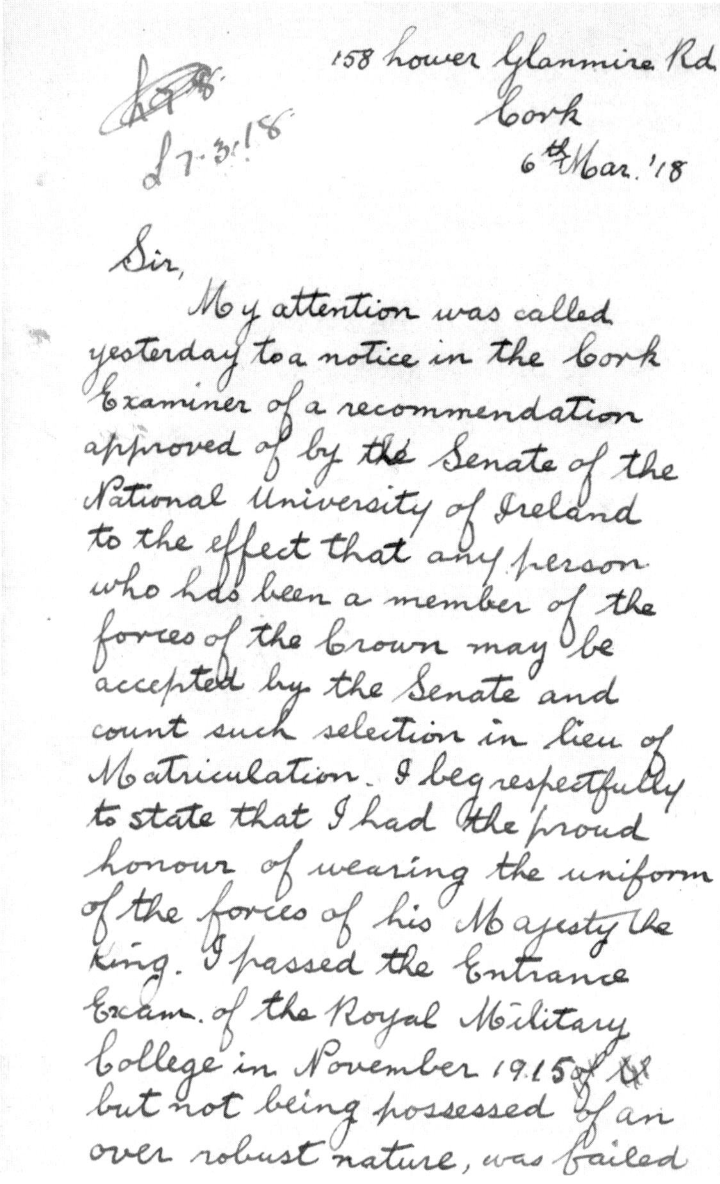

158 Lower Glanmire Rd
Cork
6th Mar. '18

Sir,

My attention was called yesterday to a notice in the Cork Examiner of a recommendation approved of by the Senate of the National University of Ireland to the effect that any person who has been a member of the forces of the Crown may be accepted by the Senate and count such selection in lieu of Matriculation. I beg respectfully to state that I had the proud honour of wearing the uniform of the forces of his Majesty the King. I passed the Entrance Exam. of the Royal Military College in November 1915 but not being possessed of an over robust nature, was failed

[page 1]

17. Letter from D.L. Coughlan to NUI, as he had read in the Cork Examiner of the NUI Senate recommendation that members of the forces may have their service accepted in lieu of Matriculation. He details the history of his service and attempts to obtain qualifications. 6 March 1918.

by the military doctor in ~~at~~ the King George v. Military Hospital, Arbour Hill. Dublin. However appealing against this decision I proceeded to London to appear before a Special Medical Board appointed by the War Office, to examine candidates who have been medically rejected at other centres. On their recommendation I was allowed to enter the Royal Military College. The strenuousness of the Military training to which I was subjected together with the evil effects of an operation I had to undergo broken down my health completely and acting on Medical advise I was compelled, I sincerely regret to say, to hand in my resignation. The War Council permitted me to resign and a few months later though still in imperfect health I again

[page 2]

applied. ~~the~~ to the War Office. This time to be allowed to proceed to India. Hoping that the training in the Indian Army would be less severe than in the Home Army. The Army Council however refused owing to my Physical debility, to accede to my request and finally sealed the only chance left to me of taking a share of the burden in a cause which every Christian Being believes to be a fight for Humanity & Justice. I then saw the only way left to me of entering the Army was through a profession. Over and over I have made firm resolutions of going back to College and grinding for Matriculation, but being away so long from Study, the thought of going back and starting the

[page 3]

over again the work of previous years and then again settling oneself down for the first time to learn Irish, seemed anathema to me. This resolution of the Senate gives me the opportunity of attaining to my one ambition a commission in the R.A.M.C. and comes like a Heaven sent gift. And whilst awaiting a favourable reply from the Senate I can say with all earnestness that though Nature in my case was the defaulter, I consider my conscience is quite clear when I ask myself "What have I done in the great war"? ~~I en~~ Please find enclosed my discharge ~~or~~ from the Royal Military College, Sandhurst. Apologising for the wastage of your valuable time in the perusal of this rather lengthy document, In the expectation of an early reply.

I Remain, Sir,

Your Obedient Servant,

D. L. Coughlan.

[page 4]

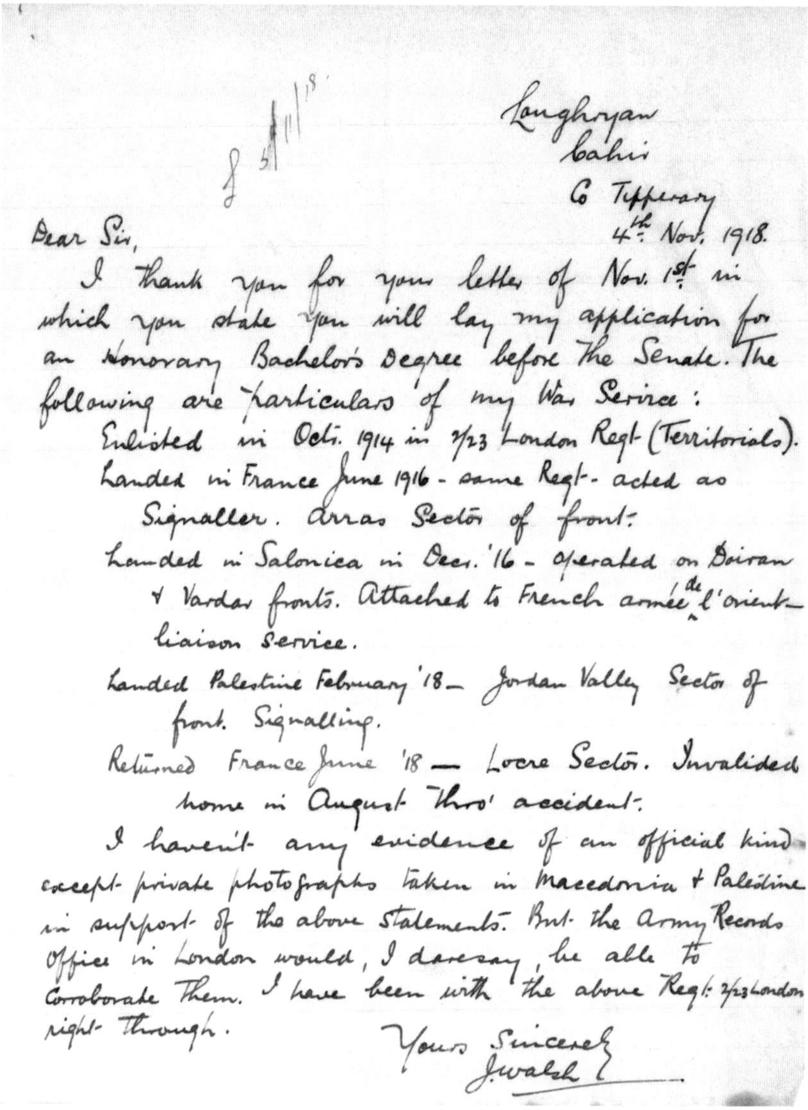

Loughryan
Cahir
Co Tipperary
4th Nov. 1918.

Dear Sir,

I thank you for your letter of Nov. 1st in which you state you will lay my application for an Honorary Bachelor's Degree before the Senate. The following are particulars of my War Service:

Enlisted in Oct. 1914 in 2/23 London Regt (Territorials).
Landed in France June 1916 – same Regt – acted as Signaller. Arras Sector of front.
Landed in Salonica in Dec. '16 – operated on Doiran & Vardar fronts. Attached to French armée de l'orient – liaison service.
Landed Palestine February '18 – Jordan Valley Sector of front. Signalling.
Returned France June '18 — Locre Sector. Invalided home in August thro' accident.

I haven't any evidence of an official kind except private photographs taken in Macedonia & Palestine in support of the above statements. But the Army Records Office in London would, I daresay, be able to corroborate them. I have been with the above Regt: 2/23 London right through.

Yours Sincerely
J. Walsh

18. Letter from J. Walsh to NUI, with regards to his application to have an Honorary War Degree conferred, he details his war service, including time in France at the front, Salonika, and the Jordan Valley in Palestine. 4 November 1918.

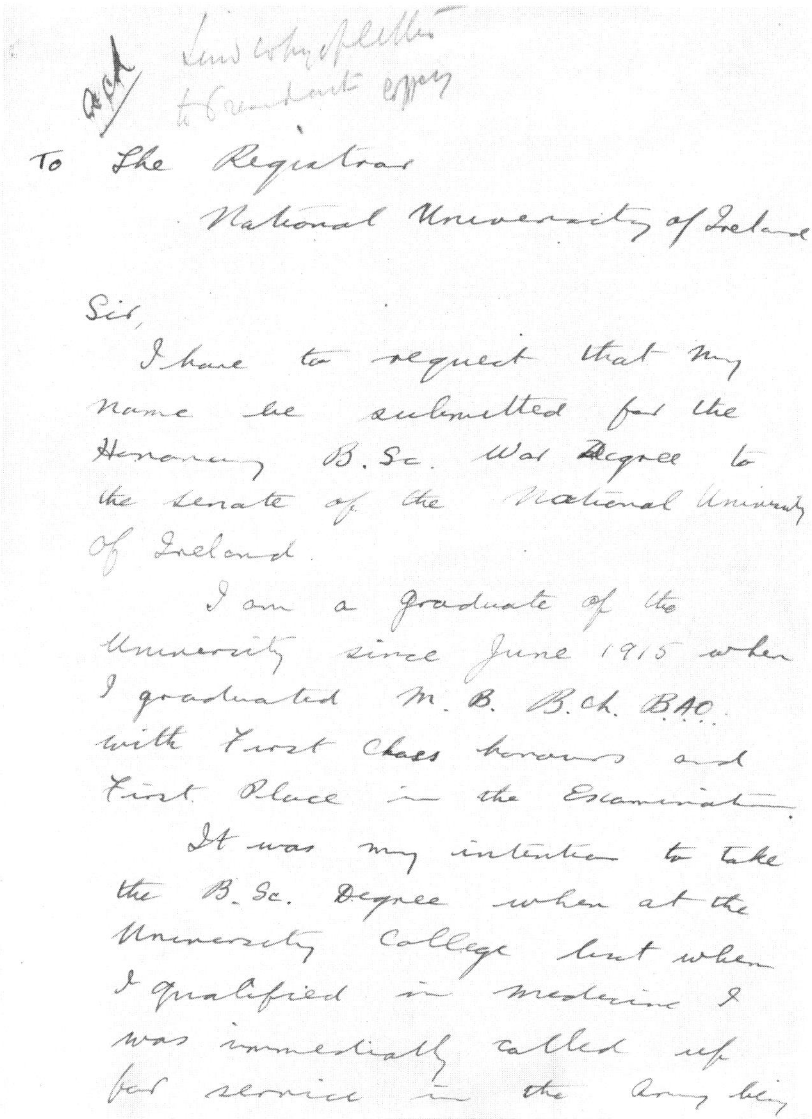

To The Registrar
National University of Ireland

Sir,
I have to request that my name be submitted for the Honorary B.Sc. War Degree to the Senate of the National University of Ireland.
I am a graduate of the University since June 1915 when I graduated M.B. B.Ch. B.A.O. with First Class honours and First Place in the Examination.
It was my intention to take the B.Sc. Degree when at the University College but when I qualified in medicine I was immediately called up for service in the Army being

[page 1]

19. Letter from Arthur Beveridge, 135 Field Ambulance, BEF, to the Registrar of NUI, requesting that his name be submitted for the Honorary BSc War Degree. He provides details of qualifications, his military cross for gallantry, and that he was mentioned in dispatches. 21 December 1918

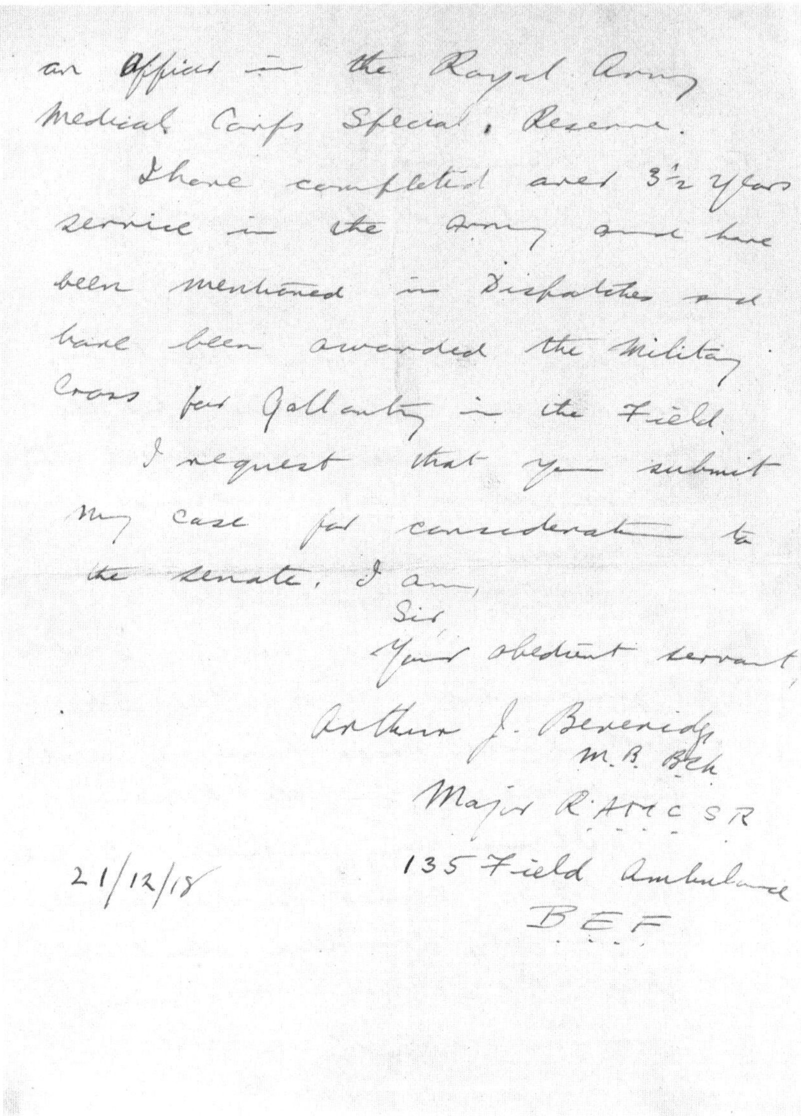

an Officer in the Royal Army
Medical Corps Special Reserve.

I have completed over 3½ years
service in the Army and have
been mentioned in Dispatches and
have been awarded the Military
Cross for Gallantry in the Field.

I request that you submit
my case for consideration to
the Senate. I am,

Sir

Your obedient servant,

Arthur J. Beveridge
M.B. B.Ch
Major R.A.M.C. S.R
135 Field Ambulance
B.E.F.

21/12/18

[page 2]

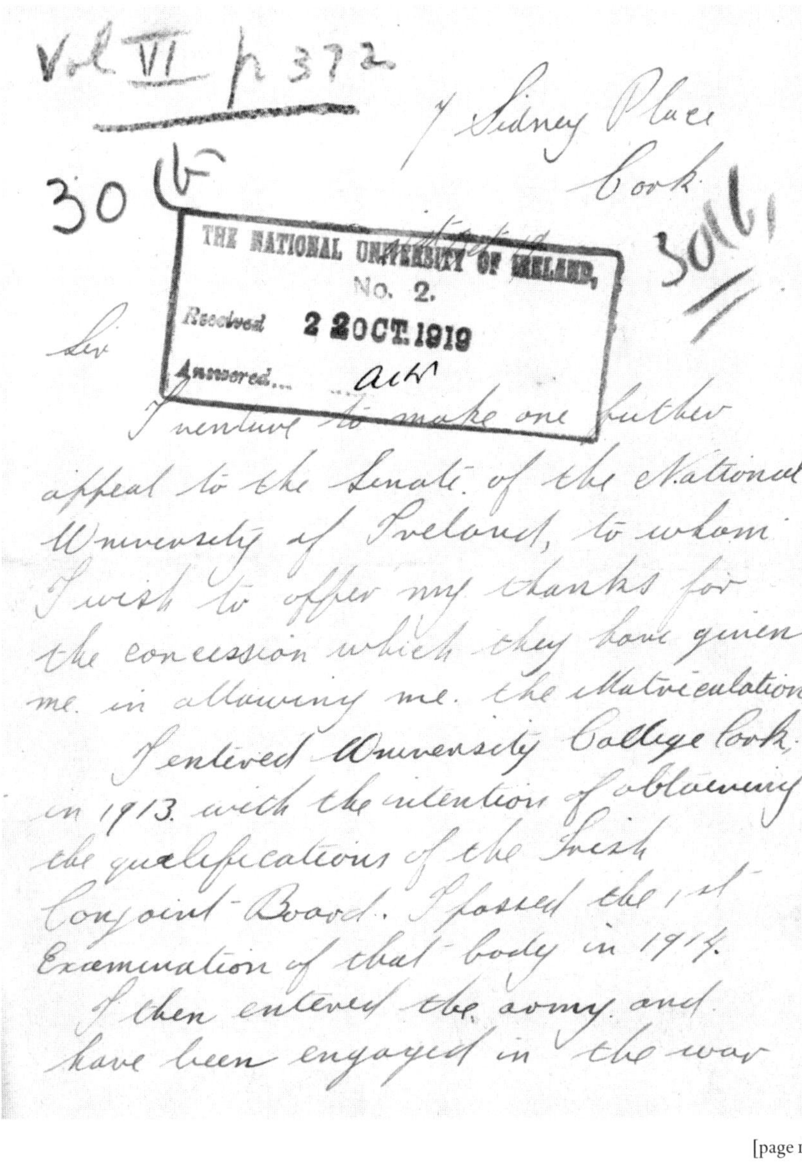

Vol VI p 372

7 Sidney Place
Cork

30 (b)

THE NATIONAL UNIVERSITY OF IRELAND,
No. 2.
Received 22 OCT. 1919
Answered... ack

3016

Sir

I venture to make one further appeal to the Senate of the National University of Ireland, to whom I wish to offer my thanks for the concession which they have given me in allowing me the Matriculation.

I entered University College Cork in 1913 with the intention of obtaining the qualifications of the Irish Conjoint Board. I passed the 1st Examination of that body in 1914.

I then entered the army and have been engaged in the war

[page 1]

20. *Letter from A.A. Townsend thanking NUI for granting him matriculation and appealing to them that he might be allowed his first examination, as he had forgotten so much of what he had learned while was 'a prisoner of war in Bulgaria'. October 1919.*

untill its conclusion having been a prisoner of War in Bulgaria. Of course during that time I forgot a good deal of what I had learned for the 1st examination.

If I have to begin it all over again it will mean adding another year to the years I have already lost through the war.

I hope that the University Senate may take this into consideration and allow me this 1st Examination in order that I may lose no more time than is absolutely necessary in obtaining my qualifications

I am Sir

your obedient servant

A H Townsend

Lt

5th Royal Irish Fus

[page 2]

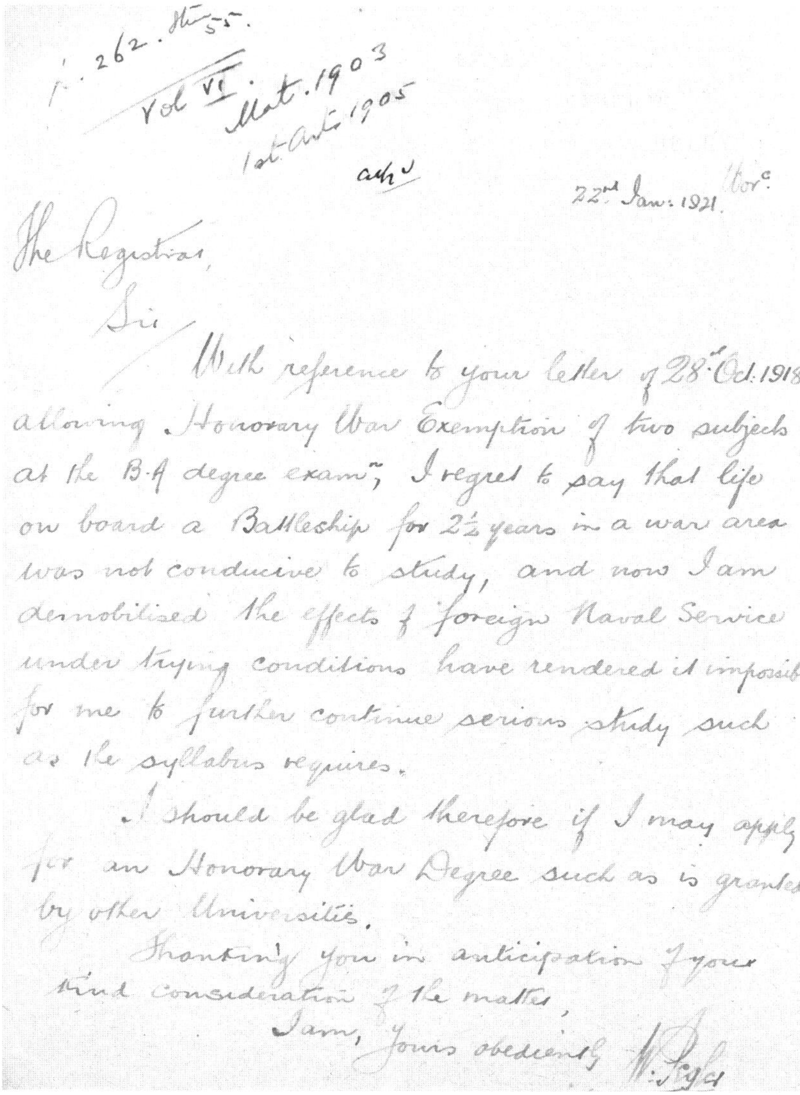

p. 262. No 55.
Vol VI Mat. 1903
1st Arts 1905
ack

22nd Jan: 1921. Wor:

The Registrar,

Sir,

With reference to your letter of 28th Oct. 1918 allowing Honorary War Exemption of two subjects at the B.A degree exam; I regret to say that life on board a Battleship for $2\frac{1}{2}$ years in a war area was not conducive to study, and now I am demobilised the effects of foreign Naval Service under trying conditions have rendered it impossible for me to further continue serious study such as the syllabus requires.

I should be glad therefore if I may apply for an Honorary War Degree such as is granted by other Universities.

Thanking you in anticipation of your kind consideration of the matter,

I am, Yours obediently W. Pegler

21. Letter from W. Pegler to the Registrar of NUI, requesting his Honorary War Exemption of two subjects at BA. 'I regret to say that life on board a battleship for $2\frac{1}{2}$ years in a war area was not conducive to study, and … the effects of foreign naval service under trying conditions have rendered it impossible … to further continue serious study'. 22 January 1921.

Further Reading

Borgonovo, John, *The Dynamics of War and Revolution: Cork City 1916–18* (Cork, 2013)

Casey, Patrick, Cullen, Kevin and Duignan, Joe, *Irish Doctors in the First World War* (Dublin, 2015)

Dunne, Tom (ed.), *The National University of Ireland 1908–2008: Centenary Essays* (Dublin, 2008),

Durnin, David and Miller, Ian (eds), *Medicine, Health and Irish Experiences of Conflict, 1914–1945* (Manchester, 2015)

Fitzpatrick, David (ed.), *Ireland and the First World War* (Dublin, 1986)

Gallagher, Niamh, *Ireland and the Great War: A Social and Political History* (Bloomsbury, 2019)

Irish, Tomás, *The University at War, 1914–1925: Britain, France and the United States* (London, 2015)

Irish, Tomás, Trinity in War and Revolution, 1912–1923 (Dublin, 2015)

Kelly, Laura, *Irish Women in Medicine, c.1880s–1920s: Origins, Education and Careers* (Manchester, 2012)

Lloyd, Nick, *Passchendaele: A New History* (London, 2017)

McCarthy, Donal, *UCD: A National Idea: The History of University College, Dublin* (Dublin, 1999)

McGreevy, Ronan, *Wherever the Firing Line Extends: Ireland and the Western Front* (2nd Edition, Stroud, 2017)

Murphy, J.A., *The College: A History of Queen's University College Cork, 1845–1995* (Cork, 1995)

Philpott, William, *Bloody Victory: The Sacrifice on the Somme* (London, 2009)

Swift, David and Wilkinson, Oliver, *Veterans of the First World War, Ex-Servicemen and Ex-Servicewomen in Post-War Britain and Ireland* (Routledge, 2019)

Taylor, Paul, *Heroes or Traitors? Experiences of Southern Irish Soldiers returning from the Great War 1919–1939* (Liverpool, 2015)

Walsh, Fionnuala, *Irish Women and the Great War* (Cambridge, 2020)

White, Gerry and O'Shea, Brendan (eds), *A Great Sacrifice. Cork Servicemen who died in the Great War* (Cork, 2010)

Notes

1. Introduction

1. John Coolahan, 'From Royal University to National University, 1879–1908' in Tom Dunne (ed.), *The National University of Ireland 1908–2008: Centenary Essays* (Dublin, 2008), pp 3–18, p. 3.
2. 1911 Census, National Archives UK: http://www.nationalarchives.gov.uk/pathways/census/living/educ/pupil.htm [accessed September 2023].
3. Coolahan, 'From Royal University to National University', p. 3.
4. A history of the National University of Ireland: http://www.nui.ie/about/history.asp [accessed September 2023].
5. The Harvard Crimson: The Irish University Bill: https://www.thecrimson.com/article/1873/3/21/the-irish-university-bill-this-bill/ [accessed September 2023].
6. Seamus Dubhghaill: Promoting Irish culture and history from Little Rock, Arkansas: Founding of the National University of Ireland: https://seamusdubhghaill.com/2017/04/27/founding-of-the-royal-university-of-ireland/ [accessed September 2023].
7. Senia Pašeta, 'Achieving Equality: Women and the foundation of the University', in Tom Dunne (ed.), *The National University of Ireland 1908–2008: Centenary Essays* (Dublin, 2008), pp 19–32, p. 22.
8. UCD website https://www.ucd.ie/president/universityhistory/ [accessed September 2023].
9. Marian Lyons and Barbara McCormack, 'On Active Service: Maynooth College, chaplains and the anti-conscription crisis', Maynooth University Library Treasure: https://mulibrarytreasures.wordpress.com/2018/08/20/on-active-service-maynooth-college-chaplains-the-anti-conscription-crisis/ [accessed September 2023].
10. See, this volume, pp 86–87, p. 277, pp 287–288.
11. 'Gratitude and Respect', Clongowes Wood College: https://clongowes.net/gratitude-respect-and-admiration/ [accessed September 2023].
12. Belvedere College war dead, Irish War Memorials: http://www.irishwarmemorials.ie/pdf/5.pdf [accessed September 2023].
13. Honour Roll, Castleknock College Union: https://www.knockunion.ie/news/svc-wwi-honour-roll-10723 [accessed September 2023].

14. Sir Michael O'Dwyer, *India as I knew it* (London, 1925), p. 18.
15. Fergus Campbell, *The Irish Establishment 1879–1914* (Oxford, 2009), p. 76.
16. Patrick Heffernan, *An Irish Doctor's Memories* (Dublin, 1958), p. 3.
17. Shawneens, also known as shoneens, was a pejorative term used in Ireland to refer to those who preferred English ways and customs to Irish ones.
18. Heffernan, *An Irish Doctor's Memories*, p. 3.
19. James P. Murray, *On Medicine in From Queen's College* in *National University: Essays on the Academic History of QCB/UCG/NUI Galway* (Dublin, 1999), p. 143.
20. Jane Ohlmeyer, *Making Empire. Ireland: Imperialism and the Early Modern World* (Oxford, 2023); *Irish Times*, 27 December 2023.
21. C.S. Andrews, *Dublin Made Me* (Dublin, 1979), pp 3–8.
22. Ibid.
23. Eugene Sheehy, *May It Please the Court* (Dublin, 1951), pp 91–92.
24. Anthony P. Quinn, *Wigs and guns: Irish barristers in the Great War* (Dublin, 2006), p. 42.
25. The National University of Ireland: Senate Minutes, 4 July 1914, p. 56.
26. The National University of Ireland: Senate Minutes, 19 August 1914, p. 52.
27. The National University of Ireland: Senate Minutes, 1 September 1914, p. 54.
28. The National University of Ireland: Senate Minutes, 1 September 1914, p. 55.
29. Senia Pašeta, 'Thomas Kettle: An Irish Soldier in the Army of Europe' in Adrian Gregory and *Senia Pašeta* (eds), *Ireland and the Great War: 'A War to Unite us All'* (Manchester, 2002), pp 8–27, p. 9.
30. Profile of Dr Denis Coffey, UCD website: https://www.ucd.ie/president/about/universityhistory/pastpresidents/drdenisjcoffey/ [accessed August 2023].
31. Andrews, *Dublin Made Me*, p. 133.
32. Donal McCarthy, *UCD: A National Idea: The History of University College, Dublin* (Dublin, 1999), p. 99.
33. Ibid.
34. Ibid.
35. UCD Governing Body Minutes, 7 April 1915 (UCD Archives).
36. UCD Governing Body Minutes, 11 May 1915 (UCD Archives).
37. Andrews, *Dublin Made Me*, p. 130.
38. Dermot and Ann Keogh, *Bertram Windle: the Honan Bequest and the Modernisation of University College Cork, 1904–1919* (Cork, 2010), p. 143.
39. Ibid., pp 144–145.
40. 'Bertram Windle, John A. Murphy,' *Dictionary of Irish Biography* [accessed online September 2023].
41. Ibid.
42. UCG Academic Council Minutes, 6 May 1915 (UCD Archives).
43. The National University of Ireland: Senate Minutes, December 1914.

44. The National University of Ireland: Senate Minutes, 26 February 1915, p. 199.
45. The National University of Ireland Senate Minutes, 8 July 1914, p. 307.
46. Ibid.
47. Joseph P. Finnan, *John Redmond and Irish Unity, 1912–1918* (Syracuse, 2004), p. 95.
48. Dermot Meleady, *John Redmond: The National Leader* (Sallins, 2013), pp 310–311. Discussed further in Chapter 2, see pp 123–123.
49. Sheehy, *May It Please the Court*, p. 86.
50. Casey et al., *Irish Doctors in the First World War*, p. 17.
51. Ibid.
52. Ronan McGreevy, *Wherever the Firing Line Extends: Ireland and the Western Front* (Stroud, 2016), p. 5.
53. David Durnin, *The Irish Medical Profession and the First World War* (London, 2019), p. 23.
54. Ibid., p. 25.
55. Ibid., p. 36.
56. Steven O'Connor, 'Imperial Continuities: Irish doctors in the British Armed Forces, 1922–1945' in David Durnin and Ian Miller (eds), *Medicine, Health and Irish Experiences of Conflict, 1914–1945* (Manchester, 2017), pp 191–205, pp 191–192.
57. Greta Jones as quoted in Steven O'Connor, *Irish Officers in the British Forces, 1922–1945* (Dublin, 2014), p. 86.
58. O'Connor, 'Imperial continuities: Irish doctors', p. 191.
59. World War 1 Casualties, Robert Schuman Centre website: http://www.centre-robert-schuman.org/userfiles/files/REPERES%20–%20module%201-1-1%20-%20explanatory%20notes%20–%20World%20War%20I%20casualties%20–%20EN.pdf [accessed September 2023].
60. McGreevy, *Wherever the Firing Line Extends*, p. 5.
61. Keith Jeffreys. 'Ireland and the First World War: The historical context', Queen's University Belfast: http://www.qub.ac.uk/sites/irishhistorylive/IrishHistoryResources/Articlesandlecturesbyourteachingstaff/IrelandandtheFirstWorldWar/ [accessed September 2023]. See p. 135, where Walsh cites 210,000 Irishmen took part in the British Armed Forces, and see p. 152, where Casey et al, cite 250,000 Irishmen in the BAF.
62. Ireland's National Roll of Honour: 1914–1921, findmypast.ie: https://www.findmypast.ie/articles/world-records/full-list-of-the-irish-family-history-records/military-service-and-conflict/irelands-memorial-record-world-war-1 [accessed September 2023].
63. *Irish Times*, 11 November 2017 (online): https://www.irishtimes.com/news/ireland/ irish-news/historian-lists-almost-30-000-irishmen-who-died-in-ww1-1.3288632 [accessed September 2023].
64. The Irish War Memorial Records lists 30,986 men who died in the First World

War who were born in Ireland. Of those 18,946 came from what is now the Republic of Ireland (59.6%) and 11,299 were from Northern Ireland (40.4%). On a 60:40 split; it indicates a figure of 49,083 dead for the island of Ireland.

65. Keith Jeffery, *Ireland and the Great War* (Cambridge, 2000), p. 7.
66. *Irish Times*, 11 November 2018.
67. Elections Ireland: 1918 British general election, NUI constituency result: https://electionsireland.org/result.cfm?election=1918&cons=189 [accessed September 2023].
68. MacNeill responded to John Redmond's call with this statement: 'Mr Redmond, addressing a body of Irish Volunteers last Sunday, has now announced for the Irish Volunteers a policy and programme fundamentally at variance with their own published and accepted aims and pledges . . . He has declared it to be the duty of the Irish Volunteers to take foreign service under a government which is not Irish. He has made his announcement without consulting the provisional committee, the Volunteers themselves or the people of Ireland, to whose service alone they are devoted', 'Manifesto to the Irish Volunteers', *The Irish Review [Dublin]*, 4 (September – November 1914), pp 281–286
69. Ernie O'Malley, *On Another's Man Wound* (Dublin, 1936), p. 34.
70. Ibid., p. 74.
71. National University of Ireland: Senate Minutes, 12 December 1918, p. 284.
72. National University of Ireland: Senate Minutes, 2 March 1917, p. 292.
73. National University of Ireland: Senate Minutes, 12 December 1918, p. 315.
74. *University College Cork Official Gazette*, vol 7. No. 26, Trinity Term, July 1919, pp 255–259.
75. In comparison, see 'The Long, Long Trail, British Army statistics of the Great War': https://www.longlongtrail.co.uk/army/some-british-army-statistics-of-the-great-war/ [accessed September 2023], where of the 5,704,416 from the British Isles, who served, 704,803 are listed as having been killed, or 12.3 % of those who served.
76. *Cork Examiner*, 14 August 1964.
77. Busteed Prize 2014. UCC news: https://www.ucc.ie/en/news/archive/2014andbeyond/2010pressreleases/busteed-prizes.html [accessed September 2023].
78. Paul Taylor, *Heroes or Traitors: Experiences of Southern Irish Soldiers Returning from the Great War, 1919–39* (Liverpool, 2015).
79. *Irish Independent*, 5 March 1930.
80. *Freeman's Journal*, 10 March 1924.
81. Peter Cottrell, *The Irish Civil War 1922–1923* (Oxford, 2008), pp 23 & 51. Richard Mulcahy Papers P7/B/195, (UCD Archives).
82. *Irish Times*, 24 November 1976.
83. Casey et al., *Irish Doctors in the First World War*, p. 166.

84. Bureau of Military History, Rev Thomas Duggan, Witness Statement [WS], No. 551. Digitised: https://www.militaryarchives.ie/collections/online-collections/bureau-of-military-history-1913–1921 [accessed August 2023].
85. See, John Borgonovo, 'Revolution, ex-servicemen and the Cork of the National Federation of Discharged and Demobilized Soldiers and Sailors, 1918–21' in David Swift and Oliver Wilkinson, *Veterans of the First World War: Ex-Servicemen and Ex-Servicewomen in Post-War Britain and Ireland* (Routledge, 2019), pp 82–109.
86. Jackie Uí Chionna, *The Queen of Codes: The Secret Life of Emily Anderson, Britain's Greatest Female Codemaker* (London, 2023), p. 98.
87. Motion by Deputy Redmond – Disabilities of British Ex-Servicemen, Dáil Eireann Debate, Wednesday, 16 November 1927: https://www.oireachtas.ie/en/debates/debate/dail/1927-11-16/42/ [accessed September 2023].
88. Keith Jeffery, 'Ireland and World War One', 3 October 2011. BBC History website: http://www.bbc.co.uk/history/british/britain_wwone/ireland_wwone_01.shtml [accessed September 2023].
89. *Irish Times*, 19 November 1998; *Irish Times*, 6 July 1927.
90. John Benignus Lyons, *The Enigma of Tom Kettle* (Dublin, 1983), p. 305.
91. *Irish Times*, 9 September 2016.
92. Speech by Professor Andrew Deeks, President of UCD, 9 September 2016, Rose Garden, UCD.
93. *Irish Times*, 9 September 2016.
94. UCD Library document of the month: https://twitter.com/UCDLibrary/status/1045657140470468608 [accessed August 2023].
95. UCC hosts First World War conference: https://www.ucc.ie/en/news/archive/2014andbeyond/2014-(jan-june)/ucc-hosts-first-world-war-conference.html [accessed September 2023].
96. 'Students and Soldiers: The University War Dead', NUI Galway: https://exhibitions.library.nuigalway.ie/s/nuigalway-1916/page/university-war-dead [accessed September 2023].
97. Marian Lyons and Barbara McCormack, 'On Active Service: Maynooth College, chaplains and the anti-conscription crisis', Maynooth University Library Treasure: https://mulibrarytreasures.wordpress.com/2018/08/20/on-active-service-maynooth-college-chaplains-the-anti-conscription-crisis/ [accessed September 2023].
98. Stephen Gwynn, *John Redmond's Last Years* (London, 1919), p. 126.
99. President Mary McAleese's speech at Messines 1998 https://president.ie/en/media-library/speeches/remarks-by-president-mary-mcaleese-at-the-inauguration-reof-the-messines-pe [accessed October 2023]
100. Casey et al., *Irish Doctors in the First World War*, p. 219, p. 271, and p. 409..

101. Tomás Irish, *The University at War, 1914–1925: Britain, France and the United States* (Basingstoke, 2015).
102. Introduction in Brian Harrison and Trevor Henry Aston (eds), *The History of the University of Oxford: Volume VIII: The Twentieth Century* (Oxford, 1994), p. 20.
103. BBC Magazine, Viewpoint: 10 big myths about World War One debunked https://www.bbc.com/news/magazine-25776836 [accessed September 2023].
104. *The Daily Express*, 14 January 2014.
105. Irish, *The University at War 1914–1925*, p. 156.
106. Trinity College Dublin (TCD) Hall of Honour Memorial: https://www.tcd.ie/news_events/articles/hall-of-honour-memorial-stone-to-remember-trinity-wwi-war-dead/ [accessed September 2023].
107. Ibid.

2. *Selected Bibliographies*

1. See introduction for a discussion of the history of NUI and its constituent universities. Graduates of the Catholic University and the Royal University of Ireland are listed in the UCD list and likewise graduates of Queen's College Cork and Queen's College Galway are listed in the UCC and UCG lists respectively. For clarity only the constituent college names as listed per college in the NUI Roll are used here.
2. Ireland's Memorial Records in Flanders Fields Museum. See www.inflandersfields.be [accessed September 2023].
3. Tom Burnell, *26 County Casualties of the Great War* (Ireland, 2017), 15 vols.
4. Patrick Casey, Kevin Cullen, and Joe Duignan, *Irish Doctors in the First World War* (Dublin, 2015). See, also this volume, Chapter 4, pp 148–166.
5. See, this volume, pp. 137–138.
6. See Róisín Healy, 'The Lives of Emily Anderson: Galway professor, music historian, and British intelligence officer', Moore Institute for Research in the Humanities and Social Studies, University of Galway: https://mooreinstitute.ie/2017/03/20/lives-emily-anderson-galway-professor-music-historian-british-intelligence-officer/ [accessed October 2023]. See more recently: Jackie Uí Chionna, *Queen of Codes: The Secret Life of Emily Anderson, Britain's Greatest Female Code Breaker* (London, 2023). Emily Anderson is also discussed by Fionnuala Walsh in this volume, see also Chapter 3, pp 137–138.
7. *Kerryman*, 26 December 1914.
8. Casey et al., *Irish Doctors in the First World War*, p. 219.
9. *Kilkenny Echo* and *South Kerry Chronicle*, 9 January 1915.

10. Casey et al., *Irish Doctors in the First World War*, p. 219.
11. 'Strong Hearts Stir Belvedere College SJ', 26 lives linking Belvedere College and the Easter Rising of 1916: http://shs-bcsj.blogspot.com/p/captain-arthur-joseph-beveridge-captain.html [accessed October 2023].
12. *Cork Examiner*, 28 September 1959.
13. Casey et al., *Irish Doctors in the First World War*, p. 225.
14. *Cork Examiner*, 13 February 1918.
15. Ronan McGreevy, *Wherever the Firing Line Extends: Ireland and the Western Front* (2nd Edition, Stroud, 2017), p. 176.
16. *Irish Times*, 14 April 2016.
17. See John Borgonovo, *The Dynamics of War and Revolution: Cork City 1916–18* (Cork, 2013), p. 188.
18. *Cork Examiner*, 13 February 1918.
19. 'They were truly bohemian in spirit', Bohemian FC website: http://bohemianfc.com/?page_id=38 [accessed October 2023].
20. Bureau of Military History, witness statement of a member of the community of the Sisters of Mercy, Mater Hospital, Dublin. WS No. 463: BMH.WS0463.pdf (militaryarchives.ie)[accessed October 2023].
21. *Irish Times*, 2 September 2008.
22. *Irish Independent*, 13 July 1925. His son, Mr Justice John Blayney, who was just three months old when his father died, became a Supreme Court judge. He died in 2018.
23. Pauric Dempsey, 'Garrett Brennan' in James McGuire and James Quinn (eds), *Dictionary of Irish Biography* (Cambridge, 2009).
24. Ibid.
25. Bureau of Military History, Statement by Deputy Commissioner Garrett Brennan (1957), WS No. 460: BMH.WS0460.pdf (militaryarchives.ie) [accessed October 2023].
26. *Cork Examiner*, 25 September 1959.
27. *Irish Times*, 28 November 2009.
28. *Irish Independent*, 12 August 1918.
29. *Weekly Irish Times*, 8 August 1924.
30. Ibid.
31. *Irish Independent*, 10 August 1964.
32. Ronan Fanning, 'Economists and the Irish Economy', *Hermathena*, vol. 135 (Winter, 1983), pp 138–156.
33. Fanning, 'Economists and the Irish economy'.
34. Ibid.
35. *Irish Times*, 15 August 1964
36. *Cork Examiner*, 14 August 1964.
37. Patricia M. Byrne, 'James Bayley Butler' in James McGuire and James Quinn (eds), *Dictionary of Irish Biography* (Cambridge, 2009).

38. *Irish Independent*, 22 February 1964.
39. Cónal Thomas, 'The Story of Lion's Head', *Dublin InQuirer*, 12 April 2017: https://www.dublininquirer.com/2017/04/12/the-story-of-lion-s-head [accessed October 2023].
40. *Irish Times*, 28 February 1964.
41. 'James Bayley Butler', *DIB*.
42. 'Patrick Anthony Langan-Byrne', Wikipedia entry: https://en.wikipedia.org/wiki/Patrick_Anthony_Langan-Byrne [accessed October 2023].
43. *London Gazette*, 14 November 1916.
44. Joe Gleeson, *Irish Aces of the RFC and RAF in the First World War: The Lives Behind the Legend* (London, 2015), pp 28–33.
45. Ibid.
46. 'Students and Soldiers: The University War Dead', Exhibition, University of Galway 2016: https://exhibitions.library.nuigalway.ie/s/nuigalway-1916/page/university-war-dead [accessed October 2023].
47. Commonwealth War Graves Commission: https://www.cwgc.org/find-war-dead/casualty/680830/campbell,-thomas-callender/ [accessed October 2023].
48. *Irish Times*, 18 April 1928.
49. *The Peerage: a Genealogical Survey of the Peerage of Britain as well the Royal Families of Europe* online #36350: http://www.thepeerage.com/p36350.htm#c363494.1 [accessed October 2023].
50. *London Gazette*, 18 June 1917: https://www.thegazette.co.uk/London/issue/30135/supplement/5987/data.pdf [accessed October 2023].
51. *Cork Examiner*, 21 April 1928.
52. *Irish Times*.
53. Johnny Doyle Blogspot, 17 September 2013: http://johnny-doyle.blogspot.com/2013/09/dr-carew-and-captain-stanley.html [accessed October 2023].
54. Obituary: Sir Arthur Chance, F.R.C.S.I., *British Medical Journal*, 4 August 1928, p. 224: https://www.ncbi.nlm.nih.gov/pmc/articles/PMC2455755/ ? page =1 [accessed October 2023].
55. Ibid.
56. *Irish Independent*, 27 July 1928.
57. BMJ, p. 224: https://www.ncbi.nlm.nih.gov/pmc/articles/PMC2455755/ ?page=1 [accessed October 2023].
58. Noel Browne, *Against the Tide* (Dublin, 1986), pp 57–58.
59. *Weekly Irish Times*, 13 October 1917.
60. Ibid.
61. *Irish Independent*, 6 October 1917.
62. *Freeman's Journal*, 6 October 1917.
63. 'Collingwood Cup: History and Winners', Irish Universities Football Union:

http://thirdlevelfootball.ie/iufu/competitions/collingwood-cup/history-and-winners/ [accessed October 2019].

64.. Obituary: Bertram Collingwood, *British Medical Journal*, 25 August 1934, p. 377: https://www.ncbi.nlm.nih.gov/pmc/articles/PMC2445073/?page=1 [accessed October 2023].

65. Irish Universities Football Union: http://thirdlevelfootball.ie/iufu/competitions/collingwood-cup/history-and-winners/ [accessed October 2023].

66. Obituary: Bertram Collingwood, *British Medical Journal*, 25 August 1934, p. 377: https: //www.ncbi.nlm.nih.gov/pmc/articles/PMC2445073/?page=1 [accessed October 2023].

67. Ibid.

68. Diarmuid Ó Cearbhaill, 'The Colahans: A Remarkable Galway Family', *Journal of the Galway Archaeological and Historical Society*, vol. 54 (2002), pp 121–140.

69. The Great War Forum: https://www.greatwarforum.org/topic/269466-dr-arthur-colahan-and-galway-bay/[accessed October 2023].

70. Find a Grave Website: https://www.findagrave.com/memorial/57138098/arthur-colahan [accessed October 2023].

71. Lynda Callaghan Blog, 'The Irish in Leicester, Prebend Street': http://lynda-callaghan.blogspot.com/2014/04/prebend-st.html [accessed October 2023].

72. David McCullagh, *The Reluctant Taoiseach: A Biography of John A. Costello* (Dublin, 2010), pp 16–18.

73. Ibid.

74. *Irish Times*, 21 July 1971.

75. 'Unproven Methods of Cancer Treatment'. Statement distributed to the American Cancer Society for their information, *A Cancer Journal for Clinicians,* July 1958: https://onlinelibrary.wiley.com/doi/pdf/10.3322/canjclin.16.6.254 [accessed October 2023].

76. Profile of Sir John Wenman Crofton, Lives of the Fellows, Royal College of Physicians: Sir John Wenman Crofton | RCP Museum (rcplondon.ac.uk) [accessed October 2023].

77. Profile of Richard Crofts, Royal Army Medical Corps in the Great War online: http://www.ramc-ww1.com/profile.php?profile_id=6198 [accessed October 2023].

78. Gerry White and Brendan O'Shea (eds), *A Great Sacrifice. Cork Servicemen who died in the Great War* (Cork, 2010), p. 220.

79. *Weekly Irish Times*, 4 August 1917.

80. Clongowes Wood College Great War Memorial, Inventory No. 689: http://www.irishwarmemorials.ie/pdf/680.pdf [accessed October 2023].

81. George Albert Dinan, Kings College London Memorial List: http://www.kings collections.org/warmemorials/guys-hospital/memorials/dinan-george-albert [accessed October 2023].

82. Pat Bracken, *Irish Cricket and the Great War, 1914–1918: Biographies of the Fallen*, Cricket Europe Ireland, 7 November, 2018: The Great War (irishcricketarchives.org) [accessed October 2023].
83. *Kerry Sentinel*, 20 September 1916.
84. White and O'Shea (eds), *A Great Sacrifice*, p. 236.
85. Casey et al., *Irish Doctors in the First World War*, p. 271.
86. S. Tharakaram, 'Charles Donovan MD, Indian Medical Service', paper delivered to the Liverpool Medical History Society, 6 May 1999.
87. Dietmar Steverding, 'The History of Leishmaniasis', *Parasit Vectors*, vol. 10 (2017), US National Library of Medicine National Institutes of Health: https://www.ncbi.nlm.nih.gov/pmc/articles/PMC5312593/ [accessed October 2023].
88. Rob Bohan and Linde Lunney, 'Charles Donovan' in James McGuire and James Quinn (eds), *Dictionary of Irish Biography* (Cambridge, 2009).
89. European Funding Guide: http://www.european-funding-guide.eu/awardprize/3082-charles-donovan-prize-dermatology [accessed October 2023].
90. *Kildare Observer*, 28 October 1915.
91. 'The UCD War List and Roll of Honour, an Armistice Centenary', Dr Conor Mulvagh, History Hub: http://historyhub.ie/ucd-war-list-roll-of-honour-armistice-centenary [accessed October 2023].
92. Profile of Lieutenant John J. Doyle, Ireland and the Great War Blog: https://irelandandthegreatwarblog.wordpress.com/2016/04/20/lieutenant-john-j-doyle/ [accessed October 2023].
93. *Irish Independent*, 17 October 1916.
94. *Kilkenny People*, 4 March 2012.
95. Profile of Archdeacon Tom Duggan, Cork, and Ross Catholic Diocese website: http://corkandross.org/priests/archdeacon-thomas-tom-f-duggan-pp-vg-2/ [accessed October 2023]. See Chapter 5, where Rev Thomas Duggan is also discussed, p. 277 and pp 287–288.
96. Letter from Meda Ryan, *History Ireland*, 12, Spring 2004: https://www.historyireland.com/20th-century-contemporary-history/tom-barry-2/ [accessed October 2023].
97. *Irish Times,* 4 July 2015: https://www.irishtimes.com/life-and-style/homes-and-property/fine-art-antiques/asian-lots-top-sheppard-s-bill-again-1.2272288 [accessed October 2023].
98. The Geograph Project aims to collect geographically representative photographs and information for Ireland. See their website: https://www.geograph.ie/photo/5830360 [accessed October 2023].
99. *Limerick Leader*, 21 June 1916.
100. *Limerick Leader*, 21 June 1916.
101. Reginald William Durdle, Southampton Cenotaph online: https://southamptoncenotaph.com/reginald-william-durdle/ [accessed May 2019].

102. James Jameson Dwyer, Find a Grave online: https://www.findagrave.com/memorial/22635447/james-jameson-dwyer [accessed October 2023].
103. *Kerryman*, 12 May 2018.
104. *Kerry News*, 1 May 1918.
105. *Kerryman*, 12 May 2018.
106. 'Killorglin's World War 1 Servicemen and Women'. A collection of information and stories about the men and women from the parish who served in the war: KILLORGLIN'S GREAT WAR SOLDIERS, SAILORS AND AIRMAN | Killorglin Archive (killorglinarchives.com) [accessed October 2023].
107. *Southern Star*, 25 November 2018.
108. 'Hong Kong Stories: a Compendium of Irish Connections'. Derek J Collins Blogpost: Two Irish Military Doctors in Hong Kong, 10 August 2014: http://derekjcollins.blogspot.com/2014/08/2-irish-military-doctors-in-hk.html [accessed October 2023].
109. *Belfast Newsletter*, 19 June 1916.
110. Ibid.
111. Flanigan Brothers, The Great War Forum: https://www.greatwarforum.org/topic/167150-flanagan-brothers/ [accessed October 2023].
112. *Connaught Telegraph*, 31 January 1917.
113. *Freeman's Journal*, 6 January 1917.
114. *Weekly Irish Times*, 8 September 1917.
115. Profile of Alexander Boyd Foott, Royal Army Medical Corps in the Great War: http://www.ramc-ww1.com/profile.php?cPath=274_98&profile_id=11175&osCsid=1dd87172aad1be38bd96aa6b3cbf8b38 [accessed October 2023].
116. 'Students and Soldiers: The University War Dead', Exhibition, University of Galway, 2016: https://exhibitions.library.nuigalway.ie/s/nuigalway-1916/page/university-war-dead [accessed October 2023].
117. *Cork Examiner*, 9 May 1916; *Cork Constitution*, 10 October 1916.
118. Sir Peter Freyer Papers, University of Galway, Irish Archives Resource: http://www.iar.ie/Archive.shtml?IE%20JHL/P057 [accessed October 2023].
119. Sir Peter Freyer Surgical Symposium: http://www.freyer.ie/index.php/about [accessed October 2023].
120. *Cork Examiner*, 11 May 1918.
121. *Drogheda Independent*, 24 July 2013.
122. *The Clare Herald* online, 7 April 2015: http://clareherald.com/2015/04/video-100-years-on-lusitanias-clare-victim-45646/ [accessed October 2023]. Joseph Garry is also discussed in Chapter 4, p. 156.
123. *Irish Independent*, 9 June 1915.
124. *Cork Examiner*, 9 September 1915.
125. Joseph Garry, People's Stories, Merseyside Maritime Museum: http://www.liver-

poolmuseums.org.uk/maritime/visit/floor-plan/lusitania/people/peoples-stories.aspx?id=13765 [accessed October 2023].

126. Jesuit Ireland photos, Flickr website: https://www.flickr.com/photos/jesuitsireland/4604258186 [accessed October 2023].
127. BBC 16 Voices. Father Henry Gill: https://www.bbc.co.uk/programmes/articles/13Koc4JFvlDLRNZDFWmlRyt/father-henry-gill [accessed October 2023].
128. Ibid.
129. *Freeman's Journal*, 5 June 1918.
130. Ibid.
131. *Freeman's Journal*, 6 May 1918.
132. *Weekly Irish Times*, 8 June 1918.
133. *Cork Examiner*, 4 October 1917.
134. *Cork Examiner*, 12 April 1971.
135. Lieutenant Denis Gwynn, Royal Munster Fusiliers, Service Record, National Archives Kew: https://discovery.nationalarchives.gov.uk/details/r/C1116071 [accessed October 2023].
136. *Cork Examiner*, 12 April 1971.
137. Stephen Gwynn, *The Lost years of Redmond* (London, 1919).
138. Denis Gwynn, *The Life of John Redmond* (London, 1932), p. 361.
139. Profile of Sir John and Lady Lavery, Michael Collins 22 website: http://www.generalmichaelcollins.com/life-times/the-struggle/sir-john-lady-lavery/ [accessed October 2023].
140. Jesuits in Ireland website: https://www.jesuit.ie/events/11oct-fr-john-gwynn-sj-memorial-mass/ [accessed October 2023].
141. Irish Jesuit Archive: http://sjarchives.tumblr.com/post/131014392865/today-12-october-marks-the-centenary-of-the [accessed October 2023].
142. Profile of Fr John Gwynn, The Sacred Heart Church Caterham, Whyteleafe and Godstone: http://www.sacred-heart.co.uk [accessed October 2023].
143. Rudyard Kipling, *The Irish Guards in the Great War* (New York, 1923), p. 118.
144. *Freeman's Journal*, 5 June 1918.
145. *Limerick Leader*, 22 March 1918.
146. *Limerick Leader*, 7 June 1918.
147. 'Would Ireland be different if de Valera had become a maths professor?', Ireland Calling website: https://ireland-calling.com/eamon-de-valera-maths-professor/ [accessed October 2023].
148. Colum Mulcahy, 'Edgar Harper: the mathematician who changed the course of Irish history?' (September 2016), Mathematics Ireland website: http://www.mathsireland.ie/blog/2016_09_cm [accessed October 2023].
149. Edgar Henry Harper and Allan Ferguson, *Aerial Locomotion*. Cambridge Manuals of Science and Literature (Cambridge, 1911).

150. George Hartley Bryan, *Stability in Aviation: An Introduction to Dynamical Stability as Applied to Motions of Aeroplanes* (London, 1911).
151. *Belfast Telegraph*, 1 May 2018.
152. *Cork Examiner*, 9 March 1917.
153. *The Indian Medical Gazette*, June 1917, p. 220: https://europepmc.org/backend/ptpmcrender.fcgi?accid=PMC5176590&blobtype=pdf [accessed October 2023].
154. *Kerry Sentinel*, 14 August 1915.
155. *Skibbereen Eagle*, 14 August 1915.
156. Profile of James Lyle Hay by Shane Flanagan, Dunmore Community School, *My Adopted Soldier*: http://legacy.myadoptedsoldier.com/archive/myarchive.php?u=16 [accessed October 2023].
157. 'Students and Soldiers: The University War Dead', Exhibition, University of Galway 2016: https://exhibitions.library.nuigalway.ie/s/nuigalway-1916/page/university-war-dead [accessed October 2023].
158. McGreevy, *Wherever the Firing Line Extends*, pp 194–195.
159. The Grave of James Lyle Hay, Commonwealth War Grave Commission website: https://www.cwgc.org/find-war-dead/casualty/191151/hay,-james-lyle/ [accessed October 2023].
160. Maurice R.J. Hayes, *The British Institute of Radiology*, vol. 3 (1930): https://www.birpublications.org/doi/abs/10.1259/0007-1285-3-30-282 [accessed October 2023].
161. David Durnin, 'Irish Doctors in the First World War', 10 April 2013. A blog by the UCD Centre for the History of Medicine in Ireland: http://historyofmedicineinireland.blogspot.com/2013/04/irish-doctors-in-first-world-war-by_10.html [accessed October 2023].
162. David Durnin, 'Ireland's British Army doctors and the treatment of Irish nationalists, 1916–1923', in David Durnin and Ian Miller (eds), *Medicine, Health and Irish Experiences of Conflict, 1914–1945* (Manchester, 2015), pp 94–108, p. 104.
163. *Irish Independent*, 5 March 1930.
164. *Irish Independent*, 3 March 1930.
165. *Weekly Irish Times*, 18 August 1917.
166. Maurice Healy, *The Old Munster Circuit: a Book of Memories and Traditions* (London, 1939; Reprint 2001).
167. Charles Lysaght, 'Maurice Francis Healy' in James McGuire and James Quinn (eds), *Dictionary of Irish Biography* (Cambridge, 2009).
168. Borgonovo, *The Dynamics of War and Revolution*, p. 32
169. Lysaght, 'Maurice Francis Healy'.
170. *Belfast Telegraph*, 13 August 1941.
171. Maurice Healy, *Stay me with Flagons: A book about wine and other things* (London, 1963).
172. *Irish Times*, 18 January 2014.

173. *Irish Independent*, 26 May 1941.
174. *Cork Examiner*, 23 July 1943.
175. Casey et al. *Irish Doctors in the First World War*, p. 121.
176. *Evening Herald*, 14 May 1954.
177. *Southern Star*, 22 May 1954.
178. 'Glasnevin's Ace, Captain Oscar Heron D.F.C.', Glasnevin Trust website: https://www.glasnevintrust.ie/visit-glasnevin/news/glasnevin-cemetery-film-0/glasnevins-ace-captain-os/ [accessed October 2023].
179. *Irish Times*, 7 August 1933.
180. 'World War 1 at Sea: Naval battles in outline': http://www.naval-history.net/WW1Battle1507KonigsbergAction.htm [accessed October 2023].
181. 'The Canadian Bank of Commerce: Letters from the Front: Volume II': http://lib.militaryarchive.co.uk/library/Biographical/library/The-Canadian-Bank-of-Commerce-Letters-from-the-Front-Volume-II/files/assets/basic-html/page267.html [accessed October 2023].
182. Casey et al. *Irish Doctors in the First World War*, p. 346. And St John's Wood Memories, 17 February 2016: https://www.stjohnswoodmemories.org.uk/content/memories/world_war_1_world_war_2/one_of_the_last_flying_bombs_25_november_1944 [accessed October 2023].
183. *London Gazette*, 25 July 1916.
184. St John's Wood Memories, London, 17 February 2016: https://www.stjohnswoodmemories.org.uk/content/memories/world_war_1_world_war_2/one_of_the_last_flying_bombs_25_november_1944 [accessed October 2023].
185. Obituary: Richard Lane Joynt, *British Medical Journal*, 21 April 1928, pp 693–694: https://www.ncbi.nlm.nih.gov/pmc/articles/PMC2455432/?page=1 [accessed October 2023].
186. Ibid.
187. *Irish Independent*, 12 September 1918.
188. 'Students and Soldiers: The University War Dead', Exhibition, University of Galway 2016: https://exhibitions.library.nuigalway.ie/s/nuigalway-1916/page/university-war-dead [accessed October 2023].
189. *Cork Examiner*, 5 July 1918.
190. Melville Henry Massue Ruvigny, *The Roll of Honour: A Biographical Record of All Members of His Majesty's Naval and Military Forces Who Have Fallen in the War* (London, 1917–1922), p. 163. Known as de Ruvigny's Roll of Honour, a digitised copy may be found at: https://archive.org/stream/rollofhonourbiog02ruvi#page /163/mode/1up/search/kelly [accessed October 2023].
191. *Tuam Herald*, September 16, 1916.
192. Ibid.

193. Ralph May, 'Lieutenant-General Sir Alfred Keogh GCB, GCVO, CH', *Journal of the Society for Army Historical Research*, 85, No. 342 (Summer 2007), pp 115–125: https://www.jstor.org/stable/44231467?seq=1#page_scan_tab_contents [accessed October 2023]. For further discussion of Keogh, see Chapter 4, p. 150, p. 156, and p. 165.
194. J.S.G. Blair, 'Sir Alfred Keogh: The Early Years', *Journal of the Royal Army Medical Corps* 154 (2008), pp 268–274: https://jramc.bmj.com/content/154/4/268 [accessed October 2023].
195. May, 'Lieutenant-General Sir Alfred Keogh', pp 115–125.
196. National Portrait Gallery: https://www.npg.org.uk/collections/search/portrait/mw94887/Sir-Alfred-Keogh [accessed October 2023].
197. Tom and Mary Kettle, *The Ways of War* (New York, 1917), p. 3.
198. Kathryn Rix, '"Died not for flag, nor King, nor Emperor": Thomas Michael Kettle (1880–1916)', The History of Parliament: https://thehistoryofparliament.wordpress.com/2016/09/09/died-not-for-flag-nor-king-nor-emperor-thomas-michael-kettle-1880–1916/ [accessed October 2023].
199. John Benignus Lyons, *The Enigma of Tom Kettle* (Dublin, 1983), pp 299–300.
200. McGreevy, *Wherever the Firing Line Extends*, p. 241.
201. Captain Richard Crofton George Moore Kinkead, Our Heroes column, *Irish Life* newspaper's digitised by South Dublin Library: https://localstudies.wordpress.com/2014/10/28/our-heroes-a-supplement-to-irish-life-1914–1918-database-now-online/ [accessed October 2023].
202. 'Students and Soldiers: The University War Dead', Exhibition, University of Galway 2016: https://exhibitions.library.nuigalway.ie/s/nuigalway-1916/page/university-war-dead [accessed October 2023].
203. *Irish Independent*, 6 November 1914.
204. Profile of Richard Kinkead, Royal Army Medical Corps in the Great War: http://www.ramc-ww1.com/profile.php?cPath=292_508&profile_id=9428&osCsid=7326968b669af351338a02e2ea3dc7c1 [accessed October 2023].
205. Casey et al., *Irish Doctors in the First World War*, p. 355.
206. *Connacht Tribune*, 12 August 1916.
207. Ibid.
208. There is no listing for this man in the Commonwealth War Graves Commission website or on the In Flanders Fields Irish Memorial Records website though he is listed in the Roll of Honour among the UCD war dead.
209. *Freeman's Journal*, 1 January 1917.
210. *Freeman's Journal*, 1 January 1917.
211. Michael MacDonagh, *The Irish on the Somme* (London, 1917), p. 134.
212. *London Gazette*, 27 July 1916.
213. *Western People*, 23 September 1916.

214. Ibid.
215. Ralph Bodkin Mahon, Plarr's Lives of the Fellows, Royal College of Surgeons: https://livesonline.rcseng.ac.uk/client/en_GB/lives/? [accessed October 2023].
216. Europeana: World War 1 Collections: https://pro.europeana.eu/project/europeana1914–1918 [accessed October 2023].
217. Great War Forum: https://www.greatwarforum.org/topic/42012-vad-other-ranks/ [accessed October 2023].
218. *Freeman's Journal*, 28 September 1917.
219. *Irish Times*, 13 July 1968.
220. *Irish Independent*, 19 July 1968.
221. Profile of Samuel Wauchope Matthews, Royal Army Medical Corps in the Great War: http://www.ramc-ww1.com/profile.php?cPath=342&profile_id=8416&osCsid=29 [accessed October 2023].
222. Casey et al. *Irish Doctors in the First World War*, pp 372–373.
223. Golfing Ireland website hosted by Eddie Costello: http://www.golfingireland.ie/index.php/search-by-county/roscommon/athlone [accessed October 2023].
224. *Irish Times*, 25 July 1973.
225. *London Gazette*, 25 July 1918: https://www.thegazette.co.uk/London/issue/30813/supplement/8824/data.pdf [accessed October 2023].
226. *Evening Herald*, 25 January 1918.
227. 'Royal Dublin Fusiliers: a Forgotten Regiment, 4th Battalion': https://www.dublin-fusiliers.com/battaliions/4-battaliion.html [accessed October 2023].
228. 'Great win for Ireland over Wales last weekend, the same match held 100 years ago has a UCC connection', 10 February 2014, UCC website: https://www.ucc.ie/en/build/news/great-win-for-ireland-over-wales-last-weekend-the-same-match-held-100-years-ago-has-a-ucc-connection.html [accessed October 2023].
229. *Cork Examiner*, 22 November 1955.
230. *Limerick Leader*, 23 July 1951.
231. *Limerick Leader*, 12 February 1951.
232. *Irish Times*, 22 November 1955.
233. Cookstown War Dead Database: http://cookstownwardead.co.uk/persondepth.asp?cas_id=269 [accessed September 2023].
234. General William Parsons, the original general commanding the 16th (Irish) Division insisted that those who had no military experience join the ranks first.
235. *Irish Times*, 24 November 1976.
236. Edmond Joseph Theophilus McWeeney, Royal College of Physicians of Ireland: http://www.iar.ie/Archive.shtml?IE%20RCPI/EJTM [accessed October 2023].
237. *Irish Times*, 24 November 1976.
238. Edmond McWeeney, Royal College of Physicians of Ireland: https://rcpi-live-cdn.

s3.amazonaws.com/wp-content/uploads/2018/12/Edmond-Joseph-Theophilus-McWeeney.pdf [accessed October 2023].

239. Deirdre McMahon, *The Moynihan Brothers in Peace and War, 1908–1918: Their own Ireland* (Dublin, 2008).

240. 'The Midst Of It All', UCD Library Cultural Heritage Collections: https://ucdculturalheritagecollections.com/2018/04/19/the-midst-of-it-all/ [accessed September 2023].

241. 'In the Midst 1917', Twitter: https://twitter.com/InTheMidst1917/status/986583921377890305 [accessed September 2023].

242. McMahon, *The Moynihan Brothers in Peace and War.*

243. Papers of Seán and Maurice Moynihan, UCD archives: https://www.ucd.ie/archives/t4media/p0122-moynihan-maurice-sean-descriptive-catalogue.pdf [accessed September 2023].

244. *Irish Independent*, 11 January 1943.

245. See also, Arthur Chance, pp 80–81.

246. *Irish Independent*, 11 January 1943.

247. *Sunday Independent*, 10 January 1943.

248. Casey et al., *Irish Doctors in the First World War*, p. 409

249. Ibid. p. 121.

250. *Weekly Irish Times*, 1 December 1917.

251. *Cork Examiner*, 7 October 1958.

252. *Cork Examiner*, 2 October 1958.

253. Nyhan also had his car taken by republicans during the Truce period. Doctors and priests were among the few professions in Ireland at the time who had cars. Doctors in particular were targeted and even inspired a humorous song 'Johnson's Motor Car' about the seizure of a car by the IRA during the War of Independence: 'But when he got to the Railway Bridge, the rebels he saw there/Ould Johnson knew the game was up for at him they did stare/He said I have a permit to travel near and far/To hell with your English permit, we want your motor car.'

254. Paul Taylor, *Heroes or Traitors? Experiences of Southern Irish Soldiers returning from the Great War 1919–1939* (Liverpool, 2015), p. 63.

255. *Limerick Leader*, 12 February 1951 and *Cork Examiner*, 4 October 1958.

256. *Irish Times*, 23 May 2013.

257. Ibid.

258. See also, Conor O'Brien, p. 118.

259. Profile of Second Lieutenant Frank Brendan O'Carroll, *Irish Life* newspaper's Our Heroes column digitised by South Dublin Library: http://ourheroes.southdublinlibraries.ie/ga/node/16332 [accessed October 2023].

260. *Freeman's Journal*, 20 October 1915.

261. *Freeman's Journal*, 1 September 1915.
262. *Cork Examiner*, 8 October 1920.
263. Lives of the Presidents, Joseph O'Carroll: www.rcpi.ie and further details from Great War Forum: https://www.greatwarforum.org/topic/271332-sons-of-dr-joseph-francis-ocarroll/ [accessed October 2023].
264. *Skibbereen Eagle*, 2 October 1915.
265. 'The O'Leary family of Curriheverin', Courtmacsherry and Barryroe History Group: http://www.courtmacsherrybarryroehistory.com/oleary-family-of-curri-heverin.html [accessed October 2023].
266. Profile of Patrick Joseph O'Reilly, Royal Army Medical Corps in the Great War: http://www.ramc-ww1.com/profile.php?profile_id=5519 [accessed October 2023].
267. 'Students and Soldiers: The University War Dead', Exhibition, University of Galway 2016: https://exhibitions.library.nuigalway.ie/s/nuigalway-1916/page/university-war-dead [accessed October 2023].
268. South-East History Boards, covering Kent, Sussex, and Surrey: http://sussexhistoryforum.co.uk/index.php?topic=15200.0 [accessed October 2023].
269. Profile of Henry Perry, Royal Army Medical Corps in the Great War: http://www.ramc-ww1.com/profile.php?profile_id=11836 [accessed October 2023].
270. Lives of the Fellows, Royal College of Physicians: https://history.rcplondon.ac.uk/ [accessed October 2023].
271. *Cork Examiner*, 29 March 1955. Obituary: H.M.J. Perry, *British Medical Journal*, 9 April 1955, p. 915: https://www.bmj.com/content/1/4918/915.3 [accessed October 2023].
272. Profile of Arthur John Kershaw Peters, Nottinghamshire Great War Roll of Honour: https://rollofhonour.nottinghamshire.gov.uk/Person/Details?id=2887 [accessed October 2023].
273. Obituary of Henry Perry, *British Medical Journal*, 9 April 1955: https://www.bmj.com/content/1/4918/915.3 [accessed October 2023].
274. *Cork Examiner*, 5 June 1916.
275. *Irish Times*, 24 May 2016.
276. Marie Coleman, 'William Archer Redmond' in James McGuire and James Quinn (eds), *Dictionary of Irish Biography* (Cambridge, 2009).
277. Timothy Bowman, 'Ireland and the First World War', in Alvin Jackson (ed.), *The Oxford Handbook of Modern Irish History* (Oxford, 2014), pp 603–620, p. 610.
278. Kipling, *The Irish Guards in the Great War,* 2 vols (London, 1923), vol 2. Digitised: http://www.telelib.com/authors/K/KiplingRudyard/prose/IrishGuardsv2/appendixa.html [accessed May 2019].
279. See Martin O'Donoghue and Emer Purcell (eds), *John Redmond and Irish Parliamentary Traditions* (Dublin, 2024).
280. *Freeman's Journal*, 3 July 1916.

281. *Freeman's Journal*, 3 July 1916.
282. Roll of Honour 1914–1918, Masonic Great War Project: https://www.masonicgreatwarproject.org.uk/legend.php?id=2593 [accessed May 2019].
283. Commonwealth War Graves Commission: https://www.cwgc.org/find-records/find-war-dead/casualty-details/21845/benjamin-richard-roberts/{accessed October 2023].
284. Profile of Paddy Roche, Sports Reference: https://www.sports-reference.com/olympics/athletes/ro/paddy-roche-1.html [accessed May 2019].
285. *Cork Weekly Examiner*, 6 January 1916.
286. Stephen Walker, *Ireland's Call: Irish Sporting Heroes who fell in the Great War* (Dublin, 2015).
287. *Irish Life* newspaper's column 'Our Heroes', digitised by South Dublin Library: http://ourheroes.southdublinlibraries.ie/node/16764 [accessed May 2019].
288. *Irish Times*, 22 October 2014: https://www.irishtimes.com/culture/heritage/irish-doctor-defends-haig-1.1950996 [accessed October 2023].
289. Eugene Ryan, *Haig's Medical Officer: The Papers of Colonel Eugene 'Micky' Ryan CMG, DSO, RAMC* (Barnsley, 2013).
290. Profile of Mgr. Joseph Augustine Scannell, Catholic Dioceses of Cork and Ross: http://corkandross.org/priests/mgr-joseph-augustine-scannell-pp-vg/ [accessed May 2019].
291. *Cork Examiner*, 28 February 1961.
192. McGreevy, *Wherever the Firing Line Extends*, p. 72.
293. Captain James Owen Shine by Sophie Shine, My Adopted Soldier, which is a project conducted by Irish secondary school history students: http://legacy.myadoptedsoldier.com/archive/myarchive.php?u=70 [accessed May 2019].
294. *Irish Times*, 7 October 2013.
295. Hogan, 'Eugene Sheehy' in James McGuire and James Quinn (eds), *Dictionary of Irish Biography* (Cambridge, 2009).
296. See also, Tom Kettle, p. pp 20–21, pp 105–107, and p. 122.
297. Eugene Sheehy, *May it Please the Court* (Dublin, 1951), p. 92.
298. Ibid., p. 92.
299. Members of the Bar of Ireland in World War 1: an Online Exhibition, The Law Library: https://www.lawlibrary.ie/News/World-War-I-centenary-exhibition.aspx [accessed May 2019].
300. Turtle Bunbury, *The Glorious Madness: Tales of the Irish and the Great War* (Dublin, 2014), p. 122.
301. Dictionary of Irish Architects 1720–1940, Irish Architectural Archive: https://www.dia.ie/architects/view/5490/waller%2C+james+hardress+de+warenne [accessed May 2019].
302. Major Bryan Cooper, *The 10th (Irish) Division in Gallipoli* (London, 1917), p. 150.
303. *Irish Times*, 9 August 2008.

304. *Irish Times*, 2 October 1915.
305. Profile of Stephen Barry: Walsh, Royal Army Medical Corps in the Great War: http://www.ramc-ww1.com/profile.php?profile_id=12192 [accessed May 2019].
306. *Limerick Leader*, 13 September 1915.
307. *Irish Times*, 18 August 1917.
308. Casey et al., *Irish Doctors in the First World War*, p. 491.
309. *Cork Examiner*, 14 September 1915.
310. Profile of Lieutenant-Colonel M.J. Whitty, Class '81, Castleknock College Union: https://www.knockunion.ie/obituary/lieutenant-colonel-m-j-whitty-class-81-11199 [accessed May 2019].
311. Profile of Major General Sir Michael Yarr, Malta Royal Army Medical Corps: https://www.maltaramc.com/ramcoff/y/yarrmt.html [accessed May 2019].
312. Profile of Michael Thomas Yarr, *Biographical Dictionary of Medical Practitioners, Hong Kong: 1841-1941* http://hkmd1841-1941.blogspot.com/2013/09/yarr-michael-thomas-1887.html [accessed May 2019].
313. M.T. Yarr, *Manual of Military Ophthalmology* (London, 1902).

3. *What has the War got to do with a dance?*

1. Kate O'Brien, 'UCD as I forget it (1916–1919)' extracted in Anne Macdona (ed.), *From Newman to New Woman: UCD Women Remember* (Dublin, 2001), p. 7.
2. *National Student*, vol. 5, no. 8, April 1915, p. 9.
3. *National Student*, vol. 6, no. 1, December 1915, p. 9.
4. *UCG College Annual*, vol. 1, no. 3, 1915, p. 70.
5. O'Brien, 'UCD as I forget it (1916–1919)', p. 7.
6. Caitriona Clear, *Social Change and Everyday Life in Ireland, 1850–1922* (Manchester, 2007), pp 46–48.
7. Senia Pašeta, 'Achieving equality: Women and the foundation of the university' in Tom Dunne (ed.), *The National University of Ireland 1908–2008: Centenary Essays* (Dublin, 2008), pp 19–20, p. 20.
8. Margaret Ó hÓgartaigh, 'Women in university education in Ireland: The historical background' in Macdona (ed.), *From Newman to New Woman*, p. iii.
9. I am grateful to the NUI IT Unit and Records Office for providing me with a list of the women graduates of the Royal University of Ireland and the National University of Ireland.
10. *University College Cork Official Gazette*, vol. 5, no. 15, June 1915, p. 147. Harper was killed in action in 1916, *University College Cork Official Gazette*, vol. 7, no. 19,

December 1916, p. 184. The *University College Gazette* was produced three times a year, once a term.

11. *University College Cork Official Gazette*, vol. 5, no. 15, June 1915, p. 147.
12. John A. Murphy, *The College: A History of Queen's University College Cork, 1845–1995* (Cork, 1995), p.199.
13. National Library of Ireland, *War Record of University College Cork* (Cork, 1919), pp 3–15.
14. Lindsey Earner-Byrne, 'Cummins, Iris Ashley' in James McGuire and James Quinn (eds), *Dictionary of Irish Biography* (Cambridge, 2009).
15. *University College Cork Official Gazette*, vol. 4, no. 13, December 1914, p. 121; vol. 5, no. 15, p. 155; vol. 7, no. 24, July 1918, p. 234.
16. *University College Cork Official Gazette*, vol. 7, no. 24, July 1918, p. 237.
17. *University College Cork Official Gazette*, vol. 7, no. 21, June 1917, p. 210.
18. *University College Cork Calendar for the session 1919–1920* (Cork, 1919), p. 325; *University College Dublin Calendar for the session 1919–1920* (Dublin, 1919), p. 770; *University College Galway Calendar for 1920–1921* (Dublin, 1920), pp 418–421.
19. *University College Dublin Calendar for the session 1916–1917* (Dublin, 1916), p. 98.
20. Keith Jeffery, *1916: A Global History* (London, 2016), pp 110–111. See also, Fionnuala Walsh, *Irish Women and the Great War* (Cambridge, 2020).
21. Murphy, *The College*, p. 199.
22. *War Record of University College Cork*, p. 20.
23. *University College Cork Official Gazette*, vol. 6, no. 17, March 1916, p. 165.
24. *University College Cork Official Gazette*, vol. 6, no. 17, March 1916, p. 166.
25. *War Record of University College Cork*, p. 20.
26. *University College Cork Official Gazette*, vol. 7, no. 19, December 1916, p. 185. British Red Cross Archives, service record for Eileen Duke.
27. 'Memoranda on Red Cross Work in Ireland' in *Reports by the Joint War Committee and the Joint War Finance Committee of the British Red Cross Society and the Order of St John of Jerusalem 1914–1919* (London, 1921), p. 727.
28. Clara Cullen, 'War work on the home front: The Central Sphagnum Depot for Ireland at the Royal College of Science for Ireland, 1915–19' in David Durnin and Ian Miller (eds), *Medicine, Health and Irish Experiences of Conflict, 1914–45* (Manchester, 2017), pp 158–163.
29. British Red Cross Archives, service record for Una Magner.
30. *University College Cork Official Gazette*, vol. 7, no. 24, July 1918, p. 235.
31. *UCG College Annual*, vol.1, no. 4, 1916, p. 61.
32. I am grateful to the British Red Cross Archives for providing me with a database of all the Red Cross membership records from the First World War, and to Daniel Purcell for his assistance with the data analysis. See also, Walsh, *Irish Women and the Great War*, p. 25.
33. Mary Clancy, 'It was our joy to keep the flag flying: a study of the women's suffrage

campaign in county Galway' in *UCG Women's Studies Centre Review*, vol. 3 (1995), p. 99.

34. Marie Coleman, 'Donovan Sullivan, Mary', in James McGuire and James Quinn (eds), *Dictionary of Irish Biography* (Cambridge, 2009). See also University of Galway, 'Path breaking Women' exhibition brochure, March 2017.
35. *Galway Advertiser*, 30 March 2016.
36. *UCG College Annual*, vol. 1, no. 4, 1916, p. 62.
37. *UCD College Annual*, vol. 1, no. 5, 1917, p. 25.
38. Fionnuala Walsh, 'We work with shells all day and night: Irish female munitions workers during the First World War', *Saothar*, vol. 42 (2017), pp 19–30, p. 20.
39. See for example, *UCG College Annual*, vol. 1, no. 3, 1915, p. 57.
40. University of Galway 'Path breaking Women', Exhibition brochure, March 2017. Coleman, 'Donovan Sullivan, Mary', *DIB*.
41. Mary Clancy, 'The "Western outpost": local government and women's suffrage in County Galway 1898–1918' in Gerard Moran and Raymond Gillespie (eds), *Galway History and Society: Interdisciplinary Essays in the History of an Irish County* (Dublin, 1996), pp 557–587, pp 573–574.
42. Lindie Lunney, 'Anderson, Emily' in McGuire and Quinn (eds), *Dictionary of Irish Biography*. Also, now the subject of a recent biography by Jackie Uí Chionna, *Queen of Codes: The Secret Life of Emily Anderson, Britain's Greatest Female Code Breaker* (London, 2023).
43. British Red Cross Archives, service record for Emily Anderson.
44. Lunney, 'Anderson, Emily'. Anderson is also discussed by Ronan McGreevy, see Chapter 2, p. 73.
45. Leah Leneman, 'Medical women in the First World War—ranking nowhere', *British Medical Journal*, vol. 307, no. 6919 (December, 1993), p. 1592.
46. Keith Jeffery, *Ireland and the Great War* (Cambridge, 2000), p. 32.
47. Imperial War Museum, Women War and Society Collection: BRCS 24.10/23 and 24.10/21, 'Women in medicine', May 1918 and January 1917.
48. Laura Kelly, *Irish Women in Medicine, c. 1880s–1920s: Origins, Education and Careers* (Manchester, 2015), p. 139.
49. Kelly, *Irish Women in Medicine, c. 1880s–1920s*, p. 69.
50. Murphy, *The College*, p. 130.
51. *UCG College Annual*, vol. 1, no. 4, 1916, p. 62.
52. See for example, *Lady of the House*, 15 February 1917, 15 October 1917, 15 November 1917.
53. Dr C.M. Benson, 'The effect of war on the medical profession', *Dublin Journal of Medical Science*, vol. 141 (1916), pp 90–92.
54. Bouchier-Hayes census returns for Limerick, 1901, available at http://www.census.nationalarchives.ie/pages/1901/Limerick/Rathkeale_Urban/Main_Street/1512870/ / [accessed October 2023].
55. *British Medical Journal*, vol. 284, 6 March 1982.

56. Kelly, *Irish Women in Medicine, c. 1880s–1920s*, p. 212; UCD School of Medicine website: http://www.ucd.ie/medicine/ourcommunity/ouralumni/alumniprofiles-interviews/drmaryjfarrell/ [accessed October 2023].
57. British Red Cross Archives, service record for Dr Ella Webb, 1914–1919.
58. British Red Cross Archives, service record for Dr Ella Webb, 1914–1919, additional record.
59. Helen Andrews, 'Webb, Isabella ("Ella") Gertrude Amy' in McGuire and Quinn (eds), *Dictionary of Irish Biography*.
60. Margaret Ó hÓgartaigh, 'Lynn, Kathleen', in McGuire and Quinn (eds), *Dictionary of Irish Biography*. Lynn's diaries have recently been published, see Mary McAuliffe and Harriet Wheelock (eds), *The Diaries of Kathleen Lynn: A Life Revealed through Personal Writing* (Dublin, 2023).
61. UCD Archives, UCDA NUWGA 2/2 Minute book of the NUWGA Dublin branch 1913–1917, 7 February 1917.
62. UCDA NUWGA 2/2: Minute book of the NUWGA Dublin Branch 1913–1917, 30 October 1914 and 23 April 1915.
63. See for example references to the participation of women in college affairs in *National Student*, vol. 6, no. 2, March 1916, p. 8.
64. *National Student*, vol. 6, no. 1, December 1915, p. 25.
65. *National Student*, November 1914, p. 3.
66. *National Student*, vol. 5, no. 8, April 1915, p. 14.
67. *National Student*, vol. 5, no. 8, April 1915, pp 1, 4–5.
68. Pašeta, 'Achieving equality: women and the foundation of the university', pp 22, 31. See also, Joyce Padbury, *Mary Hayden: Irish Historian and Feminist, 1862–1942* (Dublin, 2020).
69. *Irish Citizen*, 31 October 1914.
70. *Irish Citizen*, 31 October 1914; 10 October 1914; 14 November 1914.
71. Margaret Ward, *Hanna Sheehy-Skeffington: A Life* (Dublin, 1997) and more recently by the same author, *Fearless Women: Hanna Sheehy-Skeffington, Feminism and the Irish Revolution* (Dublin, 2019)
72. *Irish Citizen*, 15 August 1914; 10 October 1914.
73. See also Chapter 2, p. 127, where Francis Sheehy-Skeffington is discussed.
74. *Irish Citizen*, 22 August 1914.
75. *Irish Citizen*, 19 September 1914.
76. *Irish Citizen*, 22 August 1914; 19 September 1914; 30 January 1915.
77. Pašeta, 'Achieving equality: women and the foundation of the university', p. 31.
78. *National Student*, vol. 6, no. 6, June 1914, p. 135.
79. *National Student*, vol. 6, no. 6, June 1914, p. 157.
80. Diarmaid Ferriter, *The Transformation of Modern Ireland 1900–2000* (London, 2004), pp 126–127 and Walsh, *Irish Women and the Great War*, p. 170.

81. *Irish Volunteer*, 15 August 1914.
82. *Irish Volunteer*, 17 October 1914.
83. Cal McCarthy, *Cumann na mBan and the Irish Revolution* (Cork, 2007), p. 36.
84. *National Volunteer*, 21 November 1914.
85. *National Volunteer*, 31 October 1914, 28 November 1914.
86. Senia Pašeta, *Irish Nationalist Women 1900–1918* (Cambridge, 2013), p. 149.
87. Bureau of Military History (BMH) Witness Statement (WS) 541, Nancy Wyse Power.
88. BMH WS 333, Aine O'Rahilly, p. 2.
89. BMH WS 216, Louise Gavan Duffy, p. 2.
90. David Fitzpatrick, *The two Irelands 1912–1939* (Oxford, 1998), p. 36.
91. Pašeta, *Irish Nationalist Women*, p. 244 and Walsh, *Irish Women and the Great War*, p. 184.
92. BMH WS 587, Nancy Wyse-Power, p. 9.
93. Mathews, pp 214–218; *Irish Citizen,* July 1918; *Freeman's Journal*, 10 June 1918.
94. *Irish Citizen*, May–June 1918.
95. Ó hÓgartaigh, 'Women in university education in Ireland: the historical back ground', p. x.
96. *Irish Times*, 23 November 1921, cited in Kelly, *Irish Women in Medicine c.1800s–1920s*, p. 139.
97. Kelly, *Irish Women in Medicine c.1800s–1920s*, p. 172.
98. Ibid., pp 155–156.

4. *NUI Doctors*

1. For a more detailed treatment of doctors in the First World War see, Patrick Casey, Kevin Cullen and Joe Duignan, *Irish Doctors in the First World War* (Dublin, 2015). The maps and images are reproduced from that publication with the consent of the authors.
2. See also, Chapter 1, p. 9 and p. 24.

5. *Maynooth Chaplains*

1. The material presented here forms part of a broader doctoral study, the working title of which is 'St Patrick's College, Maynooth and Irish politics and society, 1891–1923'. Under the supervision of Professor Terence Dooley, Department of History, Maynooth University.

2. Jane Leonard, 'The Catholic Chaplaincy' in David Fitzpatrick (ed.), *Ireland and the First World War* (Dublin, 1986), pp 1–2.
3. Hugh O'Neill, 'Irish Catholic Chaplains in the British Armed Forces during the First World War' in *Seanchas Ardmhacha: Journal of the Armagh Diocesan Historical Society*, vol. 23, no. 2 (2011), pp 203–230, p. 214.
4. Damien Burke, *Irish Jesuit Chaplains in the First World War* (2015), James Hagerty, *Priests in Uniform: Catholic Chaplains to the British Forces in the First World War* (Herefordshire, 2017); Oliver Rafferty, 'Catholic Chaplains to the British Forces in the First World War' in *Religion, State and Society*, vol. 34, no. 1 (2011), pp 33–62, p. 42.
5. Patrick Callan, 'Recruiting for the British Army in Ireland during the First World War' in *Irish Sword*, vol. 17, no. 66 (1987), pp 42–56.
6. Thomas P. Dooley, *Irishmen or English soldiers? The times and world of a southern Catholic Irish man (1876–1916) enlisting in the British army during the First World War* (Liverpool, 1995).
7. Ibid., p. [1].
8. Ibid., p. [1].
9. Ibid., pp [1]–2.
10. Tom Johnstone and James Hagerty, *The Cross on the Sword: Catholic Chaplains in the Forces* (London, 1996).
11. Edward Madigan, *Faith Under Fire: Anglican Army Chaplains and the Great War* (Basingstoke, 2011).
12. Jérôme aan de Wiel, *The Catholic Church in Ireland, 1914–1918: War and Politics* (Dublin, 2003).
13. Ibid., p. xv.
14. O'Neill, 'Irish Catholic Chaplains'.
15. Patrick J. Hamell, *Maynooth Students and Ordinations Index, 1795–1895* (Maynooth, 1982); Patrick J. Hamell, *Maynooth Students and Ordinations Index, 1895–1984* (Maynooth, 1984).
16. James O'Shea, *Priest, Politics and Society in Post-Famine Ireland: A Study of County Tipperary, 1850–1891* (Dublin, 1983), p. 14; Rafferty, 'Catholic Chaplains to the British Forces in the First World War',p. 42.
17. Rafferty, 'Catholic chaplains to the British Forces', p. 42.
18. *Irish Times*, 25 June 1915.
19. Report of the President for the year 1914–1915, St Patrick's College, Maynooth Archives, Box 132, p. 7.
20. Ibid.
21. Report of Special Committee on the Finances of St Patrick's College in 1915, St Patrick's College, Maynooth Archives, 132/4/41.
22. Ibid.

23. Report of the President for the year 1914–1915, p. 2.
24. J.M. Harty to J.F. Hogan, 9 September 1914, St Patrick's College, Maynooth Archives, Hogan papers, 21/4/9.
25. Report of the President for the year 1914–1915.
26. H. Bewerunge to D. O'Doherty, 21 February 1915, St Patrick's College, Maynooth, Salamanca Archives, Doherty papers, SP/S/103/5.
27. Report of the President for the year 1914–1915, p. 5.
28. *The Tablet*, 24 October 1914.
29. T. Gilmartin to J. F. Hogan, 1 March 1915, St Patrick's College, Maynooth Archives, Hogan papers, 21/6/20.
30. Minute book of the League of St Columba, St Patrick's College, Maynooth Archives [unlisted], p. 32.
31. 'Maynooth in World War I – and After' in *Vexillia Regis* (1966), p. 24.
32. Captain George S. Gordon to Hogan, 5 November 1917, St Patrick's College, Maynooth Archives, Hogan papers, 23/45/5.
33. 'Unilever House London – Unilever PLC', *http://unilever-archives.com/Record.aspx?src=CalmView.Catalog&id=GB1752.UNI%2FPLC%2FUH* [accessed on 25 August 2020].
34. Patrick Corish, *Maynooth College, 1795–1995* (Dublin, 1995), p. 302.
35. *The Nation*, 12 May 1877.
36. *Freeman's Journal*, 7 October 1902.
37. *New Zealand Tablet*, xxix, no. 35 (29 August 1901).
38. Annette Becker, *War and Faith: The Religious Imagination in France, 1914–1930* (Oxford, 1998), p. 40. Translated from the original by Helen McPhail [*La Guerre et la Foi. De la Mort à la mémoire* (1994)]
39. Gary Sheffield, 'Chaplains in context: British Army padres and the "Bureaucracy of Paternalism" in the First World War' in Michael Snape and Edward Madigan (eds), *The Clergy in Khaki: New Perspectives on British Army Chaplaincy in the First World War* (London, 2016), pp 111–126, p. 115.
40. J.E. Nelson, 'Irish soldiers in the Great War: some personal experiences' in *Irish Sword*, 11 (1973–74), pp 166–172, p. 167. See also, Timothy Bowman, *The Irish regiments in the Great War: Discipline and Morale* (Manchester, 2003), p. 27.
41. Hagerty, *Priests in Uniform: Catholic Chaplains to the British Forces in the First World War*, pp 22–23.
42. *Cork Examiner*, 29 November 1948.
43. *Irish Independent*, 6 February 1943.
44. 'Catholic Army chaplains – a diary', in *Catholic Bulletin*, vol. 7, no. 4 (1917), p. 250.
45. In October 1914, *The Tablet* reported that fourteen chaplains were at the Front, compared to twenty-five newly commissioned chaplains serving in Britain.
46. *The Tablet*, 14 October 1914.

47. *Cork Examiner*, 14 October 1914.
48. Rafferty, 'Catholic chaplains to the British Forces', p. 42.
49. *Catholic Bulletin*, vol. 7, no. 4 (1917), p. 250.
50. *Irish Independent*, 19 October 1914.
51. *Irish Independent*, 27 October 1914.
52. *Irish Independent*, 28 October 1914.
53. *Irish Independent*, 25 November 1914.
54. T. Gilmartin to J.F. Hogan, 15 December 1914, St Patrick's College, Maynooth Archives, Hogan papers, 21/6/19.
55. *Irish Times*, 25 June 1915.
56. *The Tablet*, 29 May 1915.
57. Circular from Cardinal Bourne to bishops of United Kingdom, 16 September 1915, St Patrick's College Maynooth Archives, Hogan papers, 22/31/30.
58. F. Bourne to J.F. Hogan, 28 September 1915, St Patrick's College, Maynooth Archives, Hogan papers, 22/31/30.
59. *Cork Examiner*, 13 October 1915.
60. Madigan, *Faith Under Fire*, p. 90.
61. *Irish Independent*, 11 February 1916.
62. *Freemans Journal*, 4 March 1916.
63. D. Kelly to J. F. Hogan, 19 May 1916, St Patrick's College, Maynooth Archives, Hogan papers, 22/25/3.
64. Journal of the Administrative Council, 30 October 1916, St Patrick's College, Maynooth Archives, B4/3/3, p. 27.
65. Ibid.
66. WO 374/35916, Service File: Chaplain Timothy Aloysius Hurley, Army Chaplains' Department, The National Archives of the UK, hereafter TNA(UK).
67. *Irish Independent*, 1 December 1956.
68. Ibid.
69. WO 374/49557, Service File: Reverend Michael Joseph Mullins, Army Chaplains' Department, TNA(UK).
70. *Sligo Champion*, 24 December 1976.
71. *Cork Examiner*, 6 March 1973.
72. R. Browne to J.F. Hogan, 21 April 1917, St Patrick's College, Maynooth Archives, Hogan Papers, 21/7/13.
73. Ibid.
74. Journal of the Administrative Council, 23 April 1917, St Patrick's College, Maynooth Archives, B4/3/3, p. 36.
75. *Irish Examiner*, 9 March 1965.
76. Journal of the Administrative Council, 1 October 1917, St Patrick's College, Maynooth Archives, B4/3/3, p. 46.

77. Journal of the Administrative Council 17 December 1917, St Patrick's College, Maynooth Archives, B4/3/3, p. 50.
78. *Ulster Herald*, 19 February 1966.
79. *Fermanagh Herald*, 20 June 1964.
80. Hagerty, *Priests in Uniform*, p. xxv.
81. *The Tablet*, 22 July 1916.
82. Ibid.
83. *Freemans Journal*, 12 July 1916.
84. *Southern Star*, 22 July 1916.
85. *Irish Catholic Directory*, 1917, p. 519.
86. *Kerry Weekly Reporter*, 22 July 1916.
87. *Anglo-Celt*, 20 October 1917.
88. WO 339/127875, Service File: Captain Reverend Stephen Clark, The Lancashire Fusiliers, The National Archives of the UK.
89. *Anglo-Celt*, 20 October 1917.
90. *The Tablet*, 20 October 1917.
91. WO 339/127875, Service File: Captain Reverend Stephen Clark.
92. 1901 Census, National Archives of Ireland: *http://www.census.nationalarchives.ie/pages/1901/Waterford/Waterford_Urban_No__4/William_Street/1762824/* [accessed 10 October 2023].
93. WO 339/1327, Service File: Captain Matthew Vincent Prendergast, Army Chaplains' Department, TNA(UK).
94. Ibid.
95. Snape and Madigan, *The Clergy in Khaki*, p. 3.
96. John Martin Brennan, 'Irish Catholic chaplains in the First World War' (M.Phil. thesis, University of Birmingham, 2011), p. 142.
97. Patrick Callan, 'Recruiting for the British Army in Ireland during the First World War' in *Irish Sword*, vol. 27 no. 66 (1987), pp 42–56, p. 42.
98. Ibid., p. 43.
99. Hagerty, *Priests in Uniform*, p. xxv.
100. *Irish Press*, 5 September 1940.
101. *Irish Press*, 17 April 1963.
102. *Cork Examiner*, 27 October 1978; *Irish Independent*, 24 November 1950.
103. Jane Leonard, 'The Catholic Chaplaincy', p. 6.
104. Michael McKernan, 'Devine, William (1887–1959)', Australian Dictionary of Biography, *http://adb.anu.edu.au/biography/devine-william-5971/text10187* [accessed 19 October 2023].
105. Recorded in *The Gazette* (Seventh Supplement to the London Gazette), no. 30598, 22 March 1918; ibid. no. 30997, 5 November 1918.
106. *Monthly Navy List*, May 1920, p. 806.

107. *Irish Independent*, 19 January 1934.
108. *Southern Star*, 20 May 1944.
109. Brian Heffernan, *Freedom and the Fifth Commandment. Catholic Priests and Political Violence in Ireland, 1919–21* (Manchester, 2014), pp 17–18.
110. R.F. Foster, *Vivid Faces: The Revolutionary Generation in Ireland 1890–1923* (London, 2014), p. 34.
111. Becker, *War and Faith*, p. 42.
112. *Maynooth College Calendar: 1903–4*, p. 106.
113. *The Gazette* (Fourth Supplement to the London Gazette), no. 29595, 23 May 1916.
114. *The Gazette* (Third Supplement to the London Gazette), no. 30834, 6 August 1918.
115. *The Gazette* (Fifth Supplement to the London Gazette), no. 30997, 5 November 1918.
116. WO 374/5132, Service File: Reverend Henry Beauchamp, Army Chaplain's Department, TNA(UK).
117. *The Gazette* (London Gazette), no. 32017, 13 August 1920.
118. Matriculation Returns, St Patrick's College, Maynooth Archives, B4/7/4.
119. Information provided by the National University of Ireland.
120. *The Gazette* (Supplement to the London Gazette), no. 30410, 30 November 1917.
121. *The Gazette* (Second Supplement to the London Gazette), no. 32630, 6 March 1922.
122. WO 374/8027, Service File: Chaplain John Francis Bowen, Army Chaplain's Department, TNA(UK).
123. Matriculation Returns, St Patrick's College, Maynooth Archives, B4/7/3.
124. *The Gazette* (London Gazette), no. 29689, 1 August 1916.
125. *The Gazette* (Third Supplement to the London Gazette), no. 31723, 6 January 1920.
126. Matriculation Returns, St Patrick's College, Maynooth Archives, B4/7/4.
127. *The Gazette* (Third Supplement to the London Gazette), no. 29807, 27 October 1916.
128. WO 374/8768, Service File: Chaplain Francis Breen, Army Chaplain's Department, TNA(UK).
129. Matriculation Returns, St Patrick's College, Maynooth Archives, B4/7/4.
130. *The Gazette* (Second Supplement to the London Gazette), no. 29216, 2 July 1915.
131. *The Gazette* (Supplement to the London Gazette), no. 31148, 28 January 1919.
132. Information provided by the National University of Ireland.
133. *The Gazette* (Supplement to the London Gazette), no. 29451, 25 January 1916.
134. *The Gazette* (Seventh Supplement to the London Gazette), no. 30598, 22 March 1918.
135. *The Gazette* (Supplement to the London Gazette), no. 32197, 18 January 1921.
136. Matriculation Returns, St Patrick's College, Maynooth Archives, B4/7/4.
137. *The Gazette* (London Gazette), no. 29547, 14 April 1916.
138. *The Gazette* (Second Supplement to the London Gazette), no. 31204, 25 February 1919.

139. Matriculation Returns, St Patrick's College, Maynooth Archives, B4/7/4.
140. *The Gazette* (London Gazette), no. 29534, 4 April 1916.
141. *The Gazette* (Supplement to the London Gazette), no. 30832, 6 August 1918.
142. Matriculation Returns, St Patrick's College, Maynooth Archives, B4/7/4.
143. Information provided by the National University of Ireland.
144. *The Gazette* (London Gazette), no. 29547, 14 April 1916.
145. Chaplain 4th Class The Rev. Stephen Clarke, *https://www.cwgc.org/find-war-dead/casualty/1628914/clarke,-the-rev.-stephen/* [accessed 9 October 2023].
146. Matriculation Returns, St Patrick's College, Maynooth Archives, B4/7/4.
147. *The Gazette* (Second Supplement to the London Gazette), no. 29585, 16 May 1916.
148. *The Gazette* (Supplement to the London Gazette), no. 31479, 29 July 1919.
149. John Coffey was ordained on 22 June 1902 and left for service on Easter Monday 1916 (*Nenagh News*, 21 August 1920). The name appears as 'James Coffey' in the London Gazette.
150. *The Gazette* (Fourth Supplement to the London Gazette), no. 29595, 23 May 1916.
151. *The Gazette* (Supplement to the London Gazette), no. 30777, 2 July 1918.
152. Matriculation Returns, St Patrick's College, Maynooth Archives, B4/7/4.
153. Information provided by the National University of Ireland.
154. *The Gazette* (Supplement to the London Gazette), no. 29176, 29 May 1915.
155. *The Gazette* (Second Supplement to the London Gazette), no. 29956, 20 February 1917.
156. *The Gazette* (Second Supplement to the London Gazette), no. 29534, 4 April 1916.
157. *The Gazette* (London Gazette), no. 29547, 14 April 1916.
158. *The Gazette* (Second Supplement to the London Gazette), no. 30275, 7 September 1917.
159. Matriculation Returns, St Patrick's College, Maynooth Archives, B4/7/4.
160. Information provided by the National University of Ireland.
161. *The Gazette* (Supplement to the London Gazette), no. 29045, 19 January 1915.
162. *The Gazette* (Supplement to the London Gazette), no. 31148, 28 January 1919.
163. Information provided by the National University of Ireland.
164. Matriculation Returns, St Patrick's College, Maynooth Archives, B4/7/4.
165. *The Gazette* (Sixth Supplement to the London Gazette), no. 30090, 22 May 1917.
166. *The Gazette* (Second Supplement to the London Gazette), no. 32470, 27 September 1921.
167. Matriculation Returns, St Patrick's College, Maynooth Archives, B4/7/4.
168. Information provided by the National University of Ireland.
169. *The Gazette* (London Gazette), no. 29972, 6 March 1917.
170. *The Gazette* (Supplement to the London Gazette), no. 31699, 19 December 1919.
171. *The Gazette* (London Gazette), no. 29547, 14 April 1916.
172. *The Gazette* (Fifth Supplement to the London Gazette), no. 31370, 30 May 1919.

173. *The Gazette* (Fifth Supplement to the London Gazette), no. 31502, 12 August 1919.
174. Information provided by the National University of Ireland.
175. *The Gazette* (London Gazette), no. 28995, 4 December 1914.
176. *The Gazette* (Third Supplement to the London Gazette), no. 31711, 30 December 1919.
177. *The Gazette* (Second Supplement to the London Gazette), no. 29890, 2 January 1917.
178. Information provided by the National University of Ireland.
179. Matriculation Returns, St Patrick's College, Maynooth Archives, B4/7/4.
180. *The Gazette* (Fourth Supplement to the London Gazette), no. 30357, 26 October 1917.
181. *The Gazette* (Second Supplement to the London Gazette), no. 32608, 13 February 1922.
182. Matriculation Returns, St Patrick's College, Maynooth Archives, B4/7/3.
183. *The Gazette* (London Gazette), no. 29534, 4 April 1916.
184. *The Gazette* (Fourth Supplement to the London Gazette), no. 31210, 28 February 1919.
185. *The Gazette* (Supplement to the London Gazette), no. 31148, 28 January 1919.
186. Matriculation Returns, St Patrick's College, Maynooth Archives, B4/7/4.
187. *The Gazette* (Supplement to the London Gazette), no. 30410, 30 November 1917.
188. *The Gazette* (Second Supplement to the London Gazette), no. 31835, 23 March 1920.
189. Matriculation Returns, St Patrick's College, Maynooth Archives, B4/7/3.
190. *The Gazette* (Second Supplement to the London Gazette), no. 29585, 16 May 1916.
191. *The Gazette* (Second Supplement to the London Gazette), no. 30955, 15 October 1918.
192. *The Gazette* (London Gazette), no. 28995, 4 December 1914; Recorded in *The Gazette* (Third Supplement to the London Gazette), no. 30129, 12 June 1917.
193. *The Gazette* (Fourth Supplement to the London Gazette), no. 31410, 17 June1919.
194. *The Gazette* (Sixth Supplement to the London Gazette), no. 30288, 14 September 1917.
195. *The Gazette* (London Gazette), no. 30973, 25 October 1918.
196. *The Gazette* (London Gazette), no. 29972, 6 March 1917.
197. *The Gazette* (Second Supplement to the London Gazette), no. 31566, 23 September 1919.
198. *The Gazette* (London Gazette), no. 29744, 12 September 1916.
199. *The Gazette* (Second Supplement to the London Gazette), no. 32496, 21 October 1921.
200. *The Gazette* (London Gazette), no. 29162, 14 May 1915.
201. *The Gazette* (Fourth Supplement to the London Gazette), no. 30561, 5 March 1918.

202. *The Gazette* (Second Supplement to the London Gazette), no. 32496, 21 October 1921.
203. Information provided by the National University of Ireland.
204. *The Gazette* (London Gazette), no. 29534, 4 April 1916.
205. *The Gazette* (Supplement to the London Gazette), no. 31479, 29 July 1919.
206. *The Gazette* (London Gazette), no. 29547, 14 April 1916.
207. *The Gazette* (Fourth Supplement to the London Gazette), no. 30718, 31 May 1918.
208. *The Gazette* (Second Supplement to the London Gazette), no. 32506, 2 November 1921.
209. Matriculation Returns, St Patrick's College, Maynooth Archives, B4/7/4.
210. Information provided by the National University of Ireland.
211. *The Gazette* (Second Supplement to the London Gazette), no. 30955, 15 October 1918.
212. *The Gazette* (Second Supplement to the London Gazette), no. 31753, 23 January 1920.
213. *Irish Press*, 1 June 1965.
214. *The Gazette* (Supplement to the London Gazette), no. 30375, 9 November 1917.
215. *The Gazette* (Supplement to the London Gazette), no. 32062, 24 September 1920.
216. Matriculation Returns, St Patrick's College, Maynooth Archives, B4/7/4.
217. Information provided by the National University of Ireland.
218. *The Gazette* (Supplement to the London Gazette), no. 30375, 9 November 1917.
219. *The Gazette* (Fourth Supplement to the London Gazette), no. 31641, 11 November 1919.
220. *The Gazette* (Third Supplement to the London Gazette), no. 30129, 12 June 1917.
221. *The Gazette* (Second Supplement to the London Gazette), no. 32618, 22 February 1922.
222. Matriculation Returns, St Patrick's College, Maynooth Archives, B4/7/3.
223. *The Gazette* (Supplement to the London Gazette), no. 30429, 14 December 1917.
224. *The Gazette* (Second Supplement to the London Gazette), no. 32506, 2 November 1921.
225. Matriculation Returns, St Patrick's College, Maynooth Archives, B4/7/4.
226. *The Gazette* (Supplement to the London Gazette), no. 29391, 3 December 1915.
227. *The Gazette* (Second Supplement to the London Gazette), no. 30467, 8 January 1918.
228. Matriculation Returns, St Patrick's College, Maynooth Archives, B4/7/4.
229. *Connaught Telegraph*, 16 December 1916.
230. *The Gazette* (London Gazette), no. 29972, 6 March 1917
231. *The Gazette* (Second Supplement to the London Gazette, no. 32506, 2 November 1921.
232. Matriculation Returns, St Patrick's College, Maynooth Archives, B4/7/3.
233. WO 374/49557, Service File: Reverend Michael Joseph Mullins, Army Chaplains' Department, TNA(UK).
234. *The Gazette* (Fourth Supplement to the London Gazette), no. 31017, 15 November 1918.

235. *The Gazette* (Supplement to the London Gazette), no. 31105, 3 January 1919.
236. Matriculation Returns, St Patrick's College, Maynooth Archives, B4/7/4.
237. Information provided by the National University of Ireland.
238. *The Gazette* (Fourth Supplement to the London Gazette), no. 29734, 1 September. 1916.
239. *The Gazette* (Second Supplement to the London Gazette), no. 31133, 17 January 1919.
240. *Western People*, 16 December 1916.
241. *The Gazette* (London Gazette), no. 29972, 6 March 1917.
242. *The Gazette* (Fourth Supplement to the London Gazette), no. 31728, 9 January 1920.
243. *The Gazette* (Supplement to the London Gazette), no. 29045, 19 January 1915.
244. *The Gazette* (London Gazette), no. 29689, 1 August 1916.
245. *The Gazette* (Third Supplement to the London Gazette), no. 29886, 29 December 1916.
246. *The Gazette* (Second Supplement to the London Gazette), no. 31550, 12 September 1919.
247. *The Gazette* (Third Supplement to the London Gazette), no. 31711, 30 December 1919.
248. *The Gazette* (London Gazette), no. 29140, 23 April 1915.
249. *The Gazette* (Second Supplement to the London Gazette), no. 32517, 14 November 1921.
250. Matriculation Returns, St Patrick's College, Maynooth Archives, B4/7/3.
251. *The Gazette* (London Gazette), no. 29140, 23 April 1915.
252. *The Gazette* (Sixth Supplement to the London Gazette), no. 30111, 1 June 1917.
253. *The Gazette* (Supplement to the London Gazette), no. 30832, 6 August 1918.
254. *Irish Independent*, 5 September 1950.
255. *The Gazette* (Supplement to the London Gazette), no. 30410, 30 November 1917.
256. *The Gazette* (Second Supplement to the London Gazette), no. 31133, 17 January 1919.
257. *The Gazette* (Sixth Supplement to the London Gazette), no. 30090, 22 May 1917.
258. *The Gazette* (Tenth Supplement to the London Gazette), no. 30724, 31 May 1918.
259. *Connacht Tribune*, 11 October 1919.
260. *The Gazette* (London Gazette), no. 29534, 4 April 1916.
261. *The Gazette* (Second Supplement to the London Gazette), no. 30955, 15 October 1918.
262. Matriculation Returns, St Patrick's College, Maynooth Archives, B4/7/4.
263. Information provided by the National University of Ireland.
264. Recorded in *The Gazette* (Supplement to the London Gazette), no. 29517, 21 March 1916.
265. Chaplain 4th Class The Rev. Donal Vincent O'Sullivan, *https://www.cwgc.org/find-war-dead/casualty/202424/o'sullivan,-the-rev.-donal-vincent/* [accessed 9 August 2023].

266. Hamell, *Maynooth Students, 1795–1895*, p. 148.
267. Ibid.
268. *The Gazette* (Supplement to the London Gazette), no. 29270, 20 August 1915.
269. Matriculation Returns St Patrick's College, Maynooth Archives, B4/7/4.
270. *The Gazette* (Supplement to the London Gazette), no. 29176, 28 May 1915.
271. *The Gazette* (London Gazette), no. 29547, 14 April 1916.
272. Matriculation Returns, St Patrick's College, Maynooth Archives, B4/7/4.
273. Information provided by the National University of Ireland.
274. *The Gazette* (London Gazette), no. 29972, 6 March 1917.
275. *The Gazette* (Fourth Supplement to the London Gazette), no. 31095, 31 December 1918.
276. *The Gazette* (Supplement to the London Gazette), no. 31699, 19 December 1919.
277. Matriculation Returns, St Patrick's College, Maynooth Archives, B4/7/3.
278. *The Gazette* (Fourth Supplement to the London Gazette), no. 29734, 1 September 1916.
279. *The Gazette* (Fourth Supplement to the London Gazette), no. 31135, 17 January 1919.
280. *The Gazette* (London Gazette), no. 29247, 30 July 1915.
281. Chaplain 4th Class The Rev. Mathew Vincent Prendergast, *https://www.cwgc.org/find-war-dead/casualty/113424/prendergast,-the-rev.-mathew-vincent/* [accessed 9 October 2023].
282. *The Gazette* (Sixth Supplement to the London Gazette), no. 30090, 22 May 1917.
283. *The Gazette* (Third Supplement to the London Gazette), no. 30744, 11 June 1918.
284. Matriculation Returns, St Patrick's College, Maynooth Archives, B4/7/4.
285. *The Gazette* (London Gazette), no. 29262, 13 August 1915.
286. *The Gazette* (Second Supplement to the London Gazette), no. 29956, 20 February 1917.
287. *The Gazette* (Second Supplement to the London Gazette), no. 29824, 14 November 1916.
288. *The Gazette* (Supplement to the London Gazette), no. 30558, 5 March 1918.
289. *The Gazette* (Second Supplement to the London Gazette), no. 30773, 28 June 1918.
290. Matriculation Returns, St Patrick's College, Maynooth Archives, B4/7/4.
291. Information provided by the National University of Ireland.
292. *The Gazette* (London Gazette), no. 29534, 4 April 1916.
293. *The Gazette* (Second Supplement to the London Gazette), no. 32535, 30 November 1921.
294. *The Gazette* (Third Supplement to the London Gazette), no. 30171, 7 July 1917.
295. *The Gazette* (Second Supplement to the London Gazette), no. 31566, 23 September 1919.
296. *The Gazette* (London Gazette), no. 29972, 6 March 1917.
297. WO 374/63447, Service File: Chaplain Hugh Smith, Royal Army Chaplains' Department, TNA(UK).
298. *The Gazette* (Fourth Supplement to the London Gazette), no. 29090, 2 March 1915.
299. *The Gazette* (Supplement to the London Gazette), no. 30304, 25 September 1917.
300. *The Gazette* (Second Supplement to the London Gazette), no. 30367, 2 November 1917.

301. *The Gazette* (Third Supplement to the London Gazette), no. 31530, 29 August 1919.
302. Matriculation Returns, St Patrick's College, Maynooth Archives, B4/7/4.
303. Information provided by the National University of Ireland.
304. *The Gazette* (Third Supplement to the London Gazette), no. 29641, 27 June 1916.
305. Matriculation Returns, St Patrick's College, Maynooth Archives, B4/7/4.
306. *The Gazette* (Third Supplement to the London Gazette), no. 31035, 26 November 1918.
307. Chaplain 4th Class The Rev John Watters, *https://www.cwgc.org/find-war-dead/casualty/536912/watters,-the-rev.-john/* [accessed 9 October 2023].
308. WO 374/5132, Service File: Reverend Henry Beauchamp, Army Chaplain's Department, TNA(UK); Ann Power, 'Kildare and Leighlin Roman Catholic Chaplains in World War 1 'If the men can't go to the church, then the church must go to the men'' in *Carloviana: Carlow Historical and Archaeological Society*, 64 (2016), pp 145–152, p. 148.
309. *http://www.portarlingtongolfclub.ie/archive/web/History/founders.htm* [accessed 23 October 2023].
310. Power, 'Kildare and Leighlin Roman Catholic Chaplains in World War 1', p. 148.
311. 1901 Census Return: *http://www.census.nationalarchives.ie/pages/1901/Carlow/Carlow/College_Street/1040810/* [accessed 23 October 2023]; Hamell, *Maynooth Students,1895–1984*, p. 37.
312. WO 374/5132, Service File: Reverend Henry Beauchamp.
313. *The Gazette* (Fifth Supplement to the London Gazette), no. 30997, 5 November 1918.
314. *Irish Press*, 28 June 1940.
315. *Cork Examiner*, 27 April 1948.
316. 1901 Census Return: *http://www.census.nationalarchives.ie/pages/1901/Dublin/Howth/Howth/1270734/* [accessed 22 October 2023].
317. *Freemans Journal*, 23 June 1913.
318. WO 374/8027, Service File: Chaplain John Francis Bowen, Army Chaplain's Department, TNA(UK).
319. Ibid.
320. Ibid.
321. Ibid.
322. Ibid.
323. *Irish Times*, 29 January 1945.
324. *Irish Press*, 29 January 1945.
325. 1901 Census Return: *http://www.census.nationalarchives.ie/pages/1901/Meath/Kilmainham/Edengora/1615476/* [accessed 23 October2023].
326. Hamell, *Maynooth Students,1895–1984*, p. 43; *Meath Chronicle*, 10 January 1920.
327. WO 374/8446, Service File: Captain (Chaplain) Thomas Joseph Bradley, Army Chaplains' Department, TNA(UK).

328. Ibid.
329. *Irish Press*, 5 November 1937.
330. 1901 Census Return: *http://www.census.nationalarchives.ie/pages/1901/Kerry/Killarney/High_Street_East_Side/1415358/* [accessed 22 October 2023].
331. *Kerry Reporter*, 20 June 1931.
332. *Kerry Reporter*, 20 June 1931; Hamell, *Maynooth Students, 1895–1984*, p. 35.
333. *Kerry Reporter*, 20 June 1931.
334. Ibid.
335. WO 374/8768, Service File: Chaplain Francis Breen, Army Chaplain's Department, TNA(UK).
336. Ibid.
337. *Kerry Reporter*, 20 June 1931.
338. Ibid.
339. *Connaught Telegraph*, 25 June 1910.
340. Ibid., 6 May 1916.
341. WO 339/43173, Service File: Reverend Michael Carney, Army Chaplains Department, TNA(UK).
342. Ibid.
343. 'Ignotus', 'Pastoral work in war-time' in *Irish Ecclesiastical Record*, vol. 8 (1916), pp 352–357, p. 353.
344. *Irish Independent*, 14 May 1969.
345. *Connacht Tribune*, 16 May 1969.
346. Ibid., 12 April 1958.
347. *Western People*, 24 May 1969.
348. *Irish Independent*, 14 May 1969.
349. Candidates for Matriculation, 1895 (A–L), National University of Ireland.
350. *Nenagh News*, 21 August 1920.
351. *Irish Catholic*, 28 August 1920.
352. 1911 Census Return: *www.census.nationalarchives.ie/pages/1911/Cork/St__Mary_s/Farranferris/403166/* [accessed 22 August 2020].
353. 1901 Census Return: *http://www.census.nationalarchives.ie/pages/1901/Cork/Bealanageary/Illauninagh_West/1141196/* [accessed 22 August 2020].
354. WO 339/93551, Service File: Reverend Cornelius Michael Creed, Royal Army Chaplains' Department, TNA(UK).
355. Ibid.
356. Ibid.
357. Ibid.
358. Ibid.
359. Ibid.

360. Ibid.
361. Ibid.
362. Ibid.
363. Ibid.
364. *Cork Examiner*, 25 August 1958.
365. 1901 Census, National Archives of Ireland: *http://www.census.nationalarchives.ie/pages/1901/Kilkenny/Kilkenny_Urban/New_Road_from_Callan/1450964/* [accessed 22 October 2023]; Hamell, *Maynooth Students, 1895–1984*, p. 49.
366. 1901 Census, National Archives of Ireland: *http://www.census.nationalarchives.ie/pages/1901/Kilkenny/Rathpatrick/Kilmurry/1457620/* [accessed 22 October 2023].
367. *Irish Times*, 26 December 2014; *Irish Independent*, 25 January 1917.
368. WO 374/20529, Service File: Chaplain Edward Dowling, Army Chaplain's Department, TNA(UK).
369. *Munster Express*, 15 October 1921.
370. WO 374/20529, Service File: Chaplain Edward Dowling.
371. *Nationalist and Leinster Times*, 11 June 1960.
372. See also Chapter 2, p. 86-87.
373. *Cork Examiner*, 5 July 1940, pp. 86-87.
374. Witness Statement, Bureau of Military History (hereafter WS, BMH) Very Rev. Thomas Canon Duggan, WS 551 (available online at https://www.militaryarchives.ie/en/home/).
375. Ibid.
376. *Cork Examiner*, 5 July 1940.
377. Ibid.
378. WS, BMH, Very Rev Thomas Canon Duggan, WS 551.
379. Thomas Duggan, Cork County Library: Local Studies Digital Library. *https://www.corklocalstudies.ie/items/show/5191* [accessed 27 January 2019].
380. *Cork Examiner*, 3 August 1939.
381. *Munster Express*, 6 March 1953.
382. *Irish Independent*, 9 March 1965.
383. Hamell, *Maynooth students, 1795–1895*, p. 64.
384. Ibid., p. 139.
385. WO 374/23670, Service File: Reverend Bernard Farrell, Army Chaplain's Department, TNA(UK).
386. Ibid.
387. *The Gazette* (Fourth Supplement to the London Gazette), no. 31210, 28 February 1919.
388. *Meath Chronicle*, 12 February 1921.
389. WO 374/26071, Service File: Chaplain Joseph Furlong. Army Chaplain's Department, TNA(UK).

390. *Evening Herald*, 17 June 1967
391. *Irish Press*, 4 January 1967.
392. *Nationalist and Leinster Times*, 22 October 1971.
393. *Irish Independent*, 27 June 1959.
394. WO 339/115524, Service File: Rev Francis A Gleeson, Royal Army Chaplains' Department, TNA(UK).
395. *The Tablet*, 29 May 1915.
396. WO 339/115524, Service File: Rev Francis A Gleeson.
397. Ibid.
398. Ibid.
399. Ibid.
400. Ibid.
401. B.D.H. Clark, 'The Dirty Shirts' in *Irish Sword*, 11 (1973–1974), pp 1–2, p. 2.
402. See, for example, the 'Diary of Fr. Francis A. Gleeson 17 January 1915 – 4 October 1915', Dublin Diocesan Archives, P101/4.
403. Diary entry for 21 March 1915 in 'Diary of Fr. Francis A. Gleeson 7 February 1915–3 May 1915', Dublin Diocesan Archives, P101/5.
404. Diary of Fr. Francis A. Gleeson 12–25 December 1917, Dublin Diocesan Archives, P101/8.
405. *Cork Examiner*, 12 October 1955.
406. *Freemans Journal*, 17 June 1899.
407. *Freemans Journal*, 27 October 1917.
408. Leonard, 'The Catholic Chaplaincy', p. 9.
409. *Cork Examiner*, 4 May 1915.
410. Ibid., 18 June 1917.
411. *Cork Examiner*, 31 October 1917; *The Gazette* (Fourth Supplement to the London Gazette), no. 30561, 5 March 1918.
412. *Weekly Irish Times*, 29 March 1919.
413. *Limerick Leader*, 25 April 1936; *Cork Examiner*, 13 March 1947.
414. WO 374/39395, Service File: The Reverend Patrick Kerr, Army Chaplains' Department, TNA(UK).
415. Pádraig Mac Giolla Cheara, 'From the Valley of Death' in *An Crann*, 4 (1917), pp 10–12 in Fionntán de Brún, 'Litreacha ón Chéad Chogadh Domhanda leis an Athair Pádraig Mac Giolla Cheara' in *Taighde agus Teagasc*, 4 (2004), pp 1–19.
416. *All Hallows Annual*, 34 (1957–8), p. 43.
417. WO 374/49558, Service File: Reverend William Mullins, Army Chaplains' Department, TNA(UK).
418. Ibid.
419. *Tuam Herald*, 1 February 1919; *Irish Independent*, 22 June 1951.

420. Hamell, *Maynooth Students, 1895–1984*, p. 16.
421. *Irish Press*, 15 June 1964.
422. 1911 Census Return: *http://www.census.nationalarchives.ie/pages/1901/Monaghan/Aghabog/Corranewy/1632772/* [accessed on 22 October 2023].
423. WO 374/50787, Service File: Chaplain James Nolan, Army Chaplains' Department, TNA(UK).
424. Ibid.
425. Ibid.
426. Ibid.
427. *Irish Press*, 15 June 1964.
428. *Fermanagh Herald*, 13 October 1934.
429. *Irish Press*, 15 June 1964.
430. 1901 Census Return: *http://www.census.nationalarchives.ie/pages/1901/Monaghan/Enagh/Tonygarvey/1636473/* [accessed 22 October 2023].
431. WO 374/51231, Service File: Reverend Edward O'Hart, Army Chaplains' Department, TNA(UK).
432. Ibid.
433. *Donegal Democrat*, 11 November 1949.
434. *Irish Independent*, 9 November 1949.
435. *Connacht Tribune*, 11 October 1919.
436. 1901 Census Return: *http://www.census.nationalarchives.ie/pages/1901/Galway/Craughwell/Craughwell/1385980/* [accessed 22 October 2023].
437. WO 339/94696, Service File: Reverent John T. O'Kelly, Royal Army Chaplains' Department, TNA(UK).
438. Ibid.
439. Ibid.
440. 1901 Census Return: *http://www.census.nationalarchives.ie/pages/1901/Longford/Longford_No__1_Urban/Deanscurragh/1555690/* [accessed 22 October 2023]; Hamell, *Maynooth Students, 1895–1984*, p. 14.
441. 1901 Census return: *http://www.census.nationalarchives.ie/pages/1901/Longford/Rathcline/Lisnacush/1554180/* [accessed 22 October 2023].
442. WO 374/51166, Service File: Reverend (Captain) Peter O'Farrell, Army Chaplains' Department, TNA(UK).
443. Terry Denman, The 10th (Irish) Division 1914–15: a study in military and political interaction', in *Irish Sword*, 17, no. 66 (Summer 1987), pp 16–24, p. 25.
444. 1901 Census Return: *http://www.census.nationalarchives.ie/pages/1901/Cavan/Bally jamesduff/Ballyjamesduff/1051231/* [accessed 22 August 2023]; 1911 Census Return: *http://www.census.nationalarchives.ie/pages/1911/Cavan/Ballyjamesduff/Cornahilt/348486* [accessed 22 October 2023].

445. WO 374/61997, Service File: Captain James Sheridan, Army Chaplains' Department, TNA(UK).

446. Ibid.

447. Ibid.

448. *Anglo-Celt*, 18 January 1947.

449. WO 374/62969, Service File: Chaplain Terence Small, Army Chaplains' Department, TNA(UK).

450. Ibid.

451. *Fermanagh Herald*, 18 January 1947.

452. 1901 Census Return: *http://www.census.nationalarchives.ie/pages/1901/Donegal/Moville/Malin_Street/1186002/* [accessed 22 October 2023].

453. 1901 Census Return: *http://www.census.nationalarchives.ie/pages/1901/Londonderry/South_Ward_No__2_Urban/Bishop_Street/1528968/* [accessed 22 October 2023]; Hamell, *Maynooth Students, 1895–1984*, p. 26.

454. WO 374/63447, Service File: Chaplain Hugh Smith, Royal Army Chaplains' Department, TNA(UK).

455. Ibid.

456. Ibid.

457. Ibid.

458. *Munster Express*, 30 November 1951.

459. *Irish Independent*, 18 May 1943.

460. BMH, Joseph V. Lawless, WS 1043, p. 179.

461. M.J. Curran to William Walsh, 23 July 1916 (Dublin Diocesan Archive, Walsh papers, 385/4).

462. BMH, John J (Sean) Murphy, WS 0204, pp 14–15.

463. BMH, James Kavanagh, WS 0889, p. 83.

464. WO 339/56857, Service File: Reverend Laurence Joseph Stafford, Royal Army Chaplains' Department, TNA(UK).

465. Ibid.

466. Ibid.

467. *Irish Press*, 18 May 1943.

Index